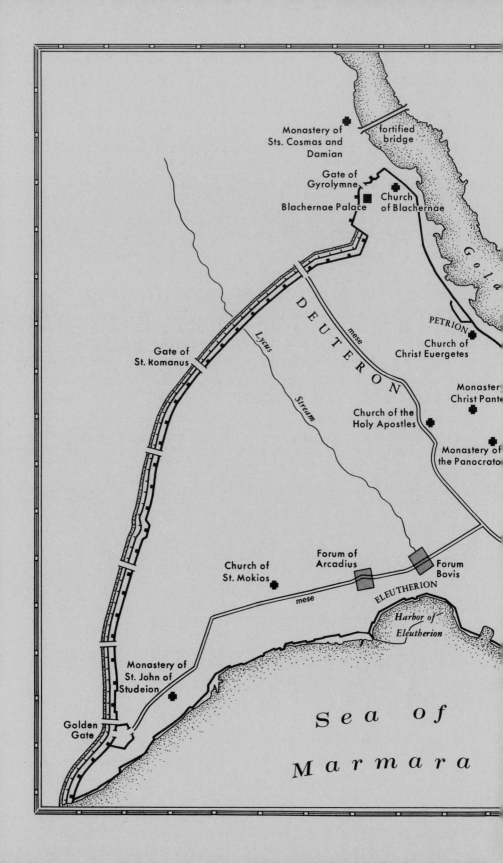

Monastery of
Sts. Cosmas and
Damian

fortified
bridge

Gate of
Gyrolymne

Blachernae Palace

Church
of Blachernae

G o l d

PETRION

Church of
Christ Euergetes

D E U T E R O N

mese

Gate of
St. Romanus

Monaster
Christ Pante

Lycus

Church of the
Holy Apostles

Stream

Monastery of
the Panocrato

Forum of
Arcadius

Forum
Bovis

Church of
St. Mokios

ELEUTHERION

mese

Harbor of
Eleutherion

Monastery of
St. John of
Studeion

Golden
Gate

S e a   o f

M a r m a r a

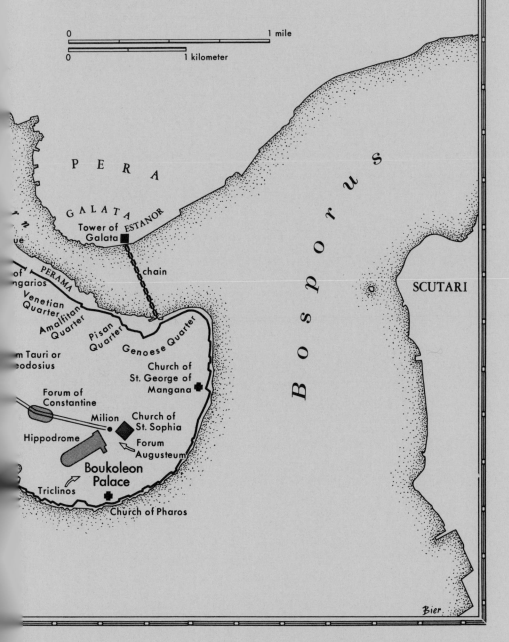

CONSTANTINOPLE

In the Time of the Fourth Crusade
1203-1204

0 — 1 mile

0 — 1 kilometer

PERA

GALATA ESTANOR

Tower of
Galata

PERAMA

chain

of
ngarios

Venetian
Quarter

Amalfitan
Quarter

Pisan
Quarter

Genoese Quarter

m Tauri or
eodosius

Church of
St. George of
Mangana

Forum of
Constantine

Milion

Church of
St. Sophia

Hippodrome

Forum
Augusteum

Boukoleon
Palace

Triclinos

Church of Pharos

Bosporus

SCUTARI

Bier.

The Fourth Crusade

The Middle Ages
Edward Peters, *General Editor*

The Fourth Crusade

The Conquest of Constantinople
1201-1204

Donald E. Queller

University of Pennsylvania Press
1977

Library of Congress Cataloging in Publication Data
Queller, Donald E
    The Fourth Crusade.
    (The Middle ages)
    Bibliography: p.
    Includes index.
    1. Crusades—Fourth, 1202-1204.   2. Istanbul—
Siege, 1203–1204. I. Title. II. Series.
D164.Q38   940.1'8   77-81454
ISBN 0-8122-7730-9

Dedicated in love and appreciation to my mother and father

Contents

Preface

For many years I have been intrigued by the controversy over the so-called "diversion" of the Fourth Crusade. Since Comte Louis de Mas Latrie first assailed the "theory of accidents" of Geoffrey of Villehardouin in the mid-nineteenth century numerous distinguished historians have debated the reasons why the crusaders attacked and conquered Constantinople. Susan J. Stratton and I published in 1969 an historiographical article tracing the development of the controversy. There we wrote of the simple theory of accidents of Villehardouin and all those who followed him uncritically until the nineteenth century. We described the development of the treason theories, which attribute the attack upon Constantinople to the self-serving schemes of Venetians, the Hohenstaufen, or even the pope. Around the turn of the century occurred a new development, the elaboration of a modified theory of accidents, basically upholding the truthfulness of Villehardouin, but setting the Fourth Crusade firmly in a context of deteriorating Greek relations with the West. Finally, we wrote of the few recent scholars who have attempted to capture the inner motivations of the crusaders.

Since the publication of that article—or slightly before it, but too late for inclusion—have appeared a number of additional contributions, which may be found in the present bibliography. I would be remiss, however, not to call the reader's attention particularly to the following: B. Ebels-Hoving, *Byzantium in Westerse Ogen*; Sibyll Kindlimann, *Die Eroberung von Konstantinopel als politische Forderung des Westens im Hochmittelalter*; Helmut Roscher, *Papst Innocenz III. und die Kreuzzuge*; the various works of Benjamin Hendrickx; and, above all, the fine book by Charles M. Brand, *Byzantium Confronts the West, 1180–1204*.

Obviously and properly, historians have not followed the well-known dictum of Achille Luchaire: "we will never know, and science has truly something better to do than to discuss indefinitely an insoluble problem." In view of the rich literature on the Fourth Crusade, and especially considering the excellence of the English treatments by McNeal and Wolff in the Pennsylvania (now Wisconsin) *History of the Crusades*, and by Brand, it may well be asked whether another book on the subject is needed. I have concluded that it is, for several reasons. There still is no modern scholarly work in English devoted wholly to the Fourth Crusade. Much which I think is wrong, moreover, continues to be written, even by scholarly authors. The differences in Brand's approach and mine seem sufficiently great to justify my own effort to interpret these much-debated events. Brand is a Byzantinist, and, although well-versed in the non-Byzantine sources as well, he stands in Constantinople looking westward, a perfectly natural and justifiable position. I, on the other hand, am a Western Europeanist, and the focus of my interest is within the army of the Latins. Brand also paints on a larger canvas than I have chosen. He covers a quarter of a century, dealing at length with the background of conflict between the Latins and the Greeks. I concentrate upon five years or less, telling the story of the crusade itself in greater detail, especially in the earlier chapters, with only occasional allusions to preceding events.

I have not attempted to deal with the history of the crusades in general or the relationship of the Fourth Crusade to other crusades except insofar as earlier events cast light upon the conquest of Constantinople by the Latins. Neither have I described the demographic, economic, and political forces which lie behind the crusading movement. The reader will have no trouble finding information about these in the modern general histories of the crusades, or, indeed, in any recent textbook. It has seemed to me justifiable, while recognizing the importance of these matters, to concentrate upon a full narrative account of how the Fourth Crusaders came to conquer the capital of Eastern Christendom.

It would be exciting to regale the reader with a tale of a dark plot to conquer Constantinople concocted at Hagenau by Philip of Swabia, Boniface of Montferrat, and the young Alexius, but I am absolutely convinced that it was not so. A retelling of the myth of the Venetians who had no religion but profit and the state, and of the devious Dandolo who spun a web to entrap the naive northerners to achieve his ends, also would be intriguing, but it too is not true. The documentation for these views, as I hope my text will prove, is weak. Their authors, moreover, have overestimated, in my opinion, the power of men to control events and have underestimated the complexity, unpredictability, and recalcitrance of the events themselves. They have fallen prey to that "mania for making judgments" which Marc Bloch called the satanic enemy of history. Besides such colorful versions my account may seem overly complex and at times even self-contradictory. If so, it is because I believe that the events were highly complicated and that the crusaders were driven by a variety of sometimes contradictory motives. To me there is much excitement in viewing the host caught up in a chain of events which overwhelmed their best intentions, leading them step by step to the Christian city on the Bosporus.

As Brand stands in Byzantium, I move with the crusading army and the Venetian fleet, trying to understand the various forces and personalities at work there. I have tried to view the participants as real and whole men, blessed with noble aspirations and cursed with ambition and greed, as I find men to be. I have colored the narrative here and there with descriptions of sites, ceremonies, battle scenes, and the like, which may seem unnecessary or even unduly romantic to some. One cannot read the sources, however, without realizing that these matters were important to the participants. I contend that to ignore the tears which flowed from the eyes of grown men at the thought of Christ's sacrifice, to leave out the thrill which the crusaders experienced at the sight of banners and the sound of battle-cries is to distort the history of the crusades. These emotions, not merely rational calculations of political or economic advantage, motivated the cross-bearers. It is part of my thesis that much modern scholarship has erred in viewing the crusades within modern frames of reference, particularly nationalism and economic determinism. My attempt, on the contrary, has been to capture from the sources the views, motives, and feelings of the early thirteenth century crusaders, who were not so very different from us moderns, but yet some different.

Several times I have used the Fourth Crusade as the subject of my seminar. It has great advantages for this purpose. The known contemporary or nearly contemporary sources are all published and readily available. The library at the University of Illinois possesses all of them, and most are within arm's reach on the shelves of the medieval seminar room. The modern scholarly literature is also profuse, controversial, of high quality, and distributed over more than a century, so that the students begin to gain command of a magnificent scholarly tradition. The efforts of my students have profited me, as well as them, and I wish here to thank them collectively for their contributions to this book. In particular I wish to express my appreciation to the research assistants who have aided me year by year, George Stow, Gary Blumenshine, James Curtis, Donald Campbell, and especially Gerald Day. My colleague, Bennett Hill, has read part of a draft, and has made valuable suggestions. Eugenia Petridis has kindly undertaken the task of transferring my citations of Nicetas Choniates from the Bekker edition to the new one. She, Deno Geanakoplos and Constance Head have kindly read the epilogue.

Since all the major sources of the Fourth Crusade are readily at hand, its history can be written from one's study. My two years in Venice working on other subjects, thanks to a Fulbright research fellowship, a Rockefeller Foundation fellowship, and a Guggenheim fellowship, however, contributed to my understanding of the early stages of the crusade and even resulted in a few notes from rare Venetian books and manuscripts. I am very grateful for the opportunity. The National Endowment for the Humanities also honored me with a grant to facilitate a journey along the coast of the Eastern Adriatic, a visit to Zara, and to Constantinople to study the topography and the remains. In my own mind, at least, these examinations of the sites have lent an aura of reality, which I hope I have been able to pass on to the reader.

"If you consider the matter carefully, you cannot deny that Fortune has great power over human affairs. We see these affairs constantly being affected by fortuitous circumstances that men could neither foresee nor avoid."

Francesco Guicciardini, *Maxims and Reflections of a Renaissance Statesman*

1

The Preaching
and Taking of the Cross

In his letter announcing to the patriarch of Jerusalem the death of his predecessor and his own elevation to the papacy on 8 January 1198, Innocent III proclaimed his intention to work for the cause of the Holy Land and the deliverance of Jerusalem.[1] Infidel possession of the Holy City offended the hearts and minds of medieval Christians in a way scarcely comprehensible even to the most religious among us. The young pope, acutely conscious of his responsibility as the head of Christendom, intended to reassume papal leadership of the Holy War.[2] On 15 August he proclaimed a new crusade, summoning the *militia Christi* for March of 1199. All towns, as well as counts and barons, should provide crusaders for two years at their own expense according to their resources. Kings were not mentioned, for he meant this crusade to be wholly under papal control.[3] Prelates of the church should also contribute either men or money according to their means. Both those who would undertake the pilgrimage and those who would provide the means were offered the crusading indulgence for the remission of sins. Crusaders would also receive the usual protection of their goods and a moratorium on the interest of their debts. The pope named Cardinal-priest Soffredo and Cardinal-deacon Peter Capuano as his legates to direct the enterprise.[4]

Political conditions in Latin Europe, however, were not auspicious for a crusade. England and France were at war, as they had been on and off since Richard Lion-Heart's return from captivity in 1194. The powerful and wealthy Count Baldwin of Flanders was also at loggerheads with his French suzerain. Germany was rent by two rival claimants to the imperial crown, Philip of Swabia, allied with France, and Otto of Brunswick, allied with England. Sicily was unsettled under the boy-king Frederick and his regent mother, Constance, struggling to maintain Hohenstaufen rule. Genoa and Pisa, two of the great maritime powers, were also at war. Innocent III pursued a policy aimed at solving or stabilizing the conflicts of the secular powers. The Fourth Crusade was both the end toward which this policy was directed and a means intended to achieve it by enlisting the contentious powers in the war against the infidel.[5]

1

To the bitter disappointment of the pope the appointed time passed, but there was no response to his summons or to his repeated demands for men and money. In late December and early January Innocent took the unprecedented step of levying a general papal tax upon the clergy. The pope and cardinals taxed themselves a tenth of their incomes for the following year; other clergy were to pay a fortieth of their revenues, with the exception of certain privileged monastic orders, the Cistercians, Carthusians, Premonstratensians, and Grandmontines, who had to pay only a fiftieth. Although we have no records which enable us to determine how much money was collected, various sources indicate considerable clerical opposition.[6] Other measures to gain financial support for the Holy Land were also taken. A chest was placed in each church for weekly offerings, in return for which donors would receive the remission of sins and a weekly public mass said for them. Bishops converted penances into cash for the Holy Land.[7]

Results were disappointing until religious fervor was fanned by the preaching of the charismatic Fulk of Neuilly. Before he acquired his fame Fulk had been rector or curate of the country church of Neuilly near Paris. Discouraged by his lack of success he had turned for improvement to the university. Fortified with new learning and confidence, his sermons gained popularity. It seemed to many that the Holy Spirit spoke through him.[8] Jacques of Vitry wrote: "Come and hear the priest Fulk, because he is another Paul."[9] Intent upon reforming the moral abuses of his day, he harangued huge crowds in the open air, focusing his denunciations upon the sins of usury and lechery.[10] Clerical concubinage was a favorite target. Fulk not only condemned priests and their concubines generically, but he pointed them out in the crowd.[11] He had considerable success in redeeming prostitutes, either settling them under vows of celibacy in the convent of Saint Anthony near Paris or finding them doweries and husbands.[12] When Fulk denounced sin he filled the streets with innumerable penitents. His followers believed that he worked miracles, giving sight to the blind, hearing to the deaf, walking to the lame. As he journeyed, the sick were carried from long distances to lie along his route, so that they might touch his clothes as he passed.[13] Great as his eloquence and the force of his personality were, however, his success was also due to the foibles of his hearers. Readily moved to a high pitch of emotion, all too often they proved to be the shallow soil, on which the seed sprouted quickly, but as quickly withered, for it had no root.[14]

Just how Fulk became a preacher of the crusade remains obscure. Some believed that the Blessed Virgin appeared to him, commanding this mission.[15] We know that in September 1198 Fulk sought the aid of the white monks in preaching the crusade, but was refused.[16] Less than two months later, however, Innocent III authorized him to enlist both black and white monks in his campaign.[17] He traveled abroad, beyond his parish and the environs of Paris, subject only to the jurisdiction of the legate Peter. Fulk's crusade preaching recalls the fervor of Peter the Hermit and the First Crusade.[18] He touched the hearts of the common people. Although he also enlisted nobles, Fulk bestowed the crusader's cross upon many thousands of the poor.[19]

Cardinal-legate Peter Capuano, meanwhile, had proceeded to France where at Dijon he had promulgated the papal bull offering the full remission of sins to those who would take the cross or bear its financial burden. He succeeded in negotiating a truce between Philip Augustus and Richard, probably because Philip found himself in difficult straits and therefore ready to listen to the legate's proposals.[20] Peter, however, soon clashed with Philip over the king's displacement of the queen, Ingeborg of Denmark, in favor of Agnes of Meran. After the legate had placed France under the interdict he was withdrawn by the pope.[21]

The enlistment of a real crusading army of knights finally began at a tournament held by Count Thibaut of Champagne at his castle at Ecry-sur-Aisne in the Ardennes region of northern France on 28 November 1199.[22] This was fifteen months after Innocent had proclaimed the crusade, a year after he had authorized Fulk to enlist monks to preach it, and six months after the pope's original scheduled date of departure for the crusading army. From Champagne itself and from nearby lands a numerous and illustrious assemblage of knights had gathered to test their military prowess, to win honor before the ladies, and to enjoy the banqueting, the minstrelsy, and other social amenities of their class. Suddenly, when they were all armed and ready for the sport, the knights, led by Count Thibaut himself and by his cousin, Count Louis of Blois, put aside their weapons, and, swept by a common enthusiasm, committed themselves instead to the crusade.[23] Older historians painted a colorful picture of Fulk of Neuilly denouncing the frivolity in which they were engaged and turning their souls toward Christ. It is regrettable to have to give up such a romantic scene, but there is no evidence that he was present.[24] We do not know, in fact, what sparked their ardor: perhaps some preacher did take advantage of the gathering to issue his plea; or perhaps the fervor sprang spontaneously from Thibaut and Louis, for such waves of enthusiasm were not uncommon in the Middle Ages. In any case, the knights, uttering solemn oaths, converted the momentary passion into vows of a lasting and enforceable obligation.[25] As an outward sign of their commitment they received crosses of cloth to be worn proudly on their shoulders. They also gained the spiritual and temporal privileges of crusaders, the most important of which was the indulgence—the remission of the temporal penalties for sins.[26] Those who died on crusade were believed to enter straightway into the kingdom of heaven, rising from the dust of battle to the company of the saints. In popular estimation, the fallen heroes of the crusades were regarded as Christian martyrs.[27]

By this time the Latin church possessed a well developed doctrine of the crusade. The concept of Christian war appears alien to the thought and personality of Jesus, and, in fact, it was not looked upon favorably by the Greek church.[28] Throughout its history, however, the Christian church has survived and flourished by adaptation to its cultural milieu. As the Germanic tribes began to sweep over the Roman Empire, Saint Augustine had discussed the just war.[29] At the time of the disintegration of the Carolingian Empire and the invasions by Vikings, Magyars, and Muslims, the Christians of Western Europe, who were not far removed from their warlike barbaric ancestors, quite understandably had asserted the virtue of Holy War in defense of the interests of the church.[30] The Cluniacs of the eleventh century had extended the concept to the offensive war in Spain against the infidel.[31]

Another important component of the crusading idea was the pilgrimage, the journey of the penitent to sacred shrines to gain religious benefit. Originally pilgrims went unarmed, and as late as 1065 a devout band of pilgrims had refused to defend their lives with arms.[32] To Gregory VII's zeal for a holy war belongs the credit for sanctifying the armed pilgrimage by transforming the meaning of *militia Christi* from monastic asceticism to military combat, from a figurative to a quite literal interpretation.[33] The concept of a holy pilgrimage remained vital; medieval writers do not refer to the armed pilgrimage as a "crusade," but as an *expeditio, iter in terram sanctam,* or *peregrinatio,* the technical term for pilgrimage.[34] When the First Crusade had set out for Jerusalem the concept was not fully formed, but it had developed during the course of the movement. In the middle and late twelfth century the canonists had elaborated a quite specific doctrine of the crusade, which was summoned and authorized by the pope for a definite period against a specific enemy.[35]

Not all the knights who assumed the cross at Ecry, to be sure, were moved solely by religious considerations. The feudal noble's position in society, his code of honor, and his chivalric self-esteem urged him to the crusade. No measure of success in the lists could win for a knight such admiration from the ladies as he gained by taking the cross.[36] To men reared for warfare, moreover, the sheer joy of battle was a strong motive often neglected by bookish scholars. The winning of lands and, for the greater men, an enhanced role in power politics joined in the complex of motives that led men to devote themselves to a dangerous campaign in a distant land.

The two young counts, Thibaut and Louis, were among the most powerful and distinguished French nobles. Grandsons of Louis VII and Eleanor of Aquitaine, they were double cousins, for the two daughters of the royal marriage had married two noble brothers.[37] Thibaut and Louis, of course, were also nephews of Philip II Augustus and of Richard Lion-Heart and John. They were both young men in their twenties.[38] Thibaut's mother was Marie of Champagne, famed patroness of the gentled chivalry of the twelfth century, and from her circle he imbibed the code of the Arthurian romances, in which the armed pilgrimage played a prominent part. Thibaut's brother, Count Henry II, had earlier taken the cross, received the government of the Kingdom of Jerusalem in 1192, and died in the Levant in 1197.[39] Louis, too, was a model of crusading chivalry, who later proved his mettle by a valorous, if foolhardy, death in 1205.[40] The example of the two young barons, therefore, encouraged many to follow them in taking the crusaders' vow.[41] The tournament at Ecry provided the first tangible nucleus for a crusading army.

Soon after Ecry, other nobles of northern France were also inspired to join the Holy War. On Ash Wednesday, 23 February 1200, at the city of Bruges where several drops of the blood of Christ were treasured, Count Baldwin of Flanders took the cross.[42] Baldwin was known as a pious and just man, charitable to the poor, and generous to the clergy.[43] His beloved wife Marie, sister of Thibaut of Champagne, was also moved by the Lenten spirit of sacrifice and assumed the crusader's burden along with her husband. Afterwards, Baldwin's two brothers, Henry and Eustace, his nephew Thierry, and other Flemish nobles took their vows.[44] The count of Flanders was perhaps the most powerful of all the vassals of the French king. At twenty-eight years of age, ruler of his country since 1194, he had achieved a reputation for political sagacity, which was respected throughout Europe.[45] He had proven his military ability by defeating Philip Augustus and had shown great diplomatic alacrity in entering into an alliance with England, thereby forcing Philip to accept the provisions of the Treaty of Péronne.[46]

In Perche, Count Geoffrey and his brother, Stephen, who were also cousins of Thibaut and Louis, enlisted in the growing ranks of the crusade.[47] The interrelationships among the great nobles of France help to account for the wave of those taking up the cross, as the crusade took on something of the character of a family affair. But other great nobles, unrelated to the above, also enlisted. In Picardy, the powerful Count Hugh of Saint Pol, a veteran crusader, committed himself to the new enterprise, and naturally, many lesser nobles followed suit.[48] At Ecry, Renaud of Montmirail, cousin to the counts of Champagne and Blois, Simon de Montfort, future leader of the Albigensian Crusade, Geoffrey of Villehardouin, marshall of Champagne and chronicler of the Fourth Crusade, and many other knights had taken up the cross.[49] In Flanders, there were John of Nesle, the châtelain of Bruges, Conon of Béthune, and Baldwin of Beauvoir.[50] Perche supplied Rotrou of Montfort, Yves of La Jaille, and many others.[51] And from Picardy came Nicholas of Mailly, Walter of Nesle, and his son, Peter.[52]

It has been estimated that the initial wave of enlistments, which began with Ecry, netted about a hundred companies of eighty to a hundred men each. These were not, of course, all knights: many were commoners. The usual proportions for armies of that time were one heavily armored knight to two lightly armed squires or sergeants on horseback to four foot soldiers or sergeants on foot.[53]

In consequence of this popular response to the crusading call, the leading nobles held a *"parlament"* in early 1200 at Soissons.[54] Honored as guests of the city's bishop, Nivelon, one of the earliest ecclesiastics to enlist in the crusade, they met in order to settle upon a time of departure and a route.[55] Because a sufficient number had not yet enlisted, however, they disbanded without achieving anything.[56] Later in the year every count and baron who had been crossed met at Compiègne, on the border of Vermandois and the Ile-de-France, to deal with the organization and strategy of the coming expedition.[57] However, they found themselves in disagreement on many points and few conclusive decisions were made. Since earlier pilgrimages, most recently that of Frederick Barbarossa, however, had demonstrated the innumerable difficulties of the journey by land, its slowness, physical fatigue, and spiritual *ennui*, it was decided to go by sea. Many crusaders in the past had come to the same conclusion. Venice, Genoa and Pisa regularly sent two fleets a year to the Levant carrying crusaders and supplies for the settlers.[58] None of the feudal nobles possessed a fleet, of course, and only the count of Flanders could readily obtain one. Thus, they determined to seek transportation from one of the great Mediterranean maritime cities. The meeting ended with an agreement to appoint the best envoys they could find, give them full diplomatic powers to act in the names of their lords, and send them to secure transportation for the crusading army.[59]

The counts of Flanders, Champagne, and Blois appointed six plenipotentiaries for this purpose, among whom were Conon of Béthune and Geoffrey of Villehardouin.[60] Conon was a member of an illustrious family of Artois, a famed troubadour, and a veteran of the Third Crusade.[61] Geoffrey, the marshal of Champagne, a mature man of about fifty, was well known for his wisdom in council.[62] His chronicle of the Fourth Crusade reveals to us a mind well-organized and clear, though not profound.[63] Among the leaders of the crusade, he falls into a rank just below the great counts of Flanders, Blois and Champagne, a position of leadership higher than his relatively modest estate would in itself suggest.[64] The count of Champagne trusted none of his men more than the marshall, and, on this and other occasions when diplomatic skill was required, the crusaders invariably turned to Villehardouin for his counsel.[65]

Great trust was placed in these six envoys. Their principals, the counts of Flanders, Champagne, and Blois, had left all the details to be worked out by them: the envoys' agreements would be as binding as their own. As was not uncommon in medieval diplomacy, the principals did not even specify the parties with whom their representatives should negotiate, but agreed to be bound by whatever conventions they might make "in all the ports of the sea, in whatever place they might go."[66] Since no French port was capable of providing the number of ships they believed they would need, the envoys were left with a choice among the three great Italian maritime cities, Genoa, Pisa, and Venice, whose flourishing commerce contributed so much to the revival of Western Europe.[67] Robert of Clari contends that the envoys first sought aid from Genoa and Pisa before turning to Venice,[68] but the Picard knight is notoriously misinformed about the preliminaries of the crusade, confusing, in this case, actual visits to Pisa and Genoa by four of the envoys on the return trip.[69] These two western ports, weakened by their long struggles for maritime supremacy against each other, were in no condition at this time to undertake new ventures.[70] Genoa may also have been opposed by the French knights, for there had been numerous complaints concerning Genoese fulfillment of their contract to transport the army of Philip Augustus on the Third Crusade.[71] The envoys decided, therefore, in favor of the great port at the head of the Adriatic, the only one where they could find available the maritime resources required to meet their needs.[72]

There has been considerable debate over the attitude of Pope Innocent III toward the choice of Venice. One group of historians has argued that the pontiff not only favored the choice, but ordered it, trusting the Venetians more than the Genoese or Pisans.[73] The *Gesta Innocentii*, a Roman *apologia* for Innocent III, which is by no means a pro-Venetian source, tells of a papal legation sent to the two warring western ports in an effort to make peace between them in the interest of the crusade: the Genoese and Pisans, however, would not accept "the word of peace, because they were not sons of peace."[74] This, of course, left no alternative to Venice. A few of the pro-Venetian authorities, misinterpreting a passage in the *Devastatio Constantinopolitana*, hold that Innocent ordered the crusaders to take passage from Venice. He did do this, but it was two years later in 1202, long after a contract with Venice had been made and while crusaders were hesitating in Lombardy.[75] Innocent had urged the Venetians, in fact, to take the cross, both through a legate and in a letter of December 1198.[76] The letter is important for it demonstrates Innocent's willingness to compromise on certain issues in order to assure the future success of the crusade. Undoubtedly conceding to Venetian demands, the pope granted them permission to carry on trade with Egypt in nonstrategic goods. Until the crusaders had committed themselves to the Venetians, however, there is no solid evidence that Innocent III favored Venice rather than other Italian seaports.[77] That he ordered or demanded its selection is, indeed, a myth.

A larger group of historians has taken exactly the opposite approach. [78] They find a history of papal complaints against the Venetians throughout the crusades because of their refusal to give up their trade with the enemy. Venice showed greater interest in commercial privileges, they assert, than in the Holy War. The pope, therefore, according to this line of reasoning, was displeased with the choice of Venice, foreseeing a conflict between the mercantile spirit of the Republic of Saint Mark and the aims of the crusade. However, when the historian goes below the surface of this seemingly logical argument, the error of their interpretation becomes apparent. Although Venice had maintained profitable relations with the infidel for some time, commerce with the Muslim East was neither limited nor peculiar to Venice.[79] A generation earlier, Benjamin of Tudela had declared that people from all parts of Christendom frequented Alexandria for trade. His extensive list includes Tuscany, Lombardy, Apulia, Amalfi, Sicily, Genoa, and Pisa, but not (incorrectly, of course) Venice.[80] It is evident that other Italian sea powers were just as interested as the Venetians in taking advantage of lucrative trade with the infidel. While the church might well distrust the profit motive, Venetian merchants were not unique in pursuing it.[81] Innocent III neither encouraged nor discouraged the choice of Venice, which was the only port able to serve the crusaders' purposes.

The pope's preferences, in fact, had little or no bearing on the course of the crusade. Innocent's vision of papal leadership was already anachronistic in an increasingly secular society. The crusading leaders faced a practical problem of transportation, and they dealt with it in their own way, seeking counsel from neither the pope nor his legate. Venice seemed more likely to be able to supply what they needed, and so the envoys decided to go there.[82]

2

The Ill-fated Treaty
of Venice, 1201

In the dead of winter of 1200–1201 the crusaders' envoys struggled through the Mount Cenis Pass into the north Italian marquisate of Montferrat. Passing through Piacenza on the Po, they traversed the length of the Lombard Plain, and arrived at Venice during the first week of Lent.[1] They came to the great port at the head of the Adriatic seeking ships to bear their armies to the Levant for the reconquest of Jerusalem. They were welcomed warmly and honorably, as befitted ambassadors of great feudal lords, by the venerable doge Enrico Dandolo, garbed in almost imperial splendor and preceded by a sword, a chair of state draped in cloth of gold, and a parasol.[2]

Dandolo was a very old man in 1201— sources vary, but it is generally agreed that he was nearly eighty when he was elected doge in 1193. Some estimates are even higher. Marino Sanudo, the great sixteenth-century chronicler of Venetian affairs, declares that he was eighty-five at the time of his election.[3] He was a most distinguished old statesman, dignified and made wise with the years. He was also blind or nearly blind. Villehardouin, who was closely associated with him for four years, says that he did not see at all, but this is difficult to accept in the light of his exploits.[4] Old and handicapped as he was, Enrico Dandolo still possessed remarkable energy and had lost nothing of his mental acuity, but had indeed continued to sharpen it upon the whetstone of experience. The sources which reflect a direct acquaintance with the man reveal him as benevolent, eloquent, and universally respected.[5] Of course he possessed vast experience in affairs of commerce and of state. Novices were not elected to head the Venetian state. He possessed a great and penetrating sense of politics. He was also an ingenious and skilled diplomat and an equally skilled strategist and tactician. He was one of those men whose qualities make others turn naturally to them for leadership, as the young crusading barons were to learn to do. Many historians picture him as extraordinarily ruthless and unscrupulous when the glory, wealth, and power of the republic were at stake.[6] He was certainly an ardent Venetian patriot: he was

9

also not a saint, but a man of the world. As a Venetian and a bourgeois his values were not identical with those of northern European chivalry, nor should that be expected. No absolute scale, however, places chivalric virtues on a higher plane than those of the bourgeoisie.[7] Dandolo was ambitious for his own glory and for the prosperity and power of the republic; he was not, however, the unscrupulous manipulator that some historians have depicted.

The envoys delivered to the doge their letters of credence to which were appended clauses giving them full powers to commit their principals. When Dandolo had seen them, he appointed an audience for the envoys on the fourth day.[8] At the agreed time Villehardouin and his companions were led before the doge and his Small Council (the Council of Six) in the ducal palace. There they presented their request: "Lord, we have come to you on behalf of the great barons of France, who have taken the sign of the cross to avenge the shame done to Jesus Christ and to conquer Jerusalem, if God permits. And because they know that no one has as great power as you and your people, they beg you for the love of God to have pity on the land beyond the sea and on the shame done to Jesus Christ, and to consider how they can obtain vessels and a fleet."[9] Villehardouin does not record giving any estimation of the number of crusaders for whom transportation would be needed, but it is not believable that the envoys had failed to receive such an estimate from the magnates at Compiègne or that they neglected to communicate it to the doge. They could not, after all, have opened negotiations by requesting a fleet of unspecified size. The treaty subsequently concluded states that the envoys requested transportation for four thousand five hundred horses, four thousand five hundred knights, nine thousand squires, and twenty thousand foot soldiers.[10] Responsibility for the estimate of the number of crusaders is no mere detail of the dickering with the Venetians, for the overestimation was crucial to the outcome of the Fourth Crusade. The doge replied that he would respond in eight days, for this was a very serious matter which required much thought.[11]

When the French knights rejoined the doge and his council on the determined day the Venetians were ready with an offer. On condition of approval by the Great Council and the popular assembly, the doge proposed to provide horse transports (*usserii*) and transports (*naves*) for the specified numbers of men and horses. The Venetians would also provision the army for a year.[12] The doge asked in payment four marks for each knight and each horse and two marks for each squire and foot soldier, or a total of ninety-four thousand marks. In addition to the transportation that the French had requested, Dandolo offered to supply fifty war galleys at the expense of Venice on condition that the Venetians should receive a half-share in any conquests made by the combined forces. The envoys replied that they would consult together and would respond on the following day. By and large they found the offer acceptable, but, if the requested price given above is correct, they must have determined to seek a reduction in the rate for knights from four marks to two, or a new basis of four marks per horse and two marks per man. Thus, on the following day, the French and the Venetians agreed upon terms at a cost of eighty-five thousand marks of Cologne to be paid in four installments by April 1202, when the crusaders should come to Venice. The fleet would be ready to sail on the feast of Saints Peter and Paul, 29 June.[13]

Some scholars have charged that the Venetians imposed extortionate terms upon the guileless warriors from the north, but it was overestimation of the numbers of the crusaders, not the price demanded by the doge, which proved disastrous.[14] Villehardouin was no innocent babe, but a man of experience whose judgment was highly trusted. Among the entire host of crusaders and Venetians only Dandolo was more highly regarded in council than he.[15] We can also compare the treaty of 1201 with other contracts for transportation of crusaders to determine whether its terms were reasonable. In the earliest such contract that we possess, Genoa agreed in 1184 to carry a small band of thirteen knights, twenty-six horses, and twenty-six squires with provisions for eight months at a cost of eight-and-one-half marks per unit of one knight, two horses, and two squires.[16] The treaty of 1201 would have charged fourteen marks for a knight, two horses, and two squires, but for a year. The price of the contract of 1184 for a comparable time would presumably have been twelve-and-three-fourths marks. In 1190 Philip Augustus contracted with Genoa for an army of 650 knights, 1,300 horses, and 1,300 squires at a rate of nine marks per unit of one knight, two horses, and two squires for eight months, or, presumably, thirteen-and-a-half marks for a year. Moreover, under the contract of 1190, wine was to be provided for only four months. The Genoese were also to receive concessions in the conquered cities.[17] Genoese performance of the earlier contract, furthermore, was a source of French complaints,[18] while our sources on the Fourth Crusade have only praise for the fleet prepared by Venice.[19] The treaty of the crusaders with the Venetians, therefore, while a bit more costly than the contracts of 1184 and 1194, cannot be called extortionate.[20]

As the doge had told the envoys, he now had to seek the assent of the Great Council and the people. In former days a doge could have acted on the basis of the consent of the popular assembly alone, but little by little the ducal power, like that of the people, was eroding before the rise of the Venetian oligarchy. Now, apart from his powers as commander-in-chief, the doge could do nothing without the Great Council's approval.[21] Enrico Dandolo, of course, was no common doge. His age, his great ability, and his reputation earned him an extraordinary influence upon his countrymen. When the treaty was presented to the Great Council it was applauded and approved. Then Dandolo summoned increasingly larger groups, first one hundred, then two hundred, finally a thousand, according to Villehardouin, which approved in their turn.22

At last, for the final acceptance of the treaty on the part of the Venetians, Dandolo assembled the *arengo* or popular assembly, consisting of ten thousand persons, according to Villehardouin. They met in the dim golden glow of Saint Mark's. The venerable doge spoke to the people, explaining the question before them and how the proposed treaty would redound to the honor and profit of the city. He then bade them hear a mass of the Holy Spirit, as was appropriate upon such a solemn occasion, and to pray to God for guidance concerning the request of the crusaders. After the mass had been said Dandolo invited the crusaders to address the people. Villehardouin tells how the crowd stared curiously at the French envoys, who were the center of attention, since few Venetians until this moment had seen these strangers whose request promised to transform their lives for good or ill. Villehardouin himself spoke for the envoys, telling his hearers how the most powerful lords in France had sent him and his colleagues to Venice, knowing that no other city had such great power on the sea.23 Moved by the solemn setting and his zeal for the cross, the marshal of Champagne implored his hearers to have mercy on the Holy City and to avenge the shame done to Jesus Christ by the desecration of the Holy Places. Finishing his plea, Villehardouin, joined by the other envoys, fell to his knees, weeping copiously, and swearing that they would not arise until their request was granted. Such a display was not regarded as unseemly in the Middle Ages, for men showed their emotions more openly then than we do today. Dandolo and his Venetians, equally moved by the plight of the Holy Land, also wept and stretched their arms on high, crying, "We grant it! We grant it!" And then there went up such a shout, says Villehardouin, that the earth itself seemed to tremble. Finally the doge spoke once more from the lectern, telling his people how highly honored they were that the greatest men in the world had chosen them as their companions in this exalted enterprise.24 The envoys had fulfilled their mission, and more than fulfilled it, in that the Venetians had agreed not only to provide transportation, but to join the expedition as allies. Only details and formalities remained.

On the following day, according to Geoffrey, the treaty was officially redacted.25 Two copies of it, both in the name of the doge, survive. We do not possess the complementary copies in the names of the crusaders, but the envoys bore with them blank parchments previously sealed by their principals, which were undoubtedly used for this purpose. Villehardouin and his colleagues met with the doge and his Great and Small Councils in the ducal palace for the concluding ceremonies. When the doge delivered the treaty to the envoys he fell to his knees in tears swearing to maintain the covenants in good faith. The French, who had used some of their blank sealed parchments to inscribe oaths on behalf of the counts of Flanders, Champagne, and Blois, also were in tears as they swore their adherence.[26]

The treaty did not name a specific destination, although the envoys had secretly agreed with the doge and the Small Council that the crusade should land in Egypt (*Babilloine*), because they believed that the Holy Land could be recovered more easily from the Muslims in this way than by direct assault.[27] The idea was not new. There were hints of it during the First Crusade. King Amalric of Jerusalem (1163–1174) had later made five unsuccessful assaults upon Egypt, and Renaud of Châtillon, lord of Transjordan, had incensed Saladin in 1183 by his foray into the Red Sea area. The idea of an attack by Western crusaders upon this center of Muslim power had gained increasing support after Richard Lion-Heart had considered it, and it was to prevail in the crusades of the coming century.[28] Gradually, the single-minded zeal of the earlier crusaders was giving way to the development of a strategy. It has been argued that the failure of the Westerners to seize and hold the great interior cities, such as Damascus and Aleppo, possession of which would have posed a threat to Baghdad itself and to the valley of the Tigris-Euphrates, was responsible for the ultimate defeat of the crusaders. The failure to gain a foothold in Egypt, however, was more important. The crusaders themselves were aware of the precarious nature of their possessions along the Syrian coast, vulnerable to a pincer movement from Egypt in the South and from upper Mesopotamia in the North. The Egyptian littoral, on the other hand, was critical to communications among the Muslims. Not for nothing was Alexandria called the market of the two worlds. If the crusaders could cut the lines between North Africa and the eastern Muslim world, the whole of Islam would be in jeopardy, and Jerusalem would fall like ripe fruit into their hands. As it turned out, of course, neither the Fourth Crusade nor subsequent attempts upon the Delta succeeded, and ultimately a Muslim offensive launched from Egypt drove the Latins from the Levant.[29] To the crusaders and the Venetians in 1201, however, there seemed every promise of success. They knew that Egypt was in the midst of hard times. For five years the Nile had failed to deliver its fruitful flood, and the land was in a weakened state, overwhelmed by famine and poverty.[30]

Prospects for the crusade in the Holy Land itself, moreover, did not present an encouraging aspect. The Christians of the Levant had entered into a five-year truce with the Muslims in 1198, and were not disposed to violate it.[31] When Renaud of Dampierre, one of the French crusaders who was to sail directly from Apulia to the Holy Land in 1202, arrived there, he pleaded with King Aimery to break the truce, which the king would not do.[32] Such incidents as this confirmed in the minds of the crusaders their distrust for their coreligionists of Syria. Decades of dwelling in the East as conquerors had softened their natures and dulled their ardor for war. The religious zeal that had driven their ancestors had given way to the enjoyment of the good life. Their great concern in these matters was that what they possessed should not be put in jeopardy. They were even suspected of having set a trap with the Muslims for earlier crusaders out of a fear that the newcomers would dispossess them, a charge which is probably extreme and ill-founded, but which reflects the attitude of some of the new crusaders. Certainly no one counted upon the Christians of the Levant for much help.[33] To the leading men, therefore, the plan to attack the Nile Delta made a great deal of sense. If they succeeded in seizing one of the great port cities, the sultan would be compelled to yield Jerusalem to protect his more vital interests.

Strategic considerations were supported by a shift in religious attitude. In the course of a century of crusading the Holy Land had ceased to be the specific and unique objective of some of those who bore the cross. The concept of the crusade had become less specifically associated with the places consecrated by the life of Christ. A Christian who made war at the behest of the Church against the enemies of Christendom in Spain or elsewhere was conceived to be fighting for the heavenly Jerusalem and to be entitled to the privileges of a crusader. For those who saw the crusade in these broader terms, therefore, it was no less sacred a task to attack Egypt than Palestine.[34]

This liberal view, however, had failed to capture the minds of many crusaders, particularly those in the ranks. Simple men were still drawn to the actual places where the Lord had lived and died and they felt bound, as we shall see, to a literal accomplishment of their vows. For this reason, although the negotiators agreed upon Egypt, the treaty was deliberately vague concerning the destination. The envoys did not wish to arouse dissension among the mass of crusaders when the terms of the treaty became known to them. In general, the great barons, more inclined to strategic considerations, favored Egypt, while many of the lesser men simply assumed that their single and immediate goal was Jerusalem. Probably not even the barons were all of one mind. We know that the councils at Compiègne in 1200 had been so fraught with dissension that the envoys had been entrusted with remarkable power of discretion, because the barons themselves were unable to agree. The question of the destination of the host was almost certainly one of the chief points of dispute. A crusading army was a rather disorderly mass. Each man, certainly each of the more powerful men, remained free to follow the dictates of his own will or his own conscience. In order to attract as many of the crusaders as possible to Venice, therefore, deliberate obscurity concerning the destination was sound policy. Announcement that they planned to sail for Egypt could only cause disaccord and defection. Once all were gathered in Venice, however, a certain commitment to the common enterprise would already have been made and the influence of the leaders would be stronger.[35]

Before leaving Venice the envoys borrowed two thousand marks to pay the Venetians to begin construction of the fleet.[36] They may have used blanks presealed by the three counts for this also.[37] It is true that the terms of the treaty do not seem to require any payment before August, but Villehardouin tells of borrowing the money from a Venetian bank near the Rialto bridge.[38] This earnest money permitted the building of the fleet to begin.

The preparation of ships to transport an army of 33,500 men, plus the fifty galleys that Venice was to provide at her own cost, was a massive undertaking, even for the great Adriatic maritime republic. Robert of Clari reports that the doge suspended Venetian commerce for eighteen months in order to concentrate upon preparing the fleet.[39] Payment for the labor involved in the construction of the fleet stimulated the issuance of a new coin, probably the quarter-penny or quartarolo.[40] Provision of the ships required for the expedition, as foreseen by the treaty, was an enormous task. We know that the fleet before Constantinople numbered approximately two hundred ships.[41] Villehardouin tells us, however, and there is every reason to believe him, that the Venetians had prepared ships for at least three times as many crusaders as appeared in Venice.[42] We must conclude, therefore, that the Venetians had prepared, in addition to the fifty galleys, some four hundred fifty transports. It obviously required all the resources Venice could muster to make ready such an imposing fleet, even if it numbered considerably less than the five hundred vessels we have calculated.[43] Lane further asserts that Venice's commitment of transportation and warships would obligate at least one-half the city's able-bodied men.[44] These facts have been too little noted by critics of the Venetian role in the Fourth Crusade. The city had made a tremendous effort and had committed itself very deeply to the enterprise. Its failure would be a disaster for the merchants of the Rialto and the city whose well-being depended upon them.

No one could then anticipate it, but this treaty of transportation of 1201 set the crusade on the course which was to lead to Constantinople. It was not that the Venetians took advantage of the knights from beyond the Alps, but that the envoys of the crusaders committed themselves to conventions impossible of fulfillment. Contracting for ships and supplies for an army of thirty-three thousand five hundred men was extravagantly optimistic, to say the least. Presumably the envoys were not completely uninstructed by their principals, so the full blame does not rest upon them, but must be shouldered in large measure by the young counts of Flanders, Champagne, and Blois. Probably no ruler of the time, no king or emperor, could raise such a force, certainly not without the very greatest difficulty.[45] Events were to prove that the leaders of the crusade could not. As a result of their failure necessity and circumstance would draw the Fourth Crusade step by step to the shores of the Bosporus.

The marshal of Champagne, Geoffrey of Villehardouin, has often been indicted as an official historian of the crusade, cleverly appearing to tell the whole story, but actually concealing devious plots to divert the army to Constantinople. Revelation of the whole truth, according to this view, would have been most embarrassing to the small circle of leaders to which he belonged.[46] Where Villehardouin's account can be checked against official documents, however, he proves to be relatively accurate and quite specific, if somewhat superficial. His description of the negotiations at Venice in early 1201 can be verified in considerable detail by the treaty itself and other official documents. In spite of a few minor deviations, which do not appear to reflect any desire to mislead, he analyzes the conventions carefully and accurately. His chronology is also detailed and relatively precise, although his date for the conclusion of the treaty is difficult to reconcile with the date which the official document bears. Again, however, there seems to be no deep significance in the discrepancy. The tone and style of certain passages, moreover, particularly those recounting the speeches of the envoys, suggest that he was working with documents or notes in hand. It has been suggested that when he wrote his account some years later he possessed copies of numerous official documents and possibly a journal that he had kept day by day.[47] Certainly the style of his chronicle is very different from the impressionistic one of Robert of Clari. The evidence brought against his honesty is not convincing. He does not probe underlying causes and motives, it is true, for his approach, while detailed, is not profound. It is the style of a soldier, not that of a trained historian. If, as the fate of the crusade unfolds, he appears to be pleading for the defense, it is not because he is concealing some secret plot, but because he himself played such a prominent role in making the treaty from which all subsequent difficulties followed.[48]

Finally the envoys joined the Venetians in dispatching messengers to Rome to obtain papal confirmation of the treaty. This would lend added sanction to their covenants. Such confirmation was granted between 5 May and 8 May. Opinions differ, however, concerning Innocent's reaction to the news brought by the envoys from Venice.[49] Villehardouin reports simply that the pope confirmed the treaty "very willingly".[50] Innocent's clerical biographer, however, describes the attitude of the pope in quite different terms. Foreseeing the future, Innocent cautiously replied that he would confirm those conventions, provided the crusaders should not harm

Christians, unless they would wrongfully impede the passage of the crusade or another just or necessary cause would occur. The consent of the papal legate would be required before any such attack on Christians could be undertaken. The author of the *Gesta Innocentii* continues that the Venetians would not accept the confirmation with these provisions, from which he concludes that they planned an attack upon Christian territory from the beginning.[51] Which of the two, the marshal of Champagne or the Roman cleric, tells the truth? Supporters of the *Gesta* (those who blame Venetian greed for the outcome of the crusade) point to the long-standing Venetian trade with the infidel and the reluctance of the merchants of the lagoons to give up their profits in spite of repeated papal prohibitions. Innocent, according to this view, saw the Venetians as dangerous and untrustworthy allies, and granted even qualified approval to the pact only very reluctantly. Those who support Villehardouin reply that the papacy had not shown itself fearful of the Venetians, that Innocent had sought their participation in the crusade, that he had conceded them the right to deal with Egypt in nonmilitary goods, and that his letter to them of 8 May 1201 spoke in warm terms of their commitment to the crusade. These historians concede that the *Gesta* is a generally reliable source often based directly upon papal letters. It was not written until 1208, however, seven years after the events in question, and it is an *apologia* for Innocent III, who may have inspired its composition himself. Writing long after the conquest of Constantinople and after Innocent had finally recognized the failure of the Fourth Crusade, and unwilling to burden the pope with any share of responsibility for the outcome, the author, according to this view, knowingly or unknowingly transferred to May 1201 the prohibition against attacking Christians first actually delivered in November 1202. In doing so he not only sought to avoid embarassment for the pope, but attributed to him a remarkable foresight of things to come.[52]

It is possible, however, to believe that the pope confirmed the treaty very willingly, yet also imposed conditions, although Innocent's prescience must be dismissed as the overly enthusiastic praise of an apologist. A letter of the pope to Dandolo of 25 February 1204, recounts "how we gave warning to your envoys, who came to the Apostolic See seeking that the pacts undertaken between you should be confirmed, and through them to you and to the Venetians, lest you should harm the lands of that king [of Hungary] in any way." This can scarcely refer to any other agreements than those of 1201. The prohibition seems to have been verbal and it is not identical with the prohibition in the *Gesta*, since it deals specifically with the Hungarian kingdom. The papal letter, however, continues, that "through our letters" the Venetians had been strictly admonished not to invade or harm the lands of Christians with the exceptions and conditions given in the *Gesta*.[53] It is possible, of course, that the pope here refers to a document considerably later than the verbal prohibition, but it is probably not so. Very likely, given the record of earlier crusaders in becoming involved in peripheral campaigns and interventions, Innocent did deliver a specific oral warning to the envoys in an effort to protect the king of Hungary, and then shortly in the written confirmation of the treaty broadened the prohibition to include attacks upon any Christian lands. Since the *Gesta* is, in general, a reliable source, it seems preferable to adopt this interpretation, which is in no way contradictory to Villehardouin.

Innocent's prescience and his distrust of the Venetians, however, need not be accepted. For one thing, the author of the *Gesta* is not here writing from documents, but speculating concerning his hero's frame of mind. For another, no specific foresight and suspicion need be predicated, for the crusades had already given ample evidence of the likelihood that conflicts among Christians would arise. The papal prohibition was simply the product of experience and common sense.[54]

Papal confirmation could not make a bad treaty a good one. No doubt the pope rejoiced at the huge army that was intended to assemble at Venice in the spring of 1202, but Innocent had no power to transform unrealistic plans into realities. The fateful treaty of 1201 was to lead to one crisis after another for the crusaders who did assemble in Venice, and they had to meet these crises one by one, as best they could, papal prohibitions notwithstanding.

3

The Election of Boniface
of Montferrat

After Villehardouin and his five colleagues had arranged for transportation of the crusade, they set out for home to report the success of their mission. When they reached Piacenza the party divided, Geoffrey the marshal and Alard Maquereau continuing toward France, while the other four journeyed to Genoa and Pisa to discover what those cities would do to aid Jerusalem. Since the envoys had already entered into a binding contract with the Venetians for ships to convey an enormous army, they could not have been seeking in Genoa and Pisa additional transportation or more favorable terms. Possibly they considered it worth the detour to see if they might gain Genoese or Pisan participation in the crusade, or it might have been merely a courteous gesture in the hope of averting any adverse reaction to the alliance with Venice on the part of the great Ligurian and Tyrrhenian ports. In any case, the Genoese and Pisans replied that they could do nothing.[1]

While their colleagues were occupied with this fruitless journey Geoffrey and his companion retraced their way home via the western Alps. Between Piacenza and the Mont Cenis pass they would have had to pass through the marquisate of Monteferrat, and it is highly probable that there they visited with Marquis Boniface.[2] The crusader-envoys were seeking men and money in support of their enterprise. Boniface was a famous knight, and, moreover, a relative by marriage of Count Thibaut of Champagne. The court of Montferrat, in addition, was a center for chivalric entertainment. Noble visitors gathered there to hear the songs of some of the most famous troubadours in Europe. Considering Villehardouin's own status, connections, and interests it is hardly likely that he would pass by the court of Marquis Boniface without stopping. In all probability he told the marquis of the mission to Venice, and Boniface may have shown himself inclined to join the French crusaders. Perhaps Geoffrey and Boniface established then the friendly relationship which was to become so strong and enduring. All of this, of course, is merely reasonable speculation. A month or so later, however, when the crusaders were seeking a new chief, Ville-

19

hardouin was entirely confident that the lord of Montferrat would accept
a summons to lead the crusade. It seems plausible to conclude, therefore,
that there was a meeting at the time of Geoffrey's return from Venice.[3]

Resuming their homeward journey, Villehardouin and Maquereau
traversed the Mont Cenis pass. On their way they encountered Walter of
Brienne, accompanied by a considerable number of crusaders from Champagne and elsewhere. The count of Brienne had been enlisted by Pope Innocent as an instrument in the faltering papal struggle against the party of
the Hohenstaufen for control of Italy and Sicily. Walter had married the
eldest daughter of Tancred, last of the Norman kings of Naples and Sicily,
the foe of the imperial Hohenstaufen. The pope promised support for Walter's efforts to conquer, in the name of his wife, the county of Lecce and
the principality of Taranto in Apulia, the heel of the Italian boot.[4] Innocent regarded his war against the Germans in Italy as a quasi-crusade, and
once even threatened to divert the entire Fourth Crusade to Sicily, though
he probably did not really mean it.[5] In exchange for news of Walter's affairs Villehardouin recounted the accomplishments of the crusader-envoys
at Venice. He reports that the count of Brienne and his companions rejoiced at the news and congratulated the negotiators. Walter declared that
he and his men were already en route, and that when the main body of
crusaders would come they would find him and his followers quite ready.[6]
It appears that the count and his men regarded the campaign in Apulia as
a side-journey on their expedition to the Holy Land, which offers a key to
the understanding of the later excursions to Zara and Constantinople. Villehardouin tells of the encounter with joy, but it was fraught with evil portents. Although Innocent did not, like some pontiffs, cynically sacrifice the
cause of the Holy Land to other interests, he was here making use of crusaders pledged to the pilgrimage overseas for papal warfare in Italy.[7] This
hardly comported with his pleas to other rulers to cease their wars in the
interest of the crusade. No doubt he hoped and Walter confidently expected that their battle would be swiftly won and that these crusaders
would indeed be ready within a year to fulfill their vows, but, if so, they
were tragically wrong. Furthermore, Villehardouin does not record, nor is
it logical to expect, that the count promised to lead his men back up the
peninsula to the rendezvous at Venice. If he were able to join the crusading army at all, he would naturally embark his troops directly from an
Apulian port. Thus there was already lost to the future assemblage at Venice a number of men described as "a great part of the crusaders from
Champagne."[8] As it turned out, the pope was able to lend Walter of Brienne only a little support. Even so, within a few months he had marched
to a victory near Capua and he gained a great part of Apulia. Later he put
his German foe to flight upon the historic field at Cannae. Many enthusiastic Italians flocked to follow his banners, including the young Francis of

Assisi, who fell out, however, upon the way, overcome by the call to a new and greater cause.[9] Provençal and Italian troubadours, who hated the Germans, sang the praises of the count of Brienne.[10] In the end, however, Walter was surprised in his camp and slain by the enemy in June of 1205, long after the departure of the crusade from Venice.[11] A considerable body of good fighting men was thus lost to the crusade. And by so much the chances of fulfilling the newly made compact with the Venetians were diminished.[12]

Without further incident Geoffrey and Alard hastened by way of Burgundy to Troyes to report their success to Count Thibaut. They found the young count very ill, but he received the news of the progress of his plans with such joy that he rose from his bed and mounted his horse. He had not ridden since his illness. The exercise exacerbated the ailment, which, in any case, may have been fatal, and he took once more to his bed, never to rise again. Anticipating death, the count made what preparations he could. Deprived of the opportunity of fulfilling his pilgrimage to the Holy Land, he appointed a knight, Renaud of Dampierre, and provided him with sufficient money to go in his place. Then he made his testament. Of the money that he had gathered for the crusade, he distributed some among his followers for their expenses of the journey.[13] He made each of them swear to follow the army assembling at Venice. Many of these, Villehardouin complains, later violated that trust. The remainder of this money was reserved for the army to be used for the crusade. Having made what preparations were possible for the repose of his soul and for the holy cause to which he had dedicated himself, on 24 May the young count of Champagne died. He left mourning his widow Blanche and a small daughter, and only a few days later, perhaps 30 May, Blanche gave birth to a son, the famous Thibaut IV of Champagne. Thibaut III's body was laid to rest with great pomp beside that of his father in the Church of Saint Stephen, which the latter had built at Troyes.[14] Over the new tomb they raised an inscription:

> Intent upon making amends for the injuries of the Cross
>   and the land of the Crucified
> He paved a way with expenses, an army, a fleet.
> Seeking the terrestrial city, he finds the one celestial;
> While he is obtaining his goal far away,
>   he finds it at home.[15]

The precise role of leadership of Thibaut in the Fourth Crusade is not clear. Robert of Clari declares that the count was elected to lead the enterprise shortly before his death, which Robert incorrectly places before the Treaty of Venice.[16] Ernoul-Bernard reports that the election took place after the treaty at an assembly of the crusaders at Corbie.[17] Robert, however, cannot be trusted until his own arrival in Venice in the summer of 1202 and Ernoul-Bernard cannot be counted upon for details of events in far away France. Both are obviously confused on the various assemblies of the barons. It is quite clear that Thibaut was not sole commander prior to the spring of 1201.[18] Despite Villehardouin's prominence, the six envoys to Venice were of equal status in a formal sense, and the Treaty of Venice lists the counts of Flanders, Champagne, and Blois in that order.[19] If Thibaut had been elected chief between the time of Villehardouin's and Maquereau's return and his death, it seems almost certain that Geoffrey, one of the vassals and companions who admired him so highly, would have recorded it, but he does not. The marshal does report, however, that the duke of Burgundy was offered Thibaut's place, the money reserved for the crusade, and the obedience that the crusaders owed to the count of Champagne.[20] The offer finally accepted by Boniface of Montferrat included taking the place of the count of Champagne and command of the army.[21] After Thibaut's death it does seem as if he was recognized as having been the chief among the leaders, whether or not this was the result of a formal election. It may have been merely an informal recognition of his initiative at Ecry, his power and prestige, his influence over Louis of Blois, and perhaps his generous testament. It has been suggested, on the other hand, that Thibaut's last and fatal ride was the journey to Corbie, where, as Ernoul-Bernard declares, he was elected to leadership as a final tribute to a dying man.[22]

Although Villehardouin does not mention an assembly at Corbie, and it is not possible to determine whether Count Thibaut was elected to command there, it does seem reasonable to believe that the leading men gathered to hear the report of the envoys to Venice and to ratify the treaty. The Venetians had included in the document requirements that the three principals must ratify it and that the other crusaders should swear their own adherence to its terms.[23]

After Thibaut's burial the crusaders sought a new leader. Matthew of Montmorency, Simon de Montfort, Geoffrey of Joinville (the seneschal of Champagne), and Villehardouin were sent to offer the position to Duke Eudes of Burgundy, a cousin of Thibaut. They requested him to take the cross and come to the succor of the Holy Land. If he consented he would receive the allegiance of the crusaders and the money that Thibaut had left for the crusade. When the duke of Burgundy refused, Joinville then was sent to make the same offer to Count Thibaut of Bar-le-Duc, also a cousin of the deceased count of Champagne. He in turn declined.[24] So in late June another assembly was held at Soissons to determine what should be done. All the chief men of the French crusaders were present, Baldwin of Flanders, Louis of Blois, Geoffrey of Perche, Hugh of Saint Pol, and many others. Villehardouin proposed that the leadership should be offered to Boniface, marquis of Montferrat, a very worthy and one of the most highly regarded men alive, and he assured the assembled barons that the marquis would accept.[25] Villehardouin's confidence has been interpreted as a sign of prior collusion between the Italian marquis and the marshal of Champagne to place Boniface at the head of the crusade, but there is no evidence of this.[26] The two had probably conferred at the time of the marshal's return from Venice, but it is not at all credible that Geoffrey and Boniface could have foreseen the tangled skein of events, the death of the count of Champagne and the refusals of the duke of Burgundy and the count of Bar-le-Duc, which led to the choice at Soissons. There was much debate among the crusaders, now troubled by their failure to obtain a leader, but they finally agreed upon the Italian marquis.[27]

One may well ask why the command was not offered to the powerful and popular Baldwin of Flanders. After the death of the count of Champagne no one would seem to possess a better claim to leadership than he. Two reasons for overlooking Baldwin may be cited. The offers to the duke of Burgundy, the count of Bar-le-Duc, and the marquis of Montferrat, none of whom had at that time joined the crusade, suggest that the barons were seeking to use the vacant post to add to their ranks. The enlistment of a prominent baron with his followers would entail a sizable increase in the numbers of the crusaders. Perhaps they already had premonition of difficulty in fulfilling the treaty with the Venetians. Baldwin, moreover, was no favorite of the king of France, whom he had humiliated.[28] Apart from personal feelings, the king would have a natural reluctance to enhance so greatly the prestige of one of his most powerful vassals. If it is true, as it appears to be, that Philip Augustus intervened on behalf of Boniface, his opposition to the count of Flanders provides a motive.[29]

The marquis of Montferrat, to be sure, had imposing qualifications on his own account to attract the attention of the leaderless crusaders. He belonged to the great international aristocracy. The house of Montferrat was related to both the German Hohenstaufens and the French Capetians and it had played a celebrated role in the earlier crusades.[30] In his early fifties, Boniface was a mature leader with long experience of command. He had governed Montferrat since 1183, and had been marquis since 1192, when his brother Conrad died in the East.[31] His aptitude in diplomacy is proved by his ability to retain the trust of the pope in spite of his loyalty to the Hohenstaufen.[32] He was widely regarded as an ideal Christian knight. His impetuous valor finally brought about his death in 1207 when he rushed into battle armed only with a sword.[33] He was one of the best fighting men and commanders of his day. According to his faithful troubadour, Raimbaut de Vaqueiras, Boniface was also renowned for compassion toward the weak and distressed and respect toward ladies. As young men Boniface and Raimbaut had shared romantic expeditions in the service of ladies, emulating the heroes of romance. The court of Montferrat was a center of chivalry. In his *Epic Letter* Raimbaut celebrates the courtly life, the fine raiment and armor, the jousts and song, the hospitality of Montferrat.[34]

The marquis of Montferrat was without question a brilliant choice. Recognized as the greatest of the Italian nobles, he possessed formidable power and large numbers of fighting men. His marquisate lay in the Piedmont, straddling the banks of the Tanaro River between Turin on the west and Tortona on the east. As a Lombard prince, Boniface would be relatively acceptable to the various national components of the crusading army, the Italians, the Germans, and the many French.[35]

The *Gesta* of Innocent III informs us, in fact, that the selection of Boniface was made upon the advice of Philip Augustus, the king of France.[36] Contrary to the opinion of those who believe that many crusaders enlisted to escape the wrath of Philip, it was quite natural that the French barons should consult with their king on so important a matter.[37] That the Venetians recognized the king's influence among the crusaders is proved by their demand that his oath be sought in support of the treaty for transportation.[38] Boniface's visit to the court of France immediately before his acceptance of the command also lends support to the belief that Philip Augustus influenced the selection.[39]

Philip of Swabia, Hohenstaufen claimant to the German kingship and the Holy Roman Empire, also was favorably inclined, since the house of Montferrat had a heritage of allegiance to the Ghibelline cause. During Frederick Barbarossa's wars against the Lombard League, Boniface and his brothers joined in defending the marquisate against the attacks of the antiimperial communes of Piedmont and Lombardy.[40] In these wars the young nobleman grew up, disciplined by experience in battle to the duties of his position in life. At the Reichstag at Mainz in February of 1194 the Piedmontese marquis Boniface ranked among the great princes of the empire, the duke of Austria, the duke of Swabia, and others.[41] He joined Henry VI's campaign of the same year against the Normans of Naples and Sicily, received the title of imperial legate, and, along with the podestà of Genoa, was placed in command of the fleet. He nearly was killed at Messina for the Ghibelline cause, but survived to enjoy Henry's coronation at Palermo on Christmas of 1194.[42] After the premature death of Henry VI Boniface continued to enjoy the friendship and favor of Philip of Swabia.

Boniface was a choice agreeable also to Pope Innocent. In 1199 the pontiff had chosen the marquis of Montferrat as a colleague of the highly regarded Conrad, cardinal-archbishop of Mainz, in a vain effort to settle the struggle over the German throne between the Hohenstaufen Philip of Swabia and the Welf Otto of Brunswick, or at least to try to obtain a truce of five years.[43] In light of the well-known Hohenstaufen loyalties of the marquis of Montferrat his employment by the pope in this prominent role is surprising. Innocent must have had great confidence in Boniface, a relative, vassal, and friend of the feared German dynasty, to entrust him with this task.[44]

Few families could rival the reputation of the house of Montferrat in the Levant. Boniface's father, William the Old, had fought with distinction on the Second Crusade. When the barons of the kingdom of Jerusalem decided to seek a successor from Europe for the leper Baldwin IV, who had no hope of an heir of his body, the renown of the marquis William and his flourishing family attracted their attention. Boniface's eldest brother, William Longsword, was therefore called to Palestine in 1176 to marry Baldwin's sister Sibyl and to provide for the succession to the crown. William's energy, intelligence and valor soon gained a predominant influence over the sick king, arousing the envy of some of the magnates. A bare three months after his marriage William died mysteriously. The posthumous son of this brief marriage was the future king, Baldwin V.[45] William the Old himself returned to the Holy Land, falling captive in 1187 to the victorious Saladin at the fateful Battle of Hattin, which sealed the fate of Jerusalem.[46] In the midst of the shock of this disaster for the Christians of the Levant William's second son, Conrad, arrived at Tyre. He, too, was a knight of renown, highly praised for valor and wisdom. When the people of Tyre heard that the son of the marquis of Montferrat was at hand they went forth in joyous procession to welcome him and rendered the city into his hands. His defense of Tyre, both before and after the fall of Jerusalem, earned him the highest glory. He flung into the city's ditch the standards that Saladin had sent to be flown from Tyre's walls after its surrender, which had already been arranged.[47] When Saladin, confident that he held a trump card in the person of Conrad's captive father, tried to bargain with the son, Conrad refused to surrender the smallest stone in order to gain the liberation of William the Old.[48] Conrad married Isabel, the other sister of Baldwin IV, and succeeded in gaining election as king. That he was already married to the Byzantine princess Theodora Angelina he conveniently ignored. Very soon after his election, however, Conrad was murdered in the streets of Tyre by the minions of the Old Man of the Mountain, the chief of the feared sect of the Assassins.[49]

The house of Montferrat also had played an exalted role in Byzantium. In 1179 the emperor Manuel Comnenus had proposed the marriage of his daughter Maria to one of the sons of the illustrious William the Old. The emperor's aim was to win over to his Italian policy a powerful family which had been loyal to his enemies, the Hohenstaufen. At this time the house of Montferrat had been left by Barbarossa's capitulation in the Treaty of Venice of 1177 to face alone the fury of the nearby towns. The inducement offered by Manuel was high indeed—his own daughter, second in succession to the throne.[50] The lord of Montferrat leaped at the opportunity, giving up for a time his support of the German emperor who had abandoned him. Since William Longsword was dead in Palestine, Conrad and Boniface were already married, and Frederick had donned clerical vestments, the honor fell to the youngest son, Renier.[51] This seventeen year old youth married the princess Maria, a strong-minded woman of thirty. Renier received the title of "Caesar" and the high honors of a member of the imperial family. Although two Latin sources declare that Renier became king of Thessalonica, the youth in fact received little if any real authority. No doubt, however, the Latin sources do reflect a fact in distorted form. Manuel very likely granted him Thessaloncia as a *pronoia*, an estate for life normally given as payment for high military command.[52] The princess Maria could not forget that she had been deprived of the right of succession to the throne by the birth of her much younger half-brother Alexius. By her maturity and her determined and energetic character she gained domination over her younger spouse, who became caught up in affairs too great for his limited experience. When Emperor Manuel died and the throne passed to the youngster Alexius II in September 1180, Maria found her chance. Manuel's young, beautiful, frivolous, and spoiled widow abandoned herself and the empire into the hands of Alexius the *protosebastos*, a high official and a member of the imperial family. This scandalous liaison upset the entire court. The lover of the empress-dowager arrogantly assumed an almost imperial role. He also foolishly alienated his subjects, particularly the more ambitious courtiers, by his reliance upon the Latins, whose wealth and influence aroused bitter resentment. This pro-Latin policy had been Manuel's as well, but a policy disliked under a strong emperor became intolerable in the hands of the despicable paramour. Maria seized the opportunity. With Renier and many nobles of the court she plotted to overthrow the *protosebastos*, secretly harboring the aim of usurping her brother's throne for herself. Renier of Montferrat seems to have been a passive follower of his ambitious wife. The conspiracy was prematurely exposed, and some of the conspirators were arrested. Maria and Renier with about a hundred and fifty followers, mostly Latin, perhaps Renier's own Piedmontese, took refuge in Sancta Sophia. Reduced to these desperate straits, young Renier proved his mettle as a fighter. He led his little band out of the sanctuary to repulse the imperial army, at least for the time, before returning to the churchly fortress. In the morning the embattled conspirators received an offer of amnesty from the *protosebastos*, which they willingly accepted. A few years later, however, Maria, Renier, and Alexius II alike fell victims to the usurper Andronicus I.[53] The call of the East proved fatal to all four of the brave sons of William of Montferrat who answered it. One learned scholar believed that Boniface was present in Constantinople with Renier while these events unfolded, but this is quite unsupported by evidence, so it cannot be accepted[54] At any rate, Boniface no doubt harbored against Byzantium a desire for revenge for the murder of his youngest brother. He may also have dreamed of reclaiming what he conceived to be Renier's rights to Thessalonica, if not to the Byzantine throne. This is not to say that revenge and ambition were necessarily in the forefront of Boniface's mind when he took the cross. The tragic career of Renier, however, must have constituted a significant portion of the memories which influenced the mind of Boniface of Montferrat.

Conrad of Montferrat, too, before his brilliant and ill-fated career in the kingdom of Jerusalem, had played a prominent role in Constantinople. It was probably late in the year of 1186 when the emperor Isaac II Angelus, seeking an able Latin commander for the imperial troops, turned once more to the house of Montferrat. He first offered the hand of his sister Theodora to Boniface, and, discovering that he had a wife, willingly accepted Conrad, then a widower, as a substitute. Conrad was already known for his military exploits and had previously paid an extended visit to Constantinople. Almost immediately after his marriage Conrad proved himself the main support of the emperor against the revolt of Alexius Branas. Not long after his victory over the popular rebel, however, Conrad began to find his position at court uncomfortable. Many of the nobels were relatives or friends of Branas. He could not have remained unaware, moreover, of the popular hatred of Westerners, even though it was not directed against him personally. He even failed to receive from the emperor rewards commensurate with his success. He had gained from Isaac the title of Caesar, formerly borne by his brother, but he was not permitted to don the blue buskins which signified that office, and his title appeared an empty honor. Unpopular at court, cheated of the full recognition he deserved, and apparently not enamoured of Theodora, when Conrad heard that Saladin threatened to sweep the Christians of Palestine into the sea, he answered the call of adventure without a by-your-leave to either emperor or wife.[55] There, as mentioned previously, he won renown at Tyre, but shortly suffered assassination. Boniface of Montferrat's three brothers who had gained glory and met their deaths in the East marked him as a likely leader of the crusading host.

So emissaries were sent from the crusaders at Soissons to offer command of the army to the marquis of Montferrat. They found him at Castagnola delle Lanze, a castle in the territory of Asti. They requested him to come to Soissons on a certain day to consult with the leaders about accepting the command, and he agreed with thanks.[56]

Journeying to Soissons where the nobles awaited him in the late summer of 1201, Boniface stopped in Paris to consult with Philip Augustus.[57]

Apart from his relationship with the French king and the latter's role in promoting the offer which Boniface had just received, there were other reasons for speaking with Philip before proceeding. Prior to accepting command of an army dominated by French nobles it was certainly appropriate for a Lombard prince to confer with the king of France, not only as a mark of courtesy, but because the king would be able to tell him much about the men he was asked to lead. There were also matters not directly related to the crusade, but to the general political background in which it was set. Philip received Boniface warmly. The marquis did not let pass the opportunity to intercede with the French monarch on behalf of the Hohenstaufen faction in the struggle for the German throne. The king convinced Boniface that he remained attached to the cause of Philip of Swabia and had no understanding with his rival Otto of Brunswick. It was probably at this time, in fact, that Philip Augustus entrusted Boniface with a message for the pope in which he complained strongly of Innocent's support of Otto. If the pope feared Hohenstaufen policy, the king of France wrote, he himself would serve as a guarantor for Philip of Swabia[58]

Boniface then proceeded to Soissons to meet the French crusaders. Accompanying him, as the crusaders had no doubt hoped , were various Lombard nobles who had elected to share the work of God. Also included in the group were two abbots of the white-garbed Cistercian order, one of whom was Peter of Locedio, who was to play a prominent role in the crusade. The proceedings took place in an orchard adjoining the Benedictine abbey of Notre Dame. Here the crusading barons offered the Lombard marquis the command of the whole army, as well as the money left by Thibaut and the latter's men. Kneeling in tears before him, they begged him to accept. Falling in turn at their feet, Boniface declared that he would do as they wished.[59] On his knees before the nobles he committed himself to them and their cause. Yet it was not for the crusading ideal alone that he assumed the cross. Most crusaders were driven by a complex of religious and secular motives, and ambition ran deep in the souls of the Montferrats. No doubt he envisioned for himself a powerful position in Palestine, and the thought of the honors his brothers had enjoyed in Constantinople may also have passed through his mind.[60]

The assembled knights and clergy moved to the abbey church to solemnize the work of giving the host a commander. It is surely not coincidental that the abbey church of Nôtre Dame at Soissons contained the tomb of Saint Drausius, seventh-century bishop of Soissons, who was venerated, among other things, as the protector of those who were preparing to fight the infidel.[61] Then the bishop of Soissons, Nivelon, together with the popular crusade preacher Fulk of Neuilly and the two Cistercian abbots, fastened the cross on the shoulder of the marquis. After the ceremony they consulted over their plans and agreed to meet in Venice in the following summer. On the next day the marquis took his leave to return and settle his affairs.[62]

On his homeward journey the marquis visited the great abbey of Cîteaux in the Burgundian wilderness, mother-house of the white monks, whose annual general chapter met on 13 September, the eve of the Exaltation of the Holy Cross.[63] For the occasion were assembled at Cîteaux not only abbots of the order, but many nobles, for the focus of attention of the general chapter of 1201 was the forthcoming crusade. Since their foundation at the time of the First Crusade the white monks, who came largely from aristocratic and military backgrounds, had been deeply involved in the crusading movement. Their own Saint Bernard of Clairvaux had been closely associated with the Knights Templars and he had been the heart and soul of the Second Crusade. His preaching had called it into being and its failure was his greatest disappointment. Cistercians had thrown themselves into the Third Crusade as well. Discouraged, perhaps, at the outcome of their earlier efforts, they had not been active in Innocent III's endeavors to promote the Fourth Crusade, but once the tournament at Ecry had given distinguished leaders for a Holy War, the white monks rallied enthusiastically to the new effort. They not only provided preachers to exhort the faithful to take the Cross, but some of them joined the crusaders to care for their spiritual needs. The wealthy Cistercian Order also lent its financial support to the enterprise.[64]

Perhaps Fulk, the miracle-working preacher of the crusade, accompanied Boniface on his journey to Burgundy, for he too was present at the general chapter, and in fact the main attraction. Before the assembled monks and nobles the fiery evangelist preached the cross, as he had done so successfully over the past three years. During this period Fulk is said to have crossed some two hundred thousand soldiers of Christ.[65] All too many of them, however, were the untrained and the unarmed, the poor and the sick. He had gained much praise for awaking this mass enthusiasm, but it is doubtful that many of these enlistments were to be taken seriously by the secular leaders responsible for planning the crusade in practical terms. Many enthusiasts would have been worse than useless for reasons of sex, age, debility, or poverty. Others had come forward under the influence of the immediate fervor aroused by the spell-binding Fulk, but their commitment was not firm. Not even the overly sanguine counts of Flanders, Champagne, and Blois had dared to think in numbers of anything like this magnitude. Perhaps it was hoped that many who did not participate as crusaders would redeem their vows with money for the undertaking. Had they done so, the history of the crusade might have taken a different course.

Greater men were not immune to Fulk's eloquence. At the general chapter of September of 1201 his emotional summons to succor the land sanctified by the feet of Christ resulted in the enlistment of many additional knights from Burgundy, Champagne, and elsewhere, who had perhaps come to Cîteaux for this purpose.[66] Each of the greater men who took his vows naturally attracted the enlistment of lesser folk. The monks at Cîteaux, of course, were not allowed to take the cross without the approval of their superiors, but Fulk had brought a letter from Innocent III designating certain white abbots to assist him in the spiritual care of the crusaders.[67] Boniface made a special plea in addition for the company of Abbot Peter of Locedio, whose counsel he required, and permission was granted.[68]

Upon leaving Cîteaux the new leader of the crusade did not return directly to Montferrat, but instead paid a visit to his lord and cousin, Philip of Swabia. At the court of the German king at Hagenau he passed the Christmas holidays, attending an assembly of the king's vassals of the left bank of the Rhine.[69] Boniface and Philip were on familiar terms. The marquis had served the Hohenstaufen well, and after Philip's election to succeed his brother Boniface had visited Germany as a papal envoy to attempt to settle the struggle over the German throne. Very recently Boniface had represented the Hohenstaufen cause at Paris, and wished to report to Philip of Swabia his success there. As chief of the crusade, moreover, the marquis had reason to visit Germany to discover what aid the German barons might lend to the venture. There had been relatively few enlistments from Germany because of the struggle between the Hohenstaufen and the Welf, which divided Germany into armed camps. Most of the German nobles had their attention focused upon this conflict instead of the crusade, which was one reason, of course, why Pope Innocent had been anxious to seek a truce, if a true peace was not possible. Not much was to be hoped from Germany, perhaps, but it was incumbent upon the new leader, who was himself a vassal of the empire, to make a try.

At Hagenau Boniface encountered an unexpected guest, the refugee Byzantine prince Alexius, son of the deposed emperor Isaac II Angelus.[70] Alexius, consistently referred to as a youth in the sources, was a late adolescent; he was not porphyrogenitus, so his birth must be dated prior to Isaac's ascent to the throne in 1185.[71] He was the brother of Irene, Philip's Greek wife. Their father Isaac had been dethroned in 1195 by the treachery of his older brother, also named Alexius, whom Isaac had completely trusted and highly honored. Early in Isaac's reign the emperor had sought and gained through Saladin his brother's release from prison. Returned to Constantinople, the elder Alexius had been given high office and is said to have received the imperial palace of Boukoleon and the revenues of the adjacent port, which provided an enormous income. Those hostile to Isaac, however, sought to turn the older brother against him, and in time they worked upon his ambitions and a palace coup was plotted. Reports of the conspiracy frequently reached the emperor, but he trusted his brother too blindly to investigate. The conspirators found their opportunity when Isaac and his brother were encamped in southern Thrace in early April 1195. The emperor had decided to go hunting, accompanied by only a small retinue. The conspirators seized the opportune moment. Alexius, the treacherous brother, had excused himself from the hunt, saying that he did not feel well. As soon as Isaac was a short distance from the camp the conspirators led his brother to the imperial tent and hailed him emperor. Attracted by the uproar, the whole camp ran to the scene, and finding the soldiers ready to accept the result, all others had perforce to accept it. Isaac, still within earshot, heard the tumult, and attendants quickly brought him the news. His first reaction was to attack the camp, calling upon Christ and an icon of the Virgin for heavenly aid. His companions, however, seeing how things stood, refused to follow him in a hopeless cause, so he was forced to flee. Across the Maritza River and down the main road to the west the frightened emperor fled, closely pursued by his brother's men. Shortly he was taken, led to a nearby monastery, and was there blinded, the usual fate of deposed rulers, since blindness was conceived as a disqualification for rule. Later he was imprisoned in a palace in Constantinople near the two columns in the vicinity of the crossing of the harbor to Pera.[72]

The new emperor Alexius III was surprisingly careless in keeping his blinded brother and young nephew under surveillance. His own treacherous ascent to the throne should have put him fully on his guard against treachery, for one who rises to power by an act of violence sets a dangerous precedent against himself. As Nicetas puts it in his ornate style, however, Alexius III forgot that "great misfortunes sear themselves indelibly into the minds of men" and that "revenge ... loves to crash dowm unexpectedly upon those committing unjust deeds."[73] The blinded Isaac enjoyed considerable freedom. Anybody could visit him in his palace without fear, and there flocked all those with grievances against the government. Among the callers were disgruntled Latin inhabitants of the capital and visiting merchants from the West, jealous of their economic privileges, who proposed schemes to overthrow the usurper. Not at all surprisingly Isaac welcomed these overtures, and he wrote to his daughter Irene in Germany urging her to avenge her wronged father. On the plea of Isaac the emperor allowed much freedom to young Alexius, who was not blinded, but young and ambitious, although not very clever. Father and son willingly promised not to plot against the throne, a declaration upon which the elder Alexius foolishly placed his trust. Bare promises, insufficiently sanctioned by an appropriate balance of benefits, are frequently broken. In fact, Isaac and his son conspired that young Alexius should escape to the West and with the aid of Irene and her German husband should attempt to overthrow the treacherous emperor. When Alexius III was engaged in repressing the rebellion of Michael Camytzes in the late summer and early fall of 1201 young Alexius accompanied his uncle to Damokraneia in Thrace. The young prince had come to an agreement with two prominent Pisan merchants of Constantinople to assist his escape by sea. Their great ship set sail at the appropriate time for Athyra on the Sea of Marmara, where it anchored, ostensibly to load sand for ballast. Young Alexius, at the first opportunity, fled his uncle's camp, and hurried to Athyra, where a skiff awaited to row him to the merchant ship. The emperor soon learned of his nephew's escape, of course, and ordered that all outgoing ships should be searched for the fugitive. When the emperor's agents searched the Pisan vessel, however, the young prince had cut off his long hair, put on Western clothing, and was mingling with the Pisans aboard, so they did not discover him.[74] The merchantman then conveyed the prince to the Adriatic port of Ancona, from where he sent word of his escape to Irene in Germany. Irene sought her husband's aid for her brother, who, as Nicetas tells us, "without shelter and fatherland, was traveling, like the floating stars and had nothing with him but his own body."[75] Philip, who was a gracious, gentle, and generous prince, sent for his unfortunate brother-in-law to come to Germany.[76]

Thus Alexius journeyed from Ancona to Germany, arriving in late September or October of 1201, and met Boniface at Hagenau. The young prince and the Italian veteran had in common their resentments against Byzantium. Alexius had seen his father deposed and blinded, himself deprived of the succession and forced to become a refugee without possessions or power, dependent upon the aid of others. Boniface recalled the fate of his brothers in Constantinople, Renier murdered, Conrad cheated of his expectations. The question of moving the crusading army to Jerusalem by the accustomed route through Constantinople, where the young Alexius should be installed as an ally of the crusaders, could scarcely fail to arise. It is important that Alexius professed and probably believed that he would be welcomed as the rightful heir to the throne by the inhabitants of the imperial city.[77] That he was rejected when it came to the test does not alter the significance of the belief which he held and communicated to his new friends in the West. The idea of an attack upon Constantinople, however, should it be necessary, was by no means a novel one. Boniface's father, William the Old, had heard such an assault proposed in the council of Louis VII as long ago as the Second Crusade.[78]

Philip also had his reasons to join in the discussions. Frederick Barbarossa's relations with Byzantium had been so bad during his journey across Byzantine territory on the Third Crusade, that he had considered the conquest of the city. Ironically, the Byzantine emperor at that time had been Isaac II, the father of the young Alexius who now sought the aid of Frederick's son.[79] Henry VI, Philip's brother, had also threatened the conquest of Constantinople by a crusading army.[80] The notion of employing a crusade against Byzantium, therefore, was far from strange to the German king. Irene, who had received letters from her father seeking revenge, had great influence over her kind husband, and she was pleading her brother's cause.[81] Philip was in no position, however, to lend material aid, as Irene herself must have known. His struggle with Otto, the pope's protégé, was not going well. Philip had been excommunicated since March, and the anathema had deprived him of crucial supporters. The duke of Austria, the bishops of Halberstadt and Basel, the abbot of Pairis and others had taken the cross perhaps in part to escape the censure of the pope while providing justification for declining to perform their duty toward the king. Even those who took the cross, but did not actually join the army in 1202 withheld their active military support from Philip. In Italy, meanwhile, the Ghibellines were at odds among themselves, while the Germans of the Regno were taking a beating at the hands of Walter of Brienne.[82] Philip had too many problems of his own to concern himself in any effective way with the claims of his brother-in-law.

Historians who attribute the Latin conquest of Constantinople to a plot laid primarily by Philip of Swabia see in the election of Boniface of Montferrat to head the crusade precisely the instrument required by the Hohenstaufen to achieve his ends.[83] The author of the *Gesta Innocentii*, desiring not only to clear his hero of any responsibility for the sack of Constantinople, but to cast blame upon the hated house of Hohenstaufen, states that Boniface "was said" to have treated with Philip concerning the installation of Alexius in Constantinople by means of the crusading army.[84] Some such discussion undoubtedly took place. Historians, however, sometimes leap too readily from discussions to deeds, from idle talk to careful plans to successful execution. Bookish men themselves, they tend to overestimate the powers of leaders of men to grasp the various threads of an already evolving pattern of events and to weave them into a desired design. Philip, it is agreed, was powerless; so, these historians contend, he worked his way by wile through Boniface.[85] But neither Philip nor Boniface had any way of foreseeing the fortuitous concatenation of circumstances which ultimately led the crusade to Constantinople. Boniface did not have a crusading army at his disposal, just because he had been elected commander. A crusading army was not like a modern army, disciplined, and ruled by a fixed and well-organized chain of command. Nor, in fact, is even a modern army so rational an instrument of the commander's will as would appear from the tables of organization. A crusading army was an inchoate mass of men moved unpredictably by enthusiasms, fears, ambitions, superstitions, lusts.[86] Boniface could not reasonably anticipate any effective authority over such barons as Baldwin of Flanders or Simon de Montfort. They in turn had not much more real control over those below them.[87] The commander of such an army was rather like a man shooting a rapids in a canoe. He cannot control the stream, and he has only a very limited control over the course of the canoe. Hopefully, by energetic and constant care, he can keep it headed in the right direction, avoid the rocks, and come safely through. Boniface would have been not only arrogant, but foolish, if he believed at Christmas of 1201 that he had power to manage the crusade according to his will.[88]

Having found commiseration, but no promise of aid at Philip's court, young Alexius now journeyed to Rome to seek the pope's assistance. This visit took place shortly after the meeting at Hagenau, perhaps in late February 1202, not immediatly upon the arrival of Alexius in the West.[89] Innocent himself later described it in a letter to Alexius III of 16 November 1202. His word *olim* (formerly), which, it has been argued, must refer to a time at some distance in the past, could certainly refer as well to early 1202 as to late 1201.[90] Alexius complained to the pontiff of the wrongs he had suffered at the hands of his uncle. The pope should condemn his former captor and help him to regain his rightful place. The whole city of Constantinople, he asserted, desired him as emperor. Innocent, however, turned a deaf ear and sent the young man back to Germany.[91] The pope was not prepared to risk the outcome of the crusade, to which he was committed so deeply, upon this young man. Supporting him would be hazardous, a risk not well calculated. Why should the pope, moreover, do anything to aid the relatives of the Hohenstaufen? Something might still be hoped, too, from Alexius III, who now and again dangled before Innocent some faint hopes concerning the unification of the churches under Rome.[92]

Not long after the departure of Alexius, Boniface of Montferrat also journeyed to Rome, probably about the middle of March.[93] He wished to consult with the head of the Church concerning the great enterprise over which he had recently assumed command. The visit had been planned before Boniface had gone to Germany and had met young Alexius, for he had agreed during his visit to Paris to become the emissary of Philip Augustus to the pope.[94] The original purpose of the journey to Rome was not, therefore, to win the pope for a Constantinopolitan adventure. On the basis of his conversations with Alexius, Philip of Swabia, and Irene, however, Boniface did by indirection sound out the pope concerning the route of Constantinople, not directly proposing this modification of plans but hinting at it. Innocent had already become acquainted with the idea, of course, and it did not please him. He had not been impressed by young Alexius and his claims, a judgment which proved in the outcome extremely sound. Innocent therefore expressed his displeasure to Boniface, warning that the crusade must not attack Christians, but should proceed as quickly as possible to the Holy Land. Wishing to retain the favor of the Holy See, Boniface renounced the idea, at least for the moment. He curtailed the discussion and dealt with various details concerning the crusade which required attention.[95] One of these was probably the continuing enmity between Genoa and Pisa, for in late April we find him at Lerici, a coastal town about midway between the feuding cities, no doubt on his return journey, attempting to mediate a peace between them. If it is true that Boniface did this as a collaborator with the pope, an assumption it would seem difficult to avoid, it indicates that his hints concerning the route of Constantinople did not drive a wedge between Innocent and the marquis. From Lerici Boniface returned to Montferrat, where he had none too much time to make his personal preparations for departure.[96]

4

The Poverty of the Army
at Venice

The failing spirits of the crusaders, depressed by the death of the count of Champagne and the difficulty of finding a new leader, revived when Boniface accepted the command at Soissons. Once again the preparations for the crusade were moving forward. The gathering at Cîteaux shortly afterwards provided a grand opportunity to whip up enthusiasm and to gain recruits, a chance which Fulk the preacher did not fail to seize. Abbot Martin of Pairis and other ecclesiastics also sounded again and again the call to arms against the infidel.[1] In the aftermath of the journey of Boniface to the assembly at Hagenau, German troops under the bishop of Halberstadt, the count of Katzenellenbogen, and other nobles, took the cross.[2] Raimbaut de Vaqueiras and his fellow troubadours did their part too in propagandizing the venture in song.[3]

In the spring of 1202 the marquis of Montferrat and all those who were destined to serve under his command, from the highest baron to the lowest sergeant, had much to do. In the great castles of the barons and in the solitary towers of lesser nobles complex preparations were underway.[4] Lands were sold or pledged to raise money for the journey, horses and arms were made ready. In anticipation of a long absence affairs at home had to be put in order. Facing the likelihood of death, for they well knew that many of them would never return, they had also to look to their spiritual state. Some just grievances against them might yet be satisfied to the easing of their souls. With an eye to sins that could no longer be remedied nobles of wealth about to depart on an undertaking of great danger made gifts to monasteries and provided for prayers and masses to insure their well-being in this life or in the life to come. The preparations of crusaders of lower rank, who had less of this world's goods and power, were on a smaller scale. But they too had money and equipment to provide, families to leave, and death to fear.[5]

Their spirits were cast down again by the loss of another of the leaders. About the middle of April, Count Geoffrey of Perche took ill and died. By his testament he provided that his brother Stephen should receive the money he had gathered for the crusade in order to lead his men and fulfill his vow. There was great grief for his loss within his own lands and among the ranks of the crusaders.[6]

Between Easter (14 April) and Pentecost (2 June) of 1202 the most timely pilgrims said good-bye to homes and families, and many were the tears and laments, as both Villehardouin and Robert of Clari inform us.[7] Some consideration of the emotions of the crusaders and their loved ones is not amiss if we are to understand these men to the extent that we can comprehend the crusade, as much as possible, from their point of view. The poets, always sensitive to the interplay of emotion between the lover and his beloved, describe the lady trembling at the thought of the danger facing her lover, and fearing that she will die of grief or go insane. Months ago, when he took the cross, it seemed a romantic adventure, undertaken in part, perhaps, to display his chivalry before her. Now harsh reality was at hand: the vow had been taken, and the lover must depart, perhaps never to return.[8] The poets also show the crusader himself torn between love and duty. Duty prevails, but though his body goes to Palestine, his heart will never leave his kind and beautiful lady.[9] The troubadour Raimbaut, friend and comrade in arms of the marquis of Montferrat, describes his own emotions and reveals incidentally some of the motivations which led these men to abandon their loved ones. The insufferable thought of leaving his sweetheart, Beatrice, warred against the pride he felt in the honor that had been paid his friend and patron. He had not been enthusiastic about the crusade, and he had agreed to go only out of loyalty to Boniface. Romantic devotee of knighthood that he was, Raimbaut pictured to himself the banners of the knights of Champagne, he imagined the count of Flanders crying "Flanders!" and the marquis shouting "Montferrat and the lion!" as they charged. He also thought of the joy of serving God and the reward of Paradise should he die in His service. Yet over against the imagined joys of battle appeared the beauty of Beatrice, and he did not know whether he should go or stay. He, in fact, delayed until the spring of 1203 before joining the expedition.[10]

Although many delayed, a multitude of soldiers of the cross parted from their loved ones and set out toward the south.[11] At last the *militia Christi* were on the march. Some were small bands, like that of Villehardouin; some were great, like Baldwin's. The French crusaders followed the customary route via the Mont Cenis pass and Lombardy.[12] As they marched they sang crusading songs, whiling away the tiresome hours and reinforcing the bonds that linked them together and bound them to a common cause. On their journey they visited centers of piety, such as Clairvaux and Cîteaux, to venerate the precious relics and to renew their faith that their fearful venture was indeed the will of God.[13] Many of those coming from France, including Count Baldwin, must have stopped at

Montferrat to pay their respects to their leader, for his lands were on their route of march, and they would not have passed up the opportunity to visit him and rehearse their plans.[14]

The departures were tardy. It had been agreed in the treaty that the journeys should be made during the month of April in order to be prepared for embarkation on 29 June,[15] but, as Villehardouin informs us, many crusaders did not get underway until toward Pentecost, which was 2 June.[16] Many, in fact, did not leave so soon. Synchronizing the movements of any army is enormously difficult; for a crusading army it was impossible. Some started earlier, some later. Some enjoyed a more leisurely journey than others. While the most prompt, therefore, departed early enough to arrive in Venice before the scheduled date for sailing, they would have to wait for the late-comers. In this respect, as well as for lack of numbers, the crusaders were to fail the Venetians and to get into a predicament from which they were never able to extricate themselves.

About 1 June the first crusaders began to arrive at the rendezvous in the city on the lagoons.[17] From Flanders, Picardy, the Ile de France, Blois, Chartres, Champagne, Burgundy, the lands bordering the Rhine, and the subalpine provinces of Italy they came, their varied languages mingling in the confusion of tongues common in this city of international commerce. If they kept to the old tradition, the crusaders from various lands wore crosses of different colors, such as red for the French and green for the Flemings.[18] There were few or no English, for King John was deeply engaged in a struggle for his throne with his nephew Arthur, who had the support of Philip Augustus. The English king, therefore, had not only declined to take the cross himself, but had placed obstacles in the way of English enlistments.[19] Some of the Germans arrived early, and so did Baldwin of Flanders, Hugh of Saint Pol, and Geoffrey of Villehardouin.[20] They pitched their tents on the island of Saint Nicholas (the Lido), the long narrow sandbar fronting the Adriatic behind which the lagoons of Venice are formed. Robert of Clari states that the crusaders decided to encamp on the Lido after discovering that they could not find quarters on Rialto, the main island.[21] The anonymous author of the *Devastatio Constantinopolitana*, on the other hand, complains that the Venetians deliberately isolated the crusaders there.[22] Each states the same basic truth, although from different points of view. It simply was not feasible to host a large alien army in the city proper. After all, they were expecting an army of thirty-three thousand five hundred men to descend upon a city of perhaps one hundred thousand population.[23] Housing could have been found only by expelling the rightful possessors, a means used freely enough in conquered places, but not even to be considered in the allied city, which was to supply the essential fleet. No city, morever, certainly not proud Venice, would tolerate even a friendly army within its confines over a long period of time, and it now appeared that the assembling of the crusaders was to be a drawn out process. The burgesses, and their wives and daughters, could sleep more soundly if the lagoon separated them from the host. Some of the crusaders, no doubt, shared the piety and chastity of Count Baldwin. Others possessed the desires for drink and sex common among most soldiers throughout history and the common soldierly lack of inhibitions in seeking them. Far better that a wall of water should separate these foreigners from the homes of their allies.

Among the early arrivals was probably also the chronicler Robert of Clari, although he does not tell us exactly when he came to Venice. Robert's lord, Peter of Amiens, was related to Hugh of Saint Pol, in whose company they likely traveled, and we know that the count of Saint Pol was among the early comers.[24] Whatever its failings for the earlier period, from the time of Robert's arrival in Venice his chronicle becomes an invaluable source of information, especially about the experiences and feelings of the men in the ranks. This is a rare advantage, since most of our sources were either written by men of higher estate or composed according to their testimony. Robert continues to display some weaknesses, however. He had no head for numbers or dates, so he should never be relied upon for amounts of money, numbers of men, or chronology without the greatest caution.[25] He was a poor knight from near Amiens, an adventurer, like so many members of his class. Though a simple man, as men go, he was not uncultured. He knew the chivalric romances and through them legends about Alexander the Great, the fall of Troy, and the Trojan origin which the Franks had attributed to themselves. He possessed the gift of a fresh eye, and so he gives us clear and colorful details of battles and buildings and all sorts of things.[26]

The Venetians were prepared for their allies. Doge Enrico Dandolo had prohibited all commercial voyages, had set the whole of Venice to work on building the fleet, and everything was in readiness.[27] The Venetians had fulfilled their contract to the letter.[28] Even the anti-Venetian *Gesta Innocentii* concedes that they had ready a fleet, the like of which had not been known for a long time.[29] We may estimate it at about five hundred vessels, not counting petty auxiliary craft.[30] The vessels rode at anchor off the Lido; sails, ropes, supplies, and all the many things needed for the voyage were aboard; siege weapons were mounted in readiness; an appropriate number of passengers had been assigned to each ship. Only one thing was lacking: passengers.[31]

Already in June it was clear that the crusade was in trouble. Crusaders were not arriving soon enough or in sufficient numbers.[32] Not to speak of the two hundred thousand who received the cross from Fulk, nothing approximating the thirty-three thousand five hundred anticipated by the Treaty of Venice were to keep the rendezvous at the city on the lagoons.

Some never set out. Others coming from France gathered at Marseilles or
Genoa, and either crossed through many perils (as Robert of Auxerre puts
it) directly to Palestine or were detained by adverse circumstances.[33] Many
sought transportation from Apulian ports.[34] Some joined Walter of Brienne in his campaign against the Germans.[35] In this overestimation of the
number of the crusaders, and not in Venetian or Hohenstaufen treachery,
nor in territorial ambitions more worldly than those of Baldwin of Edessa
or Bohemond of Antioch a century before, lies the reason for the failure of
the Fourth Crusade.

Not even Count Baldwin's full strength assembled in Venice. A sizable force of Flemings, perhaps half of Baldwin's entire following, took ship
in Flanders under the command of John of Nesle, sworn to join Baldwin
in Venice or wherever else he should command.[36] All summer they struggled with contrary winds before passing through the Straits of Gibraltar.[37]
Ernoul-Bernard reports that they sacked an unnamed Muslim port on the
Mediterranean with great profit.[38] Arrived at Marseilles in the fall, they
decided to remain there for the winter.[39]

Some scholars believe that those who failed to join the host in Venice
resented the leadership of Boniface of Montferrat. The crusade was primarily a French undertaking, they contend, and he was a Lombard prince
of whom they had perhaps never heard. The Champenois, in spite of their
vows to the dying Thibaut to meet the army in Venice, smoldered at Boniface's receiving the money that Thibaut had gathered and direct command
over his followers. Some also were apprehensive over Boniface's visit to
Philip of Swabia, who was under excommunication at the hands of the
pope. Villehardouin, a leader of the Champenois mentions nothing unfa-
vorable to Boniface, of course, but according to this theory, the chronicler
deliberately obscured the real cause for the failure of the crusade, since he
himself was responsible for nominating the marquis.[40] Some crusaders, indeed, may have avoided Venice through distaste for the Italian marquis,
but this is sheer speculation and not even very plausible. It anachronisti-
cally introduces modern nationalism into the minds of the crusaders, and
it fails to take sufficient account of the medieval brotherhood of chivalry
and the renown of the marquis of Montferrat in that international community of arms. It is doubtful, moreover, that many crusaders knew anything
about his journey to Hagenau. Robert of Clari, who is our key to what
was in the minds of the mass of the crusaders, does not mention it until
Boniface himself speaks openly to the host at Zara of his meeting with
young Alexius.[41] The argument that resentment or fear of the leadership of
Boniface kept many crusaders from the rendezvous is not at all convincing.

If a plot to install young Alexius on the Byzantine throne had existed,
of course, rumors of this might have deterred from assembling at Venice

those who held a strict view of their crusading vows. It has been shown, however, that although the marquis, the German king, and the young prince undoubtedly discussed the use of the crusading army to return Alexius to Constantinople, no realistic plans could have been made. Boniface's trip to Rome was not primarily to attempt to enlist the pope's support for such a scheme, for the journey had been planned before the encounter at Hagenau.[42] If a plot had existed, moreover, surely such prominent foes of any attack upon Christians as Simon de Montfort, Enguerrand of Boves, and the abbot of Vaux-de-Cernay would have learned of it and would have abandoned the army at this time, as in fact they did later.[43]

There is no need for historians to resort to such spurious arguments, for an abundance of good reasons for the paucity of crusaders at Venice can be found. First of all, the cohesion of the crusading host must not be exaggerated. Every prominent crusader had his own goals and his own plans, and felt bound to the army only insofar as it served his purposes. The same was true to a lesser extent even of the common people.[44] Villehardouin, of course, shows an intense loyalty to the host, but his was a special case, since his own honor and reputation rested upon its success. The Treaty of Venice had not been made in the name of the army, but of the counts of Flanders, Champagne, and Blois.[45] The army, indeed, could not form a treaty, for it had no corporate character, no standing as an entity in law. The greater men had probably ratified the treaty by oaths at Corbie, but we have no way of knowing who was present on that occasion. The mass of crusaders certainly was not.[46] The cost of transportation was another factor. It was not expected to be paid from a common treasury, but, in general, each crusader was to pay his own way.[47] As they finally set themselves in motion, many probably decided to sail from Marseilles, Genoa, or Apulia simply because they thought they could find more favorable terms for passage than had been agreed upon with the Republic of Saint Mark. It is likely for this reason and to avoid the long overland journey to Venice that the force under John of Nesle took ship from Flanders. Another very important reason why many crusaders failed to keep the rendezvous at Venice may have been the codicil to the treaty providing that Egypt should be the place of debarkation.[48] Although it was to be kept secret, knowledge of the agreement had probably come into the hands of the more prominent men, at any rate. Everyone involved in the assemblies at Soissons, Compiègne, and Corbie would be seeking information on the details of the conventions with the Venetians. The six envoys and their three principals, at least, were initially privy to the plan, not counting the doge and his small council, and it is likely that rumors of the destination were abroad. Those who believed that the only legitimate goal for a man under the crusader's vow was Palestine, therefore, would be moved, if they had heard of the Egyptian codicil, to find other ways of reaching the Holy Land directly.

The lack of cohesion of a crusading army and the possible aversion to the Egyptian route were compounded by the problem of numbers itself. Knowledgeable leaders very likely had qualms about their ability to muster so large an army as anticipated by the treaty, and feared precisely what occurred in fact, the inability of the crusaders to meet their obligations to Venice. Their fears, valid enough in themselves, were also self-fulfilling. Some changed plans to save themselves from the disarray of a reduced and indebted host. Some held back, waiting to see how many others appeared, and, as the result was not encouraging, they headed for Apulian ports.[49] One of those who hesitated was the count of Blois, one of the original leaders and one of the principals of the Treaty of Venice. If even Count Louis wavered, we may imagine the hesitancy of others not so deeply obligated as he. Hugh of Saint Pol and Geoffrey of Villehardouin were sent out from Venice to meet the count of Blois, and to plead with him and others to keep the rendezvous. They found him at Pavia. Here, before the road to the south branched off at Piacenza, he vacillated. Geoffrey and Hugh prevailed upon his sense of honor, and Count Louis agreed to join his friends at Venice, but we may imagine with what trepidation. The great joy with which he and his large force were received there accentuates how crucial was the arrival of additional pilgrims. After the count and his men united with the other crusaders on the Lido, Villehardouin tells us how great and fine an army was assembled there, but he admits that it was only one third as great as anticipated.[50]

Although Count Louis had been persuaded to keep his faith, many crusaders did turn south from Piacenza to seek passage in Apulian ports. By this means several hundred knights found their way to Palestine, not at all the puissant force that was expected.[51] This was naturally a great disappointment to the more warlike of the embattled Christians of the Holy Land. Seeing that so little aid was at hand, the king, Aimery II, refused to break the truce with the Muslims, despite the pleas of Renaud of Dampierre, one of the newcomers.[52] Since Renaud was the knight who had been entrusted with the duty of fulfilling the crusading vow of the dying count of Champagne, perhaps this obligation to his dead lord weighed on his mind and influenced him toward a narrow interpretation of his duty.[53] Not content to wait for the expiration of the truce, Renaud and others departed for Antioch. Against advice he tried to force his passage, and was ambushed by the Muslims. The entire band of eighty knights was wiped out, with only one escaping. Renaud himself was made prisoner and remained in captivity for thirty years.[54]

A harsh judgment is passed by Villehardouin upon those who sailed from other ports than Venice. Here we see the bitter disappointment of our author, writing after the events and possessing a full grasp of the con-

sequences of the lack of men.[55] The crusaders could not meet their obligations to the Venetians for want of men and money, and so they were
drawn by the promises of young Alexius to Constantinople. When Alexius
could not fulfill those promises, they lacked the resources to go on to the
Holy Land, and so they conquered the city. Even after the conquest, they
could not muster a sufficient force to hold their new possessions and to
mount the long-anticipated assault upon the Holy Land, and so, after
marching through Christian blood to the Bosporus, they were unable to
perform their vows. Villehardouin's bitterness is understandable, but it is,
in part, at least, misdirected. The failure of the crusade did result from in-
sufficiency of men and money, as Villehardouin protests, but those who
sailed from Marseilles, Genoa, or Apulia were not guilty of betraying the
holy war. They reacted according to their best conscience and judgment to
a tragic train of events already set in motion and irreversible. Not those
regarded by Villehardouin as defectors, but the unrealistic treaty itself
plays the villain's role. No wonder Villehardouin does not stress it, for he
himself stands out among those responsible for the ruinous blunder.[56] We
know that some three hundred knights came directly to the Holy Land.[57]
If those taking the direct course were in the common proportions of one
knight to two squires to four sergeants, their total number would be
twenty-one hundred men.[58] Villehardouin has told us that only one third
of the thirty-three thousand five hundred expected at Venice actually assembled there.[59] If we add, therefore, the number who went directly to
Palestine to the number gathered in Venice, we find no more than about
fourteen thousand men, still far short of those for whom passage had been
prepared.

If those who failed to keep the rendezvous at Venice acted in accor-
dance with their consciences, they disobeyed, however, the will of the
pope. Innocent saw clearly enough in the fragmentation of the army the
ruination of his plans. He therefore ordered those hesitating in Lombardy
to take ship from Venice, but many did not obey.[60]

The papal legate, Cardinal Peter Capuano, did not arrive at the port
of embarkation until 22 July, nearly a month after the scheduled date of
departure.[61] Upon his arrival, according to the *Devastatio*, he took the wise
measure of sending home the poor, the sick, and the women.[62] The role of
the legates in the crusade was not to be a great one. Villehardouin mentions Peter Capuano only once (and then not by name) between his
preaching in France before the tourney at Écry and the Battle of Adrianople in 1205.[63] Papal sources tell us that the Venetians refused to allow the
cardinal to accompany the crusade as legate, although he was free to join
them as a mere preacher.[64] Capuano's late arrival and inability to control
events demonstrate that the crusading host was moved by internal drives
and necessities, not by the will of the pope.[65]

At this late date there also arrived a detachment of Germans led, according to Gunther of Pairis, by his abbot Martin of the Cistercian monastery of that name near Colmar in Alsace.[66] As Gunther, whose chronicle is a eulogy of Martin, describes the abbot, he was pleasant looking, affable, eloquent, humble among his monks, and wise in counsel. He had assumed the responsibility for preaching the crusade in the lands along the upper Rhine.[67] We have Gunther's account, possibly as recalled years later by the abbot, of Martin's crusading sermon delivered in Basel before the end of September 1201. A great crowd of clergy and laity jammed the cathedral to hear him. He began: "My word to you, lords and brothers, my word to you. Not by any means my word, but that of Christ. . . . Christ today speaks his words to you by my mouth, he laments to you his injuries." So, in the fashion of the typical crusading sermon, he deplored the plight of the Holy Land and urged the necessity of assisting its defenders. Speaking of the desecration of the sanctified places, the abbot wept, and the cathedral was filled with the groans, sobs, and sighs of his hearers. He recalled the triumphs of the crusaders of a century before. He enumerated the spiritual advantages of taking the cross. Following the example of Pope Urban II, whose sermon at Clermont had set in motion the First Crusade, he mingled with his summons to self-sacrifice an appeal to material greed. The land overseas was much more rich and fertile than the lands of his hearers. Many of those who answered the call would easily gain a fortune. The kingdom of heaven and temporal prosperity were assured to those who joined the sacred war.[68] After preaching at Basel, he had gone about the whole region, giving the cross to many. Finally, having committed himself and his followers to the protection of the Virgin, he set out for Venice by way of the upper Rhine, Innsbruck, and the Brenner Pass. Many remarked, according to Gunther, the unarmed monk riding at the head of a military array of almost 1,200 men.[69] Toward the end of the journey, Abbot Martin spent eight weeks, late May to late July, visiting with the bishop of Verona.[70] By the beginning of June, therefore, it must have been clear that the fleet would not sail on schedule on 29 June.

On 13 August, shortly after the arrival of Abbot Martin and his followers, a leading German prelate, Conrad of Krosigk, bishop of Halberstadt, joined the host on the Lido. Bishop Conrad was one of the most devoted supporters of Philip of Swabia. Pressed by the pope and his legate in Germany to support Philip's rival Otto, Conrad sought refuge in the crusader's cross, which he assumed on Palm Sunday of 1202. Within a few weeks he journeyed by way of Bohemia and Austria to the patriarchate of Aquileia and Venice.[71] The bishop was to be the informant for the narrative of the crusade by the anonymous chronicler of Halberstadt.[72]

Boniface of Montferrat himself, the leader of the crusade, did not depart from home until early August. At Pavia on the ninth he formally transferred to his son the reins of government of his marquisate. Then he left for Venice to assume command, arriving there on 15 August.[73] Had the host assembled in anything like the order planned Boniface would surely have made his appearance at a much earlier date.[74]

At the time when the crusaders were too slowly trickling into Venice, they were further disheartened by the sad news of the death in May of Fulk of Neuilly, the holy man, the popular preacher of the crusade.[75] Many of those present, and thousands who were not, had taken the cross at his exhortation. Fulk's death on the eve of the assembling of the army was an evil omen. Not even the large sum of money that he had gathered from his overwrought hearers was to aid the expedition directly. Some had been given to individual poor crusaders to enable them to fulfill their vows. The greater part, however, was destined by the Cistercians, to whom it was entrusted, for the direct aid of the Holy Land, where it was warmly welcomed. There had been an earthquake which had destroyed fortifications; much of the money raised by Fulk was used to repair the walls of Acre, Tyre, and Beirut. Ugly suspicions arose that Fulk had diverted funds to his own use. Although these were untrue, one of his associates, Peter of Rossi, was guilty of peculation. Even Innocent III felt compelled to deny publicly that the pope himself had profited at the expense of the Holy Land.[76]

Sometime during the period of assembling at Venice the refugee Byzantine prince Alexius sent messengers from Verona to the marquis of Montferrat and the barons to seek the aid of the crusading army. His envoys recounted to the barons the treachery of Alexius III toward his brother Isaac, the blinding and imprisonment of the latter, and the escape of the young prince.[77] This was the first that Villehardouin and many others had heard of all this. The envoys of young Alexius did not speak of his journeys to Germany and Rome, so the chronicler from Champagne had only a spotty knowledge of the itinerary of the prince and the chronology of events.[78] The messengers assured the barons that the magnates of the Byzantine Empire and the more powerful elements in Constantinople longed to receive the prince as emperor.[79] At no great cost or effort the crusaders could restore a rightful ruler against a wicked tyrant and obtain aid for their own enterprise in Palestine. Not blind to the advantages of the scheme, the barons agreed to send envoys with Alexius to Philip of Swabia. The word of the young refugee alone was insufficient. If substantial assistance for the faltering crusade could be gained, however, they would help Alexius to his throne.[80] The common people of the host, naturally, were not informed concerning these negotiations.

The proposals of the messengers of Alexius were extremely alluring. To carry out their crusading purpose the barons saw by now that they must have additional support. Though they were an impressive army in spite of the failure of many to keep the rendezvous, they found themselves in extreme financial straits. We do not know how conscientiously they had made their scheduled payments to the Venetians, but it looks very much as if they had paid little of what was due.[81] No doubt they expected that almost everyone would be prepared to pay his own way upon arrival in Venice unless he was a member of the retinue of one of the barons who planned to stand the cost. Crusaders trickled slowly to the port of embarkation and there simply were not enough of them, only some eleven or twelve thousand of the anticipated thirty-three thousand five hundred.[82]

When it seemed that as many had arrived as would in fact appear the doge went to talk with the barons on the Lido. He demanded that they now pay what was owed. The Venetians were prepared to embark. They had performed what was required of them; a fleet to transport thirty-three thousand five hundred men stood ready. Villehardouin and other crusading sources agree that the Venetians had indeed fulfilled their promises admirably. So the barons asked that the host, the great and the small, should pay. Some of the poorer crusaders declared that they could not, but the barons collected as much as they were able. The sum was augmented by the money that Thibaut of Champagne had reserved for the army after distributing part of his treasure among his own followers.[83] Still they could not gather half enough to pay what they owed to the Venetians. Dandolo remonstrated that the crusaders must pay the covenanted price. Venice had undergone enormous expense and disruption of her usual commerce. Shipbuilders had been paid. Owners whose merchant vessels had been requisitioned had been recompensed. Provisions had been bought. For a year and a half Venetian traders had lost their normal gain while preparing this great armada.[84] No one ought to expect the Venetians out of Christian charity and crusading zeal to have renounced payment for the fleet and to have sailed off on a wave of piety and good fellowship. The greatest commercial city in Latin Christendom faced a financial disaster. The evil consequences of the foolish treaty now stood starkly revealed. The crusaders could not pay; the Venetians could not renounce payment.

Later, after the crusaders had sacked Constantinople and failed to fulfill their pilgrims' vows, there circulated in Palestine rumors that the Venetians had been bribed with gifts and commercial concessions to form a treaty with the sultan of Egypt to divert the crusade from his lands. This rumor found its way into the continuation of William of Tyre's history. Some scholars have accepted it as a fact, and there was even an abortive attempt to identify the treaty and date it 13 May 1202, just about the time when the first crusaders were arriving in Venice. This latter effort, at least, must be definitively discarded, and, in fact, the whole story should be regarded as nothing more than an interesting example of the suspicions and accusations which would naturally arise among the Christians of Palestine, cheated of the aid upon which they had counted.[85] When affairs go badly men all too often seek a villain upon whom to dump responsibility. This not only helps them to avoid self-accusation and achieve self-righteousness, but even enables them to escape responsiblity for serious thought about the issues. The wealthy and arrogant Venetians, who gained greatly from the conquest of Constantinople, were plausible candidates for the villain's role.

Unable to pay their debt, the leading men among the crusaders conferred in desperation. The situation was clear. The Venetians had fulfilled their contract, but the crusaders could not, because they were far short of the required number of men. Some pleaded; "For the love of God, let's each give in addition as much as we can. It is better to spend all our wealth here than to default on our agreement and lose all we have spent. If this expedition does not take place, the opportunity for aiding the Holy Land will be lost."[86] But not all were agreed. The majority, in fact, argued that they had individually paid what each man owed for passage. It was not their fault if others had failed to appear. If the Venetians would transport them, they were ready. If not, they would seek ships elsewhere. Villehardouin says that they wanted to break up the army, but this is the harshness of a partisan.[87] These crusaders, who were far from villainous, took a simpler and more individualistic view of the crusade than Villehardouin and his party. They had a specific vow to fulfill, individual obligations under the contract with Venice, and rights of their own. Villehardouin's party held a more practical and collective point of view. They were the establishment, the responsible men, adaptable as to means of achieving a more generally defined end—aid to the Holy Land. These were the same leaders who had seen the practical advantages of the landing in Egypt. This party urged that it was better that they should be impoverished than that the army should disperse. So the counts of Flanders, Blois, and Saint Pol, the marquis of Montferrat, and others of their persuasion gave all they had and could borrow to make up the deficit. They not only gave their money, but their gold and silver vessels were borne to the ducal palace in payment. And yet they lacked thirty-four thousand marks of the eighty-five thousand originally owed.[88]

Was there no other source of funds? Innocent III had imposed upon all clerics the general income tax of 1199 and had established other means for gathering money for the Holy Land. Political unrest, resistance of the clergy, and the weakness of canonical sanctions, however, had hampered collections. Records which would provide us with any approximation of the sums collected are not extant.[89] Various letters of the pope prodding the clergy to pay their quotas prove, however, that collection was not easy or efficient.[90] In any case, from the beginning of the crusades the pilgrims had been expected to provide their own financial support. The Second and Third Crusades, it is true, had been largely financed by the kings, but there is no indication that the expenses of the crusading armies were regarded as a responsibility of the church.[91] In the papal mandate of 1199 there is a minor provision for the support of knights and other soldiers who did not have sufficient money of their own, but this was to come only from the alms given by the faithful into the chests placed in the churches, not from the income tax or other souces of subsidy for the Holy Land.[92] That money was to be sent to the Levant for the use of the Christians there.[93] The disposal after his death of the money garnered by Fulk of Neuilly also suggests this, for it was sent to the Holy Land and used to repair fortifications.[94] This explains why collections continued long after the Fourth Crusade had ended, because the subsidy for the Holy Land was still needed there.[95] If the crusaders at Venice had any expectation of receiving aid from the papacy, it is unlikely that the chroniclers would have failed to mention it. They knew full well that their financial predicament was their own responsibility.[96]

Matters were growing desperate for the crusaders on the Lido. The original plan had been that they should encamp there only until 29 June, the intended date of embarkation. Those who arrived on time, expecting the prompt assembling of the host, at first found no great fault with their accommodations. As summer wore on, however, life on the Lido became more trying. Although today it is a charming and famous beach resort, in the summer of 1202 the Lido was merely a sandy island baked by the subalpine sun. The Italian summer has always been hard on armies from northern Europe. Fortunately epidemic disease does not appear to have struck the crusaders, although among an army of eleven to twelve thousand encamped in a foreign land, eating unaccustomed food and drinking strange water, suffering from poor sanitation, a few naturally died over the course of the summer and early fall.[97] When the crusaders failed to pay, according to Robert of Clari, Dandolo threatened to cut off their supplies of food and water, although he did not carry through his angry ultimatum. [98] Food did become a serious problem however, for bad harvests in recent years, not only in Italy and the West, but overseas, had made food scarce and dear.[99] And so, as the army languished, their money dwindled. The greater men were grieved and angered at all they had spent without getting any nearer to their goal.[100] Some of the poorer crusaders had expended all they possessed. Those who could borrowed from Venetian merchants, and, as the days and weeks passed, the load of debt became more and more worrisome.[101] As it became apparent that the expected number of pilgrims would never arrive, their insolvency seemed irreparable. While the summer dragged on the host was threatened with dissolution. Many of the lesser people turned back and others scattered over the mainland seeking sustenance.[102] With each departure the confidence of those remaining was further shaken, sowing the seeds of future defections. Nothing is worse for the morale of an army than prolonged inactivity. Men grow frustrated and irritable. They do not know what is going on, and wild rumors circulate. A crusading army did not even have sufficient discipline to impose the contrived work that is supposed to give to simple minds the illusion of meaningful activity. So they daily diminished in numbers and spirit. And they grumbled, mostly against the Venetians. They complained that the cost of the fleet was excessive, that they were overcharged for their supplies, that they were exploited. It seemed to the men in the ranks that their hosts had been paid plenty.[103] They had no accurate information, only impressions. They had paid—most of them. They had seen the gold and silver vessels of the barons carried off to the ducal palace. They knew that Fulk of Neuilly had left money for the crusade, and they believed that this large sum had gone to fill Venetian pockets. Surely the avaricious Venetians had gained plenty. Were the crusaders their allies or their prisoners?

Looking at their situation in another way, time was becoming a crucial factor. The winter season, when medieval men did not sail the seas, even the relatively mild Mediterranean, loomed before them.

5

The Conquest of Zara

The crusading chiefs informed the doge of Venice that they were utterly
unable to pay any more, since they were impoverished by their efforts and
had scarcely enough money to live on.[1] Despite the complaints of the ill-
informed, the Venetians were not responsible for this plight. Neither Villehardouin nor Robert of Clari blames them. The merchant-republic, in fact,
suffered along with the crusaders in their crisis, having expended vast
sums and sacrificed customary profits which could not now be recovered.
Worse yet, perhaps, Venice had on its hands a destitute, disgruntled, and
ill disciplined foreign army. The Venetians too stood under the threat of
impending debacle. Enrico Dandolo searched his old head filled with experience of statecraft for a solution which would enable the crusaders to
pay Venice for the fleet which stood ready and thus permit the crusade to
get under way. Consulting with his advisors, he recognized that the crusaders in fact could pay no more. The Venetians might keep the sums already paid, but their right to them would not be universally recognized,
and if the crusade failed, Venice would receive much criticism throughout
Christendom. Perhaps the crusade could be saved by means of another
form of compensation to the Venetians. Dandolo called to the attention of
his counselors the Venetian desire to reconquer the port of Zara on the
eastern coast of the Adriatic. All efforts to subjugate Zara had failed, and
there seemed no hope of achieving this goal without outside assistance.
Now fate had provided a means. If the crusaders would help the Venetians
to conquer Zara, they in turn would postpone payment of the thirty-four
thousand marks still owed until such time as God permitted them to gain
conquests to divide as provided by the treaty. Out of their share the crusaders could then pay.[2] The crusade would be preserved. The fortune that
Venice had invested in the fleet would not be wasted. There would even
be a positive gain. The interest of Christendom in the Holy War and the
self-interest of Venice in reconquering Christian Zara coincided.

Zara was no small issue to the Venetians. After the Istrian towns it
was the first of those ports along the eastern shore of the Adriatic upon
which Venice had depended for the refurbishing and resupplying of ships

setting out for the Levant.[3] Perhaps even more important was its use as a port through which high quality oak of the Dalmatian forests could be transported to the shipyards of Venice. Oak was not available to the Venetians in quantity from their own Italian hinterland. Dalmatian oak was therefore crucial for the fleet, and hence for the maritime mastery of Venice, its trade, its wealth and power. Although other ports, such as Ragusa, could serve, they were more distant than Zara, and the supply was more vulnerable.[4]

In the last century and a half Zara had changed hands repeatedly. Every time Zara revolted against Venice the hand of the king of Hungary was seen in the background. After every loss until the last Venice had won back the vital but recalcitrant port. Finally in late 1180 or 1181 Zara again revolted and threw off the Venetian yoke. Venice was then too much hampered by the foul state of its affairs in Constantinople to take vigorous action at once. Her privileges in the Eastern Empire had been revoked and her wealth expropriated in 1171. Attempts to negotiate compensation for these losses dragged on year after year. Once agreement for compensation was reached with Isaac Angelus in 1185, Venice took the opportunity to concentrate once more upon the troubled state of Adriatic affairs. Seeing danger impending, Zara put herself under the protection of Bela III of Hungary, who constructed a strong fortress there. Vigorous efforts of the Venetian fleet to subdue Zara in the summer of 1187 failed, and a two-year truce was signed. Fearing a renewed assault, however, Zara sought additional aid, for Hungary possessed no power at sea. The Zarans thus formed an alliance with Pisa, one of the great maritime powers, which was attempting at this time to penetrate the Adriatic, considered by Venice her private sea. So when the first two-year truce expired Venice again attacked Zara in 1190, and was again repulsed. Once more in 1193 under the new and forceful doge Dandolo the war was reopened, and some smaller cities were taken, but Zara resisted. In the course of these conflicts the Zarans had become understandably hostile to Venice. Wherever they could they attacked the Venetians, plundered their goods, killed the men. Rancor ran high on both sides.[5]

The Venetians quickly grasped the advantages of Dandolo's proposal, so he presented it to the crusading leaders. He pointed to the onset of winter, which was not favorable for long voyages or extensive naval operations. He stressed the blamelessness of the Venetians, who would have transported the army overseas long ago, had it not been for the fault of the crusaders. Then he proposed that the barons make the best of a bad situation by helping the Venetians to gain their vengeance upon Zara. In return the payment of the crusaders' debt would be deferred. The Dalmatian city was a fine one, supplied with all good things, so that they could comfortably winter there and toward Easter set sail for Egypt.[6]

The chief men of the crusaders took counsel among themselves upon Dandolo's proposal. It did not take long to conclude that their options were extremely limited. They could assist the Venetian attack upon Zara, as the doge proposed, or they could return home in shame, having set out bravely to succor the Holy Land, but having gotten no further than Venice. A few, no doubt, could have proceeded to Palestine as individuals or in small groups to fulfill their vows, but the army as a whole was by this time impoverished and would have dissolved. They might lose, moreover, the large sums that had already been paid to the Venetians and spent by them in the construction of the fleet, which stood ready. By accepting Dandolo's proposal the crusade could at last get underway. The troops would soon have action and a needed change of scene. Soldiers become restive when nothing seems to be happening. The burdensome debt could be deferred until a more propitious time. And in the spring they could at last be off to fight the infidel. So the leaders agreed to aid the Venetians in conquering Zara.[7]

Robert of Clari, it is true, tells of two meetings of the doge and the crusaders. In the first of these Dandolo offered to defer the debt until the Venetians could be paid out of the first conquests, and only later, and to the leaders alone, did he raise the subject of Zara.[8] Those historians who seek to make Dandolo the villain of the piece find here a devious and successful conspiracy with the chiefs.[9] No doubt Robert of Clari tells the story as he learned it. As a simple knight in the ranks he was not involved in the councils of the mighty. He reports only what was known to the common soldiers, that the debt was to be deferred and that they were to sail overseas. Only later did the host learn of the agreement to attack Zara. It is not at all likely, however, that he has events in their true sequence. The shrewd doge would scarcely have sacrificed publicly and without advantage so strong a bargaining point as the debt before raising the issue of Zara. Villehardouin tells us of Dandolo's discussions with the Venetians, and then simply adds that the proposals were made to the crusaders.[10] Privy to the most secret councils, the marshal no doubt also reports the incident accurately from his vantage point. The proposals were made to the leaders of the crusaders. To these experienced and responsible men Dandolo's scheme made sense, but, as once before in the case of Egypt, they concealed from the rank and file the details of their plans. They saw no necessity for confiding in the common people. The stop at Zara was a minor detail, of which the host, as Robert declares, knew nothing in advance. When the deferral of the debt and their imminent departure were announced to them, the multitude naturally rejoiced, falling at the feet of the doge. That night they burned great fires on the Lido, and they attached torches to the ends of their lances and paraded about with them. It seemed as if the whole camp was aflame with joy.[11]

On a Sunday which was a great holiday, probably the Nativity of the Virgin, 8 September, Saint Mark's was filled with Venetians and crusaders. [12] Before the mass began in this solemn and awe-inspiring setting the doge in full ceremonial garb mounted the pulpit to address his people: "Sirs, you are joined with the most valiant men in the world in the greatest enterprise that anyone has ever undertaken. I am old and weak and in need of rest, and my health is failing. But I see that no one knows how to govern and direct you as I do, who am your lord. If you agree that I should take the sign of the cross to protect and lead you, and that my son should remain and guard the country, I will go to live or die with you and the pilgrims." [13] There may have been an element of Venetian domestic politics here in an effort to pass on the ducal position to Dandolo's son, [14] as there may well have been ambition for the glory of Venice and its doge, but these do not exclude the more spiritual, if misguided motive that drew all sorts of men to the holy war. Zara was a peripheral issue, a planned stop on the journey, offering the Venetians and the crusaders a means of resolving their dilemma over the contracted and unpaid cost of the fleet. The goal of their expedition was Egypt and the ultimate objective the recovery of Jerusalem. This is not to argue that more mundane motives were absent from the minds of the Venetians, but only that they shared with other Latin Christians a real enthusiasm for the crusade. In describing the crossing of the Venetians in Saint Mark's Villehardouin gives no hint of any feeling other than overpowering religious zeal. When the Venetian multitude heard the old man offering to take the cross, they cried out their approval. Dandolo then descended from the pulpit and knelt in tears before the high altar. Others too wept at the thought of this ancient warrior with failing eyesight enlisting in the cause of the Holy Land. He received his cross, not in the customary fashion, upon the shoulder, but upon the cloth crown of the Venetian doge, where it would be more prominent. [15] Enflamed with enthusiasm by this venerable hero, many Venetians hurried to cross themselves. [16] The crusaders rejoiced at Dandolo's enlistment, not only because of the numbers he drew in his train, but because of their confidence in his wisdom and prowess. [17] Time and again they were to turn to him for leadership, and in the heat of battle no man would show greater courage than his.

The crossing of the doge was a splendid event, but Gunther of Pairis tells of widespread disaffection in the army, which indicates that rumors of the agreement to coerce Zara into submission to Venice must have leaked beyond the circle of leaders. For crusaders to become involved in an attack upon a Christian city seemed to many detestable. To fall upon Christians with burning, raping, and slaughter was sinful for those marked with the cross of Christ, however commendable these activities might be when inflicted upon unbelievers. The problem was compounded in that the king of Hungary, Emeric, was also signed with the cross and enjoyed the same papal protection as themselves. Surely they risked the pope's anathema and the loss of their own crusading privileges if they attacked Hungarian possessions. Behind the proposal of the doge some crusaders saw the greed of the Venetians, the same rapacity that some of them believed they had experienced at the hands of their hosts. Many poor crusaders, having consumed what little money they had brought with them, and having nothing left for the direct journey to Palestine, abandoned the cause, sorrowfully retracing their steps toward home. The great adventure was over for them. The spiritual and worldly benefits were lost. Some of the richer men, too, not suffering from penury, but unwilling to soil their consciences, also turned back. Not only was the army deprived of these defectors, but on their homeward journey they encountered Germans and others who were either on their way to join the host or hesitating in Lombardy to see how matters developed. Hearing the news of the expedition to Zara, these remained in a waiting position, sought Apulian ports, or joined the homeward trek.[18]

Other crusaders took a quite different view of the Venetian proposal. To return home with the crusading vow unfulfilled would be a greater public disgrace and a greater sin than taking part in the attack upon Christian Zara.[19] Men often find themselves in situations where no ethically commendable choices are open to them. They must, as Dandolo said, "make the best of it."[20] Each crusader had to weigh his own values, and those who accepted the logic of the leaders placed very great weight upon the preservation of the army and effective aid to the Holy Land. If the pope himself could not embrace their decision to accept the sin of attacking Christians, he did subsequently recognize that they were driven by a necessity which mitigated their guilt.[21] His earlier prohibition against attacking Christians, moreover, contained an exception for the case of necessity.[22] The conflict within the crusaders' camp concerning the attack on Zara also reveals the contrast between two types of men. Those who turned away were inwardly responsible to their consciences. Those who chose the lesser evil, the Zaran expedition, were outwardly responsible for practical results. The best of the former are saints, but they are not the leaders of armies, states, or even the church. Villehardouin, spokesman for the practical men, stresses that even those who proceeded to the Holy Land apart from the army, as well as those who returned home, accomplished nothing.[23] His party was concerned with attainable ends and the means by which these might be reached in a world which does not run according to the dictates of conscience.

Even the clergy were not of one mind. Abbot Martin of Pairis, shocked at the prospect that the crusading army would attack Christians, not knowing where to turn or what he should do, sought out the papal legate. Torn by conscience, he begged for absolution from his crusading vow, so that he might return to the accustomed quiet of his monastery. But one cannot lightly leave the cloister to ride at the head of an army, then lightly return when threatened by the evil which engulfs the world in which armies ride. Peter Capuano, the legate, absolutely refused the abbot's request. In no case should Martin or the other monks abandon the army, but remain with it and try to prevent, as much as possible, the shedding of Christian blood. Martin, denied his wish for moral security in the womb of his monastery, submitted, as he must, with sighs and a grieving heart.[24]

Another churchman opposed to the expedition to Zara, Bishop Conrad of Halberstadt, also sought Cardinal Peter's counsel. The legate informed the bishop that the pope preferred overlooking the proposed wrong in the interest of preserving the crusade. Conrad also should not for any reason withdraw from the crusading host[25]

The papal legate was thus among those who accepted the lesser evil, as he judged it, for the sake of the greater good. At all costs Capuano wished to prevent the disintegration of the army for which he was responsible to the pope, so he used all his powers to overcome the scruples of those more squeamish than he.[26] Perhaps his moral judgment was distorted by his legatine office, for men tend to overvalue those activities for which they bear direct responsibility. Cardinal Peter has been accused of betraying Innocent's trust, but, although the pope could not condone the attack upon Zara, there is no evidence that he repudiated his legate. In fact Capuano's decision was not inconsistent with Innocent's own policy of preserving his coveted crusade by adapting himself to situations which he could not change. Capuano had acted within the terms of the papal prohibition, which forbade crusaders to attack Christians except in case of necessity and after consultation with the legate. Whether or not Peter's judgment was correct could be argued endlessly. The doctrine of necessity is fraught with moral peril—as is life itself. The legate's decision , although it may not have been right, was reasonable, defensible, and within the limits of his authority. In a way the cardinal's moral character appears more admirable than that of the pontiff, for he grasped the thistle resolutely. Innocent, on the other hand, enjoyed throughout the crusade the desirable fruits of evils for which he managed to evade responsibility.

In refusing the requests of the abbot of Pairis and the bishop of Halberstadt for release from their crusading vows Cardinal Capuano may also have been concerned to assure spiritual leadership for the host in his own absence, for he soon returned to Rome with a bundle of bad news for the pontiff. Probably uppermost in his own mind was the refusal of the Venetians to receive him in his legatine role. I think we must accept this rejection on the authority of the Roman sources, although we should discard the *Gesta*'s assertion that it was because of fear that he would hinder their wicked plan to attack Zara, for we have seen that he in fact fell in with the Zaran proposal.[27] We have also already learned that the anonymous Roman author embroiders a reliable factual narrative with a speculative and biased attribution of motives. The real intention of the Venetians may have been to make it clear that authority over the crusade rested unequivocally with them and their allies. Innocent also had to be informed of the disappointing number of crusaders arriving at Venice and the threat this posed to the army and the crusade. In this connection Peter was instructed by the crusading leaders to consult the pope concerning the initiatives of the young Alexius.[29] Finally he had to reveal to Innocent the plan to sail to Zara. Capuano was not destined to rejoin the army until after the conquest of Constantinople. Rejected as legate by the Venetians, neither he nor the pope could accept with dignity his proposed role as a mere preacher. Futhermore, Innocent had no intention of sanctifying with the presence of a legate, who represented the very person of the pope himself, the attack on a city belonging to the king of Hungary. Capuano was not in disgrace or relieved of his legatine office.[30] Innocent simply adopted that most difficult and sometimes most effective policy of watchful waiting.

On the eve of the crusaders' departure the marquis of Montferrat also journeyed to consult the pope. With him came his friend Abbot Peter of Locedio, a man who had enjoyed Innocent's confidence for a long time. Boniface also was not to rejoin the army until after the conquest of Zara. If this attack upon the lands of a crusader could not be avoided, Innocent wished, at any rate, to disassociate the official leader of the crusade from it.[31]

However justifiable the attack upon Zara might seem to the crusaders and Venetians in their plight, and however inevitable it might appear even to the legate, who had to make his decision when confronted by the abbot of Pairis and the bishop of Halberstadt, the pope could not condone it. A letter was entrusted to the abbot of Locedio threatening religious sanctions against crusaders who should attack Christians.[32] The letter did not reach the army, however, until it stood before Zara. It has been charged that Innocent's prohibition was merely for the record, that he knew that it would not arrive in time to have any effect. He, like Peter Capuano, may have been willing to accept the evil for the sake of the crusade.[33] Whether the pontiff tried his hardest to prevent the aggression does not really matter, as far as the outcome is concerned. Timely intervention, if he could have accomplished it, would have encouraged additional crusaders to abandon the army, but would not have prevented the remainder from going through with the plan. The fewer their number, the greater was their necessity. The pope had no control and only a little influence over the course of events. The combination of the extravagant treaty and the paucity of crusaders had given to the Fourth Crusade an impetus of its own, not much subject to the fulminations of priests.[34]

Before many weeks had passed Innocent was again faced with the issue posed by the presence of the Byzantine prince Alexius in the West. An embassy arrived from his uncle, Alexius III, seeking to dissuade the pontiff from lending any support or encouragement to the refugee. The emperor was uncomfortably aware of the army poised on the Lido. Byzantine rulers had long learned to dread the unpredictable hordes of Latin warriors whose ostensible goal was the Holy Land. They had become obsessed with the fear, reinforced sometimes by the words and deeds of crusaders camped under the walls of their capital, that the real goal was the conquest of Constantinople. From the time of the Norman attacks upon the Byzantine Empire in the days of Robert Guiscard this threat had hung over the Greeks.[35] Nicetas Choniates tells us of Alexius III, about the time of the crusading fleet's departure from Venice, making light of the dangers the expedition posed to Byzantium as fairy tales.[36] He was talking to quell his own fears. Young Alexius in the West was a potential catalyst for all the forces that threatened the Greeks from that direction. So the envoys of the emperor sought to neutralize the efforts of the refugee prince. They appealed both to Innocent's religious ideals and his political sense. They argued that he should prevent any attack upon Christians by an army dedicated to war against the infidel. They also presented the constitutional arguments against the claims of young Alexius: he had not been elected by the nobles; and he had no hereditary claim, since he was born before his father's coronation.[37] They appealed to the pope's own political interests, since the connection between the young prince and the antipapal Hohenstaufen was obvious to all. Innocent was even reminded that Philip of Swabia, the brother-in-law of Alexius and his sponsor in the West, was under the ban of excommunication as a cleric who had put aside his robe for the sword of knighthood. The envoys of the emperor did not, however, touch upon the two subjects closest to Innocent's heart, aid to the crusade and the reunion of the Greek and Latin churches. The pontiff, as we know, already had made his decision not to assist young Alexius. On 16 November Innocent replied with a letter which contained both a friendly response and a thinly veiled threat. While he assured the emperor that after consultation with the cardinals he had come to a decision that would please him, Innocent took care to point out that young Alexius offered aid to the Holy Land and reunion of the churches. He also suggested how serious a matter the triumph of Philip of Swabia in Germany would be for the Byzantine Empire, since the Hohenstaufen would be freed to lend effective support to his brother-in-law.[38]

The crusaders and the Venetians meanwhile were pressing forward the final preparations for their belated departure. The transports and horse transports were turned over to the various leaders. Food and other supplies were loaded on board. Petraries and mangonels, three hundred of them, were mounted on the vessels.[39] The crusaders got themselves and their gear ready for embarkation. Baldwin of Flanders, who had contributed generously of his wealth to the sums paid Venice, at the last moment borrowed from four Venetian merchants a sum of over one hundred and eighteen marks sterling.[40] The odd figure suggests that it was for some specific purchase.

There is a slight disagreement in the sources on the date of departure. Villehardouin says that they sailed in the octave of Saint Remi, 2-8 October, while the authors of the *Gesta episcoporum Halberstadensium* and the *Devastatio* say 1 October.[41] Since Baldwin's loan from Venetian merchants bears October as the date, we probably ought to conclude that he did not contract the loan on the very day of departure.[42] It has been suggested that the fleet sailed in two sections, and this is a possibility.[43]

The sources are also in disagreement concerning the size of the fleet, ranging from about two hundred vessels to four hundred eighty, and modern scholars follow one or another without consensus.[44] The eyewitnesses, however, are in approximate agreement. The author of the *Devastatio*, probably a German or Italian follower of Marquis Boniface, counted forty transports, a hundred horse transports, and sixty-two galleys, for a total of two hundred two ships. Hugh of Saint Pol described the fleet before Constantinople in 1203 as numbering two hundred vessels, and he has specifically accounted for the loss of four transports and two horse transports, so this is good confirmation of the *Devastatio*. Moreover, from the walls of Constantinople Nicetas counted in the fleet of the enemy more than seventy transports, a hundred ten horse transports, and sixty galleys, for a total of two hundred forty or slightly more, which remains in the same range. Hugh of Saint Pol specifically excludes small auxiliary craft, as I assume the others do also.[45] We may safely accept a figure, then, of slightly over two hundred major vessels, approximately half of which were horse transports, and very roughly one quarter transports and the other quarter galleys.

The galley was the fighting ship of the Middle Ages, long, narrow, low, light, and swift. It was some one hundred to one hundred and thirty feet long and only fifteen to seventeen feet wide. Its long narrow *corsia* or deck stood no more than five or six feet above the keel. In action it was propelled by rowers, although it used an auxiliary sail for cruising. A typical galley of the period had a hundred and twenty rowers seated two to a bench with thirty benches on each side, although there were larger and smaller galleys.[46] In battle or other urgent need the rowers could propel a galley with great speed. They were protected from sun and rain by a large awning, which was removed for combat. Two great lateral oars near the stern served as a double rudder. There was a single mast about a third of the length from the bow surmounted by a cage for lookouts or for marines. When the galley was under canvas a triangular lateen sail was spread on a yard which was often longer than the vessel. Along the length of the galley ran the *corsia* or deck. There was a boarding platform on the prow, which might be furnished with a catapult, mangonel, or other artillery piece. In older times ramming had been more important, and in some cases the platform had not replaced the pointed ram. Sometimes, too, a heavy metal spike was suspended from the yard to be dropped on opposing galleys to bilge them. In addition to the rowers there were forty or fifty officers and marines to each galley, and the rowers, as well, were armed.[47]

The transports were converted roundships, which were normally used for carrying goods. They were large, high, and broad in the beam, as much as two hundred feet long and thirty or forty feet wide. They were sailing ships, normally two-masters, although some bore three. Their raised castles fore and aft gave them a crescent shape. Here siege weapons were mounted. In battle they were primarily useful for assailing walled ports, although they could also be used in the open sea to protect the galleys with a sort of floating fortress. They bore a relatively small force of marines. A few of them were of enormous size, able to carry a thousand or more passengers.[48] These giants were exceptional: among them the fleet sailing from Venice numbered the *Paradise*, assigned to the bishop of Soissons; the *Pilgrim*, assigned to the bishop of Troyes; the *Violet*, assigned to Stephen of Perche; and the *Eagle*, surnamed *The Entire World*, which bore Venetians. Robert of Clari counted only four or five ships in April 1204, great enough to assault the wooden towers which the defenders of Constantinople had built atop the stone ones.[49] These were the few giant transports.

A generation earlier the Byzantines had introduced the horse transport to the Latins. Loading and unloading horses was a ticklish business. When one tried to walk a horse up or down the narrow inclined plank used to embark men upon a transport the animal became very nervous and tended to shy. There was no efficient means of putting them aboard by sling. Once on board there was a difficulty in placing them in the hold. To meet these problems the Byzantines devised the technique of cutting a door in the side of the vessel not much above the water, which opened to form a ramp. Not having to face a steep incline, the horses remained somewhat more calm, and they walked directly to the proper level. The horse transports were also fitted out to handle these extremely valuable beasts so as to bring them to their destination in reasonably good shape. They were transported in individual box stalls, each horse suspended by leather straps so that its feet barely touched the deck. They were thus protected against the pitching and rolling of the ship, and their immobility also helped preserve the stability of the vessel. They suffered greatly from chafing and other discomforts, and from the enforced immobility, but this method of transport was the best available. The Byzantine type of horse transport was simply a roundship with a door in the side. The Westerners also employed a horse transport which was long and low, more like a galley, although much larger. Actually it was a cross between a transport and a galley, having two masts, but also a hundred and fifty rowers.[50] The manner in which the horse transports were used in the assault upon Constantinople in April 1204, alongside the galleys and in contrast to the transports, strongly suggests that these were of the latter model.[51]

The departure of the fleet was a magnificent spectacle. The impressionable Robert of Clari calls it the finest sight since the creation of the world. The almost blind doge, garbed in his colorful robes of state and wearing the cloth crown with the prominent crusader's cross, boarded his galley, painted vermilion like that of an emperor. A canopy of vermilion samite sheltered him on board. Above him fluttered the banner of Saint Mark. Four silver trumpets used on solemn occasions blared before him and drums rattled to attract attention to the show.[52] The various colored banners were raised and the sides of the ships and the castles were girt around with the shields of the crusaders, each painted brilliantly to distinguish its owner. These belts of steel around the ships provided at once a measure of defense and an ornament. When the pilgrims were all aboard the clergy mounted the castles or poops of the ships to chant the *Veni creator spiritus*. As Dandolo's vermilion galley began to move followed by the rest of the fleet a hundred trumpets of silver and brass signalled the departure and countless drums and tabors beat excitedly. Never was there such rejoicing among great and small, clergy and laymen, who all wept, according to Robert of Clari, with joy. Soon they passed the familiar Lido on the right and moved out of the lagoon into the Adriatic. Then the sails of the galleys were raised. With the whole fleet of over two hundred vessels dancing under sail, with the banners and ensigns snapping in the breeze, the sea, Robert says, seemed swarming with life.[53]

The departure was not without its foreboding aspect, however. The hugh transport *Violet*, which had been assigned to Stephen of Perche, sank. Stephen himself remained ill at Venice, either not having embarked with the others or perhaps having been injured in the sinking of the *Violet*. He was lost to the army until after the conquest of Constantinople. In March of 1203, after his recovery, he proceeded to Apulia, and thence took ship with many others directly for Palestine.[54] After the fall of the Byzantine capital he rejoined the host to serve in defense of the conquest and to claim a part in the division of fiefs.[55] Another of the barons, Matthew of Montmorency, also remained behind, sick and incapable of travel, but he shortly resumed his place in the army before Zara.[56] The marquis of Montferrat, too, was absent. Under the transparent excuse that his affairs detained him, the titular head of the crusade held back in conformity with the papal policy of avoiding, as far as possible, the apppearance of sanction to a crusaders' attack on Zara.[57]

Actually Zara was not an isolated problem for Venice, but only the most acute of her concerns for her Adriatic empire. The subject cities of Istria, Dalmatia, and of the entire eastern Adriatic coast were indispensable to Venetian shipping and prosperity. In recent years Venetian control had become very precarious. Other maritime powers were seeking to penetrate *Mare nostrum* and pirates preyed on Venetian commerce.[58] Before the doge left the Adriatic for distant adventures leading with him so much of the power of Venice he had to attempt to secure the loyalty of the coastal towns. The imposing armada sailing from Venice provided the opportunity for a convincing show of force. At the same time, since these cities owed military service to Venice, the doge could fill out his complement of rowers and marines and put aboard additional supplies.[59] Part of the fleet under command of the doge sailed directly across the Gulf of Venice at the head of the Adriatic to Pirano in western Istria, arriving on 9 October.[60] Trieste, the greatest of the Istrian ports, and Muggia, a smaller town about five miles down the coast, fearing the power the doge had assembled, hurriedly dispatched large embassies of prominent citizens to do him honor. Overlooking their wrongdoings, which both towns were forced to acknowledge in new treaties, Dandolo received them into his grace, sending the emissaries back to their cities to prepare his reception. Shortly thereafter the doge sailed up the coast to the port huddled beneath the rocky, wooded hills overlooking the Gulf of Trieste. Here the citizens of Trieste received him with all the honors due a determined man whose will was backed by a large fleet. The priests turned out in their finest vestments, innumerable candles were burned, and all the bells of the city rang noisily. In a solemn pact Trieste pledged its loyalty to Venice.[61] The ceremony was then repeated at Muggia. The pacts are almost identical.[62]

The other portion of the fleet, if we believe Robert of Clari, who does not mention the events described above, sailed directly for Pola near the southern tip of the Istrian peninsula. Here they landed, refreshed themselves, bought provisions, and stayed a little while.[63] Pola too owed Venice rowers and marines, and these were no doubt claimed.[64] The vessels then set sail for Zara, making as spectacular a display as when they departed Venice, as Robert tells it, so that the people of Pola were amazed at the show of power and splendor.[65] We hear nothing more of them until their arrival before Zara on 10 November.

Venice has been charged by Riant and other historians with deliberately delaying the fleet between the sailing from Venice and the arrival at Zara, so that winter would be facing them and it would no longer be possible to sail overseas.[66] They overlook the announcement prior to the departure from Venice of the plan to winter at Zara.[67] Early October was too late for the regular sailing season in the Mediterranean, especially for voyages from the Western European ports to Alexandria. The scholarly critics of Venice, moreover, are unaware of what was going on at Pirano, Trieste, Muggia, Pola, and perhaps other cities not recorded in the documents. Rowers and marines, as well as provisions, were being put on board. This was the service owed by the subject cities (the *servitium debitum* familiar to medievalists) to the Republic of Saint Mark. This took considerable time, for the obligation became effective only when the Venetian fleet set forth from the lagoons. The enlistment of men and gathering of provisions could not be accomplished overnight. This accounts, I think, for the slowness of this part of the voyage.[68]

The first division of ships lowered their anchors within sight of Zara on 10 November. On the next morning, the feast of Saint Martin, which was bright and clear, the remainder of the fleet joined them. Zara is sheltered from the waves, like so much of the Eastern coast of the Adriatic, by a range of generally submerged mountains protruding from the sea. The ancient Roman city, the richest in Dalmatia itself, is situated on a near-island linked to the continent by a tongue of land.[69] The crusaders took note of Zara's high walls and formidable towers, and they said to one another: "How could such a city be taken by force except with the help of God."[70] The fleet indeed received here a far different reception than in the Istrian ports. When the inhabitants of Zara saw ranged before their city the greatest naval force they had ever beheld they were filled with fear. But they prepared to resist. They raised their great chain across the mouth of the harbor, closed the gates of the city, and made ready for the impending assault.

The Venetian galleys straightaway ran upon the chain obstructing their entry and broke it; Venetian ships swarmed into the harbor. Knights and sergeants were put ashore. The doors in the sides of the horse transports were opened and the horses were led blindfolded to land. Siege machinery to be set up ashore was also disembarked. Tents and pavilions were unloaded. The Zarans did not oppose the landing, so the Venetians and the crusaders encamped.[71]

On 12 November a deputation of Zarans came to the crimson pavilion of the doge. Having calculated the force of their foes and their own powers of resistance, they offered the surrender of the city and its goods to his discretion with the sole condition that the lives of its inhabitants should be spared. Dandolo replied that he could not accept the surrender without the counsel of his allies, so he took leave of the emissaries to consult the barons.[72]

Among the crusaders qualms of conscience had again arisen over the

attack upon Catholic Zara. Among those who set their faces against it
were a number of clergy and white monks, led by Abbot Guy of Vaux-de-
Cernay, and some laymen, of whom the most important were Count Simon de Montfort and Lord Enguerrand of Boves. These dissenters, especially Simon, later renowned as the relentless leader of the Albigensian
crusade, [73] were possibly more unbending than the pope himself, for they
had to answer before God only for their own conscience, while the pontiff
bore also the burden, as he perceived his responsibilities, for the success or
failure of the crusade.[74] These zealots undercut the negotiations for the
surrender of the city. Simon and others spoke to the representatives of
Zara, reassuring them that the crusaders would not do harm to Christians.
If the Zarans could only resist the Venetians, they would be safe enough.
They should not surrender their city. The dissidents also sent Robert of
Boves, Enguerrand's brother, under the walls of Zara to declare the same
to those within. The relieved envoys departed without taking leave, uncer-
emoniously ending negotiations.[75] In the meantime the council had met to
hear the offer of surrender made to the doge and had agreed to accept it.
The crusading chieftains and the doge returned to Dandolo's pavilion to
conclude the agreement, only to discover that the Zarans had left.[76] At
this point the abbot of Vaux-de-Cernay stood forth to forbid the attack in
the name of the pope under threat of excommunication. They were pilgrims, and might not attack Christians; specifically, they must not attack
Zara.[77] Abbot Guy probably had in his hands at this point the pope's negative response to the news of the planned attack upon Zara brought to
Rome by Peter Capuano and Boniface of Montferrat. Since the legate had
not been allowed to return to the host, the message from Innocent was
borne by the abbot of Locedio.[78] The prohibition voiced by Guy of Vaux-
de-Cernay caused a violent scene. The doge was understandably outraged.
Angrily he charged the crusaders that some of their number had deprived
him of the city that lay within his grasp in spite of their promise to help
him recover it. He demanded that the knights honor their word with their
arms.[79] According to the abbot's nephew, the enraged Venetians were
about to fall upon Guy when Count Simon interposed himself to protect
him.[80] The doge angrily declared that he would not give up his revenge
upon Zara, excommunication or not. Again he demanded that the crusaders keep their word.[81] The abbot's denunciation, however, had given heart
to many who opposed the attack. To some considerable extent scarcely
conceivable to modern men pilgrims had enlisted in the crusade to win the
heavenly Jerusalem by means of the crusading indulgence.[82] If they went
against the pope's will, not only did many believe that they would lose the
indulgence and other privileges of crusaders, but that they would be cut
off utterly from the sacraments of the church, the instruments of grace.

Others saw matters differently. A state of emergency existed. The papal legate had been consulted, as required by the pope, before they left Venice, and he had not opposed the project. Abbot Guy did not possess the authority of a papal legate, although it would have made no difference if he had. It was the responsibility of the crusading leaders to make a decision which answered to the straits in which they found themselves. Their sense of emergency combined with their sense of honor to carry the day for the decision to join the Venetians in the attack.[83]

Among the magnates only Simon de Montfort and Enguerrand of Boves declared that they would not go against the command of the pope, and they withdrew from the camp and set up their tents at a distance, disassociating themselves from the sinful act.[84]

The citizens of Zara, disarmed by the false assurances of Montfort's party, scorned the threats of the Venetians. The king of Hungary had surrounded their city with formidable walls and towers and had placed there a garrison of troops.[85] In order to work upon the consciences and weaken the morale of the attackers, the Zarans suspended crucifixes from their walls.[86] Their confidence in their military and moral defense, however, was short-lived, for the Venetians and the majority of the crusaders did not hesitate to attack the city.

The Venetian fleet assaulted the walls from the harbor to the west, from the Val di Maestro to the Porta Terraferma. The vessels were equipped with projectile weapons which battered the fortifications and with ladders prepared for scaling the battlements of the defenders. To the east, from the Porta Terraferma back around to the Val di Maestro, the crusaders dug siege trenches around the walls. With mangonels, petraries, and other engines of war they hammered the city's defenses from the landward side.[87] Martin, the abbot of Pairis, who had been denied release from his crusading vow when the attack on Zara was first proposed, informed his monk Gunther that the crusaders went about their work sadly and with heavy hearts, but all the more vigorously in order to get the hateful business finished as quickly as possible.[88] The abbot undoubtedly speaks for his own frame of mind and for some others. Whatever their feelings, they did a thorough job. The city was surrounded without communication by land or sea and without hope of succor or supplies. The defenders cast javelins and stones at their tormentors from the walls, but without inflicting many casualties. The defenders saw that they could not resist the superior force which faced them. They demanded that their quarrel with the Venetians be submitted to the pope. This was ignored. Finally the crusaders began to undermine the walls of the city. Unable to beat off the sappers, the terrified Zarans saw that they were lost, that the walls would soon fall open. They were constrained to offer once more to surrender the city to the mercy of the attackers on the sole condition that their lives should be spared. It was accepted. On 24 November, the feast of Saint Chrysogonus, whose body rested within the walls of Zara helpless to protect them, the city was occupied and put to sack.[89] A poverty-stricken soldiery was unleashed upon the defenseless town. They snatched everything of value they could find; they destroyed buildings; they even plundered and profaned churches. The city was divided then between the Venetians and the crusaders, the Venetians occupying the harbor and the crusaders the inland portion.[90]

Evidence concerning Zaran casualties is conflicting. Gunther reports that there was little bloodshed or destruction, but he has an ulterior motive for giving this impression, since Abbot Martin lent his presence to an attack which he thought sinful, but was powerless to halt.[91] Pope Innocent, castigating the crusaders after the fact, declares that the conquest of Zara was not achieved without considerable effusion of blood.[92] And Thomas, archdeacon of Spalato, reports that mortality in the city was so great that there were not enough healthy men to bury the dead, so that corpses lay exposed in homes and churches.[93] Thomas wrote after 1268, however, and was a mere infant in 1202. Moreover, his unburied corpses have more the odor of literary convention than of decaying flesh.

At any rate, the terms of surrender were not honored by the conquerors. Dandolo ordered various citizens especially hateful to the Venetians decapitated and others exiled. Many sought refuge in Belgrade or Arbe or in the monastery of Saints Cosmas and Damian of the Mountain. The more adventurous men of Zara took to the hills as partisans, and an expedition from Venice under Dandolo's son eventually was necessary to suppress them.[94]

Much later, possibly in 1205, the doge wrote to Innocent attempting to justify the conquest of Zara.[95] He mentioned that it had been necessary because of the approach of bad weather to winter there. Since the Zarans were rebels of long standing against Venice, having betrayed their oaths, he deemed it just to wreak vengeance upon them as enemies. It had been reported to him that Zara was under papal protection, but he did not believe it. He was sure that neither the pope nor his predecessors would receive under the papal mantle those who did not take the cross as genuine pilgrims, but as a cover for the seizure and detention of the goods of others. We may dismiss much of Dandolo's argument as special pleading, of course, yet the conquest of Zara was not the simple, one-sided moral abomination that many historians have represented.[96] If we resist the temptation to oversimplify moral issues, a case can be made for the Venetians, as well as for their allies.[97] Zara was a former Venetian dependency, which had revolted. Zaran pirates preyed on Venetian shipping within the Adriatic, control of which was absolutely vital to Venetian prosperity. The Zarans had even allied with Pisa to challenge Saint Mark's domination of that sea. Venice, moreover, had made a massive financial commitment to the crusade, which was in danger of collapse. Abandonment of the enterprise would mean a real financial disaster. The attack upon Zara preserved the crusade and protected the investment of the Venetians. If we do not find them guiltless, we should at least comprehend sympathetically the Venetian's point of view.

6

The Treaty of Zara

The interest of the Venetians and the intention of Dandolo, of course, was not merely to take Zara, but to secure it under their own hegemony. The fleet and the army must remain there for a time, therefore, on guard against any effort by the king of Hungary to retake the city. In any case travel in the Mediterranean Sea customarily came to an almost complete halt in the winter months from November until March. Venetian commerce with the Levant was organized around two great voyages each year. The spring fleet was scheduled to leave Venice about Easter, although it often was delayed until perhaps mid-May. The summer fleet was expected to depart on the feast of John the Baptist (24 June), but sometimes was held up until as late as August or even September.[1] In conformity with this pattern of sailing and in view of the need to protect the newly won city Dandolo informed the barons that they must winter at Zara, as, indeed, had already been planned.[2] As the doge had claimed, a more suitable place would be hard to find. Around the city were numerous olive groves, ample vineyards, and rich grainfields. Game and fish were found in abundance. The winter climate was more mild than that of Venice, not to mention the crusaders' northern homelands. The Mediterranean sun almost always warmed the winter days. Only rarely was Zara afflicted with icy winds and snow: sometimes it did not snow or freeze through an entire winter. As early as January the flowering of the almond trees would foretell the advent of spring.[3]

Pleasant as the site of Zara was, however, it was now many months since the crusaders had left their homes, and Jerusalem remained distant. Even among those who accepted the necessity of the attack on Zara frustration and discontent against their leaders and the Venetians were great. Although Villehardouin tells us that the houses in the conquered city were allotted equitably, from the *Devastatio* we hear the common complaint that the rich and powerful seized all the best places, leaving nothing for the poor.[4] The Venetians chose for themselves the part of the city nearest the port.[5] The crusaders could undoubtedly observe them stacking goods on the shore for shipment to Venice and concluded that their allies had gotten the better of them.[6] The Venetians were enriching themselves. What had they, the poor crusaders, gained? Had the Venetians not already received more than was just? The mass of crusaders probably believed that the large sums left by Fulk of Neuilly had gone into Venetian purses. Many felt exploited by their allies. Also there hovered over them the shadow of guilt for their attack upon Christians.

On the third day after the conquest about the hour of vespers a bloody fight erupted in the city between the disgruntled crusaders and the Venetians. From both sides men ran to arms to join the widespread conflict in the streets. The chief men donned their armor and rushed into the midst of the melee to separate the combatants. No sooner did they quench the flames in one quarter, however, than fighting broke out anew in another. Everywhere the Venetians had the worst of it, not being able to resist the resentful fury of the French. According to the *Devastatio* about a hundred were killed and many more were wounded. Most were among the common folk, but a prominent Flemish knight named Giles of Landas was slain, struck in the eye by a Venetian shaft. The night had nearly ended before the barons were able to calm the excited troops. The doge and the leaders of the crusade spent the rest of the week soothing bitter feelings and restoring peace.[7] Even so, the fray added to the animosities between opposing factions and increased disaffection among the conquerors.

When the king of Hungary heard that the crusaders had joined in the sack of Zara he was very angry, sending messengers to reproach them for this unjustifiable deed. He had taken the cross, as they had, to deliver the Holy Land, only to be attacked by brothers-in-arms. They should give up Zara at once. If they wanted anything from him, he was prepared to give it freely, and he would then go overseas with them. The barons replied that they would not yield the city, for they had sworn to help the Venetians. The king then sent to the pope, pleading for protection against these pilgrims who were pillaging his lands.[8] Innocent's reaction to the rape of Zara and the plea of the Hungarian king is contained in a letter undated, but written at the end of 1202 or the very beginning of 1203. He denounced the crusaders for their conquest and plundering of Zara and for the great effusion of blood which they had caused. They had refused the Zarans' appeal for papal judgment of their dispute with the Venetians. They had assaulted walls from which the inhabitants had suspended the sign of the cross. They had attacked the lands of a crusader. They had ignored the strict prohibition of the pope, which was backed by the sanctions of excommunication and withdrawal of crusading indulgences. He enjoined them most strictly not to harm the city further, but to restore it to representatives of the aggrieved king, lest they incur the aforesaid sanctions.[9] It has often been assumed that Innocent launched a formal bull of excommunication, but he did not.[10] The papal letter, while vigorously condemning the attack, reveals once more the ambiguous situation in which Innocent was placed by his moral duty and his desire to preserve the crusade. He was severe, but he carefully restrained himself from employing his most stringent weapons. He was deliberately vague on the question of excommunication and withdrawal of indulgences, fearing to destroy the host.[11]

About mid-December the leader of the crusade, Boniface of Montferrat, with Matthew of Montmorency and others, rejoined the army.[12] He found a very unstable situation. Simon de Montfort, Enguerrand of Boves, the abbot of Vaux-de-Cernay, and a number of lesser men who had objected to the attack upon a Christian city were disaffected. The men in the ranks mistrusted their leaders and hated and envied the Venetians. The Venetians, in turn, were angered by the heavy losses they had suffered in the recent outburst of violence and by the repeated failure of the crusaders to honor their obligations. The latter continued to owe a very large sum to their allies, for the agreement to conquer Zara had merely postponed the day of reckoning. The army remained extremely short of money, since the unexpected delays had consumed so much of their resources. The crusade was not to set sail from Zara until about Easter, moreover, and by that time the year for which the Venetians owed support would be half gone.[13] There is no evidence that this state of affairs was either sought or desired by Boniface, or that it could have been anticipated by him a year earlier. It did provide an opportunity, however, to revive the project of an alliance with the young Greek pretender, which had earlier seemed so attractive to the scion of the house of Montferrat. In return for aid in gaining the Byzantine throne Alexius would provide the needed financial support and would assist the crusaders to attain their ultimate objective. Since most of the army had been persuaded to fight Christians at Zara, they might well consent also to intervene in Byzantine politics in order to save the crusade. Constantinople, of course, was a much more formidable city, and the Byzantine emperor was more feared than the king of Hungary, but Boniface probably thought that it would not be necessary to take the Greek capital by assault, for he believed that the inhabitants would welcome young Alexius as their rightful ruler. Since there had been contention among the crusaders over the attack upon Zara, however, care must be taken to minimize the divisiveness of the proposed alliance. Before the assembled host, therefore, the Venetian doge first pointed out the need for supplies and the possibility of acquiring them from the Greeks. Then Boniface recalled his meeting with the young prince at Hagenau a year before. If they could get hold of this youth, they would have an excuse for going to Constantinople to obtain the provisions they needed.[14]

In Germany Philip of Swabia too had learned of the plight of the crusading army and grasped how he could take advantage of it. He had received kindly the envoys whom the barons had sent from Venice in company with young Alexius and his counsellors. They discussed the restoration of the Greek prince by the crusading army in return for Byzantine aid to the crusade and the Holy Land. When the emissaries of the crusaders took their leave to rejoin their companions in arms they were accompanied by envoys from Philip bearing a specific and highly attractive offer. Two weeks after Boniface had joined the host at Zara the embassy from King Philip arrived. The barons received the German emissaries in the palace occupied by the doge.[15] The representatives of King Philip sought to move the crusaders to sympathy for Isaac II, the imprisoned father, and Alexius, his exiled son. The soldiers of the cross could perform a work of charity and justice, and, at the same time, one which would greatly further their own undertaking, by helping the prince to the throne of Constantinople. In return, first of all, young Alexius would place the Greek church in obedience to Rome. He would supply the crusading army and provide them in addition with two hundred thousand marks. He himself would raise an army of ten thousand to join in the crusade for one year, and throughout his life he promised to maintain five hundred knights in the Holy Land. The envoys possessed full powers to conclude a treaty on these terms.[16] Nicetas implies that the inexperienced young prince did not comprehend the enormity of the commitment he was making.[17] This may well be true. In any case, desperate men are disposed to promise anything, leaving the fulfillment to be worried about at a later time. Not only did Alexius overestimate his potential military and financial resources and his influence over the Byzantine church, but the envoys assured the crusaders that the magnates of the empire and the greater part of the population of the capital desired the overthrow of the usurper who occupied the throne. [18]

On the following day the leaders met again in the palace where the doge was lodged to discuss the German proposal. Gathered were the bishops and abbots accompanying the army, the barons from France and Flanders and their most important vassals, the German princes, Boniface and the other Lombard lords, and the Venetian doge with his council. The assembly was polarized. The Venetians, the marquis, and the counts of Flanders, Blois, and St. Pol had already the previous summer more or less committed themselves to the project, providing that Philip of Swabia would guarantee the word of his young brother-in-law, as he now did through his emissaries.[19] Naturally the most faithful followers of these great barons, such as the officials of their courts and the former envoys to Venice, were of their party. The Germans had been ordered by the emissaries of Philip of Swabia to support his initiative, although we do not know how vigorously they did so.[20] Some of them had joined the crusade to escape excommunication for their support of the Hohenstaufen, and they perhaps still feared the papal ban.[21] The opposing faction was led by Simon de Montfort, who, as later in the Albigensian Crusade, saw himself as the staunch defender of papal policy.[22] Some of the knights from Champagne, jealous of the leadership of Montferrat and the money he had received from Count Thibaut's legacy, stood against the German proposals.[23] The churchmen divided along similar lines. Abbot Simon of Loos, a follower of the count of Flanders, was prominent in the party favoring young Alexius.[24] Abbot Peter of Locedio followed his lord and friend Boniface, although he was also attached to Innocent and trusted by him. Martin of Pairis was a declared partisan of the Hohenstaufen king, but he had shown himself at Venice apprehensive of papal censure, so he was opposed to the proposal. Abbot Guy of Vaux-de-Cernay, follower of the count of Montfort, was chief of the clerical foes of the undertaking. As in his courageous opposition to the attack upon Zara, he conceived himself as representing the papal will.[25] The abbot of Cercanceaux was also of this faction.[26] The five bishops in the army similarly stood on different sides of the issue. Nivelon of Soissons, who had helped to negotiate the treaty of 1198 between Philip Augustus and Philip of Swabia, was favorable to the policy of the Hohenstaufen. John Faicete, bishop of Acre and chancellor of Flanders, followed Baldwin. Conrad Krosigk of Halberstadt, who had gone on crusade to avoid excommunication for his support of Philip of Swabia against the pope, had, like Abbot Martin, shown at Venice a fear of ecclesiastical censure for failure to proceed directly to the Holy Land. Now, however, he learned from the German emissaries that Otto of Brunswick had ravaged his lands and that the papal legate in Germany was trying to force the canons of Halberstadt to elect a new bishop in his place. This undoubtedly drove him back to his fundamental loyalty to Philip and to support of the German proposal. Bishop Garnier of Troyes may not have been active in the debate, for he was so old that Innocent had sought to relieve him of his crusading vow three years earlier. The only prelate who could be counted upon to oppose the German blandishments was Peter, bishop-elect of Bethlehem.[27]

The greater men thus were hopelessly divided over the German proposal, and its merits and demerits were argued abroad in the camp. The abbot of Vaux-de-Cernay and those of his party urged that the crusaders should proceed directly to Jerusalem to accomplish whatever they could. In no way would his partisans consent to the German plan.[28] They called to the minds of the crusaders the vows that they had sworn so long ago, which remained unfulfilled. Men could not with impunity forswear those promises made in the sight of God. Their arms had been blessed to fight the infidel, not to shed Christian blood.[29] In Constantinople there existed a legitimate emperor, Alexius III, who was on good terms with the Holy See, and they had no acceptable motive for attacking him.[30] To turn from the Holy War to seek booty in a Christian city could bring only disgrace. If they did it they would have to face the wrath of the pope, who possessed the keys of heaven. Moreover, how could they put their trust in the deposed and blinded Isaac and his son? The father had allied with Saladin, greatest of the Muslim foes of the crusade, against Frederick Barbarossa.[31] The son was a refugee without power, money, or subjects, who could only be a hindrance to them. Their strength, moreover, was not sufficient for the task proposed by the German envoys. The prospect of an assault upon Constantinople by water was particularly awesome to landsmen with little taste for the sea and possessing a grossly exaggerated opinion of the naval power of Byzantium.[32]

Abbot Simon of Loos and those on his side begged that the army accept the proposed treaty in order to survive. The essential thing was to prevent the dissolution of the crusading army.[33] Before his departure from Venice for Rome the papal legate himself had recognized the overwhelming importance of this objective, to which he had been willing to sacrifice his qualms concerning the attack upon Zara.[34] This faction argued that the crusaders must bow before the ineluctable facts. Their contract with the Venetians for provisions had only about six months to run, and they had not even paid what they already owed. They could not help the Holy Land without money and supplies. Those of their number who had gone directly to Palestine from other ports had accomplished nothing there. Only via Egypt or Constantinople could they aid the Christians of the Levant and fulfill their vows. Alexius provided an excuse to go to the Greek capital and an expectation of easy success.[35] Constantinople seemed to them as acceptable a step as Cairo on the way to Jerusalem. The Byzantines had been indifferent to the cause of Christ from the beginning of the crusades and had increasingly become an obstacle to the crusaders from the West. The empire was very rich, however, and if the Greeks under young Alexius would renounce their schism and throw their resources into the common cause, victory over the infidel would be facilitated. Such an outcome would not only save the present expedition, but would establish secure lines of communication and supply for the future. In the circumstances in which they found themselves the offer of young Alexius and Philip of Swabia appeared nothing less than providential. The restoration would not be an end of the crusade, but a means to attain Jerusalem, their ultimate goal.

To many of the pilgrims who interpreted their vows more liberally than others the appeal of Alexius appeared to coincide with their Christian duty. They believed that the young prince was the legitimate heir to the Byzantine throne. Their chivalric code committed them to the defense of the weak and the oppressed, and they were moved by his dolorous account of his blinded father.[36] They were told, moreover, that Alexius had the support of a large and powerful party in Constantinople, so the crusaders would come to his aid, not as conquerors, but as restorers and liberators.[37] To romantic minds, like the troubadours Conon of Bèthune and Raimbaut of Vaqueiras, aiding Alexius could appear a point of honor. Boniface also was no stranger to chivalric adventure. Even most of the bishops accepted the restoration of the Greek youth as legitimate and just.[38]

Whether or not an open appeal was made to the attractiveness of Constantinople as a center for sacred relics we do not know. Since at least the days of the Venerable Bede in the eighth century, however, Constantinople had been known as a holy city, sanctified by its relics, a great center of pilgrimage.[39] The renown of the relics resting in the Byzantine capital had been exalted by the popular legend of *The Voyage of Charlemagne to Jerusalem*. In the twelfth century the imperial capital was one of the holy places listed on the pilgrimage route. The crusaders regarded themselves as pilgrims, of course, and many probably considered the religious benefits to be gained by visiting and venerating so many holy objects.[40]

Certainly the proponents of the German proposal urged the virtue of reuniting the Greek church to Rome. Bishops and nobles joined in their enthusiasm for the return of the schismatics to the true fold and the genuine pastor. Although it was a distortion of papal views, it was argued that the pope himself regarded Alexius III as a schismatic and a heretic. Surely he would not punish the crusaders for opposing such a foe.[41] During the course of the crusades, moreover, the view was gaining currency that war upon heretics by the orthodox was a work favored in the sight of God.[42] Any who denied the authority of Rome, moreover, according to Gregory VII, were heretics.[43]

Still there was no consensus in the host. The greatest of the barons, therefore, Boniface of Montferrat, Baldwin of Flanders, Louis of Blois, and Hugh of Saint Pol, with a few of their followers who favored the expedition to Constantinople, met once more with the German envoys in the doge's palace and accepted the offer. They would be shamed, they said, if they refused it.[44] Boniface and Hugh would both later claim that they had been moved by the shortage of provisions in the army of which they were leaders.[45] Boniface also professed that he was following the advice of Peter Capuano, the papal legate.[46] The agreement of the Venetians was essential, of course, for the army could go nowhere without the fleet, but no opposition was expected from that quarter.[47] The conventions were therefore drawn up, sanctioned by oaths, and sealed. The German envoys, as they had said, possessed full powers to seal the treaty in the name of young Alexius. On the side of the crusaders not many could be found to support the oaths of the four barons, only eight according to Villehardouin, so great was the opposition and apprehension in the army. Among these, not unpredictably, was the marshal of Champagne.[48] Throughout his chronicle runs the theme of the necessity of keeping the army intact and the bad faith of those "who wished to destroy it."[49] Whatever the decision of the chosen leader of the army, Villehardouin would follow him, laying aside every consideration, even the fear of excommunication, in the interest of the unity and preservation of the crusade. The treaty to restore the refugee Greek prince was thus concluded, at least with a small group of leaders, and the German envoys, accompanied by two crusaders, returned to their king. Young Alexius was to join the host at Zara before 20 April.[50]

Nicetas and more modern admirers of Byzantium have pointed the finger of blame for the decision to go to Constantinople at the old doge, Enrico Dandolo. The Greek chronicler draws a portrait of a man bent upon vengeance: "a most jealous and treacherous opponent . . . who, being clever at cheating and calling himself the subtlest of the subtle . . . counted and calculated in his heart how many evils the Venetians were troubled with from the ruling Angeli brothers, and from Andronicus before them, and further back still when Manuel wielded the scepter"[51] This is, of course, the hostile judgment of the vanquished, but it acknowledges the genuine grievances of the doge. The imprisonment of Venetians and the confiscation of their property in 1171 and the increasing favor shown by the emperors to the Genoese and Pisans had understandably aroused Venetian fear and mistrust. Popular Greek resentment against the wealthy Venetians, moreover, always threatened to erupt in attacks upon the Venetian quarter.[52] Many historians have seen Dandolo as the only calculating realist in the midst of confusion.[53] Clearly, as an old hand at Byzantine affairs, he knew very well the value to Venice of her privileged status in the Eastern Empire. Like any skillful politician, he was capable of perceiving and grasping decisively the opportunity that fleetingly presents itself. This was one of those rare occasions. By installing upon the Byzantine throne a young emperor indebted to the crusaders and the Venetians he could guarantee the precious Venetian privileges. The chance had not been foreseeable before the envoys of Alexius came to Venice in the summer of 1202; now Alexius and Philip presented a firm offer. It is scarcely surprising that Dandolo and the Venetians were eager to grasp it.

The decision of the Venetians and a few of the chief crusaders to accept the German offer by no means put an end to the debate. There was great dissatisfaction in the camp, especially among the poorer and simpler men, who naturally suffered more from the delays and the financial difficulties of the army than did the rich. They might have borne their privations more readily if they could see that they suffered them in pursuit of their vows, but these remained as far from fulfillment as ever. Some of the pilgrims, moreover, who had not been able to meet the cost of the journey had been subsidized with funds collected by the church. These had obligated themselves not to return home without letters from the king of Jerusalem, the patriarch, the master of the Hospital or the Temple, or the papal legate attesting that they had performed their pilgrimage to the Holy Land. Otherwise they had to repay the money.[54] This weighed on their minds. The poor crusaders mistrusted the Venetians and their own leaders, all of whom, they were coming to believe, were more interested in material gains than in religious ideals. But discontent was rampant also among the barons themselves. Like the poor, the dissident nobles had not joined the expedition to fight against Christians, but for Christ. They too feared the censure of the church. They suspected that they had already incurred automatic excommunication for the conquest of Zara, and certainly they had done nothing to restore the city, as the pope had commanded under threat of the severest sanctions. They believed that the proposed intervention in Byzantine affairs was foolish and rash. Alexius would not be accepted with rejoicing, as he claimed, and Constantinople would have to be purchased with the blood of crusaders, if, indeed, they would be able to win so strong and great a city. They swore that they would not go to Greece.[55]

Under pressure the leaders granted permission for about a thousand to leave the host and find their own way to fulfill their crusading vows. Orders were then given that no more should leave the camp, but orders could not check the flight of dissident nobles and undisciplined masses. More than another thousand deserted.[56] Many embarked upon merchant vessels, two of which were lost at sea. One of the ships that sank, undoubtedly overloaded with pilgrims, took all five hundred aboard to watery deaths.[57] Other crusaders departed by land through Slavonia, where the inhabitants attacked and murdered many of them, and the survivors had to return to the army at Zara.[58]

One of the leading dissidents, Renaud of Montmirail, with the support of Louis of Blois, his kinsman, was made head of an embassy to the Christians of the Holy Land. Why a member of this faction was entrusted with such a charge is a puzzle. Perhaps the leaders hoped that Renaud would become convinced himself, and then convince his friends, that at that time nothing really could be accomplished in Palestine by the crusading army. They also may have wished to give evidence to the dissidents that the ultimate goal of the expedition, the Holy Land, remained unchanged. At any rate, although Renaud and the knights who accompanied him swore on relics that they would return within fifteen days after delivering their messages, they did not, and nothing more was heard from them until after the conquest of Constantinople.[59]

The famous and powerful Simon de Montfort was one of those who vigorously opposed the Hohenstaufen proposals, and he too departed to find his own way to the Holy Land and to fulfill his vow.[60] Simon, according to Peter of Vaux-de-Cernay, whose uncle, the abbot, was very close to the count, was a man of orthodox faith, a virtuous way of life, and great bravery.[61] What we know of his life and deeds confirms this judgment, but we may also conclude that he was a narrow-minded zealot. It is not absolutely clear when Simon and his followers left the host, but it was probably some time in the winter after the conclusion of the treaty with young Alexius.[62] He had made a treaty with the king of Hungary, presumably for safe conduct. Simon's brother Guy and the abbots of Vaux-de-Cernay and Cercanceaux were among the important men who followed him. Enguerrand of Boves, who had opposed the attack on Zara, also defected a little later.[63] According to Peter, Simon de Montfort and his party made their way with great suffering by land up the rugged coast of the Adriatic to regain Italy. In Apulia Simon hired ships to take his men to Palestine.[64] This was a most grievous loss to the army.

Another serious setback was the failure of the fleet that had sailed from Flanders under John of Nesle to join the army of Venice. The count of Flanders and his allies counted heavily upon it, for it contained a great number of sergeants. The Flemish fleet had arrived safely at Marseilles to pass the winter. Messengers seeking instructions from the count came from there to Zara not long after the debate over the Alexian proposals. Baldwin commanded the fleet to set sail at the end of March to rendezvous with the main body off the town of Modon at the southwestern corner of Morea just before the routes for Egypt and Constantinople diverged. It may be assumed, however, that the messengers carried back to the Flemish fleet news of the decision to go to Constantinople, and that the heated debate of Zara was reenacted at Marseilles. This time, though, those who were determined to go directly to Palestine prevailed, and when warm weather arrived the Flemings sailed for Syrian waters. Villehardouin, always conscious of the diminishing size of the main host, bitterly laments this loss.[65] The total number who abandoned the army at Venice or Zara, or who sailed with the Flemish fleet, he declares, was greater than those who followed the leaders to Constantinople. No good could come of their desertion. The unhealthy climate of Syria proved fatal to some, he says. Others returned home. None accomplished anything.[66]

Not all of those who defected from the army of Zara and Constantinople were single-minded zealots for the Holy Land like Simon de Montfort and Renaud of Dampierre. Some of them, too, like some of those who favored the route of Constantinople, can be charged with confusing lucrative private undertakings with the crusading venture. Walter of Brienne's campaign in south Italy to claim the inheritance of his wife was of this sort.[67] A bizarre private enterprise was pursued by a knight in the Flemish fleet. A daughter of the last Greek emperor of Cyprus of the Comnenian line had been carried off to the West by Richard Lion-Heart. This Flemish knight, a relative of Count Baldwin, encountered her in Marseilles and promptly married her to gain a claim upon the fertile island. Although he was among those who failed to obey Baldwin's order to rendezvous with the main army, Ernoul-Bernard tells us that the knight had every confidence that he would have the support of the count and the Flemings in his endeavor. This reveals a lot, I think, about the lack of discipline and fixed purpose in a crusading army. Not only was the commander's order ignored, but it was assumed that he would not mind, and would even assist the private venture. Our ambitious—and naive—knight hurried to Jerusalem to demand Cyprus of King Aimery. "Who is this beggar?" asked the king. "Let him clear out of here fast, if he values his life." And so he did, joining other crusaders in the war between Christian Antioch and Christian Armenia.[68]

Ernoul-Bernard, our source from the Christian community of the Levant, confirms that those who proceeded to Palestine failed to achieve anything, because of the truce between the two religions in the Holy Land.[69] Apart from a few unproductive skirmishes against Muslims, they became entangled in the internecine wars which the Christian states of the East waged against one another. Although their accomplishments were meager or even negative, however, we should not accept Villehardouin's attribution of bad faith to those who disagreed with his party. Most of them were motivated by a strong desire to fulfill their vows, which they interpreted simply and rigorously. When many of those who had gone to Palestine returned home in September of 1204, some of the dissenters most bitterly attacked by the marshal, Simon and Guy de Montfort, John of Nesle, and Robert of Boves, remained in the Holy Land still determined to do their duty for Christ.[70]

Even the crusaders who had supported the attack upon Christians at Zara as the lesser of two evils were not unaware that it had put them on weak ground with regard to the church. At a later date, anyway, the barons professed to regard Zara with grief as "the city of transgression."[71] They feared, if they were not certain, that they had incurred excommunication. With a show, at least, of remorse they had promptly obtained absolution from the bishops in the army.[72] With some awareness, however, that a papal excommunication could be raised only by the pope, about the end of 1202 they had decided to send emissaries to Innocent. These should excuse their act, insofar as possible, and beg his mercy. Two clerks and two laymen were appointed, according to Villehardouin: the eloquent and pious bishop Nivelon of Soissons; John Faicete of Noyon;[73] John of Friaise, who had helped to negotiate the Treaty of Venice; and Robert of Boves.[74] The first three were committed to their mission, but the fourth was not; Robert of Boves was a stupid choice for such a task. It is scarcely likely that the leaders were ignorant of his opposition to the attack upon Zara and his role under the walls in subverting the proposed surrender. Robert seized the opportunity of the mission to Rome to defect, not returning to the army, but going directly to Acre.[75] Only Gunther of Pairis names Abbot Martin as a member of the mission, and he seems confused on the subject, for he names only the clerics.[76] It is clear, however, that Martin did go to Rome at this time. Riant and others have suggested plausibly that he represented only the German contingent, whereas Villehardouin names those representing the whole army or, perhaps, since all four were from the French-Flemish group, only that segment of it.[77] Martin too had possessed serious moral misgivings about Zara and had vainly sought to be released from his crusading vow.[78] Cardinal Peter Capuano, who had refused him, was no longer with the army. The abbot, who had been left with responsibility for the Germans, likely seized this opportunity to represent them before the pope and to seek papal guidance for his own troubled conscience. There were no Venetian representatives, for they would not confess the sinfulness of the attack.[79]

The emissaries of the crusaders, who left Zara before the arrival of the German ambassadors, arrived in Rome during the early weeks of 1203.[80] Admitted to audience by the pope, they begged his absolution for the sin that they had committed with grief and compelled by necessity. According to Villehardouin, they pleaded that the barons had acted "as men who could not do better, given the defection of those who sailed from other ports. If they had not done it, they would not have able to hold the army together."[81] They were prepared to make amends.[82] If the pope, their good father, would now instruct them, they were ready to do his will.[83]

Once more the master statesman who occupied Saint Peter's throne had to weigh his objectives, curb his impulses, and muster all his great diplomatic skill. He could not, as spiritual head of Christendom, condone the conquest of Zara by the crusading army. As chief priest he had to show his displeasure toward the transgression of the crusaders. In a letter written a year later he recalls to the bishop of Soissons how severely Nivelon and his fellow envoys were received by the pope, saddened by the sin of his sons.[84] Papal grief, however, could not be allowed to jeopardize further the success of the crusade, so Innocent, as was his custom, bowed before the force of events, hoping to salvage as much good as possible from a bad situation. A righteous rigidity would cause the failure of his plans for the crusade, and so the pope was prepared to be indulgent toward his wayward sons, if only they would give him the opportunity by honoring the forms, at least, of penitence.

The envoys' plea for absolution satisfied Innocent's religious scruples and allowed him some show of severity without risking by the imposition of sanctions the dissolution of the army. The pope's letters to the crusaders showed his displeasure with them by the omission of the customary salutation. The penitents, he wrote, must beg the pardon of the king of Hungary and return the spoils of Zara. These things were not actually done, but appearances were saved, since the pope had required it. The crusaders must also desist, of course, from any further attack upon Christians. Their guilt for attacking Zara, however, was mitigated by the plight into which they had fallen. Innocent recognized, as the envoys stressed, that, constrained by necessity, they had not conquered Zara of their own will. Nevertheless, this did not entirely excuse them, because they had gotten into the predicament themselves. In reality Innocent was more concerned by the affront to papal authority than with the wrongs committed against the Hungarian king. The pope's honor and his rights under canon law must be preserved.[85] The absolution which the crusaders had received from the bishops in the army was declared null, since no sentence of the apostolic see could be relaxed by any lesser authority. Despite the outward forms of severity, though, the letter on the whole is remarkably lenient. Having nullified the absolution by the crusading bishops, Innocent then authorized the legate or someone delegated by him to receive oaths of obedience to the apostolic see from the crusaders, and then to absolve them by papal authority.[86]

The Venetians, however, had not repented their sin, but were rejoicing in the results of their attack upon Christians. Jean of Noyon tried to persuade the pope of the inconveniences that would follow from the Venetians being publicly excommunicated, for this would give a pretext to them or to dissident crusaders for breaking up the expedition.[87] On this issue, however, Innocent would not yield. The men of Venice had rejected his legate, ignored his command, corrupted his crusade—and would not even feign repentance. They were thus formally excommunicated.[88]

This created a problem, as Jean of Noyon had foreseen, for good Christians were not allowed to deal with those under the ban. Innocent therefore entrusted another letter to Bishop Nivelon, showing his flexibility, even where he had seemed adamant. The pope's overriding concern was to maintain the army in being and enable it to arrive at its destination. If the Venetians were utterly cut off from communication with crusaders the expedition would collapse, so he authorized the host to proceed with their allies, although they must keep their contacts to a minimum and bear them with grief and bitterness of heart.[89] In the same letter Innocent authorized the crusaders to seize the food they needed, if Alexius III would not provide it, as he had promised. "Necessity," wrote Innocent, "especially when an important cause is at stake, excuses many things." He did not mean to grant a right of robbery, but only to tolerate it, "for one cannot escape grave necessity without great cost."[90] This is a most interesting document. On two issues the pope seriously compromises his religion, and, in the case of authorizing (or tolerating) the seizure of food, the argument from necessity is dubious and fraught with danger for any meaningful moral code. We must bear in mind, of course, the enormous value that Innocent placed upon the success of the crusade. He was compelled to choose the lesser evil, as he saw it. He was no saintly fanatic, but a practical man who knew how to survive and thrive amidst life's moral ambiguities. The irony and his tragedy is that all the compromising did not achieve his aim. The crusaders, as they saw it, had conquered Zara under the dictate of necessity, and under the same stern command they would conquer Constantinople and fail to fulfill their pilgrimage. They can hardly be condemned, as so often they have been, for following papal teaching. I do not mean to condemn Innocent too strongly. His moral predicament calls for understanding and compassion—as do the quandaries of Dandolo, Montferrat, Villehardouin and other protagonists who were faced with hard choices.

Innocent was by no means so naive as to believe that he had now gained effective control of the crusading army. He had merely done his best to keep it in existence. He knew that a new test faced his crusaders, for news of the Hohenstaufen proposals at Zara had by this time reached Rome. The papal legate, Peter Capuano, did not rejoin the host at Zara, but awaited the response of the crusaders to Innocent's letters at Benevento.[91] From there he could proceed to an Apulian port to join the army on its journey or take ship on his own for the Levant. The pope sent him twelve hundred pounds for his expenses in either event.[92] Only if the army were prepared to obey like the true army of Christ did the pope and the legate intend that the latter should take his place as its spiritual head. They had little faith, however, in spite of protestations of repentance, that this would come about. From Benevento the cardinal appealed to the pope for instructions in case the Venetians would not seek absolution, would continue to refuse to receive him as legate, and would adopt with their allies the scheme to place young Alexius on the Byzantine throne. Innocent replied that Capuano should in that case go straight to the kingdom of Jerusalem. As for absolving the French leaders, should they not be obedient to the papacy in these matters, the cardinal should do as God inspired him.[93] If the legate had been illuminated with divine inspiration, presumably, he would not have felt the need for papal instructions, but he did the best he could on the basis of human judgment. In return for *pro forma* submission the legate did have the crusaders absolved, but the Venetians, who remained obdurate as expected, continued under the ban.[94] The very minimal influence that the pope and his legate could exercise over the crusade, though, is shown by Boniface of Montferrat's suppression of the bull of excommunication against the Venetians. Believing that its publication would destroy the army and the fleet, and recalling the pope's own advice that it was often necessary to conceal some things, he turned the bull over to one of the abbots in favor of the German proposals for safekeeping, while awaiting the further orders of the pope.[95] Everything that Capuano had feared was coming to pass. The crusade was clearly out of control, so the legate sailed for Palestine.[96] He would only rejoin the army some months after the sack of Constantinople in 1204.[97]

Abbot Martin of Pairis also failed to return to the host at Zara with the envoys. He was troubled in conscience about the course of the expedition, and had tried to gain relief from his vow when the attack upon Zara had first been broached.[98] At the Roman curia he had again begged permission to return to the quiet of the claustral life, but the pope had insisted that he could not return to Pairis until he had touched the Holy Land, as he had vowed to do.[99] So, when he departed from the court, the abbot and some companions went to Benevento and there joined the legate to await the outcome of events at Zara. Together they later sailed for Acre from Siponto on the Gulf of Manfredonia.[100] In time Martin was to rejoin the army at Constantinople to share in the looting of relics.[101]

On 7 April, the Monday after Easter, when the winter had drawn to an end and the season for sailing was at hand, the crusaders evacuated Zara and encamped near the harbor, while the Venetians leveled the city to its foundations.[102] No more, they vowed, should pirates from Zara oppress Venetian shipping in the Adriatic. They destroyed not only fortifications, but palaces and other buildings, leaving only churches and bell towers above the rubble, calling no one to worship, presiding over a dead city.[103] Not long afterwards Dandolo's son sent a force from Venice to build a castle on the island called Malconsiglio to prevent the return of the Zarans to the site.[104]

Young Alexius was expected to join the crusaders at Zara by 20 April.[105] The leaders, having made their decision, were eager to get the army underway. Soldiers become restive unless they are making recognizable progress toward a goal, and the bitter dispute over the course to be taken had left many of them in a mood to desert. So, when the date of Alexius' expected arrival came without the appearance of the prince, the fleet was ordered to sail for Corfu, leaving Dandolo and Montferrat behind at Zara to await him.[106] The chronicler of Halberstadt tells of the fleet's stop at Ragusa where Bishop Conrad met a hermit who prophesied the capture of Constantinople and its subjection to the crusaders.[107] About 1 May they reached the Greek island where they were to await the others. They pitched their tents and pavilions in front of the city and led the horses out of their transports to graze on fresh grass and to exercise. There they remained for three weeks awaiting their leaders and the Greek pretender.[108]

At Zara, meanwhile, the marquis and the doge expected day by day the coming of Alexius. On 25 April he arrived and was received with great joy and what solemnity the small number of those remaining there could muster.[109] They promptly set sail before a favorable wind to rejoin the host. At various Greek ports along the way, such as Durazzo, the western terminus of the ancient road from the Adriatic to the Bosporus, they stopped to claim the citizens' allegiance to the pretender.[110] Late in May they cast anchor before Corfu. When the chief men in the camp heard that their claimant was at hand they hurried to the shore to greet and honor him. The common soldiers too, of course, flocked to see the young prince who had provided the occasion for the change in strategy of the leaders. Alexius took great pleasure, not only in the honors that were paid him, but in the power of the host that he beheld. His tent was raised in the place of honor and security in the middle of the camp, and right beside it the tent of the marquis of Montferrat, into whose care the German king had commended the youth.[111]

Although the crusaders initially had been well-received on the island, there was a foreshadowing of the acrimony to come, not only at Corfu, but at Constantinople. As the anonymous chronicler of Halberstadt reports it, the archbishop of Corfu had invited some of the Latin clergy to lunch, presumably including Bishop Conrad. As might have been expected where churchmen from the East and West were gathered, the subject of papal supremacy came under discussion, and the Greek prelate commented sarcastically that the only justification for it that he could see was that Roman soldiers had crucified Christ.[112] This small incident gives a hint of the Greek attitude toward Rome. The Byzantine church would never accept the submission to the pope that Alexius, who lacked authority and responsibility to match his ambition, had so glibly promised. The pretender's appearance at Corfu, in fact, aroused violent resistance. The natives shelled the Venetian armada with their petraries, so that the ships had to withdraw from the harbor in haste with large stones splashing in the water about them. In revenge the Latins wasted the island.[113] If the crusaders could sense in this conflict only the isolated perversity of Corfu, the historian, who has the advantage of hindsight, can easily discern the real depth of the bitterness between East and West and the hostility which any Latin-supported pretender would enkindle among the Greeks.[114]

Although a few of the chief men of the crusade had sealed convenants embodying the plan to place young Alexius on the Byzantine throne, this project did not have the support of all the loading men, not to speak of the lesser knights and ordinary crusaders, who were more inclined to press on to Palestine. The pretender sought to appeal to the compassion of these rough warriors, who were accustomed, as we have seen, to be easily moved to weeping and other signs of emotion, by appearing before them as a suppliant begging their aid on his knees.[115]

The renewed proposal to assist the Greek prince to mount the Byzantine throne aroused an uproar in the camp. There was the deepest dissension between the supporters of young Alexius and those who bitterly opposed the Constantinopolitan adventure. The assembly got out of hand, the majority clamoring tumultuously to go to Acre, shouting down the speakers for the other side. Robert of Clari quotes them as saying: "Bah! what have we to do in Constantinople? We have our pilgrimage to make, and also our plan of going to Babylon or Alexandria. Moreover, our navy is to follow us for only a year, and half the year is already past."[116] The proposed enterprise was fraught with peril. Let those who were determined to be foresworn by sidetracking the crusade go to Constantinople. The majority would remain at Corfu, and send word to Walter of Brienne in Apulia that he should send ships to bring them to Brindisi to join him.[117] The crusade was still after seven months little nearer than Walter's forces to the goal of Jerusalem. To proceed to Apulia would not necessarily represent a turning back or giving up. Even Villehardouin, who would have every reason to minimize this opposition and fix the blame upon a few malcontents, admits that more than half of the crusaders refused to follow the official leadership—one more sign, by the way, of the chronicler's essential veracity.[118] Now the leaders were faced, not merely with defections which weakened their army, but with its utter collapse.

The leaders, and above all Boniface of Montferrat, used every imaginable argument to win supporters to the cause of Alexius. The prophecy of the hermit of Ragusa was probably recounted. They tried in vain to persuade the army that it was profitless and dangerous to go to Jerusalem. They were short of money and supplies. The chief men could not pay their knights and sergeants or afford the construction of additional machines of war.[119] Most of the ecclesiastics, seduced perhaps by the hope of rich Byzantine sees, preached the justice of the undertaking. They declared that the enthronement of young Alexius, who had been wronged by his uncle, was a righteous cause, as was the unification of the churches under Rome.[120] Constantinople, moreover, the home of sacred relics since the days of Constantine's mother, Saint Helena, was a worthy goal of pilgrimage. Religious benefits could be gained without sacrificing those already possessed as crusaders.

To no avail. The dissident majority withdrew from the camp before the city and pitched their tents in a valley at a distance, firmly intending to send word to Walter of Brienne that they were prepared to serve him. The situation was desperate, since it now appeared that the army was doomed to dissolve. Boniface urged those who wished to go to Constantinople to go to the camp of the dissidents, and to beg them humbly, for God's sake, to have pity on the army and not to dishonor themselves by being responsible for the failure of the crusade. So the leaders of the expedition, along with Alexius and all the bishops and abbots, went together to the valley where the dissidents were encamped.[121] When they arrived they dismounted, and the dissidents, who were also mounted, possibly even fearing attack, also descended from their horses to greet their comrades. The leaders then fell to their knees protesting with many tears that they would not rise until those who had withdrawn would promise not to abandon the army. According to Villehardouin, the dissidents had great pity on the suppliants, as well they might, seeing their own lords and their relatives and friends there weeping at their feet. So they agreed to talk it over among themselves, and they withdrew to a distance. Then they told the marquis and others of his party that they would agree, after all, to go to Constantinople, but only on condition that they should remain there no more than a month unless they consented to an extension of time. The leaders should swear on the Gospels, moreover, that at any time after Saint Michael's day, 29 September, when ships for transportation to the Holy Land should be demanded, they should be provided within fifteen days in good faith and without any tricks. The leaders protested that the intention of so brief a delay in Constantinople should not be published, because it would encourage the resistance of the Greeks. Those who wished to push on to Jerusalem, however, were adamant, and so the terms of the agreement were made public.[122]

The army was saved from its latest crisis and its gravest so far. They would go to Constantinople to gain the throne for Alexius and to obtain the money, troops, and supplies he promised for the recovery of the Holy Land. The young prince was required to swear upon relics that he would keep his convenants.[123]

7

The Taking of The Tower
of Galata

That necessity that is said to know no law had once more prevailed, and on 24 May, the eve of Pentecost, the fleet bearing the crusading host turned its prows toward the Christian capital on the shores of the Bosporus.[1] It was a beautiful day with bright sunshine and a gentle, favoring wind. The pilgrims committed themselves to the protection of Saint Nicholas of Bari, the protector of those who voyage by sea, and the Venetians set their sails to catch the breeze.[2] The usually reserved marshal of Champagne tells enthusiastically of the beauty of the spectacle. The water was crowded with the galleys, the transports, the horse transports, and the merchant ships which had joined to take advantage of the escort; their sails filled the sea from the shore to the edge of the horizon. The hearts of men rejoiced at the sight. The mind of Villehardouin, however, never dwelt for long upon pure spectacle, but always returned promptly to practical matters. This thing of splendor, the host of dancing sails moved gently by wind and wave, seemed to him, as it was, an instrument fit for conquering lands.[3]

The marquis of Montferrat and the counts of Flanders, Blois, and Saint Pol could not possibly have received prior to their sailing from Corfu a letter which Pope Innocent probably did not even send until after that date. Having learned from Boniface that his bull of excommunication against the Venetians had been suppressed, the pope ordered its immediate publication. He also expressly forbade the crusaders to intervene in the affairs of the Greeks, either on the grounds of the reunion of the churches under Rome or of the misdeeds of Alexius III. He wanted to hear no more of these frivolous side issues or of fake necessities. Neither the subjugation of the Byzantine church to Rome nor the punishment of the crimes of the Byzantine emperor were the causes for which crusaders had taken the cross.[4]

Much controversy concerning the papal role in the crusade has focused upon the tardiness of this prohibition. Some modern scholars, especially those under the influence of the Byzantine tradition, find Innocent guilty of conspiring in the misuse of the crusade against Eastern Christendom in order to gain papal supremacy over the Greek churches.[5] Even Gunther, whose information comes from within the crusading army, tells us that Innocent hated the Greeks and would have liked to see a son of the Latin church ruling in Constantinople, if this could be accomplished without bloodshed.[6] A Catholic emperor in Constantinople, moreover, would be a support, rather than an obstacle, in the conquest of the Holy Land. The pope was deterred from pursuing this goal, however, partly by fear of failure. He believed that the Byzantines had enough fishing vessels alone to repel the crusading fleet, a very erroneous bit of intelligence.[7] Lacking modern instrumentalities for distant intelligence, communications, and command, the pope, whatever his personal qualities, could not control a crusade once it had gotten underway. The best interpretation of Innocent's role at this point in the course of the crusade is that he allowed to happen what he had no power to prevent.[8] Because the pope feared the outcome of an attack upon the Greeks, and because he valued Jerusalem above Constantinople, he wished the crusade to proceed directly to Palestine or Egypt, but he was powerless. The tardy letter was, as the Byzantinists charge, for the record. Innocent maintained a proper diplomatic posture by prohibiting the attack upon the capital of Eastern Christendom. Now let come what must. If the pope should draw advantage from the unexpected success of the undertaking that he had prohibited, he had nonetheless fulfilled his moral and religious duty.

The fleet sailed for Byzantium, and none could have wished for a more fortunate journey. The canvas bulged before a favoring breeze bearing the Western warriors toward Constantinople.[9] As they rounded Cape Malea they encountered two ships filled with pilgrims returning from Syria, among whom were some of those who had sailed from Marseilles rather than join the main body of the army at Venice.[10] Like others who had proceeded directly to the Holy Land, they had encountered a serious plague at Acre. They had soon despaired of the arrival of their comrades from Venice, and had decided to return home. According to Villehardouin, who was prejudiced against them, they were so ashamed that they did not want to make themselves known to those whom they had betrayed. Count Baldwin, however, sent the small boat from his ship to inquire who they were, and they replied. One sergeant jumped over the side of his ship into the small boat. He shouted back to his companions on board: "You men can do what you like with anything I've left behind. I'm going with these people, for it certainly seems to me they'll win some land for themselves." The crusaders naturally rejoiced over this prodigal son, returned to his duty.[11]

They sailed on to Negroponte on the island of Euboea, where first the young prince received the submission of the inhabitants. The barons next held a council, and decided to send Alexius with a large part of the fleet under the marquis of Montferrat and the count of Flanders southward again to the island of Andros to gain its adherence to their cause. When they landed there the knights armed themselves and ravaged the land until its people surrendered to the pretender. They provided him with money and goods, and the ships filled their water barrels from the island's abundant springs. Then they sailed off once more to rejoin the remainder of the fleet. On this voyage they suffered the loss of Guy the castellan of Coucy, who was buried at sea.[12]

The portion of the fleet that had remained at Negroponte arrived first at the Dardanelles, called by the crusaders, along with the Sea of Marmara and the Bosporus, the Straits of Saint George from the monastery of Saint George of Mangana. They found the straits undefended, and the armada sailed up as far as the ancient town of Abydos, a beautiful and well-situated city on the Asiatic side. The crusaders left their ships in the harbor and went ashore, where the people of the city surrendered at once, earning the contempt of Villehardouin for lacking the courage to defend themselves. The inhabitants achieved their purpose, however, for the crusaders placed a guard over the city to prevent looting. The peasants were not so fortunate. Supplies in the fleet were running dangerously low, so the pilgrims spent the time while they were awaiting the detachment from Negroponte in seizing the harvest of winter wheat, which now stood ripe in the fields.[13] About mid-June at Abydos the two sections of the fleet were reunited.[14]

Emperor Alexius III meanwhile awaited the Latin attack helplessly. By his treachery to his brother he had gained rule over a social and political system in decay.[15] The process of feudalization and disintegration of the empire was in full swing. Virtually independent political entities had sprung up on both sides of the straits and in the islands. Revolts and disorders in the provinces almost nullified imperial authority outside the capital, and even there it was feeble. The senate, clergy, and artisans of Constantinople had refused to contribute part of their capital to a special fund for defense against the German Henry VI.[16]

A better man could not have halted the decline; Alexius did not even try. Nicetas can find little good to say of this emperor: he was gracious, approachable, and opposed to cruel punishments and tortures, but he was cowardly and incompetent.[17] Nicetas, of course, despised Alexius III for his flight from the beleaguered city in the hour of danger, but there is little reason to reverse his opinion of the emperor.[18] Alexius had come to the throne amidst hopes for a warlike and strong rule, but at the test he proved far from valorous. His very coronation was shadowed with evil portents. The horse on which he was to ride to Sancta Sophia reared, casting the imperial crown into the street and almost unseating him.[19] As ruler he surrounded himself with flatterers and calumniators. He had no aptitude for administration, and, according to Nicetas, knew as little of the affairs of the empire as if he inhabited far-distant Thule.[20] When faced by foreign ambassadors threatening war he relied upon a dazzling show of court ceremonial to overawe them.[21] So had his predecessors, of course, but they had other more substantial resources in reserve. Such successes as he did enjoy were due to a certain subtlety that his enemies called duplicity. He spent most of his time traveling about his estates on the Sea of Marmara amusing himself with gardening and designing landscapes.[22] He was devoted to astrology like his contemporaries and undertook nothing without consulting the practitioners of this arcane art. It is alleged that he lived in terror of fate's retribution for his sin against his brother.[23] His idleness was made worse by a painful disease, which may have been gout. [24] His wife, Euphrosyne, is said to have deceived him brazenly, making the emperor a laughingstock in the eyes of his subjects.[25]

When Alexius III heard of the reception of his nephew as emperor within the empire he made what preparations he could, but it was much too late. Shaking himself out of his customary lethargy the emperor ordered the imperial fleet prepared for action.[26] What a fantasy! Manuel Comnenus in the mid-twelfth century had been able to put into the water against the Normans a fleet of five hundred galleys and more than a thousand transports.[27] Even in 1171, when Byzantine sea power was again declining before the rise of the Italian maritime states, Manuel was able to assemble a hundred fifty galleys against the Venetians.[28] After the death of Manuel in 1180, however, his successors allowed the fleet to decay. They abandoned the financial burden of it to rely upon hiring pirate vessels, which were then numerous in the eastern Mediterranean.[29] Mercenaries, however, are often unavailable when they are most needed. In 1196 only thirty vessels could be mustered for a campaign against pirates.[30] There were, indeed, a myriad of exalted naval functionaries drawing large stipends for doing nothing. These officers vaunted their proud titles and posed as admirals and captains—but there was no fleet.[31] The keeper of the imperial forests, as if these were sacred groves or the Garden of Eden planted by God himself, would not allow wood to be cut for ships.[32] An even more blatant culprit was the brother-in-law of the empress Euphrosyne, the Lord Admiral, Michael Stryphnos, who had chief responsibility for naval affairs. This venal beneficiary of Byzantine nepotism, according to Nicetas, possessed a remarkable gift for turning planks and anchors to gold and ropes to silver. He sold off from the arsenals entire ships, pocketing the proceeds. He had been prosecuted for corruption, but had survived to pull down from power his accuser. The incapable emperor, Nicetas says, did nothing to restrain these fools and criminals. So, in the spring of 1203, the successor of the Caesars could put into the water only twenty decaying and worm-eaten ships incapable of putting out into the open sea to face the Venetian fleet of some two hundred vessels.[33]

The army was not in quite such a disastrous condition, but neither was it in good order. The Greeks had become a people enslaved to luxury and unwilling to defend themselves. The army had never recovered from the disasters of the last years of the reign of Manuel Comnenus.[34] It had been further weakened by Conrad of Montferrat's victory on behalf of Isaac II over Branas.[35] There were two types of Byzantine fighting men. First were the heavily armored knights who required for support large grants of land more or less analogous to the fiefs of the Westerners.[36] These were less and less prepared to render the military service to which they were obligated. Then there were the foreign mercenaries, Slavs, Turks, Hungarians, Franks (or West Europeans), and, above all, the famed Varangian Guard. The elite Varangians, largely Scandinavians and Anglo-Saxons, possessed a tradition of loyalty to the person of the emperor, although Alexius III was scarcely an emperor to inspire devotion.[37] The mercenaries generally were poorly paid, however, and, as is the way of mercenaries, could not be depended upon to resist either the allurement of higher pay or the fury of a determined assault. So the combat effectiveness of a Byzantine army of the late twelfth century was highly dubious. On occasion it could fight with courage and discipline, but morale was low, and armies occasionally simple refused to do battle. Command, moreover, rested in the emperor himself or a trusted relative, and, while this reduced the chances of military revolt, it did not result in the appointment of the best qualified officers.[38] According to the crusading leaders, who probably exaggerated the numbers of the enemy to enhance their triumph, Alexius III did raise a force of sixty thousand men.[39] In any case, when battle was finally joined, he could really depend only upon the Varangians, who were proud professionals, and the Pisans, who volunteered through jealousy and hatred of the Venetians.[40]

The patricians and citizens of the capital would be of no use in its defense. Benjamin of Tudela had noted their softness, corruption, and incapacity for war.[41] The citizenry was also inured to the rise and fall of emperors. They felt little loyalty to Alexius III—though they hated the Latins. They could be counted upon as a raucous and obscene cheering section, but hardly for bearing arms.[42]

Perhaps there was not really much that the emperor could do. It seemed safer—or at least easier—to do nothing. After all the unconquered walls had withstood many assaults since the foundation of the city in the fourth century. Perhaps they would prevail once more.[43] Alexius inspected these doughty defenders of the imperial city and ordered razed the houses that stood between them and the shore in order to deprive the invaders of protection.[44]

Once the crusaders had reunited at Abydos they embarked once more for Constantinople. The many sails appeared like flowers blossoming on the narrow straits. Against the stiff current which flows down the Dardanelles the fleet made its way into the tranquil Sea of Marmara. On the eve of Saint John the Baptist, 23 June, they cast anchor before the abbey of Saint Stephen about seven miles southwest of Constantinople. Here they were in full view of their destination.[45] Although St. Stephen's does not offer the most picturesque of the many panoramas of Constantinople, the crusaders were astounded by the grandeur of the scene before their eyes. They had never imagined there could be such a beautiful city in all the world. They had never beheld so many and such magnificent palaces, and the many domes of Orthodox churches were also a strange and marvelous sight. Since they were not mere sightseers, but men with a mission, they were awed by the high walls and loftier towers encircling the city. No man, says Villehardouin, was so brave and daring that he did not shudder at the sight.[46] After they had landed they held a conference to determine what they should do next. There were many opinions, but the doge, who was no stranger to Constantinople, advised that they must not go overland, for they were once more short of food, and it would be impossible to keep the men from scattering in search of provisions. He pointed out the Isles of the Monks (now called Princes' Islands) to the southeast of the city where they should put ashore to lay in stores. These would be much less well-defended than either shore of the Bosporus, and so could be more easily seized and used as a base of operations to attack Constantinople from the sea. A regular siege of the land walls, the tactic to which the Western knights were accustomed and which they would have preferred, was impossible, since they did not have sufficient numbers for such a great and well-fortified city. The barons agreed with the plan of the doge and returned to their ships.[47]

On the day of Saint John the Baptist, 24 June, they boarded their vessels, which were now arrayed so finely that the fleet seemed to the crusaders the most beautiful thing in the world. The pennons and banners of all the lords with their lively and variegated colors were unfurled. The shields, each furbished with the arms of its owner, were ranged around the bulwarks like a wall of steel. Each man had looked to his arms to see that all was in readiness, for the hour of battle was near and might be at hand.[48]

Why the ships did not sail to the Isles of the Monks as agreed we do not know. Sir Edwin Pears, who was not a very good historian, but who knew Constantinople and its surroundings extremely well, believed that a southerly wind negated that possibility.[49] At any rate, the ships in a long line, banners in the wind, ran right under the towering walls of the capital.

The galleys led, canvas furled and propelled by rowers, as in combat, followed by the larger transports under sail. Some of the bowmen shot at Greek ships from a distance as they sailed by, but their shots fell short into the water. The sea wall of the city stands right at the water's edge, so crowds of Greeks mounted the walls and others climbed to the roofs of houses to behold the approach of the Latin enemy. They gazed in wonder at this splendid and fearful spectacle of two hundred ships. Those in the ships were also struck with awe as they sailed under the domineering walls.[50]

Entering the Bosporus they beheld the beautiful scenery along its banks. On the Asiatic side, opposite Constantinople, picturesque cliffs and gentler slopes alternated. They viewed luxurious gardens, handsome houses, and magnificent palaces, some of them imperial summer residences, where the emperor was accustomed to withdraw from the noisome city to enjoy the fresh air and the beauties of nature.[51] The fleet made port at Chalcedon across the straits from the imperial city. There some of the crusaders took up quarters in a splendid palace belonging to the emperor, some appropriated houses in the town, and others pitched their pavilions. At the first opportunity they led the horses from their transports to graze and regain the use of their legs. Only the Venetian sailors were left aboard the ships. Foragers were put to work. The country was not only beautiful, but fertile, and the harvest of winter wheat had been gathered and stood in stacks in the fields.[52] From their encampment Constantinople stood in full view at the distance of only a mile. The crusaders were not yet ready, however, to engage the Byzantine soldiers who were observed on the walls.

The rapid current which emanates from the Black Sea and courses through the straits makes it easier to cross from the Asiatic side to Constantinople from above the city, and so the Latins decided to move their quarters another mile or so to the north to the town of Scutari. On the third day, 26 June, the Venetians sailed the ships up the straits, while the crusaders marched by land along the shore. At Scutari the leaders occupied another of the usurper's summer palaces.[53] Upon learning of the crusaders' movement Alexius arrayed his army on the European side of the straits opposite them to resist an attempted landing.[54] The crusaders, meanwhile, were deeply disturbed that no relatives or friends of the young pretender had come to welcome him. They had not even received any messages from his supposed supporters within the capital. They had been led to believe that they would be greeted as restorers and friends of the rightful emperor. Now that they had arrived before the capital no one came to reveal to them the minds of its citizens and magnates toward the young prince.[55] With fear and trembling they gazed across the straits at the army of the enemy and those enormous walls. They could only conclude that the wicked uncle, Alexius III, had poisoned the minds of the people against them as alien invaders set on destroying Greek liberties, imposing the supremacy of the Roman pontiff and subjugation to the laws of the Latins. Thus they were regarded as if they were pagans come to destroy the Christian faith.[56] The surprise and consternation of the crusaders at this point is crucial to my interpretation of the entire crusade. The Latins had not planned to conquer the city, much less to subject it to Latin rule, but to restore a rightful ruler, who, they expected, would be welcomed by his subjects. Even Dandolo and the marquis of Montferrat, who were undoubtedly better informed concerning Constantinopolitan politics than their allies from the North, were taken in by this expectation. Isaac II, after all, had not been overthrown by a popular revolt, but by a treacherous palace coup. If his son, the young Alexius, had appeared before the walls of Constantinople with a force other than that of the hated Latins he might have been welcomed as he claimed he would be. Under the present circumstances, however, this hope was in vain, so the crusaders hesitated, remaining at Scutari for nine days while each man foraged for his provisions.[57]

During this period, on 1 July, occurred the first skirmish between Greeks and Latins. The crusaders had assigned a detachment of some eighty knights to prevent a surprise attack upon the camp and to protect the foragers. While engaged in reconnaissance this party came upon some pavilions pitched at the foot of a hill several miles east of Scutari.[58] This proved to be the encampment of a force of some five hundred Greek cavalry under the Lord Admiral, Michael Stryphnos. The Latin reconnaissance party drew up in four companies to attack, and the Greeks also drew up in battle formation in front of their tents to await the enemy. Though faced by far superior numbers, the reconnaissance party couched their pennoned lances and rode upon the foe as strongly as they could. At the shock of the first encounter the Greeks broke ranks and fled, led by their commanders, who, according the Nicetas, turned their backs and ran before these "soul-snatching angels" like frightened deer.[59] The crusaders pursued the enemy for several miles before turning back to loot the camp. They gained chargers and other horses and mules, the tents, and other booty. The horses were especially prized, for there were far more men in the host trained for cavalry warfare than there were mounts. When the reconnaissance party returned to the crusaders' camp they were welcomed warmly by their comrades, with whom they shared the booty.[60]

On the following day appeared at Scutari an embassy from the emperor Alexius III headed by a native of Lombardy, Nicholas Rosso. He found the barons and the doge conferring at the emperor's summer palace, and delivered his letters of credence to the marquis, who gave him permission to speak. Rosso inquired on behalf of the emperor why the crusaders had entered his lands, for he was a Christian, as they were, and he knew that they were bound to deliver the Holy Land, the Holy Cross, and the Holy Sepulcher. If they were poor and needed supplies, he would gladly give them provisions and money, provided that they withdraw from his land. If they would not do this, the emperor would do them harm, although reluctantly, for he had power to do this, even if they were twenty times stronger than they were. Conon of Béthune replied for the crusaders. Conon was an older man, like Villehardouin, a member of an illustrious family of Artois, and a relative of Baldwin of Flanders.[61] He was an eloquent and fervent speaker, and shared with the marshal of Champagne the heaviest diplomatic burdens of the crusade. When negotiation was required, Villehardouin usually spoke for the crusaders. When Conon spoke it was in defiance.[62] He said: "We have not entered *his* dominions, since he has wrongfully taken possession of this land, in defiance of God, and of right and justice. It belongs to his nephew, seated here on a throne amongst us, who is his brother the emperor Isaac's son. However, if your lord will consent to place himself at the mercy of his nephew, and give him back his crown and his empire, we will beg the prince to allow him enough money to live in a wealthy style. But unless you return to give us such a message, pray do not venture to come here again."[63] Rosso replied, of course, that the emperor would do nothing of the sort, and he departed.[64]

In the face of all the evidence to the contrary the crusaders continued to hope that there existed in the city a strong party of Greeks eager to receive the young prince as sovereign. On the day after Rosso's visit, therefore, the doge proposed that they should take their ward on a galley under the walls of Constantinople, show him to the people, and call upon them to receive their emperor. His faction, they believed, had been held back through fear of Alexius III. At the sight of the prince this party might erupt in his support to overthrow the usurper. So the doge ordered ten galleys to be prepared. Dandolo, Boniface, and young Alexius boarded one, probably the sumptuous vessel of the doge. All the knights who wished to accompany them climbed aboard the others. Under a flag of truce the galleys rowed back and forth right under the sea walls, perhaps as close as ten feet at times, displaying the prince to the Greeks and calling for his recognition. They cried out the crimes of Alexius III and their intention to help the Greeks to depose the tyrant, and they threatened to do their worst if he were not dethroned in favor of his nephew. The response was a torrent of hoots, whistles, and derisive insults. Each time the galleys drew too close to the walls, in spite of the flag of truce, they were showered with missiles. For once the sagacious Dandolo had given bad advice. That he did so, however, offers solid support for my belief that even Dandolo expected that the crusaders escorting the young Alexius would be received at Constantinople as liberators. In fact, presenting the young prince in such a fashion, borne on a Venetian galley and manifestly a ward of the marquis of Montferrat, only served to unify the Greeks in opposition to him. Even if Alexius III were as bad an emperor as he is depicted by Nicetas, he was bound to become a rallying point for the Greeks against the Latin puppet, a symbol of the independence of the Greek empire and, above all, of the Greek church. The shouting of abuse from the walls was so loud that the crusaders later complained that they were unable to make the Greeks understand their reasons for coming to Constantinople. So they returned to Scutari.[65] There was no choice now but to recognize that the prince's party in Constantinople was a figment of the young man's imagination. The representations of Alexius, his sister, and his German brother-in-law had probably not been consciously false. Philip of Swabia did not know the temper of the Greeks directly, but only through his wife and her brother. Irene, of course, had been long absent from Constantinople, but was quite ready to believe in the popularity of her family. We have all seen older and wiser men than young Alexius deceive themselves concerning the measure of their own support. His did not exist. In fact, the overwhelming mood of the Greeks was resentment against him as a pawn of the Latins and of Rome. The crusaders had hoped that they could use Alexius as the instrument of a bloodless coup d'état. Now they saw clearly enough that they must risk all in battle.

On the day following the abortive attempt to excite a revolt in favor of the pretender, after hearing mass, the leaders of the crusaders held a council of war on horseback in an open field.[66] They had observed that the walls of Constantinople facing the Sea of Marmara and the Bosporus rose almost immediately out of the water, leaving practically no space for attackers to gain a foothold. The tiny shore that existed there was dominated by the towers that projected from the walls, leaving assailants exposed to a rain of javelins, arrows, and stones from above. Any assault upon these walls would also be endangered by the strong current sweeping the ships southward. On the north shore of the Golden Horn, however, where the suburbs of Pera and Galata flourished, there was a larger beach defended only by the strong tower of Galata. The barons agreed that their first objective must be to gain a foothold on this north shore and control of the Golden Horn. From there they could launch an attack upon the city itself.[67]

After much discussion of details they agreed upon an order of battle for the next day's attack. The army of about ten thousand men, not counting the Venetians, was arranged in seven battalions.[68] The advance guard was given to Baldwin of Flanders, since he had under his command the most skilled and numerous archers.[69] A feudal army, while it relied upon the charge of heavily armed knights for the blow-giving victory, customarily tried to shelter that mounted mass behind a screen of infantry until the critical moment. Archers and crossbowmen were especially favored, so that they could soften up the enemy with a shower of arrows and bolts before the chivalric charge. Many of Baldwin's archers were undoubtedly well-equipped with iron caps and leather or quilted linen protection for the body, if not chain mail. Less favored infantrymen wore their ordinary clothing, having only a spear or a bow to distinquish them from peaceful pilgrims.[70] Baldwin's brother Henry commanded the second battalion. Hugh of Saint Pol, had the third. The numerous vassals and followers of Louis of Blois formed the fourth battalion. Like Baldwin's, this was an especially strong force. The valiant Matthew of Montmorency had charge of the Champenois and the fifth battalion. Geoffrey the Marshal, of course, was one of the outstanding nobles in this group, perhaps the second in command or a sort of chief of staff.[71] Much has been seen of Villehardouin already as diplomat and counselor, but he was also a noteworthy knight. In him are reflected the dominant values of his age and class. Individual honor, in the sense of renown, was foremost in his mind. "He does ill,"he wrote, "who through fear of death does anything that will cause him to be reproached forever."[72] Yet his courage was not of the foolhardy sort, but rather consisted in a firm resolution in the face of peril. It was tempered too by his consciousness of the common good and the practical problems. We find his mind always occupied with plans of operations, alignments of forces, and the availability of supplies.[73] The sixth battalion was composed of Burgundians, while the seventh embraced Lombards, Tuscans, Provençals, and Germans under the command of Boniface. The marquis's battalion was the rearguard. The Venetians, of course, were to be responsible for the fleet, which was so vital to success and the survival of all.[74]

Now it was cried through the host that everyone should arm himself. For the moment all disaffection with the course of the crusade seemed to disappear. The hour of decision had passed, and the hour of battle was upon them. Now they must either conquer or die.[75] If they conquered, their obligation to young Alexius would be fulfilled, and they need only collect their reward and continue toward Jerusalem. Yet the result of battle was uncertain and, indeed, not very promising, and the heart of many a brave man trembled at the thought of forcing a landing. The priests among them reminded the crusaders of the imminence of death and exhorted them to cast themselves upon the mercy of God. Through confession and absolution the warriors prepared to face the Eternal Judge. Many also made wills, not only to provide for the disposal of their temporal goods, but to take advantage of a possible last chance to perform works worthy to be weighed in their favor before the throne of judgment. Masses were heard, and collectively and individually the crusaders placed themselves under the protection of the saints, especially those warrior-saints who were known to join miraculously in battle in favor of their devotees. Armed as fully as could be in body and spirit, the crusaders entered the ships.[76]

Just after sunrise on the fine morning of 5 July the early stillness was broken by the blare of trumpets and the rolling of drums and tabors. When those in Constantinople heard the racket the walls filled with armed men, while householders gaped from their rooftops. The Venetian galleys were moving forward in order of battle, and each towed behind it one of the more unwieldy sailing ships in order to cross over more securely.[77] Presumably this was to take advantage of the greater maneuverability of the oared galleys against the strong current. To the Greeks it seemed that land and sea trembled, and that the sea was covered with enemy ships.[78] The attack was not against the city itself, however, but against the suburb of Galata across the Golden Horn. Near the northern shore of the entrance to the harbor, less than a mile from Scutari, the emperor disposed his forces to meet the attack. The crusaders sent barks packed with crossbowmen and archers ahead of the galleys to attempt to clear the shore for landing. As missiles cast by mangonels and petraries on the walls of Constantinople splashed in the water about them the vessels made their way across the treacherous Bosporus without mishap. As they drew near the shore each ship strained to be first to land. When they ran aground the ports in the sides of the horse transports were quickly lowered to form bridges, down which the fully armored knights rode into the water up to their waists, lances in hand. The archers followed the knights, and then the other foot-soldiers. As these lesser men clambered to shore they drew up in front of the various battalions of knights in the accustomed formation.[79]

The Greeks made only a feeble pretense of contesting the landing. Some volleys of arrows were fired from a distance at the knights with their long lances poised for the thunderous mounted charge. When Count Baldwin set in motion his vanguard under the banners bearing the lion of Flanders, and the other battles began to move forward after the Flemings, the Greeks quickly turned tail and showed their heels in such precipitous flight that not even the arrows of the crusaders could catch them. The knights chased their fleeing quarry all along the north shore of the harbor as far as the fortified bridge beyond the northwest extremity of Constantinople. Over this bridge the frightened Greeks escaped to the other shore. The warlike Westerners seized the tents and pavilions of the emperor with much booty. Without the loss of a man they had gained the whole north shore of the Golden Horn except for the suburb of Galata and its critical tower.[80]

The crusaders camped on the slope of the hill behind the tower in Estanor, the Jewish quarter.[81] Along with the surrounding shops and homes of Genoese and other foreigners it formed a wealthy suburb of Constantinople.[82] The Venetians urged that they should make an assault upon the tower on the following day, for it was essential to get the fleet out of the unsheltered straits and into the safety of the Golden Horn. The barons realized that any risk to the ships placed them all in mortal danger, so the council of war agreed with the Venetian proposal.[83] The tower was the key to the harbor, for to it was fastened one end of the great chain which barred the mouth. It was a strong fortification, well-defended by mercenary troops, the English and Danes of the elite Varangian Guard, Pisans, perhaps Genoese and others.[84] That night the crusaders kept a good watch, and on the morrow they set up their siege equipment, while the ships bearing petraries moved within range. The engineers prepared to mine the strong walls. Meanwhile the guard within the tower had been reinforced from Constantinople by small boats crossing the harbor. The defenders of the tower made several sorties, inflicting some damage upon the crusaders with their arrows. In response to the last of these, however, the crusaders successfully counterattacked, dividing the enemy force and demolishing it. Many fell bloodily under the lances and swords of the Latins. Others fled in terror into the water of the harbor, where they attempted to haul themselves hand over hand along the great chain to recover the boats which had brought reinforcements across. Many of them drowned miserably in their flight, but some regained the vessels and safety. Others still ran back toward the protecting tower. The crusaders pressed after them so hard that it was impossible to close the gate, so the pursuers crowded in. In hand-to-hand conflict the crusaders prevailed, the tower fell, and its defenders were taken prisoners.[85] Among the attackers Peter of Bracieux, a tall knight who seems always to have sought the midst of the fray, distinguished himself in the assault. Robert of Clari also boasts of the valor of his brother, the cleric Aleaumes.[86] James of Avesnes, as well, who was perilously wounded in the face with a lance and nearly killed, survived to win an abundant share of the victor's glory.[87]

Now the attackers set about the destruction of the chain which extended, supported by wooden floats, from the tower to what we now call Seraglio Point, barring the mouth of the Golden Horn. Ernoul-Bernard says that it was as thick as a man's arm.[88] The greatest ship in the armada, the *Eagle*, gaining a full head of sail before the wind and the current, ran with its reinforced and iron-cased prow upon the chain, and the chain broke.[89] Pulling hard on their oars, the rowers drove the galleys into the Golden Horn in the wake of the *Eagle*, and the other transports and horse-transports followed. The overwhelming force of the Venetian fleet fell upon the few and dilapidated Byzantine galleys, barges, and light craft drawn up behind the chain. Some were captured. Others were deliberately run aground by their crews beneath the walls, abandoned, and were later sunk.[90] The vast Venetian fleet now covered the Golden Horn, safely protected from the elements. The crusaders and Venetians were elated with their brilliant victory. A part of the broken chain was sent as a token to the Christian port of Acre in the Holy Land.[91] The Greeks were now in a much more dangerous position, for the weakest part of the encompassing wall was that which faced the Golden Horn.

8

The First Conquest
of Constantinople

A council of war held by the magnates and the leading Venetians determined to follow up their advantage with an attack before Alexius III should have time to improve his defensive position. The northern knights and the Venetians, however, disagreed upon tactics. The Venetians favored a water-borne assault across the harbor against the enemy's weaker fortifications. On the side of the Golden Horn the city was protected by a single wall about thirty feet high, flanked, of course, with many projecting towers. The Venetian sons of the sea proposed to attack the heights of these fortifications from bridges mounted upon their ships. The knights, on the other hand, naturally preferred fighting on land in the manner to which they were accustomed. The shifting foothold of a flying bridge based precariously on a ship had no attraction for feudal warriors unfamiliar with the sea. They preferred to attack the land walls, despite the greater strength of these defenses. The disagreement was settled by a compromise: the crusaders would attack the land walls near the Blachernae Palace at the northern apex of the triangle of Constantinople; the Venetians in their ships would assault the nearby harbor walls.[1] With their plans laid, the Latin invaders spent the next four days after the taking of the tower in preparing for battle, readying supplies and resting the troops.[2]

On the morning of 10 July the battalions of the crusaders in full battle array set out in line of march along the north shore of the Golden Horn. They intended to pass over the stone bridge across the Barbysis river where it enters into the harbor. By this bridge the great city was joined to its suburbs on the north shore, and by means of it Alexius III and his fleeing troops had regained the safety of the walls on the day before the tower fell.[3] It was two or three miles from the crusaders' camp at Galata. When they arrived at the bridge they discovered that the Greeks had prudently demolished it. The next crossing was several miles further upstream, and its use would necessitate the separation of the army from the fleet, which had followed the troops along the shore. The crusaders therefore set men to work the rest of the day and through the night to repair the broken bridge, and the next day it was ready for their crossing. The Byzantines ought to have defended the bridge vigorously. It was long and narrow, so narrow that three horses could scarcely cross it abreast, and long enough so that its capture against a determined defense would have been very costly. After their reverses, however, the Greeks had no heart for battle, and they offered little or no opposition to the crossing. The crusaders thus passed over in good order and set up camp facing the wall in front of a hill within the city which had the imperial palace of Blachernae at the base of its northern slope. The fleet anchored nearby.[4] This was a corner of the city where the army and the fleet could attack almost side by side.

The camp was on a hill crowned by a monastery, which the crusaders called Bohemond's castle after the bellicose Norman who had occupied it at the time of the First Crusade. It was actually the monastery of Saints Cosmas and Damian, or the Cosmidion. Between the two hills and before the wall was a small valley. Nicetas tells us that the camp was so close to the walls that the besiegers before the gate of Gyrolimne could almost converse with the defenders.[5] Conversation was not the order of the day, however; instead they fired their arrows at the windows of the palace. The walls of the city, of course, also overlooked the crusaders' camp, and the defenders returned the fire.[6] From their camp and especially from the hill behind them the attackers had a view of the awesome city. First of all, they beheld the formidable walls of Constantinople. In addition to the usual protecting towers, these were flanked by the great square tower built by Isaac Angelus to reinforce the defenses and to provide a strong residence for himself.[7] The quarter directly behind the wall, of course, was dominated by the vast and gorgeous palace. Increasingly the rulers had favored it as the imperial residence over the older Great Palace in the southeastern corner of the city.[8] Beyond the palace of Blachernae extended a vista of churches and public buildings, columns and towers. Far off the great domes of Sancta Sophia hung in the sky. From almost the very site from which Boniface, Baldwin, and the other crusaders now overlooked the capital, two and a half centuries later the Ottoman Mohammed II, the Conqueror, would gaze avidly upon the doomed city.[9]

Since the besiegers were under fire from the defenders on the walls and sallies against the camp were feared, they set to work fortifying their position. They provided it with earthworks and a palisade constructed of good heavy planks and crossbeams. Then they set up their petraries and mangonels and other siege machinery to pound the walls and the palace, which was seriously damaged.[10]

The Venetians also made ready for the assault. Dandolo ordered the construction of flying bridges on the transports. These bridges of planks with rope railings were suspended from the masts and supported by lashed yards. They hung high above the water before the vessels. The bridges could be maneuvered onto the tops of the walls, making the vessels fast and forming a passage by which as many as three soldiers abreast could advance from the ship to the ramparts.[11] The ships were covered with hides to protect them from the fearful Greek fire, the Byzantine equivalent of the flame thrower.[12] The bridges also were padded with hides and canvas to protect the attackers. Siege weapons were readied on the prow of each vessel to batter the walls and threaten the defenders. From cages aloft crossbowmen also could soften the defense for the swordsmen on the bridges.[13]

When the people of Constantinople saw the ships with ladders and bridges they trembled with fear, not only of the enemy, but of inexorable fate. In the city were two columns, probably the columns of Theodosius the Great and Arcadius, patterned upon the famous column of Trajan in Rome with sculptured reliefs representing the triumphs of the emperor spiralling from top to bottom. The credulous folk believed that on these columns were depicted all the events that had happened to Constantinople and were to happen according to Sybilline prophecy. Now they recognized in the spiralling reliefs the assailants mounted on ships with ladders, so they mutilated the sculptures in a superstitious effort to frustrate fate.[14]

Alexius III also took more practical measures. While he had the crusaders' camp pelted by archers and by whatever artillery the defenders could muster, he also ordered sorties from the gates as many as six or seven times a day.[15] In these skirmishes the Western knights had a chance to measure lances with their foes. Nicetas claims that the Greeks fought well in these engagements.[16] Even at night there was no respite, for the whole camp had to be called to arms whenever one of these sorties occurred. Day and night one of the seven divisions stood guard before the Blachernae gate to protect the siege machinery and to repulse sallies. The Latins had little rest, but they did repel the thrusts vigorously.[17] On one occasion Matthew of Wallincourt had his horse killed under him as he bravely pursued his foes upon the very drawbridge before the gate.[18] Peter of Bracieux, whose quarters were pitched right before the gate from which most of the sorties issued, again distinguished himself in combat.[19]

The sallies and the fire from the walls took their toll upon the Latins. Villehardouin tells us that it was impossible to venture in search of supplies more than four bowshots from the fortified camp. Since foraging parties could not function, provisions became painfully short, although there was a sufficient store of flour and salt meat. Fresh meat was completely lacking except for the flesh of horses killed in the skirmishing. Because of their lack of provisions the leaders knew that they could not sustain the siege beyond two or three weeks—if it can properly be called a siege when a relatively small force of attackers invests one corner of a great city. They knew that their situation was desperate. As the marshal said, "never...have so many been besieged by so few."[20]

So on 16 July the leaders decided to assault the city on the morrow. At the break of day the doge prepared his vessels to draw close to the walls on the other side of the harbor and the crusaders arrayed their divisions in the field facing the Blachernae palace.[21]

From the landward side the crossbowmen opened fire upon the part of the wall which was to be attacked. The crusaders also drew up a ram in an effort to smash a hole in the fortifications, which were not so strong as the land wall stretching to the south.[22] Three battalions of knights and infantrymen under the marquis of Montferrat stationed themselves before the camp to protect it. The four battalions assigned to the assault under Baldwin of Flanders, his brother Henry, Louis of Blois, and Hugh of Saint Pol hurled themselves at the wall with scaling ladders.[23] In spite of fierce resistance they planted two of these ladders against a barbican close to the sea. From this description it must have been some part of the citadel of Blachernae formed by the Heraclian and Leonine fortifications at the very northern extremity of the land walls.[24] Many attackers were cast down as they strove to mount the walls, their bodies broken as they tumbled from the heights. Two knights and two sergeants, whose names have not been given to us, scaled the ladders and with their swords forced their way in spite of the blows rained upon them onto the parapet. They held their foothold tenaciously—while a handful of others succeeded in following them, for a total of about fifteen men. Here they found themselves faced by the select foreign mercenaries of the Varangian Guard and by some Pisans. They fought bloodily, the swords of the crusaders against the dread double-headed axes of the Varangians. The savagery of the Varangians before long drove the attackers off the wall, and two of them were captured. These were led before the beleaguered Alexius III, who was overjoyed at the triumph. A victory it was for the emperor on this front, at least, for the assault by the crusaders on the landward side was a failure. Many of the attackers had been wounded or received broken limbs in falls from the scaling ladders. The crusaders retreated behind their protecting palisades, greatly upset by their defeat.[25]

The Venetians had more success in attacking the harbor walls. Dandolo had drawn up his ships in battle formation along the shore, a line extending the length of three crossbow shots.[26] From his vermilion galley with the banner of Saint Mark waving proudly from the bow the venerable and blind doge ordered the attack. To the Greeks within the city, according to the orator Nicholas Mesarites, the water appeared covered with trees bearing baneful and deadly fruit.[27] Upon this forest of masts the defenders showered a torrent of stones from the artillery mounted on the towers, but no ships were lost. The mangonels from the fleet returned the

Greek bombardment, and, as the ships drew within range for crossbow-men and archers, bolts and arrows filled the air. The flying bridges from some vessels came so close to the walls that the attackers, suspended precariously in the air above sea and shore, exchanged pike thrusts and sword blows with the defenders. The din was so tremendous, says Villehardouin, that it seemed as if both land and sea were crumbling into pieces.[28]

At first the galleys remained behind the larger vessels. Blind old Dandolo stood in the prow of his galley grasping the staff of the Venetian banner, which, as it is shown on coins and seals, he had received from the hands of the evangelist Mark. He shouted angrily at his men to put him on shore, threatening them with dire punishments if they failed to do so. The oarsmen drove the galleys forward in short and choppy rhythm in a series of leaps, the vermilion galley in the van. Dandolo's was the first vessel to run aground on the narrow strip between the walls and the water, and the men leaped ashore, bearing the ensign of the winged lion before the doge. When those in the other galleys saw their banner on the shore they strained to emulate their venerable leader. The crews of the galleys, who were no slaves, but free and martial Venetians, piled ashore. Under fire upon the narrow strip of beach they raised scaling ladders against the wall and mounted to attack. After a time, amidst the confusion of the fray, they saw the winged lion flying from one of the towers. More than forty men told Villehardouin that they saw it, though none could report who had borne it there.[29] Meanwhile the Venetians perhaps also breached the wall with a battering ram near the imperial landing dock and gained a foothold within the city.[30]

Some of the roundships meanwhile had maneuvered their flying bridges onto the tops of towers. The attackers on the bridges, once these were made fast, had the advantage of height, and the Venetians fought fiercely to claw their way onto the ramparts. When a large number of them had gained a footing the defenders fled, and the Venetians were able to open gates for their companions on the shore. These rushed in, and soon the attackers were in possession of twenty-five or thirty towers fronting the quarter called the Petrion.[31] Since the wall facing the Golden Horn had a hundred and ten towers the Venetians held something like one fourth of the entire harbor wall.[32] They tried to penetrate into the city, and did gain some booty from the nearby quarter, but met ferocious resistance from the Varangians. Many Venetians were wounded, and they fell back to the wall. The defenders of the city rallied to attempt to retake the captured towers, but even the axe-wielding Varangians were beaten off. Dandolo sent word of his success to the crusaders, reporting that a large section of wall was held fast, news which caused great rejoicing among the crusaders. The doge even sent horses captured in the city to his allies as a symbol of his victory and because of the known shortage of mounts among them. But the Venetians did not dare again advance beyond their section of wall into the city itself.[33]

In order to protect their position the doge's men set fire to the houses which were built against the wall. The wind blowing across the harbor fanned the flames and spread fiery destruction into the interior of Constantinople, the first and smallest of the three great fires which the city was to suffer within the next nine months.[34] Nicetas bemoans the lamentable spectacle. Everything from the hill of Blachernae to the cloister of Christ Euergetes (or Benefactor) went up in flames. In its raging fury the fire blew from building to building deep into the town as far as the district called Deuteron. Everything in the path of the inferno was turned into rubble and ashes.[35] Meanwhile Dandolo had received word from the crusaders that they were in trouble and needed help.[36]

Emperor Alexius had issued from the walls on the landward side of Constantinople at the head of a large force. All those within the city had seen the smoke, flame, and embers, and many knew that the harbor wall had been breached by the Venetians. Never had the citizens of Constantinople been faced with such peril. The people were embittered against the vacillating emperor. Amidst the confusion could be heard their shouts denouncing his negligence and inactivity and vilifying his character. Finally a group of influential men came to the emperor threatening to surrender the capital unless he would deliver them from the "dogs" who were besieging it. So the indecisive Alexius was persuaded to try to relieve the danger from the stronger foes, the Venetians, by threatening the crusaders, whom his forces had already repelled from the land walls.[37] From three gates, one of which was the gate of Saint Romanus about a mile to the south of the crusaders' camp, Alexius led the best troops he could muster in an effort to catch the crusaders in the right flank. His force was so large—although it is grossly exaggerated by most Western sources—that it threatened to envelop them and their camp.[38] It appeared so overwhelming, in fact, that the magnates sent a plea for reinforcements to the doge, who ordered his Venetians to abandon their hard-won towers and go to live or die in an effort to rescue their allies.[39]Meanwhile the emperor marshalled his troops and advanced slowly and in good order. To Villehardouin it seemed that the whole plain was covered with the enemy.[40]

One battalion of the crusaders had remained outside the palisade as usual to guard the siege equipment. Now the other six moved out and drew up in front of their fortification facing the enemy to the south, so that they could not be attacked on the flank.[41] Baldwin of Flanders asked for the vanguard, and again it was given to him. Hugh of Saint Pol commanded the second battalion and Henry, Baldwin's brother, the third. The other four under the general command of the marquis of Montferrat were assigned to guard the camp and the machines. They were not to move from their defensive stance unless the battalions of Baldwin, Hugh, and Henry should be threatened with imminent destruction. So they stood quite still in front of the palisade. Each battalion was arranged with archers and crossbowmen in front, then the mounted knights, and behind them three or four companies of squires and sergeants. There was also a company of knights on foot, for a number of them had lost their horses.[42] Robert of Clari tells us that the seven battalions included only seven hundred knights. Hugh of Saint Pol's letter to the duke of Louvain counts five hundred in "the whole army," but he had been writing about the attacking battalions and it seems probable that he was giving the number of knights in those three.[43] Opposite the emperor's common infantry, which had formed along the wall, and to protect their left, which was now the flank toward the city, the crusaders armed every man possible, horseboys, cooks, and all. These flunkies draped themselves for minimal protection in quilts and saddle cloths. In lieu of helmets they donned pots from the kitchens. They armed themselves with whatever everyday implements lay at hand with which injury could be inflicted, such as pestles and skewers. The Picard knight Robert reports that these lackeys appeared so hideous that the emperor's infantry trembled at the sight of them.[44] Indeed, they must have looked like something out of the fantastic visions of Peter Brueghel, though we may wonder whether they incited fear or amazement.

For some time the armies stood facing each other, the Greeks not daring to attack and the crusaders standing fast before their camp.[45] Robert of Clari gives a colorful account of the skirmishing that followed. The Picard knight, I think, did not really understand all the ramifications of what was going on, but he reports what he saw before his eyes and what he garnered from his companions in the ranks. His account also offers valuable insight into the minds and mores of the crusaders. He tells how two of the worthiest and wisest were appointed in each of the crusaders' attack divisions to pass on the commands. If they shouted "Spur!" all should spur. If they commanded "Trot!" all should do that. The count of Flanders, who had the honor of leading the attack, rode forward with his battalion. The battalions of Henry of Hainaut and Hugh of Saint Pol fell in behind him. Robert marvels at the glorious sight of the knights with their colorful shields and their horses all caparisoned with cloth of silk and coats of arms. They moved forward at first in a tight, disciplined formation, a feat which feudal armies were often unable to achieve, since glory-hungry knights often dug their spurs into the flanks of their horses prematurely to gallop out ahead of their comrades and get themselves killed. At the tails of the tight ranks of horses advanced the companies of infantry. The Greek emperor rode to meet them with nine battalions, each of which, according to Robert, was much larger than the battalions of the crusaders. When Baldwin's contingent had ridden two bowshots from the camp, his advisers warned him not to go further, for the crusaders in reserve before the palisades would not be able to come to his aid in case of need. They counseled that he return to the camp and await the attack of the emperor there. This seemed good advice to the count, so he turned his battalion around, and his brother Henry did the same. But the count of Saint Pol and Peter of Amiens and others in their battalion did not want to turn back, and came to a confused halt in the middle of the field. Their pride would not allow them to retreat. In their eyes the count of Flanders, who had requested the vanguard, had acted shamefully. They shouted to their men: "Now that he draws back, he leaves you the van, so let us take it, in God's name!" When the count of Flanders saw that Hugh's battalion had not followed him, he sent word beseeching them to do so, but Peter of Amiens replied that they would not. A second time Baldwin pleaded with them to follow his example, but again the counts of Saint Pol and Amiens refused. Then Peter and Eustace of Canteleux, the two assigned to issue the commands in that battalion, ordered the company to resume the advance at a trot. The crusaders guarding the palisade saw all this, and they cried out: "Look, see! The count of Saint Pol and my lord Peter of Amiens mean to attack the emperor! Lord God," they cried, "Lord God, guard them this day and all their company. Look! They have taken the van that belonged to the count of Flanders. Lord God, bring them to safety." Robert, who was probably himself in the ranks following Peter of Amiens, cannot resist remarking that the ladies and maidens of the palace were watching from the windows and others from the walls. He imagines them saying to one another, for it is his own image of himself and his companions that we read here, that the crusaders looked like angels, they were so beautifully and finely armed, and their horses were so magnificently accoutered.[46]

The knights in Baldwin's battalion were not now enjoying the glow of vanity felt by Robert and his fellows who had refused to turn back. They charged Baldwin with shame at failing to advance and threatened to withdraw their allegiance from him if he did not at once resume the attack. Baldwin was no coward, and as soon as he heard these words he spurred his charger forward, and his knights spurred after him. They pulled abreast of the count of Saint Pol's battalion with Henry's battalion riding after them. Now the opposing forces came so near that the archers and crossbowmen exchanged fire. The crusaders were coming up a small rise of ground which lay between them and the enemy. When the emperor saw them appear over the crest of the rise he ordered a halt. The imperial forces that had been sent to try to surround the camp of the crusaders rejoined him there. The Latins also came to a halt at the top of the ridge. Via messengers the leaders of the three crusader battalions took counsel. They were far from their camp and their companions, and if they advanced beyond the rise they would be out of sight of their friends, who would not be able to aid them. Moreover, between them and the emperor's forces there was a great canal conducting water into Constantinople (perhaps the Lycus), and crossing it would be dangerous.[47] While the crusaders were considering what to do, the emperor also had a decision to make. According to our Latin sources, he was overcome with fear of the courage, size, and strength of the Latins, and it is true that the Greeks had an acute awareness of the "irresistible first shock" of the feudal charge of western knights. Anna Comnena had written long ago that a Frank on horseback "would make a hole through the walls of Babylon."[48] So Alexius declined battle and turned his forces back into the city.[49] Raimbaut de Vaqueiras boasts, "We were hawks and they were herons, and we chased them as the wolf chases the sheep,"[50] but actually the crusaders did not cross the stream to pursue their foe, fearing a trap. Robert reports that Alexius was blamed by the ladies who were watching and by one and all for his failure to join battle with his greater forces against the puny numbers of the attackers.[51] This again reflects the Picard knight's simplistic understanding of events. It was not only the determined advance of the crusaders, but also the imminent arrival of Venetian reinforcements which caused the emperor to retreat. But above all, the sortie was probably from the beginning merely a tactical maneuver to draw the Venetians away from the harbor walls, and the emperor had never had the intention of joining battle. If this be true, then it was a highly successful maneuver. By threatening the crusaders and their camp he compelled the Venetians, who had won a considerable stretch of the harbor walls and had fired the city, to withdraw.[52] In spite of temporary successes, the attack upon the city was a failure. Villehardouin reveals the sense of peril among the crusaders. At day's end, as they removed their armor, they were weary and overwrought. They ate and drank sparingly, because they were short of supplies.[53] Yet the retreat of Alexius likely did bring ignominy upon him in the eyes of Greek ladies, as well as Latin knights, both of whom valued the show of glory over the accomplishment of tactical success. Perhaps reproaches against his leadership and character determined or influenced his actions during the coming night.

The retreat of the imperial forces created within Constantinople a great clamor against Alexius III.[54] The emperor had forfeited his claim to represent the national feeling. He was widely regarded as a coward. The discontent of the masses turned the minds of some toward the blinded and imprisoned Isaac Angelus, if not toward his son, the puppet of the enemy before the gates. In all probability there was a secret party of opposition among the nobles, which was emboldened by the emperor's adversities. The fall of Alexius III, however, was not the result of a palace coup. Even men who were normally indifferent to politics now demanded success, which the emperor had not provided. No one cared to defend him vigorously. In any case, the overthrow of emperors was commonplace in the Byzantine capital, and Alexius III had himself risen to the throne by betraying his brother. Conspiracy feeds conspiracy: betrayal begets betrayal. One last time his entourage summoned the emperor to give battle, and Alexius promised to take the field again the following day, blustering about what he would do to the enemy.[55]

Instead, intent upon saving his hide, near midnight he secretly fled, professing to follow the example of David, who had found safety in flight from Saul. He also imitated Moses fleeing Egypt, for he took with him a thousand pounds of gold and as many precious stones and shining pearls as he could. His favorite daughter Irene, some other relatives, and his choice concubines accompanied him. Without a word he abandoned the empress Euphrosyne and another daughter, Eudocia.[56] He did not trust the empress. Several years earlier, when Alexius was on campaign in the West, her own brother and her son-in-law had accused her to the emperor's face of dishonoring his bed like a whore, and they expressed fear lest she help her lover to usurp the throne. As a consequence, the alleged lover was assassinated, and Euphrosyne had been compelled to plea with friends of the emperor to save her, not only from public dishonor, but from death. After a brief exile in a convent, she was restored to her position, if not to the emperor's favor.[57] The anonymous chronicler of Gaeta, on what grounds we do not know, states that she had a hand in the flight of young Alexius in 1201.[58] Perhaps the emperor had reason to abandon her. A third daughter, Anna, the wife of Theodore Lascaris, also remained behind with her brave husband.[59] The fleeing emperor and his entourage hurried to a prepared refuge at the town of Develtos a hundred miles to the north near the Black Sea.[60]

The flight of the emperor filled the magnates and ministers of state with alarm. Once the enemy outside the walls learned that the capital was leaderless they would surely resume the attack. The Greeks needed a new emperor at once. No one associated with the party of Alexius III seems to have been considered. A eunuch named Constantine, the imperial treasurer, proposed the restoration of Isaac II Angelus, the blind captive who had been deposed by his brother. This was a brilliant stroke of statecraft to present the Latins with a *fait accompli*. The invaders' claim to restore the rightful ruler, the young pretender rejected by the Greeks as a Latin puppet, would be preempted by enthroning the former emperor, his father. The Latins' excuse for attacking Constantinople would be taken away.[61] Isaac too appears as a pawn in the game of power. Never a strong and dynamic person, his character had been debilitated by his adversities. He dreamed of the pomp of empire, but was by now a nonentity about whose crowned head deprived of sight the endemic intrigues of the Byzantine court could swirl without hindrance.[62] Blindness, indeed, according to Byzantine tradition, unfitted a man for the imperial role, and this was why blinding was customary for unsuccessful rivals for the purple, and why Isaac himself had lost his sight at the hands of his ungrateful brother. Under the circumstances, however, there was every reason for ignoring the tradition. And so the blind man was clothed once more in purple robes of state, borne to the Blachernae palace, placed on the throne, and honored as emperor.[63]

In the middle of the night Isaac sent news of his revived state to his son in the camp of the crusaders. The marquis, the protector of the young prince, was promptly notified, and he at once summoned a meeting of the leaders in the tent of Alexius. Here the young man informed his friends of the flight of the tyrant and the enthronement of Isaac. The news was totally unexpected, and Villehardouin tells us that their joy was full. They praised God for delivering them from the hardship and danger that was theirs in the wake of their failure of the previous day.[64] Their chivalric zeal to aid the oppressed against the powerful, which was not feigned, but real, had finally borne fruit. Of course they had thought of the young prince who was among them, not his father, as the victim of oppression. But they knew the tale of the treachery of the vile uncle, and it was apparent that the blinded father had suffered the wrongs of the tyrant to an even greater degree than his son. Jubilation did not entirely prevail over caution, however, and when dawn broke the host was ordered to don their armor and to have their weapons at hand, lest they fall into a trap. The Latins placed little trust in the Greeks, although the news now was repeatedly verified by those coming from the city. A delegation of Byzantine magnates soon appeared to ask for the prince. They were sent to find him at the tent of the marquis. There his Greek "friends," who had been so strangely silent since his appearance before the city, made a great fuss over him. They thanked the crusaders profusely for the services they had rendered him and invited them into the city and into the palace as the most welcome guests.[65]

The leaders of the host slowly realized that the situation was more complex than it had at first appeared. Assuming that Isaac had indeed been restored, their position was not so favorable as it had seemed in the middle of the night. True they were delivered from immediate danger, and were now welcomed into the imperial city, but they began to see that they had staked their lives and the future of the crusade on young Alexius, not upon his father, whom they had never met and who was not their creature. They probably recalled too that this Isaac was the very man who had entered into alliance with Saladin at the time of the Third Crusade to betray and destroy Frederick Barbarossa.[66] So they drew back in hesitation from the proffered triumphal entry with the young prince. They would keep him in the camp as a hostage until the intentions of Isaac were clear. A delegation would be sent to the emperor to demand his confirmation of the promises of his son contained in the treaty of Zara. Villehardouin, Matthew of Montmorency, and two Venetians were entrusted with the mission. They rode to the gate of Gyrolimne, where they dismounted and proceeded on foot between two lines of the awesome axe-bearing Varangians to the palace of Blachernae.[67] The palace itself was situated in a low place at the foot of the hill of Blachernae, but it was so tall that it overlooked, as we have seen, the walls and the country beyond. Its exterior was of incomparable beauty. The interior too defied description, being covered with mosaics of gold and many colors and floored with costly and colorful marbles. Led into the audience chamber, the envoys saw Isaac sitting on his throne, probably the golden and bejeweled one described by Benjamin of Tudela with a golden crown sparkling with diamonds suspended above it by a golden chain.[68] Isaac was red-haired and florid,[69] dressed in the costliest robes imaginable. Beside him was his very beautiful wife, the sister of the king of Hungary. They were surrounded by such a huge array of lords and ladies, says Villehardouin, that there was hardly room to turn around. The ladies especially were richly attired in precious cloths and adorned with gems.[70] The Byzantine court, as was its custom, put on a brilliant display of wealth in an effort to overawe the visitors. Even the marshal of Champagne, who knew well enough how to discriminate between the show of power and its reality, was impressed, although not enough to distract him from hard negotiating. The envoys were received with every honor, but soon they expressed their desire to speak privately with the emperor, and the four of them retired to a smaller room with Isaac, the empress, the chancellor, and an interpreter. As spokesman for the Latins Villehardouin stated that they could not allow Alexius to enter the city until his father had confirmed the treaty of Zara. The marshall stated its terms: submission of the Greek church to the pope; 200,000 marks for the host and provisions for a year; 10,000 men for one year to join the crusaders; and 500 knights to be maintained continually in the Holy Land. Isaac immediately recognized that the young prince had committed himself to promises that could not be fulfilled. The father knew his subjects and the resources of the state much better than did his son. He protested that the financial conditions were impossible and that he could not impose papal authority upon the Greeks. After much lively discussion gaining nothing from the Byzantine point of view, in despair and knowing full well that he could not keep his promises, Isaac yielded to their demands and ratified the conventions of young Alexius. He took an oath and had the golden seal of the Empire affixed to the ratification, which the envoys triumphantly bore back to their camp.[71]

Later in the same day the gates of the city were flung open to them, and the crusading chieftains proudly conducted young Alexius into the presence of his father. Isaac embraced the son who had restored his fortunes and seated him by his side on a golden throne.[72] The Byzantine nobles and ministers prostrated themselves before the prince who had so recently been treated with derision. Alexius and his Latin friends were outwardly received with feasting, rejoicing, and every mark of honor.[73]

The scheme hatched at Zara to extricate the crusaders from their financial difficulties and to gain Byzantine support for the Holy Land seemed after all their hardships and dangers to have succeeded. They would now have abundant resources of men and money for their sacred cause. There were, however, foreboding clouds on the crusading horizon, dimly perceived, if seen at all, by the cross-bearers. Isaac II Angelus, known to them as the betrayer of Barbarossa, held the imperial power. Alexius, their trump card, had now been played. Restored to the side of his father he would come under Greek influence. The power of the crusaders over him would inevitably decline. Even if Isaac and Alexius proved true to their deliverers, moreover, the protestations of Isaac had forewarned the Latin leaders of the obstacles in the way of performance of their promises.

9

The Uneasy Alliance
of Latins and Greeks

The risk of conflict and injury to Constantinople if the foreign army from the West remained inside the walls was immediately apparent to Isaac Angelus. The manners of Latins and Greeks were mutually abrasive, and they regarded each other as—at best—religious schismatics. Isaac also probably realized the advantages in disassociating himself as much as possible in the eyes of his subjects from the army of aliens to which he owed his imperial crown and robes. He and his son therefore prevailed upon the crusaders to withdraw outside the walls and across the Golden Horn to the quarter of Pera. The crusading leaders agreed, because they too saw the risks, according to some Western sources, and did not wish to offend.[1] Robert of Clari, who probably reflects the opinion of the rank and file, says, however, that the Latins withdrew to the opposite shore because of mistrust of the Greeks, who were traitors. Robert also tells us—and it seems unlikely that he would fabricate the details—that Peter of Bracieux remained with his men in the palace of Blachernae to safeguard the interests of the pilgrims and that about a hundred yards of wall were dismantled to discourage the Greeks from betraying their new allies.[2]

By raising Isaac from captivity to his old throne the Greek magnates and ministers had for the moment outmaneuvered the Latins and young Alexius.[3] The prince had planned to gain the crown for himself, believing his father disqualified by blindness.[4] It was the young man's claim that the crusaders had supported. It did not take the leading crusaders, who were not fools, long to grasp the political significance of the Greek maneuver. It was probably, therefore, as a price for the crusaders' withdrawal from the city that Isaac and his Greek advisors reluctantly agreed to the coronation of his son as coemperor.[5] So the crusaders and the Venetians drew back across the harbor to the neighborhood of Galata and Estanor. Here the emperor saw that they were plentifully supplied with food. On the north shore of the Golden Horn they would await Isaac's fulfillment of his promises and the resumption of their pilgrimage.[6]

The solemn coronation of young Alexius was set for 1 August, the day of Saint Peter.[7] The ceremonies were celebrated with all the pomp and circumstance which the Byzantines always employed so successfully to buttress political authority. Richly garbed, the young prince was led in procession to Sancta Sophia with crowds along the way admiring the pageantry of empire. Beneath the awe-inspiring golden dome, surrounded by the rich glow of the mosaics, before the glorious high altar, with every solemn sanction that the most ceremonious of churches could offer, Alexius received an imperial diadem as symbol of the sacred office.[8] The protégé of the marquis of Montferrat was now emperor. From this time the crusading magnates tended to ignore Isaac, speaking of only one emperor, Alexius.[9]

Not long after the taking of the city the barons were granted audience to receive the appreciation of Isaac and his son.[10] Shortly they also began to receive more tangible signs of gratitude, for the emperors began to fulfill the conditions of the treaty of Zara. Some of the money that had been promised was paid, though not all of it.[11]

Naturally the crusaders spent much of their time visiting the great city across the bustling harbor. From its hills they overlooked the awe-inspiring vista of palaces, churches, and endless houses of the greatest city in Christendom, a city, as Villehardouin describes it, "richer than any other since the beginning of time."[12] The Latins marveled at the Greeks dressed like princes in garments of silk with gold embroidery.[13] People from many lands, of many races, customs, and religions swarmed about the wharves, the streets, and the forums. Not all of the city was wealthy, of course, although tourists tend to frequent the nicer places, which please the eye and do not offend the nose. Yet some of the visitors must have wandered away from the Mese and the forums to the crowded squalor of the slums, where the imperial splendor was contradicted by unspeakable misery.[14] Most of the pilgrims, however, stuck to the centers of imperial and ecclesiastical magnificence.

They marveled at the mighty church of Sancta Sophia whose domes dominate the capital. Now given the opportunity to visit the interior, they were overwhelmed by its treasures of gold and silver, of marble and porphyry and granite. The visitors gazed in wonder upon the mosaics of its walls and vaults. They were awed by the "gold-embedded saints and emperors" towering above them in the dome.[15] Outside, between Sancta Sophia and the complex of buildings making up the Great Palace, extended the porticoed plaza called the Augusteum. Here in front of the church stood the colossal bronze statue of Justinian—the pilgrims were told it was Heraclius—the right hand extended threateningly toward the east, the left holding the orb of empire.[16] They visited the Great Palace or Boukoleon, so called for the sculpted lion and bull locked in mortal combat which decorated its landing on the Sea of Marmara at the foot of a beautiful flight of marble steps.[17] The greater men, at any rate, were admitted to the sixth century Triclinos of gold which had served as the throne room and center of the palace since the tenth century. Here was the famous tree of gold with golden birds which sang, so often reported by visitors.[18] As the rank and file of pilgrims wandered the streets and the forums they came upon many towering columns commemorating the deeds of past emperors. In the Forum Bovis the tourists could climb a winding staircase inside of the tower of Theodosius II for a view of the city. On the exterior of this column were sculpted the triumphs of the emperor, and it was surmounted by his equestrian statues in gilded bronze.[19]

The pilgrims crowded the churches, not just as sightseers, but to venerate the treasures of holy relics. Villehardouin reports that these were beyond all description, for there were as many in Constantinople as in all the rest of the world.[20] The cult of the Cross, the emblem of the crusade, had played a large role in attracting many of the crusaders to the holy war, so they hastened to view and venerate the holy wood, to gain its salutary power, and to fulfill in some measure by this veneration part of the objective of their pilgrimage. With only slightly reduced zeal they made the rounds of the many other precious relics contained in the city, accumulating spiritual benefits. Those who felt guilt over their attack on Zara and the pilgrimage not yet completed probably found considerable comfort in visiting and venerating the relics of Constantinople.[21]

No Westerner who visited Constantinople before him has given us such a detailed description of the city as the impressionable Robert of Clari.[22] An innocent sightseer, the typical tourist, open-eyed and wide-mouthed, Robert was entranced by the marvels of the imperial city. As in his accounts of battles, the simple knight, in contrast to the more aloof marshal of Champagne, displays his flair for the specific and the concrete. Sancta Sophia, the Great Palace, the Hippodrome, the Golden Gate, and other monuments are pictured for us in his words. He rhapsodizes the riches of Sancta Sophia: the magnificent columns of jasper and porphyry, the great altar of alloyed noble metals and crushed precious stones, the silver canopy over the altar supported by silver columns, the shining silver lamps. Within the confines of the Great Palace he visited the church of the Blessed Virgin of Pharos to venerate the True Cross and other relics of the Passion, including the crown of thorns, which had points, he said, as sharp as daggers, although one suspects that he was not allowed to touch them. At the church of the Holy Apostles he viewed with reverence the column against which Jesus was scourged. At the abbey of the Pantocrator he beheld the marble slab upon which the body of the Lord was laid with the visible spots of the very tears of the Holy Mother.[23] Sometimes Robert gives us a garbled account of the wonders that he saw. He tells us, for ex-

ample, of the *sydoine* which miraculously opened every Friday to reveal
the features of Christ. Here he seems to confuse the grave cloth, or *sindon*,
with the *sudarium*, or handkerchief, of Saint Veronica, which captured the
image of the Lord.[24] Robert apparently did much of his touring of the city
with the help of native guides and interpreters. They told him how the
Golden Gate was opened only for the triumphal entry of a victorious emperor, and they described the pageantry of such occasions in some detail.
Other tales they related to our gullible tourist were colored by unbridled
imagination, superstition, and local pride. Robert reports the miraculous
cures obtained by rubbing against the columns of Sancta Sophia. Indeed
the interior of the church apparently functioned like a great clinic, for various columns had their special ailments. Ignorant guides also gave imagi-
native translations of inscriptions which neither they nor their hearers
could read. At the base of the statue of Heraclius (really Justinian) they
read that "he swore that the Saracens should never have truce from him."[25]
On the mantled statue above the gate that Robert calls the Gate of the
Golden Mantle, perhaps, though not clearly, the Girolimne, Robert's
guide read the words, "Anyone who lives in Constantinople a year can
have a mantle of gold, just as I have." They told him too of the Cassan-
dra-like prophetic reliefs on the columns, which could not be understood
until after the event. The credulous knight viewed with amazement the
Hippodrome and described its wonders in some detail. He was told that
the statues of men and beasts ranged along the spina used to move by en-
chantment, although they did so no longer.

Although Villehardouin tells of the friendly relations of the crusaders
and their hosts,[26] the long-developing animosity between Greeks and Latins soon prevailed. Much of the rancor of the Greeks toward the crusaders
fell upon the immature head of Alexius IV. In their eyes the young emperor degraded by his unseemly behavior the imperial dignity so jealously
preserved by his predecessors. He wasted whole days with his Latin
friends in drinking and dicing. Nicetas complains that he allowed his
drinking companions to don the golden and bejeweled diadem. Abandoning Byzantine decorum, he gave himself over to the rude manners of the
Westerners, imitating their vulgarity.[27] In his foolishness, as Nicetas sees
it, he even tried to fill up the bottomless gulf of their desire for money.[28]
The imperial treasures, in fact, did not go far toward meeting his need to
pay his benefactors. More was gained by expropriating the wealth of Euphrosyne and others associated with Alexius III, such as the lord-admiral
Michael Stryphnos, who thus lost the gains of his corruption in office. One
by one other wealthy families were plundered of their treasures to meet
the demands of the Latins, who were eager to get on their way. Yet, although Alexius seemed from the Greek viewpoint to pour a sea of gold

upon them, they were never satisfied, for they never did receive what had been promised.[29]

When secular resources failed, imperial officials turned to the treasures of the church. Precious ecclesiastical plate was confiscated. Holy icons of gold and silver were struck with axes from the walls to the ground to be melted down for bullion. This was the source of some of the money that the crusaders spent like any other in the shops and brothels of Constantinople. Of course this was sacrilege in the eyes of pious Greeks—and even of those not so pious.[30] The effect was all the worse because the usurper Alexius III, unlike his brother, who had preceded him, had been careful to placate the church lest it support the dethroned Isaac and his son.[31]

Even more sensitive than the plundering of ecclesiastical wealth was the question of the submission of the Greek church to Rome as required by the treaty of Zara. Alexius IV and the patriarch communicated their submission to the pope, but they made no effort to impose Roman doctrine and usages upon the people.[32] While Innocent recognized here a great opportunity to reunify the churches, he had much experience with the Greeks, and he was not as sanguine as the crusaders. He urged them to require the patriarch to acknowledge publicly his submission to Rome and to seek the pallium from the pope as first steps toward real reunion.[33] Given the proud heritage of the patriarch and the climate of Greek opinion these demands were quite impossible. Many Byzantines already branded young Alexius a traitor who had sold his country and his faith to the Latins for his own advantage.[34] He was caught along with his father on the horns of a terrible dilemma: the longer the crusaders remained in Constantinople the greater the likelihood of violence between Greeks and Latins, but he could not raise the money which would send them on their way without exacerbating the hatred which many Greeks felt for the westerners.

One day young Alexius came to the camp of the crusaders to discuss his difficulties and to propose a means of solving them. When the doge and the magnates gathered in the quarters of the count of Flanders to confer with him, Alexius explained to them how the Greeks resented him because he had gained the throne through Latin aid. Many of his subjects hated him so much that if his protectors abandoned him now they would surely kill him. He knew that the term for departure set by the dissidents at Corfu was near at hand and that the crusaders' contract with the Venetians was about to expire, so that there was increasing pressure for them to depart. But he could not fulfill his conventions with them so quickly. After all, he and Isaac controlled only the capital and perhaps those few places where the crusading fleet had stopped on the way to exact submission to the young emperor. The remainder of the empire was in the hands of various claimants to the purple, including, of course, the emperor who had fled The crusaders and Venetians, Alexius proposed, should remain in his service until the following March. He would pay for the retention of the Venetian fleet for another year, *i.e.*, until 29 September 1204. He would also supply the needs of crusaders and Venetians until spring, when they would be free to pursue their pilgrimage. And, of course, he assumed that he would by then be in secure authority over the whole empire, from which would come the wealth to enable him to fulfill his obligations. In March the crusaders with the promised Greek aid could sail to Palestine, having the whole summer campaigning season before them. The leaders discussed the issue in private. They realized that the young emperor described accurately the situation in the city, and that his proposal made sense, not only from his point of view, but from theirs. After all the dissension that had racked their expedition, however, they dared not make a decision without consulting the host. On the next day, therefore, the leaders summoned all the other powerful men and most of the knights to an assembly, where they informed them of the emperor's request. Heated discussion ensued, as might have been anticipated. Those who felt strongly compelled to accomplish promptly their long deferred vows were understandably outraged. Time and again the leaders had put them off. At Corfu they had been won over only at the sight of their companions and chief on their knees and in tears, promising that as soon as Alexius was restored the pilgrimage would be resumed.[35] Now they said to their leaders, "Give us the ships as you swore to do, for we wish to go off to Syria."[36] The leaders were swayed by more complex considerations. They argued that if they sailed promptly to Palestine winter would soon be upon them and they would accomplish nothing. Moreover, they had need of provisions and the aid promised by Alexius. The Venetians also were reluctant to leave their colony in Constantinople to face alone the fury of the Greeks should Alexius fall. Finally, the imposition upon Constantinople of an emperor friendly to the West and submissive to Rome was too great an accomplishment to risk. At last they had overcome one of the major obstacles to the entire crusading movement and had provided for the crusade a firm base—at least it would be a firm base if they could make Alexius IV secure on the throne. This should not be lightly tossed away just to fulfill their vows six months earlier. Most of the dissidents were won over, however reluctantly, and they agreed to an extension of their treaty with the Venetians for another year, until Saint Michael's day, 1204.[37]

Upon the advice of his counsellors, both Greek and Latin, Alexius decided to undertake an expedition to pursue his uncle and to assert his authority over the provinces.[38] With promises of liberal pay he persuaded many of the crusaders to accompany him. It is said that the marquis of

Montferrat and his followers received sixteen hundred pounds of gold for their part in the expedition.[39] Of all the magnates Boniface was most closely tied to the interests of the young emperor, so it was natural that he should accompany his protégé and enjoy his role of king-maker and mentor. Hugh of Saint Pol, Henry of Flanders, and many others joined the march toward Thrace in mid-August. The doge, Baldwin of Flanders, Louis of Blois, and the majority of the Latins remained in the camp to protect it and to watch over the city.[40] About this time the crusaders lost to death through illness the deeply respected Matthew of Montmorency.

Alexius III, the usurper who had fled, had hastened to set up a capital at Adrianople in Thrace.[42] In their assault upon his forces the crusaders and the young emperor captured at least twenty towns and forty castles, but the usurper himself escaped them. Many of the inhabitants, though, came to offer their submission to young Alexius, and the wealth of the conquered cities was peeled off to serve the needs of the emperor and the crusaders. Ioannitsa, tsar of the Bulgars, however, did not submit.[43] He was to become an important player in the drama of the crusaders in Byzantium after the second fall of the city.

During the absence of the expeditionary force two disasters rocked the capital and undermined the fragile foundations of cooperation between Greeks and Latins.[44] On 19 August the smoldering resentment of the Greek mob flared up in a vicious attack upon the Latin inhabitants of the city. Jealous of the wealth of the aliens, embittered at the prospect of religious union, humiliated by their own weakness, in rage they fell upon the foreigners.[45] From Seraglio Point the quarters of the Italians extended to the west along the south shore of the harbor, the choicest spots in the great city for seafaring trade, first the Genoese, then the Pisans, next the Amalfitans, and finally the Venetians.[46] The xenophobic wrath of the rabble made no distinction between friend and foe, for they attacked also the Pisans, who only a mouth before had fought valiantly to defend the city against the crusaders and the Venetians, their rivalry with Venice outweighing their ethnic and religious ties with the attackers.[47] Many of the Pisans had been brought up in Constantinople and regarded it as home.[48] The outnumbered victims saw their churches, homes, hospitals, warehouses, and shops reduced to ashes.[49] Fearful for their lives, a very large number took to their ships and boats and sought refuge with their fellow countrymen on the other side of the harbor. This was a tragedy for Constantinople, as well as the Italians. Through irrational violence the city lost some of those who had been among its best defenders.[50]

A few days later occurred another incident which further worsened relations between the inhabitants of the city and the foreigners. As Nicetas tells it, a small band of Flemings, Venetians, and Pisans, acting on their own, crossed the harbor in small boats to pillage the Muslim quarter which stood not far from the shore. Muslim merchants in cosmopolitan Constantinople had been allowed their own quarter with a mosque, just as the Italians were permitted their quarters and places of worship. To the minds of simple and greedy crusaders, frustrated in their efforts to make war on the Muslims in the Holy Land, this alien quarter in the Christian city was an offense and a legitimate object of plunder. The outrages of the past days committed against Roman Catholics by the Greek mob nourished their wrath. Swords in hand they terrorized the Muslims and seized what they could. The Muslims defended themselves to the best of their ability with whatever came to hand, and soon a body of their Greek neighbors came to their assistance. The Latin pillagers were driven back. In order to cover their retreat the attackers set a fire between themselves and the Greeks. A north wind was blowing across the harbor at their backs to carry the flames right into the faces of their pursuers.[51]Many more Latins, according to the *Devastatio*, crossed the harbor to aid their comrades, and these spread the flames and pillaged much of city.[52] The fire rapidly got out of hand.

Whipped by the strong wind from the north the flames spread above the waterfront. Except for its broad main thoroughfares, Constantinople was crowded with narrow little streets jammed with the ramshackle wooden houses of the lower classes. These were tinder for the flames. As the intensity of the fire increased glowing fragments flew through the air like shooting stars. These sparks leaped over some buildings to set fire to those beyond, but the fire often turned about in its course to engulf in a burning storm areas that had once been spared. Some sparks flew over the walls to set aflame houses outside the city along the waterfront, which had been spared by Alexius III. Inhabitants separated from their loved ones could not go to them without grave danger. Even a passing ship was set ablaze. The main conflagration spread toward the south and the heart of the town, the center of population, and the imperial complex in the southeast corner. At the fire's height a girdle of flame cut across the city from the Golden Horn to the Sea of Marmara. A shift of the wind, now blowing from the south, caused the fire to spread widely to east and west. Sections of the city that had seemed safe were in turn consumed. To the northwest the most distant quarter destroyed was Perama directly across from Galata. On the southeast the flames approached the Great Palace and, according to the *Chronicle of Novgorod*, at some point reached the coast.[53] Southward the inferno engulfed the forum of Constantine and continued to the vicinity of the New Harbor (also called the harbor of Julian or Sophia) on the Sea of Marmara. In a southwesterly direction, farthest of all from the point of origin, the flames reached the quarter of Eleutherion near the harbor of that name.[54] The fire raged through the day and the night and the next day until evening.[55] Nicetas says that it made all previous fires seem insignificant. Certainly a great part of the eastern portion of the city was wasted due to the folly of the plundering Latins.

The conflagration in Constantinople in August of 1203 has the dubious distinction of ranking among the great fires of the world. Scarcely anything endured in the wide path of the flames. Everything was too weak and burned down, as Nicetas puts it, like the wick in an oil lamp.[56] Before the flames galleries gave way, forums fell in ruins, and mighty columns crumbled as if they were firewood. Buildings constructed of fired brick fell along with those made of dry and flammable wood. Hovels and mansions alike were engulfed in immense number, among the latter the beautiful home of Nicetas.[57] When he tells of the loss of precious things, he speaks as one who suffered. A number of churches were burned and the narthex of Sancta Sophia itself, where all the patriarchs were painted, was damaged. Parts of the patriarchal complex were also destroyed, including the synodal assembly hall and other structures. The west side of the Hippodrome suffered from the flames. The forum of Constantine, in the direct path of the inferno, with its adjacent arcades, shops, and mansions, was reduced to rubble.[58] The material damage, Villehardouin tells us, was beyond the power of man to calculate.[59] Nicetas says that "most" of the inhabitants lost their household goods. This is no doubt an exaggeration, although it seemed real enough to him. Large numbers of men, women, and children failed to escape the path of the storm and perished in the flames.[60] This was one of the most devastating disasters to strike the fire-prone city. Few at any rate have had such far-reaching military and political consequences, for the smoldering animosity between Greeks and Latins turned into open and bitter hatred which consumed and destroyed Greek Constantinople. Again much of the bitterness of the Greeks toward their tormentors fell upon the puppet emperor Alexius. Nicetas grumbles that while Isaac was grieved at the devastation and at the plundering of the wealth of churches (for the historian very humanly makes God the companion of his private tragedy), Alexius, the firebrand of his country, exulted in the calamity and wished the destruction might be complete.[61] The last is not true, of course, but if the intelligent and sophisticated Nicetas could believe it, we can imagine the bitterness of the ignorant anti-Latin masses. Some of the superstitious Greeks believed that the fire was a punishment from heaven upon the city on account of the pillaging of churches to fill the pockets of the foreigners.[62] Almost all amicable relations between the crusaders and their erstwhile hosts now came to an end.[63]

Numberless small boats soon dotted the Golden Horn bearing Latin inhabitants with their wives and children and whatever property they had salvaged from the flames away from the ruined city. Few westerners, no matter what their country, dared remain behind to face the retribution of the incensed populace, so they sought refuge in the crusaders' camp. Villehardouin estimates that there were fifteen thousand refugees driven from their precarious existence, permanent though it had seemed to many, as aliens dwelling in relative prosperity among the native Greeks.[64] These numbers served to bolster the pilgrims when before many months they assaulted the walls of Constantinople for the second time.

10

Hostilities Resume

The expeditionary force led by Alexius and Boniface turned back to Constantinople after about three months in the field.[1] At an even earlier date Henry of Flanders, disappointed with his pay, had led his men back to the crusaders' camp.[2] Before long the others were to follow. During their absence the Greeks had rebuilt the stretch of wall torn down by the Latins stronger than it had been before.[3] This was probably done shortly after the great fire when animosity toward the aliens was at a peak. With the walls restored and strengthened a band of the foreigners would no longer be able to enter the city easily, as had those who pillaged the Muslim quarter and set the awful blaze. Isaac II had also failed to make the agreed payments to the Latins. No doubt he could not pay them. Financially it had become more and more difficult; politically it had now become impossible. Those of the crusaders who remained in the camp, therefore, sent a message to their comrades in the field that they should return no later than 1 November.[4] The barons who had accompanied Alexius agreed to comply, and Alexius himself decided to return with them, fearing that his Greek soldiers might take his life if he no longer had the immediate protection of the marquis of Montferrat.[5] The expeditionary force did not quite make it back to Constantinople by the prescribed date, but on 11 November they returned to be greeted by a magnificent reception. The flattering lords and ladies of Constantinople rode out to meet their triumphant emperor, who, while he had not achieved his objectives, had some measure of success to show for his campaign. Emperors, after all, do not require great victories to claim a triumph. The crusaders also joyously rode forth from their camp to greet their comrades in arms. Alexius returned to the Blachernae Palace, while Boniface and his companions joined the pilgrims in the encampment on the other side of the harbor.[6]

From the day of his return the crusaders noticed a marked change in the attitude of the young emperor toward them. Villehardouin says that he was filled with pride and adopted a haughty manner toward those who were his benefactors.[7] Viewing from afar and hopefully with greater understanding, we can imagine the struggle going on in the youth's mind. He had learned to depend upon Boniface and to defer to the older man. To his protector and the other Latins he owed his rise to the throne, and he feared the outcome should he be left to face his subjects without their support. On the other hand, no man likes to see himself as the puppet of others, proud young princes least of all. Surrounded now by the ego-inflating pomp of the Byzantine court, Alexius could not help feeling that his Latin friends failed to appreciate adequately the change in his position. He was no longer the erratically wandering refugee of Zara and Corfu, but the solemnly enthroned emperor. It was easy and natural to flatter himself that he could now make it on his own—a fatal conceit.[8]

Alexius's problem, of course, was not just personal and psychological, but political. Whatever limited control over events the two emperors had possessed was slipping from their grasp. They could not issue commands with assurance that they would be obeyed. Some of the troops were undependable. The populace was demoralized by financial exactions, the loss of property, and the disruption of economic life. For all these hardships the hated foreigners were blamed. Yet, though the Greeks almost universally despised the aliens, they were divided into moderate and radical anti-Latin factions.[9] The moderate or conciliatory faction saw no hope of opposition to the foreigners, but felt compelled to appease them. Reduction and delay of the payments promised by Alexius and Isaac to the Latins was an acceptable tactic to this party, but they kept up the flow of provisions and offered occasional trifling sums on account to protect themselves against a second attack.[10] Nicetas Choniates, raised once more to high office, probably was a member of the conciliatory party.[11] They recognized the power of the Latins for better or for worse and that their own tenure in office was secured by the foreigners against the threat of the mob. If they allowed themselves to be swayed too much by anti-Latin pressures the Latins themselves would cast them out. The radical anti-Latin party included Isaac, the patriarch, and most of the nobles.[12] Joined to this group by the force of common anti-Latin sentiments was Alexius Ducas, called Mourtzouphlus from his heavy eyebrows, which grew together. Mourtzouphlus had engaged in a conspiracy of an anti-Latin nature during the reign of Alexius III and had been imprisoned by that emperor.[13] It was probably this party that was responsible for the restoration and strengthening of the wall against the pilgrims. In the wave of xenophobia that swept Constantinople after the great fire Alexius IV found adherence to his Latin benefactors more and more difficult.[14] The enmity of the foreigners might be no more dangerous to the young emperor than their friendship was proving to be. In an undelivered oration eulogizing Alexius IV the orator, Nicephorus Chrysoberges, expressed the prevalent anti-Latin sentiment: "Let them not blow their cheeks out against us like Olympic victors!"[15] It became increasingly apparent to Alexius IV that he

could gain badly needed support from his subjects only by inclining toward the popular anti-Latinism.

Within the radical anti-Latin faction and between the two emperors
there were also bitter differences. The former supporters of Alexius III
shared the guilt for Isaac II's deposition, imprisonment, and loss of sight.
These are wrongs not easily forgiven. It was clear to these nobles, as it was
to the blind emperor, that they were compelled to attempt to deprive him
of power once more, lest he vent his vengeance upon them. In this they
succeeded. As Alexius IV turned toward the radical party they gained his
support against his father. When young Alexius cast off the stigma of puppet of the invaders the scorn with which he had formerly been received by
his subjects gave way to a temporary popularity. He had led an army
against his enemies, as an emperior should, and as his blind father could
not, and he had returned with some show of victory. In the crowd's saluta-
tions the name of Alexius preceded and was louder than that of Isaac,
which was sometimes omitted completely. The vain older man, who had so
recently been restored to the imperial dignity, was jealous of the new-
found popularity of his son.[16] According to the *Chronicle of Novgorod*
Alexius taunted his father that his blindness made him unfit for rule. He,
Alexius, alone was emperor![17] The young man probably did not actually
utter these words to his father, but like the speeches in Thucydides, they
represent what might have been said to reveal the reality underlying what
actually happened. In the oration of Chrysoberges, composed in late November, Alexius is treated as if he were sole emperor.[18] Isaac was edged
out. Mourtzouphlus, who had risen to the headship of the radical anti-
Latin faction, was chamberlain (*protovestiarius*) and the principal advisor
of young Alexius.[19] Nicetas lost his high office at the hands of Mourtzouphlus and other members of the conciliatory faction were also deprived
of influence.[20]

Isaac, shunted aside from the center of power, though retaining the
imperial title, could do no more than mutter through his teeth about the
vices, recklessness, and frivolity of his son.[21] Involved in Isaac's decline, as
cause or result or, more likely, a combination of the two, was his increasing mental incapacity.[22] He had never been a strong emperor, but was
given to inconsistency, impetuosity, weakness, and mystical superstition.[23]
He had suffered much in his life, which likely contributed to the breaking
of his health. Apparently, in the period we are now discussing, he alternated between states of confusion and lucidity. Such intermittent rational-
ity in the mentally ill is not uncommon. By January he had sunk into pow-
erlessness and utter incompetence. He occupied himself in babbling with
favorite astrologers and prophets, who promised the miraculous restoration of his sight, the shedding of his aching limbs like the skin of a snake,
and his transformation into a godlike world-emperor. His foolish supersti-

tion led him to bring to the palace from the Hippodrome the statue of the Calydonian boar, in the expectation that it would destroy his enemies, as the original boar had rent in pieces the enemies it had been sent to attack. Nicetas damns the monks who fed the old man's fantasies for the sake of the choice fish and rich wines they enjoyed at his table.[24]

Immediately upon their return from the expedition into Thrace the crusaders demanded the payments that were due them. Alexius, for whom the foray had been less profitable than anticipated, pled his poverty and gained a delay. He apparently continued for a time to make rather feeble efforts to pay something of what was owed, but once more had to request a postponement.[25] The crusaders kept sending men to beg him for their money, but to little avail. The marquis of Montferrat, who had a considerable claim upon the young man's gratitude, frequently reproached Alexius that he did not repay them for the great service they had done him.[26] The emperor continued to put them off with a few paltry payments.[27] Related to the conversion of Alexius to the radical anti-Latin faction was his tardy realization that he had made extravagant promises that he could never keep. He learned, as Runciman wisely says, that an emperor cannot be as irresponsible as a pretender.[28] His new advisors, of course, were opposed even to the token payments, so these terminated.[29] Gunther reports that Alexius was forbidden to give anything at all to the crusaders.[30] The inexperienced youth, impaled firmly on the horns of a dilemma that might well have defeated the most adept politician, wrenched himself free of his former protectors and seems to have hoped vainly that the crusaders would just sail away. This hope was no more realistic than it was just.

Extreme anxiety prevailed in the crusaders' camp. They had come to Constantinople and had won the throne for Alexius at great risk in the expectation of proceeding to Palestine with the support of the Byzantine Empire. Now they were not even paid the hard cash owed them under the treaty of Zara. What could they expect of the additional sums promised to keep them at Constantinople through the winter and the military support which Alexius was to send to the aid of the Holy Land? The ordinary men saw their hopes betrayed again and again. The dissatisfaction and grumbling that is to be expected of an army in camp grew to an intensity that could not be ignored.

The crusading chiefs were at last compelled to recognize that Alexius had turned against them. So they held a conference with the doge, saying that the emperor did not intend to honor his agreements and that he lied to them. He had forfeited their loyalty and friendship. They must face the prospect of breaking with him—in fact, the prospect of war against Constantinople.[31] The code of honor of western chivalry, however, required that before drawing their swords they must confront the malefactor with his treachery and defy him. Knights by no means invariably honored this code, of course, but the requirement also was expedient in providing one last chance to recall the emperor to his duty toward them. So they decided to send envoys to Alexius for the last time to remind him of all he owed to them and to demand fulfillment of his promises. If he should agree once more to keep them, the envoys should accept. Considering his record of broken promises this was a very modest demand. If he should not, they should defy him, declaring that the crusaders would do all in their power to seize what was owed them.[32] Defiance in the Middle Ages was the formal act of renunciation of allegiance. In the eyes of the crusaders this was the honest and honorable course, in contrast to the indirect and devious dealings of the Greeks. The mores of the two peoples were mutually incomprehensible. Feeling that they acted with punctilious regard for honor, the westerners could henceforth treat the Greeks as enemies unworthy of respect or compassion.

The crusaders appointed three tough veterans, Villehardouin, Conon of Béthune, and Miles the Brabantine, and the doge chose three of his chief counsellors, who are unnamed, to deliver the defiance. The six envoys, girded with their swords, rode around the north side of the harbor and crossed the bridge near the Blachernae palace. Villehardouin tells us that they rode in fear that the treacherous Greeks would not respect the sanctity that was supposed to surround them as envoys. At the palace gate they dismounted, for it was reserved to the emperor alone to enter the palace grounds on horseback. They were promptly admitted to the audience chamber where they saw Isaac and Alexius seated on thrones side by side with the empress Margaret, Isaac's wife, and many courtiers in attendance. Since hard language and defiance were the order of the day, Conon once more assumed the role of spokesman, rather than the marshal. He appears to have addressed Alexius alone, although we know that Isaac was present. Once more he reminded him of the services performed in his behalf, of his covenants, and his failure to perform them. As the envoys had been instructed, Conon demanded that Alexius fulfill his promises. If he did not, Conon threatened, the crusaders would no longer hold him for their lord and friend, but would take by force what was owed them. They would not commence hostilities without this warning, for it was not their custom to act treacherously. (The implication of moral superiority to the Greeks, of course, is clear.) Alexius now must choose. The Greeks received these words as a great insult, and, indeed, Conon had not intended to be very polite. Alexius's scowl showed his displeasure. The angry voices of the courtiers filled the hall. Nothing is said of the reaction of Isaac, who possibly dozed on his throne, dreaming of his glorious restoration to wholeness and splendor. No one, the Greek nobles declared, had ever dared to challenge a Byzantine emperor so in his own palace. The apprehension of the envoys for their safety mounted to a new high. Alexius angrily retorted that he would not pay them anything, for he had already paid them too much. According to Robert of Clari, who was not present, he ordered them to leave his land if they valued their safety. He clearly spoke at this time on behalf of the anti-Latin party of Mourtzouphlus. The envoys, having given the emperor a last chance and having delivered their defiance, turned on their heels and left the audience chamber. No more would they return as allies or friends. They rode back to their comrades, glad to be out of the city, for they believed that they had very narrowly escaped either death or imprisonment.[33]

This interview may have been crucial, not only for the relations of Latins and Greeks, but for the internal power structure of the crusading army. The marquis of Montferrat had long been identified with the elevation of young Alexius, who was regarded as his protégé. Now this policy was bankrupt. The standing of Boniface within the crusading army, never more than that of *primus inter pares*, could hardly fail to suffer. It does not follow, however, that he was out of the running for leadership. We know that after the second conquest of the city in April 1204, the Greeks, recalling his ascendancy over the young Alexius, hailed him as emperor, and that he occupied the Great Palace and married Margaret, the widow of Isaac II.[34] But we also know that the count of Flanders had more good men and archers and crossbowmen than anyone else in the army,[35] and we have seen him claim the vanguard on several occasions.[36] Although Baldwin had faltered in the skirmish before the land walls, he redeemed himself sufficiently to avoid excessive loss of face.[37] In the ultimate election of the young Flemish count to be the new Latin emperor other factors surely played a role, but the dismal failure of the policy so closely associated with Boniface cost the marquis dearly.

From the date of the angry exchange at the Blachernae palace all pretence of friendly relations between Latins and Greeks ceased. If a contingent under Peter of Bracieux had remained in the palace they had withdrawn earlier or did so now. Throughout the winter months Latins and Greeks harassed each other. There were numerous minor skirmishes in which, according to Geoffrey the marshal, the Greeks invariably suffered greater losses than the Latins, although Nicetas claims that the results were not uniform, the Greeks winning their share of the encounters.[38] Since the emperor was no longer supplying them, the pilgrims sent foraging parties along the shores of the Golden Horn and the Bosporus near the city. They did not confine themselves to foraging, however, but plundered the rich churches and beautiful palaces in the vicinity. Many villas were wantonly burned down after the marauders had taken everything that could be carried away.[39] The depredations of the pilgrims aroused once more on 1 December a pogrom against those Latins who still remained within the city. These must have been those who had lived in Constantino-

ple longest and felt most secure among the Greeks. Without regard to age
or sex all Latins seized by the mob were barbarously murdered and their
bodies burned. The barons encamped across the harbor, not prepared for
a full-scale assault on the city, made no attempt to save the victims. When
the rioters saw this, some were audacious enough to row across the Golden Horn to taunt the foreigners, and some even attacked Venetian ships.
The Venetians and crusaders easily repelled them, killing some, driving the
others back to the city, and capturing some Greek vessels.[41]

During the cold weather the Venetians could not prepare their ships
for an attack upon the walls, so the fleet lay at anchor before their camp.
This tempted the Greeks to devise a plan to destroy it with fire ships. They
loaded a number of vessels with dry wood, old barrels, shavings, tow,
pitch, pieces of fat, and other combustibles. On a night in mid-December
or a little later, about midnight, when a strong wind blew directly toward
the enemy fleet across the harbor, they set torch to the fire ships and
launched them under full sail toward the Venetian vessels. The wind blew
the flaming ships rapidly across the Golden Horn. The danger for the pilgrims was great, for, if the fleet were destroyed, they would be able neither
to conquer nor to retreat. They were saved by the naval skill of the Venetians, who leaped aboard their ships and maneuvered them out of the path
of fiery destruction.[41] On several other occasions during December the naval skill of the Venetians again prevailed in skirmishes, in which they captured many ships and killed many of the enemy.[42]

On 1 January, within two weeks of their first futile attempt to burn
the Venetian fleet, the Greeks tried again. They loaded some fifteen to seventeen old vessels with combustibles, awaited once more the cover of a
dark night with a strong south wind, and set the fiery carriers on a course
for the enemy ships. This time they improved the tactic by chaining the
prows of the fire ships together, so that they came on in a blazing line. The
trumpets in the crusaders' camp sounded the alarm. The men sprang to
arms and tumbled out into the plain in the best order they could manage
to face a possible attack by land from the direction of the bridge. The
danger was of a different kind, of course, and in confusion and consternation they beheld the flaming line bearing down upon their fleet. It seemed,
says Villehardouin, as if the whole world were on fire. The marshal, who
specifies that he was an eyewitness, praises the heroism and skill of the Venetians. They quickly leaped aboard their galleys and other vessels. Some
struggled to maneuver their ships out of the danger. Others in small boats
and barges courageously laid hold of the fire ships with grappling irons to
divert them from their destructive course. Large numbers of Greeks had
flocked to the shore of the harbor to view the fiery spectacle and to rejoice
at the discomfort of the enemy. They raised such a tumult that it seemed
as if earth and sea would be swallowed up. When the Greeks saw the Ve-

netians grappling with the fire ships, some of them jumped into whatever boats they could find and drew near enough to shoot at them, wounding many. The seafarers from the lagoons did not panic, however, but, enduring toil and danger through the night, succeeded in drawing the whole fiery mass out of the harbor and into the strong current of the straits. There the burning ships were set free to drift spectacularly, but harmlessly, past the city and into the open sea. The westerners lost only one ship, a Pisan merchantman which caught fire and sank.[43]

Alexius Ducas Mourtzouphlus was one of the few Byzantine nobles with courage to fight the Latins. Nicetas himself says it, although he intensely disliked the *protovestiarius*, who was of the opposing radical faction and was responsible for having Nicetas himself put out of office. He charges Mourtzouphlus with showing bravery for the sake of public favor upon which he might base a bid for the throne, but still the unfriendly historian recognizes his ability and valor. He tells of an encounter near the so-called Perforated Stone and the semicircular place situated there[44] from which the bushy-browed magnate barely escaped with his life. In the combat his horse's knee was broken and the rider cast to the ground. Seeing this mishap of the Greek commander the whole enemy party fell upon him. Alexius IV had given orders that none of the commanders in the area should go out of the walls to his aid, but he was rescued by a troop of young bowmen from the city.[45] Perhaps this was the skirmish mentioned by the *Devastatio* on 7 January, where the Greeks lost quite a few men, while the Latins lost only two knights and a squire.[46]

Although the Latins won at least their share of skirmishes, there was great hardship in the camp. They were not a large enough force actually to besiege the great city, yet they were still a large number of men, more than twenty thousand, plus the refugees from the city, to be fed. Since the emperor had cut off supplies to them they had lived largely by foraging, but the same area had by now been covered many times, and less and less food was available within the range of their operations. Foraging was hampered, moreover, by the sallies of the Greeks. Robert of Clari tells of the dearth and the high cost of food in the camp: a *setier* of wine cost twelve or even fifteen sous, a hen twenty sous, an egg two pence.[47] Alberic of Trois Fontaines reports that twopenny bread three days old sold for twenty-six pence, which, if true, reflects an extremely punishing inflation of prices.[48] Robert says that they had plenty of biscuit, however, which was undoubtedly not very pleasant, but adequate to stave off starvation.[49] At any rate, a merchant vessel arrived from Brindisi loaded with food, so there was plenty for everyone for a time.[50]

Within Constantinople fear and confusion prevailed among the Greeks. Alexius IV's popularity with the anti-Latin mob proved of short duration, for the westerners did not simply disappear following his break with them, and Alexius had no power to force them. The masses, of course, were not themselves prepared to act with vigor and courage to drive the hated enemy from their gates; that in their eyes was the unfulfilled task of the young emperor who had brought them here. Everyone in Constantinople now despaired of the foolish youth and his incompetent father. The crowd demanded action against the plunderers outside their walls, and the mob was in an ugly mood. The people, Nicetas says, "began to boil violently, like a kettle on the fire, and emit a steam of curses against their rulers."[51] On 25 January an immense throng gathered in Sancta Sophia for the purpose of electing a new emperor.[52] Nobles, officials, and the principal clergy were compelled to join in the deliberations. Nicetas and his party urged the crowd not to lay hands upon Alexius IV and raise a new ruler, for if they did the Latins would once more embrace the young man's cause and exert their full force to gain his restoration. This was the voice of political insight and experience, but the crowd, like crowds generally, was not reflective, but driven by its passions of the moment. They were fed up with the Angeli, and wanted no more of their misrule. They would not disperse, they said, until they had a better emperor. In typically tumultuous fashion they cast about for a candidate for the throne. First one and then another of the leading aristocrats were suggested, but all refused, for they realized that an emperor elected under these conditions was almost certain to have a short reign with a most unpleasant end. Even threats could not compel them to accept. One of the nobles they sought to enthrone, Radinos, apparently not present, assumed the disguise of a monk in order to escape their attention. Not able to find their candidate, the mob seized his wife, led her to Sancta Sophia, and pressed her to reveal the whereabouts of her husband, but she would not.[53]

It may have been during this tumult that a drunken mob destroyed one of Constantinople's greatest treasures, the lifelike statue of Athena attributed to Phidias. The ancient goddess stood with one hand extended toward the south, which the ignorant, confused even concerning directions, took as beckoning the hated westerners.[54] So a great work, perhaps a product of the finest sculptor of classical Greece, was lost to the passions of a superstitious and besotted rabble.

The crowd continued to meet at the great church on succeeding days. On 28 January their choice fell upon a young noble named Nicholas Canabus, who seems to have been a former supporter of Alexius III. Without the participation of the patriarch and against the will of Canabus they anointed him emperor.[55] Poor emperor! His dominion never extended beyond the confines of Sancta Sophia. He ruled over his followers, chiefly people of the lower classes, for only six days before meeting his death.

Alexius IV, of course, received intelligence of the meetings in the great church and the raising of Canabus, but he was powerless to disperse the crowd. Isaac, the older emperor, was on his deathbed. He no longer possessed power, in any case, having lost it to his son. Alexius saw that his throne and his life were in serious danger, but he did not guess the direction of the gravest threat. Thinking that his only recourse was to his former protector, the marquis of Montferrat, Alexius decided to offer the Latin leader and his troops entry into the Blachernae palace to defend him and to remain there until his promises to the crusaders should be fulfilled. It was natural enough that in his peril the young emperor should seek protection wherever he could. By pursuing this scheme, however, he lost both his crown and his life. His willingness to revert to dependency upon the Latins gave Mourtzouphlus the opportunity to grasp for the throne as the defender of the Greeks against the treachery of Alexius IV.[56]

Alexius Ducas Mourtzouphlus was descended through the female line from the dynasty of the Comneni and thus could flatter himself with an imperial heritage. He had been imprisoned for conspiracy under Alexius III, but had been released and raised to the office of *protovestiarius* after the coronation of Alexius IV. The young emperor had shown more faith in him than in any other counsellor. Haughty and arrogant, he proudly wore the green shoes to which his office entitled him, though he now aspired to the scarlet ones of the emperor.[57] He is described as having a hard voice and harsh speech.[58] Mourtzouphlus was ambitious and energetic, and as we have seen, not lacking in personal courage.[59] He is understandably portrayed as a villain in the Latin sources, and Nicetas also hated him, for Mourtzouphlus had had the historian removed from office to make room for one of his own partisans.[60] Nicetas describes him as a hollow man, who confused cunning for wisdom.[61] He carried on a scandalous love affair with Eudocia, a daughter of Alexius III.[62] Few men since Pilate have received such a uniformly bad press; he made the mistake of wronging the single historian of the period on the Greek side. He was a usurper, of course, and his hands were stained with the blood of his benefactor, but many such are accounted heroes. The beetle-browed Alexius Ducas had become leader of the anti-Latin faction and had done more than any other to turn Alexius IV against his former friends.[63] Meanwhile he had secretly been pursuing support for his own ascent to the throne. Why he did not seek election by the anti-Latin mob meeting in Sancta Sophia is a question that naturally arises. Perhaps he was too closely identified with the despised Alexius IV to gain assent. Perhaps he himself perceived what a fragile basis of power was offered by the crowd. He may not have wanted Sancta Sophia and the mob, but the palace, the Varangian guard, and the treasury.

On the very day, 28 January, that the crowd in Sancta Sophia hailed Canabus as emperor, Alexius IV sent Mourtzouphlus to the crusaders to offer the Blachernae palace as security for his debts if they would save him. Mourtzouphlus went to the camp across the harbor, gained the assent of Boniface to the offer, and swore to an agreement in the emperor's name and his own. Then he betrayed his lord, for he revealed to the Greek nobles what young Alexius had done, urging that such a manifest traitor as the emperor must be overthrown if the Greeks were not to lose their freedom forever.[64] The Greek magnates were convinced; Alexius IV had forfeited his last supporters in Constantinople. Baldwin of Flanders reports that the marquis actually came to the palace, where Alexius IV mocked him.[65] Possibly at this point, having seen that his plan was discovered, he did denounce the Latin baron to the Greek nobles and deny that he had sent for him, but in vain. That very night Mourtzouphlus entered the young emperor's chamber, told him in an excited manner (which was probably genuine, but for the wrong reasons) that a crowd was on its way to the palace to tear him to pieces for his association with the Latins, and urged him to go into hiding. Young Alexius fell into the trap, thinking only of his safety. He allowed Mourtzouphlus to wrap him in a heavy robe and to lead him from the palace to a tent inside the city.[66] Later he was cast into a loathsome prison with irons on his legs. He was not to emerge alive.[67]

Mourtzouphlus had promised his supporters that he would deliver them from the Latins within a week if they would make him emperor, and they had agreed to raise him to the throne.[68] With Alexius IV safely in prison, the would-be usurper appeared before a wider audience of magnates, clergy, and people, telling them of the treacherous offer of the young emperor to introduce the Latin army into the Blachernae palace. They should have no more to do with a ruler who would deliver the imperal city to the enemy. He fired their hatred of the foreigners, promising, if he were made emperor, to conduct a stubborn defense of Constantinople and of the freedom of the Byzantine church. He may also have bribed the magnates with offers of land and money, as Alberic of Trois-Fontaines, who is not, however, reliable at this point, says he did.[69] In any case, by one means and another he inveigled the support of many. The treacherous counsellor now was ready to discard his green buskins for the scarlet ones. His coronation was set for the following week, when he would don these and the other insignia of empire and be crowned as Alexius V.[70]

The usurper began promptly a clean sweep of his rivals for the imperial throne. First he removed Nicholas Canabus, holed up in Sancta Sophia with those who had proclaimed him emperor. Nicetas has words of praise for this unfortunate young man.[71] The power of Mourtzouphlus, however, who was widely known for his hatred of the foreigners and who was one of the few military heroes the Greeks could look up to in this miserable struggle, was in the ascendant, while Canabus's pitiful base of support was waning. The *Chronicle of Novgorod* tells us that Mourtzouphlus sent messengers to Sancta Sophia to announce the fall of Alexius and his own claim to the throne. He demanded that Canabus give up the crown to assume first place among the magnates.[72] The emperor of Sancta Sophia may not have wanted the diadem in the first place, or not at the hands of an unreliable crowd, but, once he had been forced to accept it, he could not let it go. Psychologically men do not like to have taken from them titles, honors, or whatever, even though these were originally unwanted. Mourtzouphlus was not to be trusted, moreover. Whatever he promised, he would not actually allow such an obvious rival to survive without blinding, at least. The lot of Canabus was tragic, for Mourtzouphlus lured away his fickle supporters with rewards and promises. The unfortunate emperor of six days was seized by armed men sent by Mourtzouphlus and put in prison. His party dispersed, none of those who had forced the crown upon him coming to his aid. The *Devastatio* tells us that he was decapitated.[73]

The new emperor attempted to conceal from the crusaders across the Golden Horn the deposition of their former protégé, Alexius IV. He sent a stream of messengers in the name of young Alexius to the crusading leaders in an effort to lure them into his hands with prospects of payment of the money owed and additional rewards. The Latins, not suspecting treachery, almost fell into the trap. They were saved only by the counsels of the wise and wary old Dandolo, who was suspicious of the overtures, fearing either that young Alexius had fallen or that he had been persuaded by others to deal treacherously with his former friends.[74]

News of the overthrow of young Alexius could not long be kept within the city's walls, and soon the crusaders learned that Mourtzouphlus was in power.[75] After his efforts to entrap the pilgrims had failed Mourtzouphlus entered into negotiation with the crusaders. There was an interview between Mourtzouphlus and Dandolo, which took place in the open near the monastery of Saints Cosmas and Damian in the vicinity of the bridge, the doge staying afloat in his galley, while Mourtzouphlus remained mounted on the shore. From Baldwin of Flanders and Nicetas we have two different accounts of the meeting with little in common. According to the Flemish count, Dandolo objected that no peace could be made with one who had imprisoned his own lord and had snatched the government from him in defiance of faith and religion. The old doge advised the Greek that if he would restore his lord and beg his forgiveness, the Latins would intervene with prayers for his pardon. Mourtzouphlus responded with empty words, according to Baldwin, for he had nothing to say. He was unwilling to negotiate, moreover, concerning religious obedience to Rome and the aid that Alexius IV had promised for the Holy Land, so that no serious choice was offered to the Latins.[76] Nicetas, on the other hand, says that Dandolo demanded payment of five thousand pounds of gold (or ninety thousand silver marks), which probably represents what was still owed to the Latins. He also demanded several other things, including, no doubt, submission to the Roman church. Mourtzouphlus, of course, did not accept, for, apart from his personal feelings, his regime could not have survived a concession so utterly unacceptable to the Greeks. The discussions were ended, according to Nicetas, when a troop of Latin knights swept down upon Mourtzouphlus in an attempt to capture him. Some of his bodyguard were seized, but Mourtzouphlus himself fled precipitously back to Constantinople.[77]

Meanwhile, fighting raged intermittently. Hardly a day passed without some fray by land or sea.[78] Baldwin of Flanders reports a minor skirmish when the crusaders once more crossed the bridge at the head of the Golden Horn and took up a position before one of the gates near the Blachernae palace. They drew up in wedge-shaped formations with the cross borne before them. A single Byzantine noble foolishly, if valorously, sought to prove his mettle by an unsupported charge upon the enemy. He met the hero's death he apparently sought, for the crusading infantry tore him to pieces. Enjoying the taste of blood, but without anything substantial to show for their effort, the crusaders then returned to camp.[79] Mourtzouphlus lent new vigor and heart to the Greeks by buckling on his own sword frequently, taking mace in hand, and doing battle. He attacked the foraging parties of the crusaders, but did not risk a major confrontation, since the Greeks had the advantage over the vastly outnumbered Latins, whom he expected to wear down with harassment.[80] The anonymous chronicler of Soissons adds an account of a noisy Greek raid on the Latin camp in the middle of the night.[81] Even Nicetas, the mortal enemy of Mourtzouphlus, admits that the people were attracted by his energy and courage.[82]

Around Candlemass, or 2 February, Henry, the brother of the count of Flanders, and his company found themselves grievously short of food and supplies, so he decided to lead a foray to a prosperous town called Philia on the Black Sea northwest of Constantinople near the entry to the Bosporus. He took with him thirty knights and many mounted sergeants, according to Robert of Clari.[83] They left the camp around six o'clock in the evening and rode all night, arriving at Philia late the following morning. The Latins seized the town without resistance, gaining great booty, such as cattle and clothing, and many prisoners. Enough was captured to supply the army for fifteen days. Some of this they shipped down the straits to their camp. They remained in Philia for two days, enjoying the abundance of good food. Then, burdened with the remaining cattle and other booty, they set out on their return journey. Greeks who had escaped from Philia reported the raid to Mourtzouphlus, who had on 5 February been crowned as emperor. He led a thousand men at arms to attack the enemy. The patriarch Samson accompanied him with the miraculous icon of the Virgin which the emperors were accustomed to bear into battle in the belief that under its protection they could not be defeated. At the edge of the woods along the road from Philia to Constantinople Mourtzouphlus laid an ambush for the returning crusaders. Henry and his followers unsuspectingly rode right into it. When the crusaders saw themselves surrounded they were filled with fear, and they began to call upon God and Our Lady to deliver them. Although fearful, they did not panic, however, and they said to one another that if they fled they would be killed, so it would be better to die honorably fighting than to perish miserably in flight. The Greeks fell upon them furiously. When the crusaders saw the enemy coming at them from all sides, they discarded their lances, and struck about with swords, knives, and daggers. Mourtzouphlus had entrusted the van to a certain Peter of Navarre, who proudly rode into battle unhelmed, his head encircled by a band of gold. Henry of Flanders himself dealt Peter a blow on the head with his sword which cut through the circlet and penetrated the depth of two fingers into the poor man's skull. The first wave of Greeks was thrown back, but again they came on. Another of the ambushers received a blow which caved his helmet into his head. Peter of Bracieux struck the patriarch so hard on the nasal of his helmet that, in falling, the priest dropped the precious icon to the ground. Peter courageously dismounted in the swirl of battle to pick it up. Heartened by this sign the crusaders rallied. Mourtzouphlus himself was smitten so strongly that he fell upon the neck of his horse. Soon the Greeks lost all appetite for battle, and they turned to flee in terror. The Latins pursued them, killing some and capturing others. Mourtzouphlus lost about twenty knights, while not a single crusader was unhorsed. The heavy-browed conspirator himself escaped, wounded and fleeing on foot in such desperation that he tossed aside his shield and helmet and left behind the imperial standard and the miraculous icon. Robert of Clari in his simple and superstitious way accepts the powers that the Greeks attributed to this image of the Virgin, believing that Mourtzouphlus was defeated because he had no right to bear it as emperor.[84]

When the crusaders in the camp heard that Henry had been ambushed a rescue party spurred forth to aid him. They met him on the road, however, already victorious and proudly displaying the captured icon. As the returning crusaders drew near, the Latin bishops and clergy came forth from the camp to meet them and to receive the precious image with rejoicing. They carried it in solemn procession to a church, where the clergy chanted a service of thanksgiving.[85] This icon, which is lost or unidentifiable today, is described as made of gold, adorned with precious stones, and provided with most sacred relics, such as a baby tooth of Christ and a part of the sacred lance.[86] The barons agreed that the holy prize should be given to Cîteaux, but we have no record of its having arrived there.[87]

Mourtzouphlus, having regained the safety of his walls, tried to make the Greeks believe that he had been the victor. Some of them asked where the icon and the imperial standard were, and he replied that they had already been put away again in safekeeping. In a short time news of the usurper's attempt to deceive the defenders of the city came to the crusaders' camp, so they mounted the holy image and the captured standard on a galley, which rowed back and forth beneath the walls displaying the spoils lost by the emperor in his flight. Seeing these proofs of his humiliation, the Greeks derided him for his defeat and for deceiving them. He retorted with boasts of the vengeance he would wreak upon the foreign intruders.[88]

His vengeance fell in fact, however, upon the deposed young emperor. The loss of prestige that Mourtzouphlus suffered through his defeat and the abandonment of the icon seems likely to have led directly to the murder of Alexius IV. A popular tumult centered upon the young man could raise him from his prison to reascend the throne, as his father had regained it. He could not be allowed to live.[89] Two or three times Mourtzouphlus attempted to poison the prisoner, but without success.[90] On 8 February the new emperor and his captive dined together, we are told,[91] and this may have been the occasion of one of those attempts. Poison failing, Mourtzouphlus decided to risk the consequences of less subtle means to remove the troublesome youth. That very night with several sergeants he entered the place where Alexius IV was sleeping. The sergeants put a noose improvised from a bowstring around the young emperor's neck, and Mourtzouphlus himself drew it taut and strangled him. He also cruelly crushed Alexius's sides and ribs, beating him with an iron implement.[92] After such a horrendous deed the treacherous Mourtzouphlus tried to pretend that his one-time benefactor had died a natural death. He falsely honored the youth with a solemn funeral and burial in an imperial tomb.[93] No one in Constantinople, however, was deceived.

Isaac II Angelus died at about the same time as his son. He had been for some time a sick man, withdrawn from the pains of the real world into his realm of fantasies. Hearing the news of his son's imprisonment, fear exacerbated his condition, and in a very short time he passed away.[94] There have been suspicions that Mourtzouphlus had Isaac murdered as well, but it appears that this was not necessary. The old emperor was no rival to fear. His death passed almost unnoticed. History has judged Isaac harshly. He was not richly endowed with talent or prepared for the responsibilities of the imperial role.[95] His judgment was not consistently good,[96] and he made grievous errors, but he also enjoyed some successes prior to his betrayal by his brother, Alexius III.[97] He loved luxury and splendor. He never wore the same garment twice, and he bathed, says Nicetas, every other day. His chefs set a magnificent table with mountains of good food and seas of rich wine, much enjoyed by the parasites he kept about him, who, in his last months, encouraged his foolishness.[98]

Robert of Clari informs us that an arrow was shot into the camp bearing a letter with the news of the fate of the young emperor. Some of the barons said, "A curse on anyone who cares whether Alexius is dead or not!"[99] For he had not dealt honestly with them. Others, unable to argue that point, nevertheless deplored the manner of his death. Although the feudal pattern in which their minds were shaped was plenty violent, treason to one's lord ranked at the top of the catalogue of crimes in a society still held together insecurely by the personal ties between lords and vassals. Villehardouin, for example, although he never uses the words "treason" or "traitor" when he complains about the dissenters within the Latin host, condemns Mourtzouphlus and the Greeks for unspeakable treachery. [100] Anxious to regain his popularity after the debacle on the road to Philia, Mourtzouphlus sent word to the crusaders informing them that he was now emperor and ordering them to vacate his lands within a week, or he would slay them all. The crusaders angrily defied him. They would not abandon the siege of Constantinople until they had taken the city, had avenged young Alexius by punishing the traitor with death, and had secured the money which was owed them.[101]

Few hearts among the crusaders, in spite of these brave words, were not filled with fear. They were isolated in a hostile land in the midst of treacherous foes who hated them bitterly. Young Alexius, upon whom their hopes had rested, was dead, and in his place was the most malevolent of their enemies. The pact of Zara was now obviously void. Their hope that young Alexius would send them on their way to the Holy Land well-supplied with funds and other necessities was gone. The cold and stormy Constantinopolitan winter was still upon them. Even if the weather had been better, even if they had food, they would not have dared to sail for Palestine, for in the midst of the disorder of embarkation the Greeks might fall upon them.[102] They lacked the basic necessities of life, living from hand to mouth by foraging, which required ever more distant and dangerous forays, since the nearby areas had been plundered frequently.[103] Many of their horses had been eaten,[104] a thing which a feudal army would do only as a last resort, for a knight without a horse felt impoverished and degraded. Before them loomed the fortified walls, whose strength they had once already tested. Nothing was to be expected from Alexius V and the Greeks but death. What hope could they find and what could they do?

11

The Second Conquest
of Constantinople

They concluded that their best hope was in their weapons. To the Venetians this was obvious.[1] With Mourtzouphlus on the throne they faced a
mortal enemy. Their countrymen within the empire were in dire danger;
the ancient commercial privileges of Saint Mark would certainly be revoked; the prosperity and power of the queen of the Adriatic would be
threatened.[2] Experience had shown, however, that many of the northern
crusaders would not take up arms against a Christian city until convinced
that their cause was something more than a quest for power or prosperity.
They had to be persuaded that such an act possessed religious sanction.[3]
The leaders who saw that they must now conquer Constantinople, therefore, sought once more to arouse the undecided and the wavering to righteous indignation and moral fervor. The clergy rendered judgment that a
traitor who had risen to power by the murder of his lord and benefactor
had no right to rule. By his deeds Mourtzouphlus had reinforced the Latin
stereotype of the Greeks as contemptible and perfidious. The Greeks,
moreover, had seceded from the Roman church.[4] Byzantium time after
time had betrayed its vital role in the crusades. To fight against such an
emperor and such a people was a just war. The monk of San Giorgio in
Venice asserts that God wished to punish the pride and disrespect of the
Greeks even more than to avenge the wrongs committed by the Saracens.[5]
The bishops and priests pronounced that those who should die in the attempt to subjugate schismatic Constantinople to the Roman church would
enjoy the crusading indulgences granted by the pope.[6] This gave courage
to the imperilled pilgrims. And now much courage they needed! They
were a small army before the walls of the greatest city they had ever seen.
This time they could take no comfort in the thought that within the walls
there was a party waiting to welcome them as protectors of a rightful
claimant to the throne. They were the invaders of a foreign land, without
friends, greatly outnumbered, lacking provisions. Their only hope lay in
their valor and the naval skill of the Venetians.

The leading men of the crusaders and the Venetians held a conference to lay their plans. That they would attempt to conquer the city was foregone conclusion, but what would be the distribution of the spoils if they should prevail? Much discussion took place before the doge on the one hand and the marquis of Montferrat and the counts of Flanders, Blois, and Saint Pol on the other reached an agreement and fixed their seals to a treaty.[7] First they agreed that all the booty should be collected in one place for equitable division. Three fourths should be set aside for the Venetians: the other fourth should go to the crusaders. This division should prevail until the debt owed by the young Alexius, who had assumed the obligations of the crusaders toward the Venetians, should be paid. If there should be a surplus, it should be divided equally. If there should not be enough, the division into three quarters and one quarter should prevail, except for food, which should be divided equally. The treaty then passes to political arrangements and the distribution of conquests. If they succeeded in conquering the city six crusaders and six Venetians should be chosen to elect as emperor the man they found best suited for the task.[8] The emperor they chose would receive a quarter of all the conquests, and he would also have both the Boukoleon and Blachernae palaces. The remaining three quarters would be divided equally between the crusaders and the Venetians, as had been agreed in the treaty of Venice. If the emperor should be selected from among the crusaders, the Venetians should have a right to Sancta Sophia and the patriarchate, and conversely. Twelve crusaders and twelve Venetians should also be elected from among the wisest men to allocate fiefs and offices among the leaders and to establish the services that the recipients should owe the emperor in return.[9] They agreed that all pilgrims should remain by the emperor's side until the end of March 1205, at which time everyone should be free to go where he pleased.[10] When this was completed each man was required to swear with his hands on holy relics that with some minor exceptions he would bring all booty to the common hoard and that he would not use force upon any woman or despoil her of any garment she was wearing. The penalty for violating this oath was death. Each man also had to swear that he would not break into monasteries or churches.[11]

During the weeks of late winter and early spring the crusaders and Venetians busied themselves with preparations for their assault upon the imperial city. Altogether they were a host of more than twenty thousand men.[12] The number of crusaders and Venetians was reinforced by Latins who had fled the city.[13] The leadership of the brave count Louis of Blois was lost to the crusaders, however, for all winter and spring he was ill of a quartan fever and took no active part in the final conquest.[14] The army's experience in attacking Constantinople in July of 1203 had revealed the very great difficulty of scaling the land walls, whereas the Venetians had been more successful in their assault across the harbor, so they now agreed to concentrate all their forces against the walls fronting the Golden Horn, as from the outset the Venetians had advised.[15] Venetians and crusaders labored industriously to put their machines of war in working order. The northerners set up mangonels and petraries on the shore before the Blachernae palace to harass and exhaust the defenders and to raise the threat of another attack from that quarter. The leaders regarded these machines as very damaging to the enemy. They also prepared rams, catapults, tortoise shells and other devices for assaulting or mining the walls.[16] The Venetians once more set up missile throwing mechanisms on their ships to bombard the city. The assault bridges which they were accustomed to suspend from the superstructures were raised even higher than those used previously to compensate for the heightening of the walls. The fleet was covered with timbers and vines to absorb the shock of projectiles and with hides to protect against fire. Dandolo not only directed much of the preparation, but also built up confidence in the capacity of the fleet and inspired the spirits of the weak-hearted.[17]

Within the city Mourtzouphlus also made ready for the coming battle. Along the land curtain to the west he ordered many of the gates walled up with bricks.[18] He too recognized the advantage of the Venetians' assault bridges, which allowed the attackers to approach on a level with the defenders or even from above, over the scaling ladders with which the northern crusaders had attempted to mount the land walls the previous July. Along the harbor curtain, therefore, he had built of stout beams towers of several stories between the permanent stone towers and also had the latter raised by several stories of wood. These hoardings overhung the stone wall, and each story overhung the one below, so that stones, missiles, hot sand, and burning oil could be poured upon attackers at the wall's base. The temporary timbered fortifications were covered with hides against burning. Mangonels and petraries were mounted along the wall to fire upon the enemy ships. Mourtzouphlus ordered a double ditch dug between the curtain and the water, so that the attackers on foot would find it difficult to drag or push their wheeled machines to the foot of the fortifications.[19] Despite the crusaders' attempt to patrol the land wall the new emperor was able to bring into the city many additional troops. With these he amply garrisoned the towers along the harbor.[20] In order to strike terror into the hearts of the attackers, according to Alberic of Trois-Fontaines, Mourtzouphlus ordered three Venetian prisoners drawn with iron hooks and burned to death in full view of their friends and allies. The Latins could only watch helplessly their horrible deaths.[21]

Now came the tense time when the preparations were complete. The Venetian fleet was equipped and armed to the teeth, the machines of war were in place, and provisions had been put on board.[22] On Thursday, 8

April, the horses were once again loaded into the horse transports.[23] The men boarded their assigned ships to be ready for sailing with the dawn. Each division of the army had its own vessels, drawn up side by side, transports alternating with galleys and horse transports. Villehardouin notes the marvelous sight of this long line of ships awaiting the morrow.[24]

Before battle the men prepared themselves for possible death by confessing their sins with tears, receiving absolution, and partaking of the Body of Christ in the sacrament.[25] With the first light of day the ships moved forward in line of battle.[26] The galleys and horse transports were to discharge their troops ashore to attempt to undermine or scale the fortifications. The transports would try to effect a foothold on the walls with their flying bridges.[27] The ships moving forward along a front of a good mile, their colorful banners fluttering in the early light, made a spectacular sight. Soldiers crowded the decks. Some prepared to throw themselves ashore under the walls. Others stood by the machines for which they were responsible. Those on the transports made ready to clamber across the precarious bridges onto the heights of the fortifications.

From the decks the attackers could see plainly the vermilion tents of the emperor, which Mourtzouphlus had ordered pitched on the slope of the hill in front of the monastery of Christ Pantepoptos (the All-seeing).[28] His silver trumpets were ringing and timbrels were shaking, creating a great din to arouse the spirits of the defenders.[29] The voices of the Greeks raised the Emperor's battle-cry, "Jesus Christ conquers!"[30] Mourtzouphlus had chosen a good command post from which he could survey the movements of the enemy and evaluate what was done on the ships even as they came directly under the walls.[31] They were approaching the same part that the Venetians had assaulted in July 1203. In just this quarter Mourtzouphlus looked across the desolate ruins left by the fire which the Venetians had set on that occasion.[32]

As the ships neared the walls they attempted to establish a cover for the assault forces with volleys of stones, bolts, and arrows. The defenders showered the fleet with return fire, which smashed some of the equipment and made it dangerous for those exposed on the decks.[33] The galleys and horse transports drew as near the shore as they could, some beaching and others of deeper draft running aground farther out, so that the assault troops had to splash ashore burdened with scaling ladders, pickaxes, and other gear. The protective wheeled shells were carefully unloaded. These troops attacked the walls from the narrow strip of land between the fortifications and the harbor. The defenders hurled great stones down from above upon the wooden equipment for breaching the wall, smashing their protective roofs and forcing the engineers to flee.[34] While some crusaders attacked from the shore, the transports with their flying bridges flung out and burdened with brave men assaulted the heights of the walls.[35] One vessel had been assigned to each tower, and each boldly pushed forward to attempt to anchor its bridge to the top of the fortifications so that its complement could achieve a foothold.[36] An unusual south wind hampered operations, driving the ships back from the walls. Only five of them succeeded in drawing close enough to their assigned towers so that the troops suspended high above the sea and the land exchanged strokes with the Greeks.[37] The defenders fought back with energy. None of the ships succeeded in affixing its assault bridge to the wall.[38] For a good part of the day the battle raged in more than a hundred different places.[39]

Those who had landed were driven back. Amid the shower of stones and arrows they were unable to hold the shore and took to their vessels.[40] The Byzantine garrison had also been able to fight off the flying bridges of the transports. The wooden superstructures that Mourtzouphlus had raised upon the towers had been a success.[41] Abandoning much of their equipment, the leaders of the crusade were constrained to give the order to retreat.[42] As the ships pulled away from the shore the Greeks on the walls hooted and jeered at the defeated atackers. Some of them let down their clouts and showed their bare buttocks in derision to the fleeing foe.[43] The attack was a complete failure. The disheartened pilgrims had clearly had the worst of it. They lost nearly a hundred dead.[44] We do not have a figure for the Greek losses, but they seem to have been very slight. Alexius, who had supervised the defense from his hillside command post before the monastery, was overjoyed with the easy victory. Again his instruments sounded, this time in triumph. The emperor boasted to his people: "Never did you have so good an emperor. I will have them all hanged and dishonored."[45]

A wave of fear, in truth, swept through the crusading army, infecting even some of the leaders. Toward six o'clock, shortly after their retreat to the north side of the harbor, the magnates and the doge gathered in a church to determine what they should do. Many different points of view were argued back and forth. The French were particularly upset by their defeat, Villehardouin tells us, some saying that it was God's punishment upon them for their sins.[46] The bishops and abbots assured them again that the war against Byzantium was just, for the Greeks had rebelled against the true church.[47] The pope, of course, had specifically and officially repudiated this argument, but they had to make do with any justification they could find.[48] The pope was safe in Rome, while the bishops and abbots stood in a foreign land in the midst of enemies as spiritual counsellors to a defeated and demoralized army. Having been reassured of the justice of their cause, some of the barons wanted to try a new attack on another side of the city, along the Bosporus or the Sea of Marmara, where the defenses had not been so strongly reinforced. The doge, drawing upon his knowledge of naval warfare, pointed out that the strong current running down the Bosporus and the almost continual wind from the north-northeast would carry their vessels away from the walls and into the open sea. Villehardouin reports that there were some who would have been glad to be swept away to sea or anywhere else, so long as it was away from where they were. He even admits that this was not surprising, since they were indeed in great danger.[49] As they were accustomed to do, the crusaders deferred to the wisdom of Dandolo. In spite of their setback many were steadfast and courageous. They decided to allocate two days to rest, refitting the ships, and repairing the equipment, before making another assault on the same walls on Monday.[50] They had discovered in the first engagement that the garrisons of the towers were large enough to beat off the attackers trying to gain a foothold from the flying bridge of a single transport. For the next assault they determined to bind the transports together two by two, so that a greater force could be brought to bear against each point of attack.[51]

On the next day, Sunday, 11 April, the clergy sought to assuage fears, disarm discontent, and prepare the men to resume battle. It was cried through the camp that everyone, including even the excommunicated Venetians, should come to divine services. The bishops of Soissons, Troyes, and Halberstadt and other prominent clergy, such as Baldwin's chancellor, the eloquent John Faicete, preached to large gatherings.[52] They sought to persuade their hearers that the struggle was righteous, not only because of the Greek schism from Rome, but because the Greeks were traitors who had murdered their rightful lord, Alexius IV. In feudal eyes this was the worst of sins. The Greeks were enemies of God, worse than Jews. The preachers offered absolution to all who would join in the punishment of these fiends. Those who died in the attack would receive an eternal reward. Making war upon the Greeks thus became in itself an act of penance.[53] The preachers purported to speak for the church, even though the pope had expressly forbidden the army to attack Christians and had specifically named Constantinople. The pilgrims accepted what their clergy told them. Their doubts appear to have been quieted, and we hear no more for the time being of dissension among them.[54] They were called to confess themselves and to receive communion, as was customary on the eve of combat. Apparently the excommunicated Venetians also communed, for we are told that they were summoned to the sermons, and there is no indication of their exclusion from the sacrament. In order to insure that the pilgrims would go into battle on Monday free from sin—for their success or failure depended upon it—the clergy ordered all the whores from the camp. They were loaded on a ship and sent, Robert tells us, far away.[55]

At sunrise on Monday, 12 April, every available crusader and Venetian was in his place, ready to resume the assault. Forty of the large

roundships had been tied together in pairs, so that each pair might attack
a single tower, thus concentrating more men against its defenders. The
fleet approached the same section of wall from the Blachernae to the monastery of Euergetes which they had unsuccessfully assailed on Friday.⁵⁶
Alexius V also occupied the same command post on the hill below Pantepoptos. Greek stonethrowers hammered the fleet with boulders so large that
a single man could not lift one, but the Venetians had protected their ships
with timbers and grapevines, so that no serious damage was done. The
roundships came as near the walls as they could, then cast anchors and
rained arrows and stones upon the defenders. They were close enough also
to disgorge Greek fire upon the wooden towers, but these were protected
with hides, so they would not burn.⁵⁷ After their victory on Friday the
Greeks had more confidence and less fear, and the walls and towers were
now even more crowded with defenders. They fought well, according to
reporters on both sides, and amid the shouts of combat the conflict raged
more furiously than before. Until about midday the defenders stood firm
and the scale of battle remained in precarious balance.⁵⁸

Toward noon there arose a north wind which blew the ships toward
the shore. Robert of Clari tells us that only four or five of the greatest vessels could reach with their assault bridges the tops of the wooden towers
erected by Mourtzouphlus.⁵⁹ Two of these were the *Paradise* and the *Pilgrim,* which were bound together and assigned to the French bishops of Troyes
and Soissons. A gust of wind and a surge of water drove them forward, so
that for an instant the end of the flying bridge of the ship of the bishop of
Soissons, the *Pilgrim,* banged against a tower near where Alexius V
watched from his hill. A courageous Venetian grabbed hold of the tower,
clung to it with hands and feet, and somehow managed to pull himself
upon it. He was quite alone, however, and the Varangians and Greeks defending it fell upon him with axes and swords and immediately made him
a bloody corpse.⁶⁰ Tossed by wave and wind, the ship once more bumped
the tower, and a French knight named Andrew d'Ureboise of the household of Bishop Nivelon followed the example of the Venetian and clambered onto its summit on his hands and knees. The Varangians and
Greeks also attacked him with their cruel weapons, but his armor protected him enough so that he was able to struggle to his feet and draw his
own sword. With great force and valor he drove the defenders to a lower
level of the tower, gaining time for his comrades to climb upon it after
him. They secured the ship with stout ropes, and other pilgrims crossed
the flying bridge to the tower. The surge of the sea, however, pulled at the
ships so strongly that the whole tower trembled, so the ships had to cast
off for fear of pulling down the superstructure with their own men upon it.
Those who had crossed were enough. The crusaders' battle-cry, "Holy

Sepulcher!" resounded as the Varangians and the Greeks fled from the tower. The Latins who had taken it waved their hands over their heads in triumph and shouted encouragement to their comrades on the ships. Soon the banners of the two bishops were flying over the captured tower.[61] Emboldened by the success of the *Pilgrim* and the *Paradise,* Peter of Bracieux, who was not accustomed to being second to any in the fray, succeeded with his men in mounting upon another tower and taking it.[62] Other crusaders descended from their ships and from the shore scaled and took several more towers.[63] Mourtzouphlus, of course, sent reinforcements to the threatened sector, and the Latins did not dare to venture beyond their captured towers, because of the multitude of foes they saw on the walls, on neighboring towers, and upon the ground below.[64]

Robert of Clari was one of a party, about ten knights and sixty sergeants led by Peter of Amiens, who landed on a narrow strip of ground between the walls and the shore. They discovered a postern gate which the defenders had walled up. The crusaders fell upon it zealously with picks, crowbars, axes, and even swords. It was hard going and dangerous, for from above the Greeks rained quarrels upon them, almost buried them under a torrent of immense stones, poured down pots of boiling pitch, and attempted to incinerate them with Greek fire. While some picked away at the postern, other crusaders covered them with their shields. Soon they succeeded in making a small hole. Peering through it, they saw a huge crowd of Greeks on the other side, and did not dare to enter. Robert's brother, Aleaumes, the same priest in hauberk who had distinguished himself in the taking of the tower of Galata, pushed forward to claim the honor of attempting entry. Robert, fearing for his brother's life, urged that he should not be so foolhardy, but Aleaumes got down on his hands and knees to crawl through the hole. Robert thereupon grabbed his foot to prevent him, but Aleaumes kicked loose from his clinging brother and dragged himself through. On the inside a great many of the Greeks ran upon him, and those on the walls threw stones at him, but he drew his sword and ran toward his attackers, who fled like cattle. The clerk called back to his companions on the other side of the wall that the way was clear, and Peter, Robert, and the others also entered the city. They lined themselves up with their backs to the wall, fearing an overwhelming attack, but the defenders in that sector were so afraid that they fled. This occurred not far from the command post of the emperor and directly under his eyes. Mourtzouphlus sounded his trumpets and beat his timbrels, and, making a show of spurring his horse upon the invaders, he approached about halfway before halting. Peter encouraged his troops to stand bravely against the emperor and to think of their honor. According to Nicetas, this Peter of Amiens was a formidable man, a giant whose very helmet seemed like a tower-crowned city.[65] He and his small band outfaced Alexius V. When the emperor saw that the enemy was not going to flee he turned back to his command post on the hill.[66]

Granted this respite, Peter dispatched some sergeants to break open the nearest gate. In spite of the bolts and iron bars, the crusaders used axes and swords to tear it open. Seeing this, the Venetians brought the transports up to shore, and the remaining Latins and the crusaders' horses were disembarked. The attackers swarmed into the city like bees. Additional gates swung wide, and a large force of Latins gathered at the foot of the hill where Mourtzouphlus had his headquarters. The heavily armed Western knights began their charge against the emperor's troops drawn up on the hillside. The appearance of the knights in full battle array, riding forward with couched lances, struck terror into the Greeks. The larger number of defenders fled before the smaller number of attackers. Mourtzouphlus himself, unable to stem the rout, fled back into the city.[67] The crusaders were free to run here and there in the vicinity, massacring and pillaging. They slaughtered many Greeks, sparing neither age nor sex, if Nicetas is to be believed.[68] They seized horses, mules, and other possessions.[69] In the attack the crusaders lost only one man, a well known and noble knight, who was killed when his horse fell into a pit while he was hotly pursuing the enemy.[70] Peter of Amiens and his men seized the imperial camp near the monastery of Pantepoptos.[71] Mourtzouphlus took refuge in the Boukeleon, and his followers fled after him to that palace or in the opposite direction to Blachernae.[72]

As evening approached, near vespers, the leaders of the crusaders assembled in a great open square to hold a council of war. They did not yet realize how completely they had triumphed, and it was said and believed that it would take another month to subdue the city. So they decided to make camp for the night, ready to renew the fight on the morrow. They did not dare to seek quarters or disperse.[73] The main part of the army assembled outside the wall before the captured towers and near the shore, so that they could have a means of retreat in case of a sudden attack. Baldwin occupied the emperor's colorful tent on the hill of Pantepoptos. His brother Henry with a detachment spent the night in the vicinity of the Blachernae palace. Boniface of Montferrat with another small force took up a position on the other side of Baldwin near the most populous part of the town.[74] The leaders commanded that none of the crusaders should venture into the city, where, amidst the narrow streets unfamiliar to them, they would be subject to ambush. They also feared that the Greeks might set a fire behind any group of marauders to cut them off. The barons knew that the troops defending the imperial city had not been destroyed. That night, therefore, the crusaders and the Venetians, fatigued by the day's fighting and excitement, slept close by their arms, fearing the worst and fully expecting to face a hard battle the next day.[75]

During the night, near the encampment of the marquis of Montferrat, a German count, identified by some historians as Berthold of Katzenellenbogen, fearing a surprise attack, set fire to the buildings between the Latins and the Greeks.[76] The fire spread into the city and soon became a raging blaze. It burned fiercely all the night and the next day until evening, destroying everything between the monastery of Euergetes and the Drungarios quarter.[77] This was the third of the great fires in Constantinople since the arrival of the crusaders, and Villehardouin states that in all there were more houses burned than existed in three of the greatest cities in France.[78] Some Byzantinists have estimated that half the buildings of Constantinople had been destroyed.[79] At least the western three quarters of the populous district along the Golden Horn was burned in the three fires, as well as a strip north and south across the city which approached Sancta Sophia and the Boukoleon palace on the side and the harbor of Eleutherios on the other.

Mourtzouphlus strode about the narrow streets during the evening trying to rally his frightened and aimless people. The chances for victory were excellent, as he depicted them, for the Latins were now trapped within the walls where they could be annihilated.[80] But the Greeks were consumed by despair and hopelessness, so they paid no attention to his exhortations, ignored his reproaches, and ran away from him. They were more concerned with concealing and burying their possessions. Mourtzouphlus saw that his appeals were fruitless, so he returned to the Great Palace.[81] He knew that if he were captured the Latins would have no mercy on him, so he took Eudocia, the daughter of Alexius III, with whom he had a passionate liaison, and her mother Euphrosyne, and about midnight he fled, sneaking out via the Golden Gate, customarily used for the triumphal entries of emperors. Not long after at Mosynopolis he married Eudocia.[82] Many Greeks followed the example of the emperor and departed Constantinople during the night in fear of the enemy now within the walls.[83]

Others assembled in confusion amidst the threatened splendor of Sancta Sophia to choose a new leader. Nicetas informs us that two excellent young men, Constantine Ducas and Constantine Lascaris, fought over control of the state, as over the helm of a storm-threatened ship. The two rivals were finally reconciled and with the support of the clergy the mantle fell upon Lascaris.[84]

Nicetas reports somewhat cryptically that he did not assume the insignia of emperor, but hastened with the old patriarch, John Camaterus, to the Milion, the square between the Great Church and the imperial palace containing the golden milestone. Here, at the very heart of the empire, he attempted by encouragement and flattery to rally the people who were milling about. The frightened crowd, however, was beyond resistance.[85] Why should they commit their lives to this emperor or that? The repeated revolutions to which the empire had been subject had dulled the loyalty of the people. They had seen brother blind brother, nephew summon foreigners to overthrow his uncle, jealous courtier strangle his benefactor. Whether this one or another mounted the throne of the Caesars to play his pitiful role for a few years or a few days mattered little to them. They hated and feared the Latins, of course, but they had lost the will to resist, and no one could restore it to them. Lascaris then turned to the Varangians, warning them that their danger was as great as that of the Greeks should the city fall to the invaders. Even if they survived, they would lose their high pay and their exalted status and be treated, not as an elite guard, but as mere mercenaries. The Varangians, however, determined to drive a hard bargain at the moment of greatest danger, and refused to budge unless paid. Not able to gain support, Lascaris slipped down to the Boukoleon harbor and boarded a galley for Asia Minor.[86]

So there was no one to resist the Latin crusaders from the West. At the break of day on Tuesday, 13 April, the invaders donned their armor and formed their battalions, fully expecting harder fighting than on the day before.[87] They did not know of the events of the night, but, somewhat anticlimatically, Constantinople had fallen. The city of the Caesars was theirs.[88] They also did not know that their crusade had ended. Its tortuous and much-debated path had led them from their homes in Flanders, the Ile de France, the Rhineland, through Venice to Zara, the city of transgression, and now to possession of Constantine's capital, the great Eastern Christian metropolis on the Bosporus. Here they would found an ill-fated Latin Empire, whose defense would require all their energies, all their resources, and many of their lives.

Epilogue

For the next three days, 13–15 April, the victorious Latins sacked the imperial city. Regulations had been issued in an attempt to control and organize the plundering, but the army, hardened and embittered by penury and war, was transformed into a mob driven by hate, greed, and lust. Villehardouin tells us that so much booty had never been taken in any city since the creation of the world. Palaces, houses, and even churches were ransacked. Men and women were searched thoroughly and without shame. Mules and other beasts of burden were driven up to the altar of Sancta Sophia to bear away the precious ornaments of the church, desecrating it with their droppings. The tombs of ancient emperors were broken open for the sake of valuable funeral ornaments. Holy relics proved a highly desired sort of loot. Gunther of Pairis tells of the pious plundering of his abbot, Martin, who gained a rich treasure of sacred booty, including the blood-stained robe of Christ. The Venetians were sophisticated enough to seize works of art, most notably the four bronze horses which grace the facade of Saint Mark's. Many of the northern pillagers, however, destroyed famed sculptures of monsters and men, pagan gods and Christian Virgin for the mere value of the bronze from which they were made. Images of Christ, the Holy Mother, and honored saints were destroyed for no reason other than blind frenzy. As might be expected, the victors also sated their sexual lusts, although to attribute such shameful behavior to mere animal desire would too readily ignore the element of human perversity, stripped of inhibitions, committing sexual violence to satisfy twisted emotional needs. Women were raped publicly on streets and squares, even in churches. Even older women were stripped and outraged. Some Greeks were slaughtered while trying to protect their wives and daughters or their property, others for no reason. Women and children also were not spared the sword. After three days of terror, the invading army was subjected to some measure of control.

After the frightful sack of the city the Latins set about the difficult task of securing their conquest and dividing the spoils. In March outside the walls of Constantinople they had provided by treaty for this eventual-

149

ity. The selection of an emperor by an electoral body composed of six Venetians and six crusaders was delayed by the machinations of Boniface of Montferrat and Baldwin of Flanders, but six high ranking ecclesiastics were finally chosen as the non-Venetian electors. Boniface was the most obvious candidate. The marquis had been the commander of the crusading host. He had seized the Boucoleon palace, had married the widow of Isaac II, and the Greeks clearly expected his succession to the throne, hailing him, if mournfully, as emperor. The election fell, however, to the count of Flanders. Baldwin was the more powerful and had a larger body of troops; he had won the respect of all for his valor and his piety. Boniface, on the other hand, had lost support by his close connection throughout the crusade with the ill-fated Alexius IV. Most important, perhaps, the six Venetians formed a solid front against the marquis, who was associated too closely, as they saw it, with their rivals in Genoa. Baldwin of Flanders was crowned emperor in Sancta Sophia on 16 May.

The planned partition of the empire among the victorious Latins was largely ignored in the scramble for territories. Venice received its promised three eighths of the capital, including the harbor area of most significance for her commercial objectives. Next in importance for the merchants of Venice was the acquisition by purchase from Boniface of Montferrat of Crete, lying strategically across the entrances to the Aegean and on the direct route from the West to Egypt or Syria. Once again the Genoese rivals of Venice were thwarted, as in the imperial election, for the purchase of the island was snatched from their hands at the last moment. Venice, in fact, had to fight a Genoese pirate, who had some support from his government, to gain possession of the island. Venice also established itself at such other critical spots as Negroponte in the Aegean and Modon and Coron at the southwest tip of the Morea. She made no attempt to conquer the three eighths of the empire which was her lot under the terms of the treaty, although the Venetian doge proudly claimed the title of "lord of one quarter and one half [of a quarter] of the Empire of Romania." Instead Venice secured the bases for a maritime empire in the eastern Mediterranean. Other Western merchants, however, were not excluded from Constantinople and the Empire. If the Genoese were not able to reestablish themselves until 1218, that was because of the war over Crete. Meanwhile, Pisans, Amalfitans, Anconitans, and others enjoyed the same privileges that they had possessed before the Latin conquest.

Boniface of Montferrat, not wanting the promised lands in Asia, insisted on Thessalonica, which had once belonged to his brother Renier, and a large dependent territory. After violent disputes with Baldwin he succeeded in establishing the vassal kingdom of Thessalonica. Villehardouin's nephew, also named Geoffrey of Villehardouin, found allies with whom to conquer most of the Morea. A Venetian, Marco Sanudo, freelanced the conquest of islands in the central Aegean and established a duchy of Naxos. Others gained lesser conquests. Greek successor states, moreover, sprang up. Two young Comnenan princes founded a so-called empire at Trebizond. Theodore Lascaris, the son-in-law of Alexius III, established another state claiming the imperial succession at Nicaea. A Ducas founded yet another in the West at Epirus. These were to be bones in the throat and the ultimate destruction of the Latin Empire.

That event, however, lay a half-century in the future. By the end of 1204 the Emperor Baldwin and the crusaders had won a large part of the empire and could look forward hopefully to the completion of the conquest. It was only a weak structure, though, that they established, a complex and decentralized system of fiefs without a strong head. Although the Frankish barons were required to take an oath of fealty to the emperor, the doge was exempt from any feudal obligation on behalf of Venice. Cooperation of the Venetians with the new emperor, however, remained crucial, and Venetians played a significant role in his council.

Foolish as the Latins were in their failure to gain the support of at least some Greeks, they were equally unwise in their rejection of foreign alliances. They failed to grasp the advantage of Seljuq allies in Asia Minor against the Greek successor states, as they scornfully rejected an alliance proposed by Ioannitsa. In an utterly ill-considered fashion the Bulgarian monarch was given to understand that he could not deal with the Latin emperor as an equal, but that he must look up to him as a serf looks up to his master. Otherwise, the Latins would conquer Bulgaria and reduce Ioannitsa to his former servile status. The Latins were thus left without allies and compelled to fight on two fronts, in Asia Minor and the Balkans, without adequate forces. Assaults that were going well had to be interrupted to cross the straits to meet emergencies on the other side. Towns that had been once conquered fell away from allegiance and had to be taken again and again.

The Latins' disdain for political and diplomatic realities brought disaster upon them. The Greek pronoiars of Thrace rebelled and summoned the Bulgarian tsar to their aid. Ioannitsa, whose offer of alliance with Baldwin had been insultingly rejected, was pleased to oblige them. He invaded Thrace and made contact with the Latin army near Adrianople. Many of Baldwin's followers, of course, were engaged in Asia Minor, so he could not bring his full force to bear against the Bulgarians and their Cuman auxiliaries. If the Latin knights lacked tact and discretion, they were not wanting courage of a rash and foolhardy sort. They blundered into the battle of Adrianople on 14 April 1205 when Count Louis of Blois, in a knightly pique because a small harassing force of Cumans annoyed him while he was dining, dashed into an ambush, followed by the emperor Baldwin and almost the entire force. Faced with disaster, but sustained by their chivalric code, neither Louis nor Baldwin would abandon the field. The Latin emperor, overwhelmed by superior numbers, was borne to the ground and captured. He died a prisoner. Louis was killed on the field of Adrianople. So were John of Friaise, Bishop Peter of Bethlehem, Stephen of Perche, Renaud of Montmirail, and many others. The crusaders suffered this crushing defeat just a year and two days after their entry into Constantinople.

The ancient doge, Dandolo, led an expedition which rescued the remnants of Baldwin's army, including Geoffrey of Villehardouin, the chronicler. Perhaps the fatigue of the retreat ruined the old man's health, for within a month and a half the doge was dead and buried in the south gallery of Sancta Sophia. With Dandolo the guiding wisdom of the crusading force expired. Two years later Boniface of Montferrat also fell into an ambush and died fighting valiantly, the last of the great leaders of the Fourth Crusade. The imperial responsibilities of the captured Baldwin were assumed by his brother Henry, first as regent, and, from 20 August 1206, as emperor. He proved to be far the ablest of the Latin emperors, moderate, humane and conciliatory. He restored Latin control over Thrace, since the cooperation between Greeks and Bulgarians was not long lasting, and he won over to himself some of the Greek nobility. He employed Greeks in the government and the army, and he treated the common people as his own, as Byzantine sources themselves attest. Above all, he showed some understanding of Greek religious sentiment. When the assertive papal legate, Pelagius, closed Greek churches because they refused to include the pope's name in prayer during Mass, a delegation of Greeks called upon the emperor, making it clear that, while they accepted his rule, they would not compromise their faith or change their manner of worship. He gained popularity among his subjects by defying the legate and reopening the churches.

Henry died on 11 June 1216, barely forty years old, after a reign of ten years. He was the only one of the Latin emperors to whom the Greeks were willing to be subject. It is by no means certain that the Latin Empire could have become a viable state under any circumstances, but, if it had had a succession of emperors as able and conciliating as Henry, it might have become a workable reality.

Henry's successors were neither talented nor energetic, although in fairness it must be added that neither they nor he had adequate foundations upon which to build. The Latin Empire declined steadily. In 1224 Theodore Angelus, the Epirote claimant to the empire, took Thessalonica, a city second in importance only to Constantinople. The empire was effectively reduced to the neighborhood of the capital, in communication with the Frankish principalities of Greece only by means of the Venetian fleet, leaderless, and on the verge of collapse. Meanwhile the Epirote and Nicaen contenders for the Empire were increasing in strength, and for a generation the Latin Empire was preserved only by their rivalry. John Ducas Vatatzes, son-in-law of Theodore Lascaris, succeeded in reuniting under Nicaean hegemony the heart of the old Byzantine possessions. Latin Constantinople was isolated and its eventual reconquest by the Greeks was certain. This was accomplished in 1261 by Michael Paleologus, the Nicaean claimant.

For years the Latin emperors had lived in abject poverty, selling relics and stripping the lead from roofs to meet their most urgent needs. If the Greeks after 1261 found Constantinople in ruins, it was because of the penury of the Latins, not their barbarism. In fact, Latin strengthening of the structure of Sancta Sophia insured the survival of the great church. There can be no doubt, however, about the decrepitude of the city at the end of Latin rule. The failure of the Latin Empire was probably inevitable from the beginning. Founded upon alien soil with a hostile population, dependent for men and money upon the West, and provided with a weak institutional base, even the greatest statesmanship probably could not have succeeded.

The Latin conquest of Constantinople did not, of course, supply the base for the successful conclusion of a crusade against the Holy Land as the Latin leaders had anticipated in the first flush of triumph. According to Innocent III, the Muslims were struck with fear by the crusaders' victory and the sultan of Cairo declared that he would rather have seen Jerusalem fall than Constantinople. In any case, the sultan hurried to conclude a new truce with the king of Jerusalem. The crusaders themselves considered that they had wrought in the conquest a great achievement as instruments of God, an extraordinary exploit, one of the great adventures of the world. This spirit breathes in the narratives of Villehardouin and Robert of Clari. But the crusaders became enmeshed in securing, extending, and protecting their conquests, not only because they were greedy for lands, as they were, but because they could not otherwise consider proceeding to the Holy Land. In fact, the need for men and the promise of lands drew knights and sergeants away from the Kingdom of Jerusalem to the chagrin of the pope.

If the Latin conquest of Constantinople did not further the cause of the crusade, neither is it primarily responsible for the weakness of the Byzantine Empire of the Palaeologi after 1261. Some historians of the crusades tend to blame that feebleness and the ultimate fall of the Byzantine Empire in 1453 upon the Latin conquest, which preceded that of the Turks by two and a half centuries. Byzantine historians do not usually make this mistake. It is true that the Palaeologan Empire after 1261 was only a fragment of the Byzantine Empire in the days of its glory. South and Central Greece, Athens and the Morea, remained in the hands of French nobles, who were naturally inimical to the Palaeologi, and their presence, of course, must be attributed directly to the Fourth Crusade. Venice and Genoa, with their colonies scattered all over the eastern Mediterranean, dominated the trade routes to the exclusion of the Byzantines, but the Italian domination of the Mediterranean trade was clearly achieved well before the expedition of 1202–1204 and cannot be blamed on the Fourth Crusade. Independent Serbia and Bulgaria now dominated the northern Balkans and rival Greek states survived in Epirus and Trebizond, but it was not the Latin conquest which introduced separatist movements into the empire for the first time. After 1261 the government was feudalistic and the army was dependent upon mercenaries, such as the ill-famed Catalan company, but we have seen that before 1204 the feudal tendency in the Byzantine Empire was strong and the defense of Constantinople itself largely depended upon the Varangian Guard of foreign mercenaries. The Latins do not bear primary responsibility for the fact that Byzantium lacked strength to overcome the menace of the Ottoman Turks.

If the empire under the Palaeologi was a weak and disordered state, this was the result of long term and deeply rooted causes, which it is not within the limits of my task or my competence to examine here. A vigorous Byzantine state would never have been subjected to the Latin conquest. A fundamentally sound society would have recovered from the sack of Constantinople. Historians who have lived through the mid-twentieth century should be acutely aware from the examples of Germany and Japan of the ability of strong societies to resurrect themselves from disaster. If Hiroshima could rise from its ashes to become a thriving commercial and cultural center, why could not Constantinople? When the Latins drove the Greeks into Asia Minor, the exiles were able to create a government sounder and better consolidated than their old one at Constantinople. When they recovered their capital they found that Byzantium's former greatness escaped them, for they had merely restored a position which already before 1203–1204 had proved untenable.

This book, therefore, does not lay claim to the reader's interest on the grounds that the Fourth Crusade radically changed the course of history, although it undoubtedly contributed to the changes which followed and hastened them. The interest rather lies in its being a small part, isolated for close examination here, of long term historical movements. By reflecting upon a detailed examination of the Fourth Crusade within this framework we can perhaps expand our understanding of mankind caught up in the great currents of events.

Notes

Chapter 1

1. Innocent III, *Die Register Innocenz' III*, ed. Othmar Hageneder and Anton Haidacher (Graz-Cologne, 1964), I: 18–20, no. 11. Achille Luchaire, *Innocent III*, vol. IV, *La question d'Orient* (Paris, 1907), pp. 6–7. This letter did not, however, constitute the proclamation of a crusade. Helmut Roscher, *Papst Innocenz III und die Kreuzzüge* (Göttingen, 1969), pp. 51–52. In fact, the German crusade had not yet expired. Apprehensive that the last of the remaining German crusaders were about to return home, weakening the defense of the Holy Land, Innocent offered crusading privileges to those who would support a crusader. Innocent III, *Register*, I: 430–33, no. 302. The document is undated, but was probably issued about mid-year.

2. Since this study will be very much concerned with the motivations of Innocent III, Boniface of Montferrat, Enrico Dandolo, and others, let me emphasize at the outset an obvious point, which, it seems to me, many writers on the Fourth Crusade have overlooked. That Innocent stood to gain power and prestige for the papacy, Boniface lands for himself, and Dandolo wealth for Venice, does not require us to believe that they were not sincere in their crusading sentiments. Quite often men's ideals and their profits are not in conflict. Scholars, for example, are not necessarily less dedicated scholars if they also gain professional stature or money from their writings.

3. Innocent's conception of papal power made no allowance for royally directed expeditions in which his own role would be limited to issuing the summons. Hans Eberhard Mayer, *The Crusades* (1st German ed., 1965), trans. by John Gillingham, rev. and updated by the author (New York and Oxford, 1972), p. 183. See Michele Maccarrone, *Studi su Innocenzo III*, Italia sacra XVII (Padua, 1972): 88–90.

4. Innocent III, *Register*, I: 498–505, n. 336. See also, ibid., I: 743–45, n. 509, on the problem of collecting money for the Holy Land.

5. E.g., the cardinal-legate Peter Capuano was sent to France to gain a peace or a truce. Ibid., I: 531, n. 355. Also a papal legation to try to make peace between Genoa and Pisa. *Gesta Innocentii PP. III*, Migne, *PL*, CCXIV: col. 91, ch. 46. In general, see James Ross Sweeney, "Innocent III, Hungary and the Bulgarian Coronation: A Study in Medieval Papal Diplomacy," *Church History* XLII (1973): 320, and nn.

6. William E. Lunt, *Financial Relations of the Papacy with England to 1327* (Cambridge, Mass., 1939), pp. 241–42; Giuseppe Martini, "Innocenzo III ed il fi-

155

nanziamento delle crociate," *Archivio della Deputazione Romana di Storia Patria*, n.s. x (1944): 318–19. Edgar H. McNeal and Robert Lee Wolff, "The Fourth Crusade," in *A History of the Crusades*, ed. Kenneth M. Setton, et al. (Philadelphia, 1962), II: 156–57; Roscher, *Papst Innocenz III*, p. 80, n. 128; Ronald P. Grossman, "The Financing of the Crusades" (Ph.D. diss., Univ. of Chicago, 1965), pp. 91–95. Adolf Gottlob, *Die päpstlichen Kreuzzugssteuern des 13. Jahrhunderts* (Heiligenstadt, 1892), pp. 22–23.

See also Innocent III, "Rubrice Registri litterarum secretarum fel. rec. Domini Innocentii pape tertii de anno pontificatus sui III. IV. (XVIII. et XIX.)," in *Vetera monumenta slavorum meridionalium historiam illustrantia*, ed. Augustin Theiner (Rome, 1863), IV: n. 123, p. 59. After much dispute the Cistercians agreed to a fixed sum of 2,000 marks, which they were still having difficulty in collecting in 1214. Ibid., IV: no. 116, p. 59. Elizabeth A. R. Brown, "The Cistercians in the Latin Empire of Constantinople and Greece, 1204–1276," *Traditio* XIV (1958): 70–72. It seems that the pope was even accused of stealing from the Holy Land for his own use. Luchaire, *Innocent III*, IV: 10–11.

7. Innocent III, *Epistolae*, II: 268–72, Migne, *PL*, CCXIV: 826–36. McNeal and Wolff, "The Fourth Crusade," p. 156. Luchaire, *Innocent III*, IV: 8. See also Joseph R. Strayer, "The Political Crusades of the Thirteenth Century," in Setton, *History of the Crusades*, II: 347. As in other areas of papal activity, Innocent III enhanced the involvement of the papacy in the financing of the crusades. Grossman, "Financing of the Crusades," p. 87. Although it is accurate to say that the general papal tax was unprecedented, lay rulers had previously imposed crusading taxes and Clement III in 1188 had ordered the clergy of Canterbury to give alms for the Holy Land. Lunt, *Financial Relations*, I: 240 and 422; William E. Lunt, *Papal Revenues in the Middle Ages*, 2 vols. (New York, 1934), I: 71–72. Gottlob argued that late Polish sources which recounted a papal tax by Clement III in 1188 and 1189 were unbelievable, but, in light of Lunt's evidence from England, one wonders whether there was not, at any rate, an order for the levy of compulsory alms. *Die päpstlichen Kreuzzugssteuern*, pp. 18–20.

8. John M. O'Brien, "Fulk of Neuilly," *Proceedings of the Leeds Philosophical and Literary Society*, XIII (1969): 114; Paul Alphandéry, *La Chrétienté et l'idée de Croisade*, texte établi par Alphonse Dupront, 2 vols. (Paris 1954–59), II: 47.

9. Quoted in O'Brien, "Fulk of Neuilly," p. 114.

10. Ibid., 118–20. Milton R. Gutsch, "A Twelfth-Century Preacher—Fulk of Neuilly," *The Crusades and Other Historical Essays presented to Dana C. Munro by his Former Students*, ed. Louis John Paetow (New York, 1928), pp. 189–90.

11. John M. O'Brien, "Fulk of Neuilly" (Ph.D. diss. Univ. of Southern California, Los Angeles, 1964), pp. 59–61; Gutsch, "Fulk of Neuilly," p. 191.

12. O'Brien, "Fulk of Neuilly," *Proceedings*, pp. 119–20.

13. Rigord, *Gesta Philippi Augusti Francorum Regis*, in *Rec. Hist. Gaules*, XVII: 48; Robert of Clari, *La Conquête de Constantinople*, ed. Philippe Lauer (Paris, 1924), sec. 1, p. 1; O'Brien, "Fulk of Neuilly," *Proceedings*, pp. 122–23; Gutsch, "Fulk of Neuilly," pp. 193–98. Miracle seekers frequently tore pieces off his garments for medicinal purposes. On one occasion, molested by enthusiastic clothes-snatchers, Fulk proclaimed that his own garments were not sacred, but that he

hereby blessed (making the sign of the cross) the garments of one of the crowd, which were promptly torn to shreds by the mob. Jacques of Vitry, *The Historia Occidentalis of Jacques of Vitry: A Critical Edition*, ed. John F. Hinnebusch (Fribourg, 1972), pp. 97–98.

14. Robert of Auxerre, *Chronicon*, ed. O. Holder-Egger, *M.G.H., SS.*, XXVI: 258; Gutsch, "Fulk of Neuilly," p. 192; O'Brien, "Fulk of Neuilly," pp. 61–62, 69–73.

15. Otto of Saint Blaise, continuation of Otto of Freising, *Chronicon*, ed. Roger Wilmans, *M.G.H., SS.*, XX: 330.

16. Gutsch, "Fulk of Neuilly," p. 202.

17. Innocent III, *Register*, I: 597, n. 398. Gutsch, "Fulk of Neuilly," pp. 202–3, gives a translation. The exact nature of this papal letter is debated; it is clearly not a crusade commission. See O'Brien, "Fulk of Neuilly," *Proceedings*, p. 128 and n. 116.

18. O'Brien, "Fulk of Neuilly," *Proceedings*, pp. 124–25.

19. Alphandéry, *La Chrétienté et l'idée de croisade*, II: 64. O'Brien, "Fulk of Neuilly," *Proceedings*, p. 131, criticizes Norman Cohn's argument that Fulk preached a crusade exclusively for the poor. Alphandéry also comes close to Cohn's position. *La Chrétienté et l'idée de croisade*, I: 1. I think O'Brien is right. See Fulk's preaching to the Cistercian assembly, below, pp. 29–30. The ideal of poverty, however, which was to culminate in St. Francis, was already widespread. It is worth noting that Robert of Clari repeatedly refers to himself as a poor knight. Robert of Clari, *Conquête*, pp. ix–x. Also Mayer, *Crusades*, p. 185. Whether this is merely a means of identifying himself in contrast to the rich, whom he resented and envied, or whether it manifests a belief in the messianic character of the poor, we do no know. Perhaps both, for one's longings and one's ideals may be at odds, just as they may be mutually supportive.

20. McNeal and Wolff, "The Fourth Crusade," p. 155. For the efforts to gain a peace or a truce, see Innocent III, *Register*, I: 502, n. 336; I: 516, n. 345; I: 517, n. 346. Innocent's letter confirming the truce: Innocent III, *Epistolae*, II: 23–25, Migne, *PL*, CCXIV: 552–54. Philip broke the truce, however, shortly after the death of Richard.

21. Innocent III, *Register*, I: 518–20, nn. 347–48. F. M. Powicke, "The Reigns of Philip Augustus and Louis VIII of France," *Cambridge Medieval History* (hereafter *CMH*) (Cambridge, 1936), VI: 288.

22. Geoffrey of Villehardouin, *La Conquête de Constantinople*, ed. Edmond Faral, 2 vols. (Paris, 1938–39), sec. 3, I: 4. (This form of citation of Villehardouin, which will be used henceforth without comment, signifies that reference is found in sec. 3, vol. I, p. 4 of the Faral ed.) I am not unaware of E. John's ingenious article urging that the dating of the preliminaries of the crusade from the tournament at Ecry through the meeting at Compiègne should be set forward one year. "A Note on the Preliminaries of the Fourth Crusade," *Byzantion* XXVIII (1958): 95–103. It seems to me that the lapse of time between the appointment of envoys at Compiègne and their departure would be incomprehensibly long. John does not claim convincing proof for his hypothesis.

23. Villehardouin, *Conquête de Constantinople*, sec. 3, I: 4; Edgar H. McNeal,

'Fulk of Neuilly and the Tournament of Ecry," *Speculum* xxviii (1953): 374.

24. McNeal, "Fulk of Neuilly," pp. 371–75. O'Brien attempts to raise some questions about McNeal's conclusions, but not successfully, I think. "Fulk of Neuilly," *Proceedings*, pp. 130–131, and n. 136. The *Gesta Episcoporum Halberstadensium* ed. L. Weiland, *M.G.H., SS.*, xxiii: 117, does not unequivocally state that Fulk crossed Thibaut and Louis. Neither does Villehardouin "invariably" cite the name of the preacher involved when he tells of nobles taking the cross. *Conquête de Constantinople*, sec. 8, i: 10–12.

25. James Brundage, *Medieval Canon Law and the Crusader*, Madison, Milwaukee and London, 1969, pp. 32–33; Michel Villey, *La croisade: essai sur la formation d'une théorie juridique* (Paris, 1942), p. 119–127.

26. *Above*, p. 1, for the pope's declaration of the indulgence.

27. Brundage, *Medieval Canon Law and the Crusader*, pp. 149–50. For legal support of this position, see Mayer, *Crusades*, p. 16; Steven Runciman, *A History of the Crusades*, 3 vols. (Cambridge, 1954), i: 84; Frederick H. Russell, *The Just War in the Middle Ages*, (Cambridge-London-New York-Melbourne, 1975), p. 119: Raymond H. Schmandt, "The Fourth Crusade and the Just War Theory," *The Catholic Historical Review* lxi (1975): 197–98 and n. 13; also C. R. Beazley, *The Dawn of Modern Geography* (London, 1901) ii: 117–18. See the martyrdom of Cacciaguida in Dante, *Paradiso*, Canto xv, ll. 145–149. I strongly endorse Brundage's warning that we must beware of modern historians who "tend to devalue the spiritual motives" of their medieval ancestors, and who tend "to overemphasize correspondingly the force of economic, social (or antisocial), and other temporal factors in terms which for the Middle Ages may be more than a trifle anachronistic." As Brundage says: "it would be. . .foolish to write off the force of a genuine, if at times grotesque, spirituality." *Medieval Canon Law and the Crusader*, p. 144. The crusaders of the Fourth Crusade have been maligned more than any others.

28. Runciman, *Crusades*, i: 83–84.

29. Villey, *Croisade*, p. 22.

30. Runciman, *Crusades*, i: 84. Pope Leo IV declared that those dying in battle in defense of the church would receive a heavenly reward: Pope John VIII declared them martyrs. See also Villey, *La Croisade*, pp. 25–26.

31. Runciman, *Crusades*, i: 89–90.

32. Villey, *Croisade*, p. 88.

33. Russell, *Just War*, p. 35. Over the opposition of Peter Damian. Villey, *Croisade*, p. 33. See also Alphandéry, *La Chrétienté et l'idée de croisade*, i: 27.

34. Mayer, *Crusades*, p. 15.

35. Russell, *Just War*, pp. 38–39, 115–23.

36. Jules Tessier, *La quatrième croisade: la diversion sur Zara et Constantinople* (Paris, 1884), p. 37; *L'esprit de croisade*, ed. Jean Richard (Paris, 1969), p. 39, quoting Conon of Béthune.

37. Villehardouin, *Conquête de Constantinople*, sec. 3, i: 6, and especially n. 5.

38. Villehardouin says that Thibaut was not more than twenty-two, Louis not more than twenty-seven. *Conquête de Constantinople*, sec. 3, i: 4–6. Many scholars, however, follow Gislebert of Mons in dating the birth of Thibaut 13 May 1179. The best discussion of the sources is in John, "The Preliminaries of the Fourth

Crusade," pp. 98–99. See also Henri D'Arbois de Jubainville, *Histoire des ducs et des comtes de Champagne* (Paris, 1865), IV: 73, 87–88, and 88, n. (a).

39. Arbois de Jubainville, *Histoire des ducs et des comtes de Champagne*, IV: 43–46, 63–65.

40. Villehardouin, *Conquête de Constantinople*, sec. 360, II: 168–170; Robert of Clari, *Conquête*, sec. 112, p. 106; Robert Lee Wolff, "The Latin Empire of Constantinople," in *A History of the Crusades*, ed. Kenneth M. Setton, et al., II: 203.

41. Villehardouin, *Conquête de Constantinople*, secs. 4–6, I: 6–8.

42. Ibid., sec. 8, I: 10–12.

43. Benjamin Hendrickx, "Boudewijn IX van Vlaanderen, de vrome keizer van Konstantinopel," *Ons geestelijk erf* XLIV (1970): 227–29; Friedrich Hurter, *Storia di Papa Innocenzo III*, trans. from the third Germ. ed. by T. Giuseppe Gliemone, 4 vols. (Milan, 1857–58), II: 324.

44. Villehardouin, *Conquête de Constantinople*, sec. 8, I: 10–12.

45. Robert Lee Wolff, "The Latin Empire of Constantinople (1204–1261)" (Ph.D. diss. Harvard, 1947), p. 81. E.g., "cet homme doué d'une sagesse exquise." *Chronique de la conquête de Constantinople*, trans. J. A. Buchon (Paris, 1825), pp. 36–37.

46. Robert Lee Wolff, "Baldwin of Flanders and Hainaut, First Latin Emperor of Constantinople: His Life, Death and Resurrection, 1172–1225," *Speculum* XXVII (1952): 283 and 304, n. 29; Wolff, "The Latin Empire," p. 85. I am not in accord with those who believe that the great men among the French crusaders took the cross to escape the wrath of their sovereign Philip after the death of Richard Lion-Heart. It does, however, have some support in the sources: Ernoul and Bernard le Trésorier, *Chronique*, ed. Louis de Mas Latrie (Paris, 1871), p. 337; Guillaume le Bréton, *Gesta Philippi Augusti*, in *Rec. Hist. Gaules*, XVII: 76. See Leopoldo Usseglio, *I marchesi di Monferrato in Italia ed in Oriente durante i secoli XII e XIII* (Turin, 1926), II: 173; Roberto Cessi, "Venezia e la quarta crociata," *Archivio Veneto*, ser. 5 XLVIII–XLIX (1951): 9, n. 3; Cessi, "Politica, economia, religione," in *Storia di Venezia*, vol. II, *Dalle origini del ducato alla IV crociata* (Venice, n.d.): 449; Francesco Cognasso, *Storia delle crociate* (Milan, 1967), p. 701. Cognasso's statement, which includes a denial of any religious motivation to the crusaders, is almost the antithesis to my thesis. On the narrower question of the reasons for taking the cross, I do not believe that the great vassals had much to fear from Philip Augustus at this stage in his career, but, if they did, they surely had no reason to believe that ecclesiastical sanctions protecting crusaders would deter him, if he were able to take vengeance upon them. Tessier, *Quatrième Croisade*, p. 36; Sebastian Naslund, "The Crusading Policy of Innocent III in France, 1198–1202: an Evaluation from Secular and Ecclesiastical Sources" (seminar paper, Univ. of Illinois, 1969), pp. 13–14.

47. Villehardouin, *Conquête de Constantinople*, sec. 10, I: 12–14. For the relationship of Louis of Blois and Geoffrey of Perche, see p. 13, n. 7.

48. Ibid., sec. 9, I: 12; Anna Maria Nada Patrone, in Roberto di Clari, *La conquista di Costantinopli* (Genoa, 1972), p. 8, n. 28.

49. Villehardouin, *Conquête de Constantinople*, secs. 4–5, I: 6–8.

50. Ibid., sec. 8, I: 10–12.

51. Ibid., sec. 10, I: 12–14.

52. Ibid., sec. 9, I: 12.
53. McNeal and Wolff, "The Fourth Crusade," p. 160.
54. Villehardouin, *Conquête de Constantinople*, sec. 11, I: 14.
55. Ibid., sec. 7, I: 10.
56. Ibid., sec. 11, I: 14.
57. The meeting cannot be dated with certainty. See Donald E. Queller, "L'évolution du rôle de l'ambassadeur: les pleins pouvoirs et le traité de 1201 entre les Croisés et les Vénitiens," *Moyen Age* XIX (1961): 484 and n. 13. Also see this article for greater detail on the envoys and the negotiation of the treaty. H. Vriens asserted that a sort of "permanent central committee" met at Compiègne. "De kwestie van den vierden kruistocht," *Tijdschrift voor Geschiedenis* XXXVII (1922): 52. There is no documentation, and I do not follow him.
58. C. W. Previté-Orton, "The Italian Cities till c. 1200," *CMH*, V: 293; E. J. Passant, "The Effects of the Crusades upon Western Europe," *CMH*, V: 328; McNeal and Wolff, "The Fourth Crusade," p. 161.
59. Villehardouin, *Conquête de Constantinople*, sec. 11, I: 14. One would like to know who participated in the agreement: the plenipotentiaries were sent in the names of Baldwin of Flanders, Louis of Blois, and Thibaut of Champagne. The failure of many crusaders to adhere to the treaty concluded by these plenipotentiaries becomes crucial for the fate of the crusade.
60. Robert of Clari, who was ill-informed concerning the preliminaries of the crusade, names only these two. *Conquête*, sec. VI: p. 6. Villehardouin, however, gives the full list, which is confirmed by official documents: he and Milo le Brébant representing Thibaut; John of Friaise and Walter of Gaudonville, representing Louis; and Conon and Alard Maquereau, representing Baldwin. *Conquête de Constantinople*, sec. 359, II: 168. Tessier wrongly attributed preeminence to Conon, Geoffrey and John, calling the others mere aids or assessors. *Quatrième Croisade*, p. 256.
61. Villehardouin, *Conquête de Constantinople*, I: 11, n. 10; McNeal and Wolff, "The Fourth Crusade," p. 160 and n. 21. He was criticized by another troubadour, Huon III d'Oisi, for returning home early with Philip Augustus. *Kreuzzugsdichtung*, ed. Ulrich Müller, Tübingen, 1969, p. 35.
62. *Livre de la conqueste de la princée de l'Amorée: Chronique de Morée*, ed. Jean Longnon (Paris, 1911), sec. 126, p. 43; *Chronique de la Conquête de Constantinople*, p. 31. Neither of these chronicles is a reliable source for the crusade, but they may serve to show the reputation of Villehardouin. See also Faral, "Introduction," Villehardouin, *Conquête de Constantinople*, I: vii and x. Jean Longnon identifies him as the *marescallus comitis Henrici* on the Third Crusade. *Recherches sur la vie de Geoffroy de Villehardouin, suivies du catalogue des actes des Villehardouin* (Paris, 1939), pp. 59–63. He also finds him as arbiter of a dispute in 1198. Ibid., pp. 65–66.
63. Concerning organization and clarity, see Faral, "Introduction," Villehardouin, *Conquête de Constantinople*, I: xxxv. The lack of profundity is my own observation. We should remember that he was a soldier writing his memoirs, not an analytical scholar.
64. Ibid., I: vi.
65. For the list of his missions on behalf of the crusaders, see Queller, "L'é-

volution du rôle de l'ambassadeur," pp. 482–83, n. 11. The second, however, was actually Geoffrey of Joinville.

66. Villehardouin, *Conquête de Constantinople*, sec. 13, I: 16.

67. Emile Bouchet, in Geoffroy de Villehardouin, *La Conquête de Constantinople*, ed. Emile Bouchet, 2 vols. (Paris, 1891), II: 18–19.

68. Robert de Clari, *Conquête*, sec. 3, p. 7. Roberto Cessi not only accepts the prior attempts at Genoa and Pisa, but also Marseilles. "Politica, economia, religione," p. 449.

69. Villehardouin, *Conquête de Constantinople*, sec. 32, I: 32–34. Lacking compelling reason one simply does not have the option of following the confused and ill-informed Robert instead of Villehardouin, who was a participant.

70. Wilhelm von Heyd, *Histoire du commerce du Levant au moyen âge* (1st German ed., 1879), trans. by Furcy Raynaud and revised and augmented by the author (1885; reprinted, 2 vols., Leipzig, 1936), I: 204, 234–235, and 312.

71. H. Vriens, "De kwestie van den vierden kruistocht," p. 61.

72. Villehardouin, *Conquête de Constantinople*, sec. 14, I: 18.

73. Luchaire, *Innocent III*, IV: 89; Tessier, *Quatrième Croisade*, p. 105; Francesco Cerone, "Il papa e i veneziani nella quarta crociata," *Archivio Veneto*, n.s. XXXVI (1888): 61.

74. *Gesta Innocentii*, sec. 46, col. 91.

75. Queller, "L'évolution du rôle de l'ambassadeur," p. 488, n. 22.

76. Innocent III, *Register*, I: 502, n. 336; I: 513, n. 343; and I, 776, n. 536. See Cessi, "Venezia e la quarta crociata," p. 7, n. 3.

77. Queller, "L'évolution du rôle de l'ambassadeur," p. 488, n. 22.

78. For specific references to Karl Hopf, Paul Riant, Ludwig Streit, Edwin Pears, Walter Norden, F. C. Hodgson, H. Vriens, E. F. Jacob, and A. Frolow, see Donald E. Queller, "Innocent III and the Crusader-Venetian Treaty of 1201," *Medievalia et Humanistica* xv (1963): 32, n. 8. Add Bouchet, in Villehardouin, *Conquête de Constantinople* (1891), II: 20–21. Fliche not only believes that the pope had a peculiar mistrust of Venice, but that he favored Sicily as the point of concentration of troops and fleets. Augustin Fliche, Christine Thouzelliers, and Yvonne Azais, "La Chrétienté romaine," in Fliche and Martin, *Histoire de l'église* (Paris, 1950), X: 60–61.

79. See Innocent's letter authorizing the Venetians to continue the trade in nonstrategic materials. Innocent III, *Register*, I: 775–76, n. 536.

80. Benjamin of Tudela, *The Itinerary*, trans. and ed. A. Asher (London and Berlin, 1840), p. 157.

81. Francesco Cerone, "Il papa e i Veneziana nella quarta crociata," *Archivio veneto*, n.s. XXXVI (1888): 59.

82. Schmandt, "Fourth Crusade and Just War Theory," p. 221.

Chapter 2

1. Villehardouin does not give us their route to Venice, but he does provide an itinerary of the return. Villehardouin, *Conquête de Constantinople*, secs. 32–35, I: 32–36. Since this return route conforms with the route of the journey to Venice

given by the *Chronicle of Morea*, which is not in itself a reliable source for such details, and by the *Chronique de la conquête de Constantinople*, I have felt secure in adopting it. *Crusaders as Conquerors: The Chronicle of Morea*, trans. Harold E. Lurier (New York, 1964), pp. 76–77; *Chronique de la conquête de Constantinople*, p. 32. Faral's dates are slightly off, because he used 21 March, instead of 25 March, the correct date, for Easter 1201. A. Giry, *Manuel de diplomatique* (Paris, 1894), p. 197. For the date of arrival: Villehardouin, *Conquête de Constantinople*, sec. 14, I: 18. The *Cronaca Bemba*, a fifteenth-century Venetian chronicle, gives the date as March, but the author is generally inaccurate on details concerning the Fourth Crusade. Such late Venetian sources have no value when contemporary documentation is available. One might be tempted to use them when contemporary documentation is lacking if they could be shown to conform closely and in detail to contemporary documents, and especially to official documents, such as treaties, on other points, but I am not convinced that this is often the case. *Cronaca Bemba*, Biblioteca Marciana, cl. ital. VII, cod. 125 (7460), f. 33 (436) r.

2. Villehardouin, *Conquête de Constantinople*, sec. 15, I: 18.

3. Marino Sanudo, *Le vite dei dogi*, ed. G. Monticolo, *R.I.S.*[2], XXII, iv, col. 527B. Villehardouin, *Conquête de Constantinople*, sec. 67, I: 68, and *Historia ducum Venetorum*, ed. H. Simonsfeld, *M.G.H., SS.*, XIV: 90, say only that Dandolo was an old man. Sara de Mundo Lo asserts that Dandolo was around eighty at the time of his election. *Cruzados en Bizancio: la quarta cruzada a la luz de las fuentes latinas y orientales* (Buenos Aires, 1957), p. 78. Paul Rousset is of the same opinion. *Histoire des croisades* (Paris, 1957), p. 213. McNeal and Wolff find Dandolo's octogenarianism very difficult to believe since such age would make him a man over ninety during the Fourth Crusade: "The Fourth Crusade," p. 162. Nevertheless, it is safe to assume that the doge was of very considerably advanced years.

4. Villehardouin, *Conquête de Constantinople*, sec. 67, I: 68; again in sec. 351, II: 160. Some manuscripts repeat the statement in sec. 314. See II: 122, note h. Dandolo's complete blindness is the tradition handed down by the Venetian chroniclers: Ernst Gerland, "Der vierte Kreuzzug und seine Problem," *Neue Jahrbücher für das klassische Altertum und für Pädagogik* XIII (1904): 507, n. 3. Other modern historians tend to believe that the doge could still see, although very poorly. McNeal and Wolff, "The Fourth Crusade," p. 162; Rousset, *Histoire des croisades*, p. 213.

5. Villehardouin, *Conquête de Constantinople*, sec. 15, I: 18. Edgar H. McNeal, "Introduction" to Robert of Clari, *The Conquest of Constantinople* (New York, 1936), p. 223. See also *Chronique de Morée, sec. 15, p. 6*.

6. E.g., Rousset, *Histoire des croisades*, p. 213; Mundo Lo, *Cruzados en Bizancio*, p. 78; Runciman, *Crusades*, III: pp. 114–5.

7. While we must appreciate that medieval values were not the same as ours, I find it beyond my comprehension why so many scholars accept as a virtuous motivation the feudal noble's desire to slay the infidel for his wrong faith (and to seize his land), while rejecting as unworthy the merchant's quest for profit. Neither, of course, seems especially saintly to us, but the merchant's values are as medieval as the knight's and surely appear upon reflection more acceptable to

most of us. See Donald E. Queller and Gerald W. Day, "Some Arguments in Defense of the Venetians on the Fourth Crusade," *American Historical Review* LXXXI (1976): 717–37.

8. "je ai veüe vos letres." Villehardouin, *Conquête de Constantinople*, sec. 16, I: 18. This is interesting and, to my knowledge, not noticed with regard to Dandolo's supposed blindness. It need not be taken literally, of course, but on balance I doubt that Dandolo was totally blind.

9. Ibid., sec 18, I: 20–22. My translation.

10. *Urkunder zur älteren Handels-und Staatsgeschichte der Republik Venedig*, ed. G. L. Tafel and G. M. Thomas, 3 vols. (1st ed. 1856–57, reprinted Amsterdam, 1967), I: 365. The treaty is also found in Longnon, *Recherches*, pp. 179–81, and in Tessier, *Quatrième Croisade*, pp. 252–54. For a discussion of whether the squires were noncombatant servants or sergeants on horseback, see Ferdinand Lot, *L'art militaire et les armées au moyen âge* (Paris, 1949), p. 170 and p. 175 and n. 3. That horses were to be transported only for the knights argues that the squires were still servants. See also R. C. Smail, *Crusading Warfare (1097–1193)* (Cambridge, Eng., 1956), pp. 108–9. Contra: Antonio Carile, "Alle origini dell'impero d'Oriente: analisi quantitativa dell' esercito crociato e repartizione dei feudi," *Nuova rivista storica* LVI (1972): 291, n. 29. Anna Maria Nada Patrone recently wrote that the agreement was for the transportation of 100,000 men, which is probably a misreading of Robert of Clari's 104,000. *La quarta crociata e l'impero latino di Romania (1198–1261)*, p. 76. Read accurately or not, Robert still should not be followed on matters of this sort, especially when there exists an official document.

11. Villehardouin, *Conquête de Constantinople*, sec. 19, I: 22.

12. Ibid., sec. 21, I: 22. Villehardouin says that the Venetians agreed to furnish provisions for nine months, but the treaty itself says a year. So does the *Chronicon gallicum ineditum*, in Tafel and Thomas, *Urkunden*, I: 330 (improperly identified there). This is a rare example of conflict between Villehardouin's account and official documentation. Tafel and Thomas, *Urkunden* I: 365. Faral proposes two explanations: (1) Villehardouin subtracted from the year the three months of 1202 when the crusaders were at Venice and supplied by the Venetians; (2) three extra months of provisions were obtained by the envoys in subsequent negotiations. Villehardouin, *Conquête de Constantinople*, I: 216. I now believe that I was wrong in preferring the former explanation. Queller, "L'évolution du rôle de l'ambassadeur," p. 490, n. 28. The sale of grain by the Venetians to the crusaders at inflated prices during their sojourn on the Lido is mentioned, so it would seem that the Venetians did not begin supplying them until the date of embarkation. *Devastatio Constantinopolitana*, ed. Charles Hopf, *Chroniques Greco-Romanes* (Berlin, 1873), p. 87. (Also in the *Annales Herbipolenses*, *M.G.H.*, *SS.*, XVI: 9–12. The Hopf edition is considered the better, but, since the *M.G.H.*, *S.S.* is more readily available, I shall cite both.) Villehardouin also mentions that the Venetians held a market for all things needful for horses and men. *Conquête de Constantinople*, sec. 56, I: 58.

13. Villehardouin, *Conquête de Constantinople*, secs. 20–30, I: 22–30. This in-

terpretation satisfactorily reconciles the figure of 94,000 marks given by Villehardouin in describing the offer of the doge and that of 85,000 marks, which appears in the treaty, especially since the difference represents a reduction of two marks per knight. See Queller, "L'évolution du rôle de l'ambassadeur," p. 490, n. 29. Another accurate description of the treaty is given by the fifteenth century Venetian chronicler Lorenzo de Monacis, who seems to have had the document before him. *Chronicon de rebus venetis ab u. c. ad annum MCCCLIV*, ed. Fl. Cornelius (Venice, 1758), p. 134. It is unfortunate that in so prestigious a publication as the *Cambridge Medieval History*, Donald M. Nicol should have Villehardouin (presumably alone) "signing" a treaty for 94,000 marks. "The Fourth Crusade and the Greek and Latin Empires, 1204–1261," *C.M.H.*, IV, pt. 1, ed. J. M. Hussey (Cambridge, 1966), p. 277. Adolf Waas is unreliable concerning the provision for division of conquests. *Geschichte der Kreuzzüge*, 2 vols. (Freiburg, 1956), I: 244. Villehardouin's statement that the date of departure was to be St. John's day (24 June) is one of his few errors of fact, not, of course, very significant. *Conquête de Constantinople*, sec. 30, I: 30. On the mark of Cologne and the mark of Venice see Louise Buenger Robbert, "The Venetian Money Market, 1150–1229," *Studi Veneziani*, XIII (1971): 16.

14. Particularly M. Hellweg, "Die ritterliche Welt in der französichen Geschichtsschreibung des vierten Kreuzzuges," *Romanische Forschungen* LII (1938): 1–40. See also Georges Duby, *The Early Growth of the European Economy: Warriors and Peasants from the Seventh to the Twelfth Century*, trans. from the French 1st ed. of 1973 by Howard B. Clarke (Ithaca, N.Y., 1974), p. 264, on the "simple minded debtors" from the north. On the negative myth of Venice, treating the Venetians as motivated solely by avarice, see Gina Fasoli, "Nascita di un mito," *Studi storici in onore di Giacchino Volpe* (Florence, 1958), vol. I, especially p. 449. Fasoli concedes that the chroniclers prior to Martino da Canale do not show any real Venetian interest in the conquest of the Holy Land for religious ends. Ibid., 462–63. Unlike most historians, I believe that the Venetians on the Fourth Crusade had religious motives as strong as most other crusaders. See Queller and Day, "Some Arguments in Defense of the Venetians on the Fourth Crusade," pp. 719–20.

15. The respect given to Villehardouin for his diplomatic skill can be inferred from the many missions assigned to him by the French nobility. For a list of these assignments, see Queller, "L'évolution du rôle de l'ambassadeur," p. 482, n. 11.

16. Grossman, *Financing of the Crusades*, p. 17.

17. *Codice diplomatico della repubblica di Genova*, ed. Cesare di Imperiale, Font. stor. Italia, LXXIX: 264–6, doc. 191. Grossman, *Financing of the Crusades*, pp. 17–18.

18. Above, chap. 1, n. 71.

19. Villehardouin, *Conquête de Constantinople*, sec. 76, I: 76. Robert of Clari, *Conquête*, sec. 10, p. 9, and sec. 13, p. 13.

20. C. Manfroni, *Storia della marina italiana dalle invasioni barbariche alla caduta di Costantinopoli* (Livorno, 1899), I: 313. The author emphatically accuses

those who believe the contract extortionate of ignorance of such affairs. Where Manfroni gets 900 horses rather than 4,500 escapes me, but the correct figure would strengthen his argument.

21. This conclusion is the one generally accepted by historians who have studied the medieval Venetian constitution. Roberto Cessi, "Venice on the Eve of the Fourth Crusade," *CMH*, vol. IV, pt. 1, p. 272; also Charles Diehl, *Une république patricienne: Venise* (Paris, 1915), pp. 85–88 and 107. For a rather full treatment of the Venetian constitution during this period, and indeed the latest treatment, see Frederic C. Lane, *Venice: A Maritime Republic* (Baltimore, 1973), pp. 82–101.

22. Cessi, who knew far more about Venetian institutions than any of Villehardouin's critics, says that Villehardouin described the procedure absolutely accurately. "Venezia e la quarta crociata," pp. 10–11 and n. 4. Another example of the chronicler's remarkable precision.

23. It was diplomatic to say it, but it was not true. The envoys themselves had chosen Venice, as we have seen. Queller, "L'évolution du rôle de l'ambassadeur," p. 487 and n. 19.

24 Villehardouin, *Conquête de Constantinople*, secs. 25–29, I: 26–30.

25. There is a problem of dating that has not been satisfactorily resolved. Villehardouin says that the treaty was redacted on the day following the assembly at St. Mark's and that it was still Lent. *Conquête de Constantinople*, sec. 30, I: 30. The treaty is actually dated in April. Easter was 25 March. For attempted reconciliations, see C. Klimke, *Die Quellen zur Geschichte des vierten Kreuzzuges* (Breslau, 1877), p. 83, n. 2., and Faral in Villehardouin, *Conquête de Constantinople*, I: 219. Contra, see Colin Morris, "Geoffrey of Villehardouin and the Conquest of Constantinople," *History* LIII (1968): 30–31.

Villehardouin, *Conquête de Constantinople*, sec. 31, I: 32. Tafel and Thomas, *Urkunden*, nos. 89–91, I: 358–62. For the use of blank parchments, see Queller, "Diplomatic 'Blanks' in the Thirteenth Century," *English Historical Review* LXXX (1965): 477–80.

27. Villehardouin, *Conquête de Constantinople*, sec. 30, I: 30. Carl Hopf believed that Egypt was selected by the barons at Compiègne, but it appears to have been left to the envoys. *Geschichte Griechenlands* in *Encylopädie*, ed. J. S. Ersch and J. G. Gruber, LXXXV–LXXXVI (Leipzig, 1867), p. 186. More recently Nicol, "The Fourth Crusade and the Greek and Latin Empires," pp. 276–77, holds that the barons determined upon Egypt. Gunther of Pairis does not really state that Innocent III selected Egypt as the goal of the Crusade. Tessier, *Quatrième Croisade*, pp. 51–56, has read the passage out of context. Also Adolf Schaube, *Handelsgeschichte der romanischen Völker des Mittelmeergebiets bis zum Ende der Kreuzzüge* (Munich and Berlin, 1906), p. 258. The *Gesta Innocentii*, sec. 83, col. 131, followed by a few modern authors, asserts that part of the force was to go to Syria and part to Egypt. Alberic of Trois-Fontaines' use of "Constantinopolim" must be a *lapsus* for Egypt or Cairo, because he only later tells how Alexius sent letters to the crusaders asking their aid. *Chronica*, ed. P. Scheffer-Boichorst, *M.G.H., SS.*, XXIII: 880. Cessi's argument, "L'eredità di Enrico Dandolo," p. 2 and n. 2, that the intended place of debarkation was Palestine, that there was no

agreement to go to Egypt, and that Villehardouin had merely voiced privately to the doge a personal opinion on the subject of Egypt is not supported by the evidence. For identification of "Babilloine" with Cairo, see Robert of Clari, *The Conquest of Constantinople*, p. 36, n. 15.

28. Joshua Prawer, in Marino Sanudo (Torsello), *Liber secretorum fidelium crucis super Terrae Sanctae recuperatione et conservatione* (Hanover ed. of 1611; reprinted Toronto and Buffalo, 1972), p. viii; William of Tyre, *Historia rerum in partibus transmarinis gestarum a tempore successorum Mahumeth usque ad annum Domini MCLXXXIV*, in *Rec. hist. crois.: historiens occidentaux*, vol. I, pt. 2, pp. 890–94, 902–13, 948–58, 962–69, 971–79; Runciman, *History of the Crusades*, II: 436–37. Runciman dates Renaud's expedition in 1182, although other authorities give 1183. Hamilton A. R. Gibb, "The Rise of Saladin," *History of the Crusades*, ed. Setton, I: 582; Joshua Prawer, *The Crusaders' Kingdom: European Colonialism in the Middle Ages* (New York, 1972), p. 28.

29. This argument is advanced by J. J. Saunders, *Aspects of the Crusades* (Christchurch, New Zealand), 1962, p. 28.

30. Gunther of Pairis, *Historia Constantinopolitana*, ed. Paul Riant, *Exuviae*, I: 70–71. Tessier, *Quatrième Croisade*, p. 48, argues against Gunther that a country desolated by famine would offer scanty resources to invaders. See also on the famine Shaul Shaked, *A Tentative Bibliography of Geniza Documents* (Paris, 1964 [Mosseri Coll., no. 22]), p. 27. It was followed by a terrible plague. Eliahu Ashtor, *A Social and Economic History of the Near East in the Middle Ages* (Berkeley-Los Angeles-London, 1976), p. 238.

31. Gunther, *Historia Constantinopolitana*, p. 70.

32. Ernoul-Bernard, *Chronique*, pp. 340–341.

33. Tessier, *Quatrième Croisade*, pp. 48–51. Otto of Saint Blaise, *Chronicon*, p. 327. In fairness to the Latins of the Levant, however, it should be borne in mind that the martial zeal of newly arrived Westerners often jeopardized the precarious kingdom.

34. Alphandéry, *La Chrétienté et l'idée de croisade*, I: 156–57.

35. Queller, "L'évolution du rôle de l'ambassadeur," p. 495 and n. 47, for the bibliography on the secrecy concerning the Egyptian destination. Walter Norden offers the strange hypothesis that the Venetians intended to divert the crusade from Egypt to Syria. *Der vierte Kreuzzug in Rahmen der Beziehungen des Abendlandes zu Byzanz* (Berlin, 1898), pp. 86–87. See also Ludwig Streit, *Venedig und die Wendung des vierten Kreuzzugs gegen Konstantinopel* (Anklam, 1877), p. 29.

36. Villehardouin, *Conquête de Constantinople*, sec. 32, I: 32. See especially n. 5 for a brief discussion of the amount borrowed.

37. Queller, "Diplomatic "Blanks'," p. 479.

38. Tafel and Thomas, *Urkunden*, I: p. 366; Villehardouin, *Conquête de Constantinople*, sec. 32, I: 32.

39. *La Conquête*, sec. 7, p. 8, and sec. 11, pp. 9–10. The first citation is in that portion of the account prior to his own arrival in Venice, which is filled with errors. The second, though, occurs when the doge attempted to get the money owed the Venetians by the crusaders. There is, however, documentary evidence of a voyage to the Levant by the *Paradiso*, one of the great roundships which went on

the crusade. *Documenti del commercio veneziano nei secoli XI–XIII,* ed. by Raimondo Morozzo della Rocca and Antonino Lombardo, 2 vols. (Turin, 1940), I: no. 461, pp. 451–52; *Nuovi documenti del commercio veneto dei secoli XI–XIII,* ed. Raimondo Morozzo della Rocca and Antonino Lombardo, in Monumenti storici della Deputazione di Storia Patria per le Venezie, n.s. vol. VII (Venice, 1953), nos. 53–54, pp. 59–61. (Dr. Louise Buenger Robbert has called these to my attention.) I find it difficult to explain the three commercial documents if Robert of Clari is literally correct. Perhaps the fact that the *Paradiso* had made its voyage and returned to Venice in time for the sailing of the crusading fleets offers the key to a reconciliation of the sources.

Such a cancellation of trade was not without precedent. In 1162 and 1163 Genoa called off all commerce with the Levant in preparation for an attack in alliance with Frederick Barbarossa against Norman Sicily. When the emperor backed out, the Genoese directed the fleet against Sardinia, but were defeated. A revolution in Genoa resulted. Yves Renouard, *Les hommes d'affaires italiens au moyen âge* (1st ed., 1949), revised according to the author's notes by Bernard Guillemain (Paris, 1968), pp. 68–69. More to the present point, when Venice was preparing for the Third Crusade, the doge in November 1188 ordered all Venetians from various parts of the world to return to Venice by next Easter *pro eminenciori Terre Sancte subsidio,* Tafel and Thomas, *Urkunden,* I: 204–6; Andrea Dandulo, *Chronica,* ed. E. Pastorello, in *R.I.S.*[2], XII, i. 270. In 1215 the Fourth Lateran Concil attempted to cancel trade for four years to ensure sufficient shipping for the Fifth Crusade. Mayer, *Crusades,* p. 208.

40. Louise Buenger Robbert, "Reorganization of the Venetian Coinage by Doge Enrico Dandolo," *Speculum* XLIX (1974): 52. I believe, however, that in following Martino da Canale she has wrongly given the year 1202, rather than 1201. Donald E. Queller, "A Note on the Reorganization of the Venetian Coinage by Doge Enrico Dandolo," *Rivista italiana di numismatica e scienze affini* (1975): pp. 167–72.

41. *Below,* p. 58.

42. *Conquête de Constantinople,* sec. 56, I: 58.

43. The calculation is based on the assumption that they employed only the ships that were needed for the crusaders actually on hand. It is true, however, that the crusaders remained obligated to pay for the full number prepared for 33,500 crusaders. Even a fleet of two hundred ships, however, would have been a very considerable one. Not all the vessels had to be newly built, of course. Still, even after the building of the new arsenal in the fourteenth century the construction of twenty light galleys in a six month period was a rare accomplishment under pressure of extreme urgency. Frederick C. Lane, *Venetian Ships and Shipbuilders of the Renaissance* (Baltimore, 1934), pp. 132–33 and 135. Professor Lane has suggested to me that Villehardouin's "three times" may be the impressionistic guess of a landlubber, and this must be admitted, although our chronicler was not a man who used numbers carelessly.

44. *Venice,* p. 36. See Robert of Clari, *La Conquête,* sec. 11, pp. 9–10. It is not clear to me whether Lane is following Robert of Clari or arriving independently

at the same conclusion through estimations of the number of men required and the total able-bodied male population.

45. Hans Jahn, *Die Heereszahlen in den Kreuzzügen* (Berlin, 1907), p. 40. Lane, *Venice*, p. 37. Lane reminds us that Philip Augustus contracted with the Genoese, prior to his departure on the Third Crusade, to transport an army of only 650 knights and 1,300 squires. Again, in Philip's most crucial battle, Bouvines, ten years after the conquest of Constantinople, the French king mustered no more than 7,000 to 12,000 men. Similarly, Lane informs us that the 85,000 mark price for shipment amounted to nearly double the yearly income of either the king of England or the king of France. Similar opinions are expressed by Lot, *L'art militaire*, I: p. 174.

46. This view is especially expounded by Albert Pauphilet, "Robert de Clari et Villehardouin," *Mélanges de linguistique et de litterature offerts à M. Alfred Jeanroy* (Paris, 1928), pp. 562, 564.

47. Faral, "Introduction," Villehardouin, *Conquête de Constantinople*, I: xiv–xvi. C. Klimke, *Quellen*, p. 4, believed that he used a diary from 1201 on.

48. Jean Dufournet, *Les Ecrivains de la Quatrième Croisade: Villehardouin et Clari*, 2 vols. (Paris, 1973), I: 202–203. This contains an extensive and judicious evaluation of Villehardouin. The author believes that he does conceal many things, but does not go to the extreme of labeling Villehardouin an "official" historian, who is covering up a plot. See also Vriens, "De kwestie van den vierden kruistocht," p. 82.

49. Queller, "Innocent III and the Crusader-Venetian Treaty of 1201," pp. 31–34.

50. *Conquête de Constantinople*, sec. 31, I: 32.

51. *Gesta Innocenti*, chap. 83, col. cxxxi.

52. For the controversy see Queller, "Innocent III and the Crusader-Venetian Treaty of 1201," p. 32, n. 8.

53. *Epistolae*, VII: 18, in Migne, *PL*, CCXIV.

54. This is the argument of my "Innocent III and the Crusader-Venetian Treaty of 1201." When I wrote this I had not yet seen John, "The Preliminaries of the Fourth Crusade," pp. 101–3, containing a similar argument. I apologize for failing to recognize his contribution.

Chapter 3

1. Villehardouin, *Conquête de Constantinople*, sec. 32, I: 32–34. Robert of Clari, *Conquête*, sec. 6, p. 8. Once more Robert, who has them accompanied by a Venetian patrician, cannot be relied upon for details until his own arrival in Venice. Ernoul-Bernard also has Venetian envoys accompanying the crusading envoys back to France. *Chronique*, pp. 338–40.

2. Villehardouin makes no mention of a visit to Boniface, but the *Chronique de Morée*, sec. 18, p. 7, states that such a meeting did take place. The visit is also related in the *Chronique de la conquête de Constantinople*, pp. 36–37. These sources are, I know, weak reeds upon which to rely, but the visit does seem probable.

3. Villehardouin, *Conquête de Constantinople*, sec. 41, I: 42. Emile Bouchet, "Notices," in Villehardouin,*Conquête de Constantinople*, II, 25; Carl Hopf, *Bonifaz*

von Montferrat und der Troubadour Rambaut von Vaqueiras, ed. Ludwig Streit (Berlin, 1877), pp. 24–25; and Longnon, *Recherches,* p. 72, accept the visit as probable.

4. Ernoul-Bernard, *Chronique,* pp. 329–30. The latest, and indeed, a very comprehensive synthesis of the papal-Hohenstaufen struggle during Frederick II's minority can be found in Thomas C. Van Cleve, *The Emperor Frederick II of Hohenstaufen: Immutator Mundi* (Oxford, 1972), pp. 38–57.

5. Strayer, "The Political Crusades," p. 347.

6. Villehardouin, *Conquête de Constantinople,* sec. 34, I: 34.

7. Innocent also gave permission to King Imre of Hungary to leave twelve crusaders in Hungary to protect the kingdom. Innocent III, "Rubrice Registri," vol. IV, no. 109, p. 58. James Ross Sweeney has misread *duodecim* as "twenty." *Papal-Hungarian Relations during the Pontificate of Innocent III, 1198–1216,* (Ph.D. diss., Cornel Univ., 1971), p. 58.

8. Villehardouin, *Conquête de Constantinople,* sec. 33, I: 34.

9. Omer Englebert, *St. Francis of Assisi,* trans. from the 2d French ed. by Eve-Marie Cooper, 2d Eng. ed. revised and augmented by Ignatius Brady and Raphael Brown (Chicago, 1965), p. 64.

10. Ibid.

11. Van Cleve, *Frederick II,* pp. 50–51.

12. I believe that Roscher underestimates the significance of the Apulian expedition for the Fourth Crusade. *Papst Innocenz III,* p. 91. It is the first manifestation of that fragmentation of the crusading host which made it impossible for the crusaders to fulfill their contract with Venice. Villehardouin does not criticize Walter, as he does others who failed to join the army at Venice, perhaps because Walter was the chronicler's lord for the fief of Villehardouin. Jean Longnon, *L'Empire latin de Constantinpole* (Paris, 1949), p. 27; Dufournet, *Villehardouin et Clari,* II: 316.

13. Thibaut's war chest had been filled in part by extortions from the Jews of his territory. Grossman, *Financing of the Crusades,* p. 96.

14. Villehardouin, *Conquête de Constantinople,* secs. 32–37, I: 32–38.

15. "Damna redempturus Crucis et patriam Crucifixi
    Struxerat expensis, milite, classe, viam
    Terrenam quaerens, caelestam reperit urbem
    Dum procul haec potitur, obviat ille domi."

Quoted by Hurter, *Papa Innocenzo III,* II: 100, n. 224. A more complete version in Arbois de Jubainville, *Histoire des ducs et des comtes de Champagne,* IV: 96.

16. Robert of Clari, *Conquête,* sec. 2, p. 4.

17. Ernoul-Bernard, *Chronique,* pp. 339–40.

18. Contrary to Nicol, "The Fourth Crusade and the Greek and Latin Empires," p. 276.

19. Tafel and Thomas, *Urkunden,* I: 362. In the Venetian *Liber Albus* and *Liber Pactorum* the oaths of the envoys are also given in that order. Ibid., I: 358–62. See also the pope's letter listing the counts of Flanders, Champagne, and Blois. Innocent III, *The Letters of Pope Innocent III (1198–1216) concerning England and Wales,* ed. C. R. Cheney and Mary G. Cheney (Oxford, 1967), p. 52, n.

318; Roger of Hoveden, *Chronica*, ed. William Stubbs, 4 vols., *Rer. Brit. M.A. Script.* vol. LI (London, 1868–71), iv: 166; Potthast, *Regestum pontificum romanorum*, 2 vols., Berlin, 1874–1875, vol. I, no. 1346.

20. Villehardouin, *Conquête de Constantinople*, sec. 38, I: 38–40.

21. Ibid., sec. 43, I: 44.

22. See my note, "L'évolution du rôle de l'ambassadeur," p. 499, n. 63. I am no longer, however, as inclined as I was toward placing the meeting at Corbie after the death of Thibaut, though I do not exclude it as a distinct possibility. Tessier, after examining the evidence, doubts that Thibaut was ever named official leader of the crusade. *Quatrième Croisade*, pp. 76–77.

23. Tafel and Thomas, *Urkunden*, I: 367.

24. Villehardouin, *Conquête de Constantinople*, sec. 39, I: 40. The duke of Burgundy possibly refused because of the poor financial condition of the duchy, dating back to the administration of his predecessor, Hugh III. Grossman, *Financing of the Crusades*, p. 11.

25. Villehardouin, *Conquête de Constantinople*, sec. 41, I: 42.

26. McNeal and Wolff, "The Fourth Crusade," p. 164.

27. Villehardouin, *Conquête de Constantinople*, sec. 42, I: 42.

28. According to the terms of the Treaty of Peronne, Baldwin received a strip of territory from Philip containing the thriving communes of St. Omer and Aire and Baldwin was also to receive the rest of Artois, the dowry of Philip's first wife, Baldwin's sister, in case the French king's son should die without heirs. Powicke, "Philip Augustus and Louis VIII," pp. 315–316.

29. Below, p. 24.

30. Mundo Lo, *Crusados en Bizancio*, p. 120.

31. Joseph Linskill, "Introduction," Raimbaut de Vaqueiras, *The Poems of The Troubadour Raimbaut de Vaqueiras* (The Hague, 1964), pp. 9–10, 14.

32. Usseglio, *I marchesi di Monferrato*, II: 169–70.

33. Villehardouin, *Conquête de Constantinople*, sec. 498–499, II: 312–14.

34. Raimbaut de Vaqueiras, *Poems*, p. 312, and "Introduction," pp. 8–9 and 18.

35. David Brader, *Bonifaz von Montferrat bis zum Antritt der Kreuzfahrt* (Berlin, 1907), pp. 171–72; Rousset, *Histoire des croisades*, p. 208.

36. *Gesta Innocentii*, ch. 83, col. 132.

37. Louis Bréhier believes that many crusaders who had sided with Richard against Philip took the cross out of fear of reprisals, so that they would scarcely consult him concerning the leadership. *L'Eglise et l'Orient au moyen âge* (1st ed., 1906; 6th ed., Paris, 1928), p. 151. Tessier, however, points out the appropriateness of seeking royal counsel. *Quatrième Croisade, pp. 79–80.*

38. Tafel and Thomas, *Urkunden*, I: 367.

39. Below, p. 27–28.

40. Brader, *Bonifaz von Montferrat*, p. 20.

41. Ibid., p. 89.

42. Ibid., pp. 97–102.

43. *Chronica regis Coloniensis (Annales maximi Colonienses)*, ed. Georgius Waitz, *M.G.H., Script. rer. Germ.* XXX (1880): 168–69.

44. Usseglio, *I marchesi di Monferrato*, I: 170; Brader, *Bonifaz von Montferrat*, p. 157.

45. Usseglio, *I marchesi di Monferrato*, I: 148; II: 57–59.

46. Thomas Sherrer Ross Boase, *Kingdoms and Strongholds of the Crusaders* (London, 1971), p. 123.

47. Ibid., p. 128.

48. Tessier, *Quatrième Croisade*, pp. 81–82.

49. James A. Brundage, *Richard Lion Heart* (New York, 1974), pp. 159–60. A new candidate, Count Henry of Champagne, Thibaut's brother, has recently been added to the list of those suspected of complicity in the murder. The list also includes Richard of England, Saladin, Guy of Lusignan, Humphrey of Toron, and, of course, Sinan, the Grand Master of the Assassins. Patrick A. Williams, "The Assassination of Conrad of Montferrat: Another Suspect," *Traditio* XXVI (1970): 381–88.

50. Charles M. Brand. *Byzantium Confronts the West, 1180–1204* (Cambridge, Mass., 1968), pp. 18–19.

51. Or perhaps his name was Otto. See Usseglio, *I marchesi di Monferrato*, I: 161.

52. Robert Lee Wolff believes that this account is more plausible than has sometimes been supposed. "Greeks and Latins before and after 1204," *Ricerche di storia religiosa*, I (1957): 324. See also Paolo Lamma, *Comneni e Staufer: Ricerche sui rapporti fra Bisanzio e l'Occidente nel secolo XII*, 2 vols. (Rome, 1955–57), I: 302.

53. Usseglio, *I marchesi di Monferrato*, I: 151–57; II: 59–63; Lamma, *Comneni e Staufer*, I: 301–2; Brand, *Byzantium Confronts the West*, pp. 34–37.

54. Brader, *Bonifaz von Montferrat*, pp. 27, 182–84.

55. Usseglio, *I marchesi di Monferrato*, II: 80–82; Brand, *Byzantium Confronts the West*, pp. 80–84; Francesco Cognasso, "Un imperatore bizantino della decadenza: Isaaco II Angelo," *Bessarione* XXXI (1915): 48–50; Nada Patrone, *La quarta crociata*, p. 70.

56. Villehardouin, *Conquête de Constantinople*, sec. 42, I: 42; Robert of Clari, *Conquête*, sec. 3, pp. 4–5. It is the *Chronicle of Morea*, pp. 74–75, which gives the place, "Lans" in the French version, "Lantza" or "Latza" in the Greek. Usseglio identified it as Castagnola delle Lanze. *I marchesi di Monferrato*, II: 179–82.

57. Villehardouin, *Conquête de Constantinople*, sec. 43, I: 42–44; Brader, *Bonifaz von Montferrat*, p. 171; Cognasso, *Storia delle crociate*, p. 707; Robert of Clari, *Conquête*, secs. 3–4, pp. 5–6.

58. J. Folda, "The Fourth Crusade, 1201–1204: Some Reconsiderations," *Byzantino-Slavica* XXVI (1965): 277–78; Innocent III, *Regestum Innocentii III papae super negotio Romani imperii*, ed. Friedrich Kempf (Rome, 1947), no. 63, pp. 175–76; also in Migne, *PL*, CCXVI: 1068.

59. Villehardouin, *Conquête de Constantinople*, sec. 43, I: 42–44; *Devastatio Constantinopolitana*, in *M.G.H., SS.*, XVI: 10 (Hopf ed., p. 86). Robert of Clari *Conquête*, secs. 3–4, pp. 5–6; Brader, *Bonifaz von Montferrat*, p. 171; Cognasso, *Storia delle crociate*, p. 707.

60. Treason theorists dwell upon the familial connections of the house of

Montferrat in Byzantium. It should be remembered that they had equally strong connections and claims in Palestine. Boniface, the brother of William Longsword, was the uncle of the late boy-king Baldwin V. He was also brother to Conrad, who had married the heiress of the kingdom, Isabelle. Their daughter, Baldwin's niece, conveyed the kingdom to her husband, John of Brienne, and the daughter of this marriage in turn brought it to Frederick II. For genealogies, see Runciman, *History of the Crusades*, vol. ii, Appendix III, and vol. iii, Appendix III.

61. Villehardouin, *Conquête de Constantinople*, sec. 43, i: 44, and p. 45, n. 2.

62. Ibid., sec. 44, i: 44. The *Gesta* of Innocent III seems to say that Boniface had earlier taken the cross, perhaps in 1200, but the chronology is not clear ("Misit ergo praefatum Sofridum, presbyterum cardinalem, ad ducum et populum Venetorum; ad cuius exhortationem ipse dux et multi de populo crucis characterem assumpserunt. Marchio quoque Montisferrati; episcopus Cremonensis, et abbas de Lucedio, multique alii nobiles de provincia Lombardiae." *Gesta Innocentii*, ch. 46, col 90). Villehardouin's eyewitness and circumstantial account should be preferred. In both accounts Abbot Peter of Locedio receives the cross along with the marquis.

63. Villehardouin, *Conquête de Constantinople*, sec. 45, i: 46; Elizabeth A. R. Brown, "The Cistercians in the Latin Empire," p. 65, n. 12a.

64. Brown, "The Cistercians in the Latin Empire," pp. 64, 70–72. The Cistercians' crusading zeal was probably dampened at first by Innocent's attempted imposition of a tax on the order for the crusade. However, by the time of the order's Chapter General meeting in 1201, a compromise had been arranged between the monks and Pope Innocent. *Above*, p. 156, n. 6. For the problem of monks going on crusade, see James A. Brundage, "A Transformed Angel (x. 3.31.18): the Problem of the Crusading Monk," *Studies in Medieval Cistercian History Presented to Jeremiah F. O'Sullivan* (Spencer, Mass., 1971), pp. 55–62, and especially pp. 57–59 on the liberalizing policy of Innocent III.

65. Ralph of Coggeshall, *Chronicon Anglicanum*, in *Rer. Brit. M.A. script.*, lxvi: 130; Alphandéry, *La Chrétienté*, ii: 62.

66. Villehardouin, *Conquête de Constantinople*, sec. 45, i: 46, listing some of those who took the cross.

67. Brown, "The Cistercians in the Latin Empire," p. 67; Alphandéry, *La Chrétienté*, ii: 62.

68. Brown, "The Cistercians in the Latin Empire," p. 68; Usseglio, *I marchesi di Monferrato*, ii: 183; Brader, *Bonifaz von Montferrat*, p. 172.

69. Robert of Clari, *Conquête*, sec. 17, p. 16; *Gesta Innocentii*, ch. 83, col. 132; Riant, "Innocent III," p. 349; Usseglio, *I marchesi di Monferrato*, ii: 183. Villehardouin does not mention the visit to Hagenau, an important omission to those who doubt his veracity.

70. Robert of Clari, *Conquête*, sec. 17, p. 16; *Gesta Innocentii*, ch. 83, col. 132. There has been much scholarly debate about the date of young Alexius's arrival in the West. Defenders of Villehardouin and the theory of accidents have argued for the summer of 1202, while treason theorists have presented a date in 1201 to allow time for the hatching of a conspiracy. I think that the controversy has been settled by Folda and Brand, who have firmly established his arrival in the fall of

1201. Folda, "The Fourth Crusade," pp. 279–86; Brand, *Byzantium Confronts the West*, pp. 275–76. Folda also succeeds, however, in preserving the integrity of Villehardouin. The arrival in 1201 does not necessarily support the theory of conspiracy. Folda, "The Fourth Crusade," pp. 289–90.

71. Folda, "The Fourth Crusade," p. 285. Later Venetian chroniclers agree that Alexius was twelve years old in 1195 when his uncle, Alexius III, deposed the boy's father, Isaac II, and imprisoned them both. Dandolo, *Chronica*, p. 274; Marcantonio Sabellico, *Rerum venetarum ab urbe condita libri XXIII* (Venice, 1718), p. 172; Gian Giacopo Caroldo, *Historia di Venetia*, Biblioteca Marciana, cl. ital., vol. VII, cod. 127 (= 8034), 66r. (The chronicle attributed to Pietro Giustinian confuses the Venetian tradition, making Alexius twelve years old at the time of his flight to the West. *Venetiarum historia vulgo Petro Iustianiano Iustianiani filio adiudicata*, ed. Roberto Cessi and Fanny Bennato, in Deputazione di Storia Patria per le Venezie [Venice, 1964], p. 136.) Nicephorus Chrysoberges declared in his oration honoring Alexius, 6 Jan. 1204: "manhood has not altogether altered the boy, nor, measured by very long years, has it marked pleasant down upon your cheeks." Charles M. Brand, "A Byzantine Plan for the Fourth Crusade," *Speculum* XLIII (1968): 466. It is probably not helpful in our case, but it should be mentioned that Isidore of Seville (*Etymologiae*, Bk. II, chap. 2, sec. 5, defines *iuventus* as ages twenty-eight to fifty, *adolescens* as fourteen to twenty-eight. Cited by Josiah C. Russell, *Late Ancient and Medieval Population*, Transactions of the American Philosophical Society, N. S., XLVIII, iii (Philadelphia, 1958), p. 33.

72. Nicetas Choniates, *Historia*, ed. Aloysius van Dieten, 2 vols. (Berlin and New York, 1975), I: 448–52.

73. Ibid., p. 536. Trans. George B. Stow, Jr., in *The Latin Conquest of Constantinople*, ed. Donald E. Queller (New York-London-Sidney-Toronto, 1971), p. 83.

74. Ibid., pp. 536–37. There is another story according to which young Alexius was hidden in a barrel with a false bottom. The officers of Alexius III drew the plugs out of the barrels, suspecting that he might be hidden in one, but when they saw water flow, they were deceived. *The Chronicle of Novgorod, 1016–1471*, trans. Robert Michell and Nevill Forbes, Camden Third Series, XXV (London, 1914), p. 44.

75. Nicetas, *Historia*, 537. Trans. A. A. Vasiliev, *History of the Byzantine Empire, 324–1453* (1st Russian ed., 1917–25; 2nd Eng. ed. rev. Oxford and Madison, Wis., 1952), p. 455.

76. On Philip's character, see Ernst Kantorowicz, *Frederick II*, trans. E. O. Lorimer (London, 1931), p. 18.

77. *Chronicle of Novgorod*, p. 44. This belief in the popular acceptance is no more clearly demonstrated than in the incident in which the crusaders at Constantinople, naive to the political realities of Byzantium, paraded Alexius before the city's walls, fully expecting the Greeks to rise to his support and to expel the emperor in the young prince's favor. Villehardouin, *Conquête de Constantinople*, sec. 145–146, I: 146–48; Robert of Clari, *Conquête*, sec. 41, p. 41.

78. Virginia G. Berry, "The Second Crusade," in Setton, *History of the Crusades*, I: 490.

79. Edgar N. Johnson, "The Crusades of Frederick Barbarossa and Henry VI," in Setton, *History of the Crusades*, II: 91–109.

80. Ibid., pp. 118–119; Brand, *Byzantium Confronts the West*, pp. 176–82, 191 and 233.

81. Nicetas, *Historia*, pp. 536–37; Usseglio, *I marchesi di Monferrato*, II: p. 185. There is a little evidence that at an earlier date Philip had been invited by a Greek conspirator to grasp the Byzantine throne himself in the name of his wife. Paul Riant, "Innocent III, Philippe de Souabe et Boniface de Montferrat," *Revue des questions historiques* XVII: 346, with the sources cited in n. 2. Gerd Hagedorn, "Papst Innocenz III. und Byzanz am Vorabend des Vierten Kreuzzugs (1198–1203)," *Ostkirchliche Studien* XXIII (1974): 8–9, with rather stronger overtones of the German treason theory than I am prepared to accept.

82. Riant, "Innocent III," pp. 339–40.

83. E. Winkelmann, *Philipp von Schwaben und Otto IV von Braunschweig*, 2 vols. (Leipzig, 1873–78), I: 52, the first of the German treason theorists.

84. *Gesta Innocentii*, ch. 83, col. 132.

85. Riant, "Innocent III," pp. 352–56; Winkelmann, *Philipp von Schwaben*, I: p. 525.

86. Alphandéry, *La Chrétienté*, II: pp. 76–77.

87. See, for example, the story of the Flemish knight who pursued his own ambitions. Below, p. 76–77.

88. Schmandt, "Fourth Crusade and Just War Theory," p. 192.

89. Folda, "The Fourth Crusade," pp. 285–86.

90. This is the classic argument put forward by Henri Grégoire, "The Question of the Diversion of the Fourth Crusade, or, an Old Controversy Solved by a Latin Adverb," *Byzantion* XV (1941): 165.

91. Innocent III, *Epistolae*, V: 122, in Migne, *PL*, CCXIV: 1123–24.

92. Brand, *Byzantium Confronts the West*, pp. 225–30. Hagedorn points out the papal reluctance since Gregory VII to become involved in the legitimacy of Byzantine emperors. "Papst Innocenz III. und Byzanz," pp. 11–12.

93. *Gesta Innocentii*, ch. 83, cols. 131–132; Winkelmann, *Philipp von Schwaben*, I: 525; Brader, *Bonifaz von Montferrat*, pp. 172–73; Folda, "The Fourth Crusade," p. 286.

94. Brader, *Bonifaz von Montferrat*, pp. 172–73.

95. *Gesta Innocentii*, ch. 83, col. 132.

96. Usseglio, *I marchesi di Monferrato*, II: 192.

Chapter 4

1. Gunther of Pairis, *Historia*, pp. 60–64.

2. These German enlistments support the argument that at least one of the reasons for the journey to Hagenau was to attempt to gain recruits.

3. Cessi, "Venezia e la quarta crociata," pp. 17–18.

4. Hurter, *Storia di Innocenzo III*, II: 44.

5. Even in the crusading songs the praise of knightly heroism is muted by the oppressive melancholy of facing the unknown. Cessi, "Venezia e la quarta crociata," pp. 17–18.

6. Villehardouin, *Conquête de Constantinople*, sec. 46, I: 46–48.
7. Ibid., sec. 47, I: 50; Robert of Clari, *Conquête*, sec. 9, p. 8.
8. "Lai de la dame de Fayel," *Recueil de chants historiques français*, ed. Antoine Le Roux de Lincy, 1ʳᵉ série (Paris, 1841), pp. 105–8.
9. Conon de Béthune, ibid., p. 113; Luchaire, *Innocent III*, IV: 78–79.
10. Usseglio, *I marchesi di Monferrato*, II: 386–87. Raimbaut de Vaqueiras, *Poems*, pp. 31 and 304. Another poet presents a parting crusader who had a different concern:

> I have ta'en the cross, the stern crusader's token:
> To purge my sins to Palestine I fare:
> A lady's heart at parting nigh is broken:
> If e'er again I breathe my native air,
> God grant I find her honor never faltered,
> Then my dearest wish is mine:
> But if her life is altered,
> God grant to me a grave in Palestine.

Jethro Bithell, *The Minnesingers* (London, 1909), p. 31. Conon of Béthune consoles himself with the thought that ladies unfaithful to their crusading lovers can sin only with cowards, because all the good men are overseas. *Recueil de chants historiques français*, p. 114.

11. "His*d*em diebus innumera populorum milia, predicti Fulconis instantia iam annis aliquot per Gallias concitata, Iherololimitana iter arripiunt, tantaque fuit peregrinantium numerositas, ut non solum precedentibus expeditionibus equari potuerit, sed preferri." Robert of Auxerre, *Chronicon*, p. 261.
12. Villehardouin, *Conquête de Constantinople*, sec. 47, I: 50.
13. Theo Luykx. *De graven van Vlaanderen en de kruisvaarten* (Louvain, 1947), p. 171.
14. Usseglio, *I marchesi di Monferrato*, II: 193.
15. Tafel and Thomas, *Urkunden*, I: 366.
16. Villehardouin, *Conquête de Constantinople*, sec. 47, I: 50.
17. *Devastatio Constantinopolitana*, p. 10 (Hopf ed., p. 87).
18. F. de Mély, *La croix des premiers croisades, Exuviae*, III: 21.
19. Rousset, *Histoire des croisades*, p. 203; Vriens, "De kwestie van den vierten kruistocht," p. 52.
20. Villehardouin, *Conquête de Constantinople*, secs. 51–53, I: 54–56; Longnon, *Recherches*, p. 75.
21. Robert of Clari, *Conquête*, sec. 10, p. 9. The island received its medieval name from the church of St. Nicholas, which possessed that saint's relics. Robert of Clari, *Conquest of Constantinople*, trans. McNeal, p. 39, n. 21. Nada Patrone incorrectly identifies Robert's island of St. Nicholas as an isoletta near the Lido. Robert of Clari, *Conquista di Costantinopoli*, p. 134, n. 92.
22. *Devastatio Constantinopolitana*, MGH SS, XVI: 10 (Hopf ed., p. 87).
23. Lane, *Venice*, p. 36. Freddy Thiriet estimates 50,000. *La Romanie vénitienne au moyen âge* (Paris, 1959), p. 66, n. 1.
24. McNeal, *Conquest of Constantinople*, pp. 4–5; Villehardouin, *Conquête de*

Constantinople, sec. 51–53, I: 54–56. Robert and Peter did not leave before May, however, since Robert is a witness to his lord's act in Amiens during that month. Nada Patrone, *La quarta crociata*, p. 13.

25. For example, Robert of Clari places Boniface's election as commander of the crusade before the embassy of Villehardouin to Venice, and he states that the agreement between the crusaders and Venetians included transportation for one hundred thousand infantry rather than twenty thousand at a cost of eighty-seven thousand marks. *Conquête*, sec. 3–4, pp. 4–8. The eighty-seven thousand marks may be explicable, although one should not labor too hard to try to make sense of Robert's figures. He may have heard of the loan of two thousand marks made by the crusader-envoys before they left Venice and added that to the eighty-five thousand, which was probably well-known.

26. Hopf, *Chroniques Greco-Romanes*, p. ix; Nada Patrone, in Roberto di Clari, *Conquista di Costantinopoli*, pp. 26, 63–77. The introduction and the apparatus of this recent Italian translation should be used by any student of Robert of Clari.

27. Robert of Clari, *Conquête*, sec. 7, p. 8; sec. 10, p. 9; Villehardouin, *Conquête de Constantinople*, sec. 56–57, 59, I: 58–60.

28. The Venetians prided themselves on their adherence to their promises. A century later Marino Sanudo (Torsello) gave as the first reason why his projected crusade should be entrusted to the Venetians: "quia Veneta gens ita bene attendit id quod promittit, sicut aliqua gens de mundo." *Liber secretorum fidelium crucis*, bk. 2, pt. 1, chap. 2, p. 35. I do not find this hard to believe of the Venetians, for it is fundamental to bourgeois ethics.

29. "Veneti tam magnificia navigia praeparaverant, ut a longis retro temporibus nedum visus, sed nec auditus fuerit tantus navalium apparatus." *Gesta Innocentii*, chap. 85, col. 138.

30. Above, p. 15, and p. 167, n. 43.

31. Manfroni, *Storia della marina italiana*, I: 314.

32. Villehardouin, *Conquête de Constantinople*, sec. 48–55, 57, I: 50–58; Robert of Clari, *Conquête*, sec. 11, pp. 9–10.

33. Villehardouin, *Conquête de Constantinople*, sec. 49–50, 54–55, I: 52–56; Ernoul-Bernard, *Chronique*, p. 340; Robert of Auxerre, *Chronicon*, p. 261.

34. Villehardouin, *Conquête de Constantinople*, sec. 54, I:56.

35. Ibid., sec. 33, I: 34; Manfroni, *Storia della marina italiana*, I: 314; Above, p. 20.

36. Villehardouin says in sec. 103 that John of Nesle, "chevetaines" of the fleet, Thierry of Flanders, and Nicholas of Mailly sent to Baldwin for instructions. *Conquête de Constantinople*, I: 102–4. In sec. 48, however, he gives all three as "chevetaines." Ibid., I: 50–52.

37. Robert of Auxerre, *Chronicon*, p. 261.

38. *Chronique*, p. 352.

39. Ibid., p. 352; Villehardouin, *Conquête de Constantinople*, sec. 50, I: 52; Hurter, *Papa Innocenzo III*, II: 147.

40. Wailly, "Eclaircissements," in Villehardouin, *Conquête de Constantinople* (3d. ed., Paris, 1882), pp. 30, 458–59; Riant, "Innocent III," pp. 348–49. Contra:

Tessier, *Quatrième Croisade*, p. 65, n. 1.

41. Robert of Clari, *Conquête*, sec. 17, p. 16.

42. Above, pp. 33–34 and 28.

43. Below, pp. 75–76.

44. Schmandt, "Fourth Crusade and Just War Theory," p. 192. See the private adventure pursued by an obscure Flemish knight. *Below*, pp. 75–76.

45. Tafel and Thomas, *Urkunden*, I: 362.

46. Robert of Clari, our source for this assembly, says only that the crusading barons were summoned to a meeting at Corbie. *Conquête*, sec. 8, p. 8.

47. Villehardouin, *Conquête de Constantinople*, sec. 58, I: 60.

48. Heinrich Kretschmayr, *Geschichte von Venedig*, vol. I (1st ed., 1905, reprinted, Gotha, 1964): 282–83; Tessier, *Quatrième Croisade*, p. 68.

49. Villehardouin, *Conquête de Constantinople*, secs. 51–55, I: 54–56.

50. Ibid., secs. 52–53, I: 54–56; sec. 56, I: 58. Cognasso believes that Count Louis was opposed to an already concluded agreement to go to Constantinople. *Storia delle crociate*, p. 716. I do not agree. Nada Patrone is wrong in fixing Hugh's departure only in 1203. Robert of Clari, *Conquista di Costantinopoli*, p. 8, n. 28.

51. Villehardouin, *Conquête de Constantinople*, sec. 54, I: 56.

52. *Ibid.* Alberic of Trois Fontaines, on the contrary, records that Renaud left the army in the company of Simon de Montfort after the fall of Zara. *Chronica*, p. 880. It is possible that Renaud spent the winter in Apulia and there joined the forces of Simon in the spring of 1203.

53. Above, p. 21.

54. Ernoul-Bernard, *Chronique*, pp. 341–43; Hurter, *Papa Innocenzo III*, II: 240; Jean Richard, *Le royaume Latin de Jérusalem* (Paris, 1953), pp. 167–68.

55. *Conquête de Constantinople*, sec. 55, I: 56; sec. 57, I: 58–60; Donald E. Queller, Thomas K. Compton, and Donald A. Campbell, "The Fourth Crusade: The Neglected Majority," *Speculum* XLIX (1974): 441. Faral points out that this is one of several examples of Villehardouin's judging of events in the light of subsequent experience. *Conquête de Constantinople*, pp. xiii–xiv.

56. Vriens, "De kwestie van den vierden kruistocht," pp. 81–82.

57. Ernoul-Bernard, *Chronique*, p. 340.

58. This proportion is close to the unit used in the treaty of 1201 itself, although the precise figures would be one knight, two squires, and 4.4 sergeants. Tafel and Thomas, *Urkunden*, I: 365.

59. Villehardouin, *Conquête de Constantinople*, sec. 56, I: 58. Benjamin Hendrickx has recently examined the question of the number of troops gathered in Venice. "A propos du nombre des troupes de la quatrième croisade et de l'empereur Baudouin I," *Byzantina (Thessalonica)* III (1971): 29–40. He gives a minimum figure of 11,167 (Villehardouin's "one third") and a maximum of 21,750 (p. 34). I see no reason to accept the assumption upon which the latter is based, that one half of the crusaders in Venice paid two marks each of the 83,000 or 85,000 marks owed. Moreover, 21,750 must be a mistake for 21,250 (p. 33). McNeal and Wolff estimate 10,000–12,000. "The Fourth Crusade," pp. 166–67. Robert of Clari says that there were not more than a thousand knights. *Conquête*,

sec. 11, pp. 9–10. We know, however, how unreliable his numbers are. If he is correct, though, in stating that 50,000 marks remained to be paid (ibid., sec. 11, pp. 9–10), which seems reasonable and in line with Villehardouin's statement that less than half had been paid (*Conquête de Constantinople*, sec. 58, i: 60), and if those present had paid at the contracted rate, this would indicate about 13,000 crusaders. I do not have much faith in Antonio Carile's elaborate attempt to quantify the crusading army. "Alle origini dell'impero latino d'Oriente: Analisi quantitativa dell' esercito crociato e repartizione dei feudi," pp. 288–314. See my specific criticisms: Queller, Compton, and Campbell, "The Neglected Majority," pp. 446–447, n. 24.

60. *Devastatio Constantinopolitana*, *M.G.H., SS.*, xvi: 10 (Hopf ed., p. 87). This is the episode misinterpreted as Innocent's selection of Venice as the port to which the crusaders' envoys should go to obtain transportation. Above, p. 7.

61. *Devastatio Constantinopolitana*, *M.G.H., SS.*, xvi: 10 (Hopf ed., p. 87). In April the other legate, Soffredo, cardinal-priest of St. Praxis, had been dispatched to Palestine. Innocent III, *Epistolae*, v: 26, Migne, *PL*, ccxiv: 978.

62. *Devastatio Constantinopolitana*, *M.G.H., SS.*, xvi: 10 (Hopf ed., p. 87). In 1200 Innocent had decided that the indigent should not accompany a crusading army since they created additional problems for the success of the holy mission. Such people were allowed to remit their vows with a money contribution to the Holy Land equivalent to the expenses they would have incurred in the expedition and to any compensation they would have received for their labor. (This is ridiculous, of course: if they had that much money they would not have been a burden to the crusade.) Those who could afford to go on crusade and to contribute positive service to the undertaking, however, were still bound to fulfill their original vow. Lunt, *Financial Relations*, p. 426. Lunt has republished the document, which was incorporated in the *Decretales*, in *Papal Revenues*, ii: 512–14, n. 556.

63. Villehardouin, *Conquête de Constantinople*, sec. 107, i: 108.

64. *Gesta Innocentii*, ch. 84, col. 138.

65. Although Roscher, *Papst Innocenz III*, p. 60, states that there had been no papal legate on the Third Crusade or that of Henry VI, I have been informed by Professor James Brundage that there indeed were legates on both of these expeditions, Ubaldo Lanfranchi, archbishop of Pisa, for the Third Crusade, and an unnamed cleric for Henry VI's crusade. Still, as Professor Brundage points out, neither of these papal officials exercised much influence. Runciman, *Crusades*, III, 31; Sidney Painter, "The Third Crusade: Richard the Lionhearted and Philip Augustus," in Setton, *History of the Crusades*, ii: 66, 69; Johnson, "Crusades of Frederick Barbarossa and Henry VI," p. 119.

66. Gunther of Pairis, *Historia*, pp. 67 and 70. There is some reason, however, to accept Gunther's figure of twelve hundred Germans with reservations, since he uses almost the identical phrase *numero quasi mille ducenti* in a completely different context, but also to end a hexameter line in the verse portion of his prosimetric chronicle. It may derive more from metrical exigencies than numerical facts. Twelve hundred is not, however, an unreasonable figure.

67. Ibid., pp. 60–61. Nada Patrone describes Gunther as "'un' ottima fonte diretta," which is untrue. The account is Abbot Martin's.

68. Gunther of Pairis, *Historia*, pp. 61–64.

69. Ibid., pp. 66–68. I have revised this entire paragraph to take account of criticisms of Gunther's *Historia* made by Francis R. Swietek in a current seminar paper. I have not gone as far as he has in rejecting Gunther's reliability, but his arguments deserve to be taken very seriously.

70. Ibid., p. 70.

71. Villehardouin, *Conquête de Constantinople*, sec. 74, 1: 74; *Gesta episcoporum Halberstadensium*, pp. 116–117. Tessier, *Quatrième Croisade*, p. 151. Bishop Conrad, however, had retained the respect of Innocent III. Helene Tillmann, *Papst Innocenz III* (Bonn, 1954), pp. 253–54.

72. Anonymous of Halberstadt, in *Exuviae*, 1: 10–11, n. 1.

73. *Devastatio Constantinopolitana, M.G.H., SS.*, XVI: 10 (Hopf ed., p. 87); Brader, *Bonifaz von Montferrat*, pp. 177–78.

74. Tessier, *Quatrième Croisade*, pp. 115–16.

75. Villehardouin, *Conquête de Constantinople*, sec. 73, 1: 74.

76. Gutsch, "Fulk of Neuilly," p. 205. Grossman believes that Baldwin of Flanders also received some of the money collected by Fulk. *Financing of the Crusades*, pp. 95–96. The *Devastatio Constantinopolitana* reports that Odo Campaniensis and the castellanus de Colcith received custody of the money. *M.G.H., SS.*, XVI: 10 (Hopf ed., pp. 86–87). These are reasonably identified as Eudes of Champlitte and the castellan of Coucy by M. A. C. de Muschietti and B. S. Díaz-Peyrera, "Devastatio Constantinopolitana: Introducción, traducción y notas," *Anales de historia antigua y medieval*, XV (1970): 171–200.

77. Villehardouin, *Conquête de Constantinople*, sec. 70–72, 1: 70–74.

78. Folda, "The Fourth Crusade," pp. 289–90. Folda's interpretation concerning the arrival of Alexius in the West and Villehardouin's ignorance of his presence there prior to this time has solved a very troublesome problem.

79. Robert of Auxerre, *Chronicon*, pp. 265–66; *Chronicle of Novgorod*, p. 44.

80. Villehardouin, *Conquête de Constantinople*, sec. 72, 1: 72–74.

81. Robert of Clari reports a meeting at Corbie at which 25,000 marks were paid. *Conquête*, sec. 8, p. 8. According to the treaty of Venice, 25,000 marks were due by 1 November 1201. The whole sum should have been paid before the end of April 1201. Tafel and Thomas, *Urkunden*, 1: 366.

82. Above, p. 177, n. 59.

83. Villehardouin, *Conquête de Constantinople*, sec. 57, 1: 58–60; Robert of Clari, *Conquête*, sec. 11, pp. 9–10. Robert further reports that the crusaders agreed that each knight should pay 4 marks, as well as 4 marks for each horse, and each sergeant 2 marks, while nobody should give less than 1 mark. The increase from the charge of 2 marks per knight specified in the treaty may represent an effort to make up for the deficit in numbers, but more likely is just another example of Robert's carelessness with figures. On the burden of Venice, see Manfroni, *Storia della marina italiana*, 1: 315, and Mundo Lo, *Cruzados en Bizancio*, p. 124.

84. *Above*, p. 15.

85. Ernoul-Bernard, *Chronique*, pp. 343–46. Mas Latrie and others accepted it as fact. *Histoire de l'île de Chypre sous le règne des princes de la maison de Lusignan*, 3 vols. (Paris, 1852–61), 1: 161–64. The false identification was by Carl Hopf,

"Geschichte Griechenlands," ɪ: 122. Hopf's identification was demolished by Gabriel Hanotaux, "Les Vénitiens ont ils trahi la Chrétienté en 1202?" *Revue historique* ɪv (1877): 74–102. Runciman's reluctance to discard the false treaty (*Crusades*, III: 113) is surprising, as McNeal and Wolff have pointed out. "The Fourth Crusade," p. 170, n. 44.

86. Villehardouin, *Conquête de Constantinople*, sec. 59, ɪ: 60–62.

87. Ibid., sec. 60, ɪ: 62.

88. Ibid., sec. 61, ɪ: 64.

89. Above, p. 2.

90. *Gesta Innocentii*, ch. 84, col. 132. This letter was written in 1200, as Potthast thought, not in 1201, as McNeal and Wolff have it. See Queller, "Innocent III and the Crusader-Venetian Treaty of 1201," p. 32, n. 7.

91. The financial cost of crusading was enormous for the ordinary pilgrim. The rise of the economy, favoring kings and powerful lords, and the limitation of the number of crusaders by the turn to the voyage by sea, made it feasible for the wealthy, especially kings, to pay for their followers. This is one manifestation of the changing relationships between lords and vassals. Grossman, *Financing of the Crusades*, p. 165.

92. Innocent III, *Epistolae*, ɪɪ: 270, Migne, *PL*, ccxɪv: 831.

93. Some of the money raised by almsgiving was used by Innocent to purchase foodstuffs for the needy in the Holy Land, but in Sicily the cargo was converted back into money which was later distributed in Palestine. Monk, "Papal Financing of the Fourth Crusade," p. 13; Innocent III, *Epistolae*, ɪɪ: 189, Migne, *PL*, 737–38; *Gesta Innocentii*, chap. 46, cols. 89–90.

94. Ernoul-Bernard, *Chronique*, pp. 337–38.

95. C. R. Cheney, "Master Philip the Notary and the Fortieth of 1199," *English Historical Review* Lxɪɪɪ (1948): 346; Monk, "Papal Financing," p. 14.

96. Monk, "Papal Financing," p. 13. Martini failed to understand that the funds raised by the pope were not intended, for the greater part, to finance the crusading army. "Innocenzo III ed il finanziamento delle crociate," p. 319.

97. Robert of Auxerre, *Chronicon*, p. 261.

98. Robert of Clari, *Conquête*, sec. 11, p. 10. McNeal points out (Robert of Clari, *The Conquest of Constantinople*, trans. Edgar Holmes McNeal [1st ed., 1936; reprinted New York, 1966], p. 40, n. 22) that a strict translation of *laissa* would give the opposite sense, i.e., that the doge did cut off their supplies. Confusion of *laissa* and *lassa* elsewhere in the text and Robert's favorable words about the doge at precisely this point, however, lead us to follow McNeal in assuming that *lassa* was intended. Nada Patrone does the same. Roberto di Clari, *Conquista di Costantinopoli*, p. 136.

99. Robert of Auxerre, *Chronicon*, p. 261; Hurter, *Papa Innocenzo III*, ɪɪ: 149.

100. Ernoul-Bernard, *Chronique*, p. 349.

101. Robert of Auxerre, *Chronicon*, p. 261; Ernoul-Bernard, *Chronique*, p. 349; Robert of Clari, *Conquête*, sec. 12, pp. 10–11; Villehardouin, *Conquête de Constantinople*, sec. 61, ɪ: 62; Tafel and Thomas, *Urkunden*, ɪ: 385; Runciman, *Crusades*, ɪɪɪ: 114.

102. Ernoul-Bernard, *Chronique*, p. 349; Robert of Auxerre, *Chronicon*, p. 261; Gunther of Pairis, *Historia*, pp. 71–72.

103. Villehardouin, *Conquête de Constantinople*, sec. 60, I: 62; *Devastatio Constantinopolitana, M.G.H., SS.*, XVI: 10 (Hopf ed., p. 87); Anonymous of Soissons, *De terra Iherosolimitana*, in Riant, *Exuviae*, I: 5–6. Rostang de Cluni wrote of Dalmase de Sercey and his companions: "a Veneticia venenatis dolose recepti sunt, qui transitum eis neque naulo neque alio pretio ex longo tempore concedere voluerant." *Exceptio capitis S. Clementis*, in Paul Riant, *Exuviae*, I: 133.

Chapter 5

1. Robert of Clari, *Conquête*, sec. 12, pp. 10–11.

2. Villehardouin, *Conquête de Constantinople*, secs. 62–63, I: 64–66. Robert of Clari's version reads: ". . .s'il nous veullent rendre ches .xxxvi. m. mars que il nous doivent des premeraines conquestes qu'il feront et qu'il aront a leur partie, que nous les messons outre mer." *Conquête*, sec. XII: p. 11. No mention of Zara.

3. Vitaliano Brunelli, *Storia della città di Zara* (Venice, 1913), p. 361.

4. Vriens, "De kwestie van den vierden kruistocht," p. 69; Alethea Wiel, *The Navy of Venice* (London, 1910), p. 105.

5. Brunelli, *Storia di Zara*, pp. 359–63; Roberto Cessi, *La Repubblica di Venezia e il problema adriatico* (Naples, 1953), pp. 50–51; *Historia ducum Veneticorum, Supplementum*, p. 90; Thomas of Spalato, *Historia Spalatina*, ed. L. de Heinemann, *M.G.H., SS.*, XXIX: 576.

6. Robert of Clari, *Conquête*, secs. 12–14, pp. 11–12. According to the version of Ernoul-Bernard, *Chronique*, pp. 349–50, the crusaders would be quit of the sum owed. Martino da Canale, a Venetian chronicler of the late thirteenth century, states that Dandolo did not reveal to the crusaders his plan to attack Zara until the fleet was there, and he rejected the aid which the crusaders offered. *Les estoires de Venise: Cronaca veneziana in lingua francese dalle origini al 1275*, ed. Alberto Limentani (Florence, 1972), I: sec. xl, p. 48; if unavailable, see the older ed., titled *La Cronique des Veniciens*, ed. by Filippo-Luigi Polidori, Ital. trans. Giovanni Galvani, *Archivio Storico Italiano*, ser. 1, VIII (1845): 322. See also Giorgio Cracco, "Il pensiero storico di fronte ai problemi del commune veneziano," in *La storiografia veneziana fino al secolo VI: Aspetti e problemi*, ed. Agostino Pertusi (Florence, 1970), pp. 54–55.

7. Robert of Clari, *Conquête*, secs. 11–12, pp. 11–12; Villehardouin, *Conquête de Constantinople*, sec. 63, I: 66.

8. Robert of Clari, *Conquête*, secs. 12–13, pp. 11–12.

9. Cessi, on the other hand, attempts to use the same evidence to argue that the crusaders were not to participate in the attack upon Zara, which was strictly a Venetian undertaking. "Venezia e la Quarta Crociata," p. 24, n. 1, and p. 27; "L'eredità di Enrico Dandolo," p. 6, n. 1; "Politica, economia, religione, " p. 453. This interpretation does not make sense to me. Responsible leaders must have recognized that the crusading army could not accompany the Venetians to Zara without becoming involved. If Zara resisted, the crusaders would be compelled to

fight, for the defeat of their Venetian allies would have left them stranded far from their destination and far from home. If Zara submitted, it would also be because the Zarans recognized the inseparability of the fleet and the crusaders. I know of no other scholar who has accepted Cessi's view.

10. Villehardouin, *Conquête de Constantinople*, sec. 63, I: 66.

11. Robert of Clari, *Conquête*, sec. 12, pp. 11–12.

12. Some old manuscripts make it the feast of Saint Mark, 25 April, which is patently impossible. Cessi chooses the feast of the Assumption, 15 July, which I think is still too early. "Venezia e la Quarta Crociata," p. 25, n. 1. Neither of these dates, in fact, fell on a Sunday in 1202. See Villehardouin, *Conquête de Constantinople*, sec. 69, I: 70 and 71, n. 1. and sec. 64, I: 66 and n. 2.

13. Ibid., sec. 65, I: 66–68.

14. Older writers believed that the appointment of the younger Dandolo as vice-doge was contrary to law. E.g., William R. Thayer, *A Short History of Venice* (Boston and New York, 1908), p. 99. Giuseppe Maranini points out that previous doges going to war had left their sons as vice-doges. *La Costituzione di Venezia dalle origini alla Serrata del Maggior Consiglio* (Venice 1927), pp. 180–81. On the supposed Flabianican law of 1032, see ibid., p. 77. Roberto Cessi argues that there was no such law. *Storia della Repubblica di Venezia*, 2 vols. (Milan and Messina, 1944–46), I: 103.

15. Agostino Pertusi considers the crimson headgear in the form of a truncated cone depicted in the mosaic of the south transept of San Marco to be the type worn by the doge in the late twelfth century. "Quedam regalia insignia: ricerche sulle insegne del potere ducale a Venezia durante il medioevo," *Studi Veneziani* VII (1965): pp. 83–84.

16. Villehardouin, *Conquête de Constantinople*, sec. 66, I: 68. The *Gesta Innocentii*, chap. 46, col 90, reports that the doge and many Venetians had already taken the cross in mid-August 1198. Robert of Clari reports a conscription of Venetians to go with the fleet before the doge's demand for payment, the proposal to go to Zara, and the crossing of Dandolo. Pairs of waxed balls were prepared, one of each two containing a summons to service. These were blessed by a priest and drawn by him, giving one ball to each eligible male. Faral believed that this occurred after the taking of the cross, and so he doubts the Venetian zeal to take up the crusaders' burden. Villehardouin, *Conquête de Constantinople*, I: 69, n. 3. I am inclined to adhere to the primary source. Carile estimates that a fleet of this size required a complement of 17,264 men. "Alle origini dell' impero latino d'Oriente," pp. 287–88. Probably overestimated.

17. Villehardouin,*Conquête de Constantinople*, sec. 68, I: 68–70.

18. Gunther of Pairis, *Historia*, 71–72; Tessier, *Quatrième Croisade*, pp. 129–30; Riant, "Innocent III" *Revue des questions historiques* XVII: 363–64, XVIII: 40. Riant, however seems to be confused chronologically, placing these happenings before the arrival of Peter Capuano on 22 July.

19. William M. Daly, "Christian Fraternity, the Crusaders, and the Security of Constantinople, 1097–1204: The Precarious Survival of an Ideal," *Medieval Studies* XXIII (1960): 84.

20. Robert of Clari, *Conquête*, sec. 13, p. 12.

21. Innocent III, *Epistolae*, v: 162, Migne, *PL*, ccxiv: 1180.

22. Ibid., v: 161, Migne, *PL*, ccxiv: 1178-1179. See also, Donald E. Queller, "Innocent III and the Crusader-Venetian Treaty of 1201," *Medievalia et Humanistica* xv (1963): 33-34.

23. Villehardouin, *Conquête de Constantinople*, sec. 50, i: 52-54. The statement is, of course, self-serving and partisan, but nonetheless correct.

24. Gunther of Pairis, *Historia*, pp. 72-73. Gunther says that the cardinal additionally imposed upon Martin responsibility for all the Germans, but, following Swietek (above, p. 179, n. 69), I now believe that this is more Guntherian puffery. Brown argues that Peter of Vaux was among those who received in person the legate's order not to abandon the army. "The Cistercians in the Latin Empire," p. 73, n. 44. I do not think that the passage cited sustains that interpretation. *Gesta episcoporum Halberstadensium*, p. 117. For a summary of views on what the individual should do when confronted with participation in an unjust war, see Schmandt, "Fourth Crusade and Just War Theory," pp. 201-2.

25. *Gesta episcoporum Halberstadensium*, p. 117. Historians who see a well planned conspiracy among Philip of Swabia, young Alexius, and Boniface of Montferrat to divert the crusade to Constantinople need to pay some attention to this episode. The attack upon Zara would certainly have been a favorable preliminary to a subsequent diversion to Constantinople, yet Conrad, a loyal and very prominent supporter of Philip of Swabia, wished to avoid it. This does not, of course, disprove such a conspiracy, but it is a scrap of interesting evidence.

26. In a subsequent letter reproaching the crusaders for the conquest of Zara, Innocent states that Peter had taken care to expose to some of them the papal prohibition against attacking Christians. *Epistolae*, v: 61, Migne, *PL*, ccxiv: 1179. There is no indication of the date of the warning. This may refer to the prohibition sent by the hands of the abbot of Locedio after Peter and Boniface had been to Rome. Below, p. 56.

27. *Gesta Innocentii*, chap. 85, col. 138; Innocent III, *Epistolae*, ix: 139, Migne, *PL*, ccxv: 957.

28. Above, p. 17.

29. Innocent III, *Epistolae*, v: 122, Migne, *PL*, ccxiv: 1124.

30. Cerone, "Il papa e i Veneziani," p. 292. Sara de Mundo Lo is good on this point. *Cruzados en Bizancio*, p. 128.

31. I am following here Riant, "Innocent III," pp. 369-70. Also Hurter, *Papa Innocenzo III*, ii: 157. The argument is based on the *Gesta Innocentii*, chap. 85, col. 139: "et hanc inhibitionem et excommunicationem [Innocentius] fecit eis per abbatem Locedio certius intimari Marchio vero Montisferrati, qui fuerat super hoc a domino papa viva voce prohibitus, se prudenter absentans, non processit cum illis ad Jaderam expugnandam." It certainly is not explicit regarding a journey by Boniface to Rome, but I think it can sustain that interpretation. We also know from Villehardouin that Boniface left Venice at this time to take care of personal business. *Conquête de Constantinople*, sec. 79, i; 80. The argument is not compelling, but represents sound speculation, in my opinion.

32. *Gesta Innocentii*, chap. 85, col. 139. Again, those who believe Boniface instrumental in a secret plot to misdirect the crusade should pay close attention to

the selection of the messenger. Peter of Locedio, who bore the pope's prohibition against attacking Zara, and delivered it in good faith, was well known as the loyal friend and counsellor of the marquis of Montferrat. If Innocent had held Boniface in disgrace for attempting to divert the crusade, surely he would have chosen another envoy.

33. The pope probably did not count Zara as one of his favorite daughters in view of the rampant Bogomile heresy that infected the ruling class of the Dalmatian city. Gary Blumenshine, "Cardinal Peter Capuano, the Letters of Pope Innocent III, and the Diversion of the Fourth Crusade to Zara" (seminar paper, Univ. of Illinois, 1968–69), p. 5. In addition the Hungarian ruler himself was not above reproach in Innocent's eyes, for the king had impiously waged war against Christians after he had taken the cross. James Ross Sweeney, *Papal-Hungarian Relations*, p. 119.

34. In another instance James Ross Sweeney has shown that Innocent's reputation as a mover of events is in need of more modest appraisal. "Innocent III, Hungary, and the Bulgarian Coronation," p. 334.

35. Paul Lemerle, "Byzance et la croisade," in *Relazioni del X Congresso Internazionale di Scienze Storiche* (Florence, 1955) III: 598–99; Lamma, *Comneni e Staufer*, II: 270.

36. Nicetas, *Historia*, pp. 540–41.

37. Steven Runciman, *Byzantine Civilization* (London, 1933), p. 70; Charles Diehl, "The Government and Administration of the Byzantine Empire," *Cambridge Medieval History*, o.s. IV: p. 728; W. Ensslin, "The Government and Administration of the Byzantine Empire," *C.M.H.*, n.s. IV: 5.

38. Although the text of Alexius III's communication with the pope is no longer extant, we can surmise its contents from Innocent's reply of 16 November 1202. *Epistolae*, V: 122, Migne, *PL*, CCXIV: 1123–25.

39. Villehardouin, *Conquête de Constantinople*, sec. 76, I: 76.

40. Tafel and Thomas, *Urkunden*, I: 385–86; Morozzo della Rocca and Lombardo, *Documenti del commercio veneziano*, I: 452, n. 462.

41. Villehardouin, *Conquête de Constantinople*, sec. 76, I: 76; *Devastatio*, *M.G.H.*, *SS.*, XVI: 10 (Hopf ed., p. 87); *Gesta episcoporum Halberstadensium*, p. 117.

42. Tafel and Thomas, *Urkunden*, I: 385–86.

43. Edwin Pears, *The Fall of Constantinople* (London, 1885 and New York, 1886), p. 254 (New York ed.) This interpretation squares with the possibility that the fleet was divided. Below, p. 58.

44. Lot, *L'Art militaire*, I: 174.

45. *Devastatio Constantinopolitana*, *M.G.H.*, *SS.*, XVI: 10 (Hopf ed., p. 87); Hugh of Saint Pol. *Epistola*, in Tafel and Thomas, *Urkunden*, I: 306; Nicetas, *Historia*, p. 539. Antonio Carile's statement that among the thirteenth century sources only the *Devastatio* gives a figure for the size of the fleet is incorrect. "Alle origini dell'impero d'Oriente," pp. 287–88.

46. The transition to the trireme did not occur until about the end of the thirteenth century. Lane, *Venice and Its History*, p. 192, and *Venetian Ships*, p. 9, n. 14.

47. Lane, *Venetian Ships*, pp. 7–9; Manfroni, *Storia della marina italiana*, I, 452–55; McNeal, in Robert of Clari, *Conquête*, pp. 132–33. For a larger estimate of oarsmen and others, see Carile, "Alle origini dell'impero d'Oriente," p. 287, n. 3.

48. Lane, *Venetian Ships*, pp. 7–9; Manfroni, *Storia della marina italiana*, I: 458; Michel Mollat, "Problèmes navals de l'histoire des croisades," *Cahiers de civilization médiévale* X (1967): 352.

49. Robert of Clari, *La Conquête*, sec. 74, p. 73.

50. Mollat, "Problèmes navals," pp. 352–53.

51. Below, p. 141.

52. On the banner and the silver trumpets, see Pertusi, "Quedam regalia insignia," pp. 89–91.

53. Villehardouin, *Conquête de Constantinople*, sec. 75–76, I: 76–78; Robert of Clari, *Conquête*, sec. 13, p. 12–13. Robert was a romantic, of course, but such romanticism played as important a role as calculation in the crusade.

54. *Devastatio Constantinopolitana*, *M.G.H.*, *SS.*, p. 10 (Hopf ed., p. 87); Villehardouin, *Conquête de Constantinople*, sec. 79, I: 80; sec. 315–16, II: 122–24.

55. Villehardouin, *Conquête de Constantinople*, secs. 315–16, II: 122–24.

56. Ibid., sec. 79, I: 80.

57. Above, p. 56.

58. Cessi, *La Repubblica di Venezia e il problema adriatico*, p. 55. Also, above, p. 51.

59. Brunelli, *Storia di Zara*, p. 368; Cessi, "Quarta Crociata," p. 26; Wiel, *Navy of Venice*, p. 133; Robert of Clari, *Conquête*, sec. 13, p. 13. On the obligation to provide men, see Manfroni, *Storia della marina italiana*, 317–18.

60. This is on the assumption that Dandolo sailed on 8 October. If he sailed on 1 October, this would be 2 October. Tafel and Thomas, *Urkunden*, I: 387.

61. Kretschmayr, *Geschichte von Venedig*, pp. 288–89; Dandolo, *Chronica*, pp. 276–77; Tafel and Thomas, *Urkunden*, I: 387–88. This treaty is commonly misdated 5 October, even in the headnote in *Urkunden*, I: 386. This would necessitate an 1 October departure for part of the fleet and would raise disturbing questions about the elapsed time between this treaty and the arrival at Zara. The text reads: "...die quinto exeunte, mense Octubri." (The comma is an error.) This means 27 October. Historians of the period should know the meaning of *exeunte*. They also ought not follow headnotes while ignoring the texts. Sanuto, *Diarii*, VII: 447, summarizes and has the correct date. He says there were thirty-four envoys, while Andrea Dandolo lists thirty-six "et alios quam plures."

62. Tafel and Thomas, *Urkunden*, I: 386–403. Lorenzo de Monacis, *Chronicon*, pp. 134–35, accurately describes the pacts, which he probably had before him. Also see *Historia ducum Veneticorum, Supplementum*, p. 92.

63. Robert of Clari, *Conquête*, sec. 13, p. 13.

64. Manfroni, *Storia della marina italiana*, I: 317–18, and 318, n. 1.

65. Robert of Clari, *Conquête*, sec. 13, p. 13.

66. Riant, "Innocent III," XVII: 369.

67. Robert of Clari, *Conquête*, sec. 13, p. 12.

68. Manfroni, *Storia della marina italiana*, I: 317–18.

69. For a colorful description of the site of Zara, see Brunelli, *Storia di Zara*, pp. 36–37.

70. Robert of Clari, *Conquête*, sec. 14, p. 13; Villehardouin, *Conquête de Constantinople, sec. 77*, I: 78. Faral, in a note to his text of Villehardouin (I: 79, n. 4), says that the *Devastatio* mentions the sinking of a ship named the *Workhorse*. Indeed, Pertz's edition of the *Devastatio* reads: "Iaderam navigaverunt, in qua iumentum periit." "Iumentum" does mean "workhorse," but comparing this passage to one closely preceding, "Viola navis periit," we note that in our questionable passage there is no juxtaposed word, "navis." Again, Pertz undoubtedly did not consider "iumentum" to be the name of a ship, for he left the word uncapitalized. The loss of a horse would have been too insignificant an event for the author of the *Devastatio* to mention. Probably with this objection in mind, Hopf emended Pertz's text to read: "Iaderam navigaverunt, in qua iuramentum periit." The passage is then translated not as, "They sailed to Zara, where the *Workhorse* sank," but rather as, "They sailed to Zara, where their (crusading) oath went for naught."

71. Villehardouin, *Conquête de Constantinople*, sec. 78, I: 78.

72. Ibid., sec. 80, I: 80. Zaran narrative sources name the heads of the delegation, Damiano de Varicassi and Berto de Matafarri. Brunelli, *Storia di Zara*, p. 375, n. 56.

73. Guy of Vaux-de-Cernay was also a promoter of the Albigensian Crusade. His nephew, Peter, who accompanied him on the Fourth Crusade, inserts in his history of the Albigensian Crusade an account of the expedition from the viewpoint of those who interpreted their vows strictly. Peter of Vaux-de-Cernay, *Petri Vallium Sarnaii monachi hystoria Albigensis*, ed. Pascal Guébin and Ernest Lyon, 3 vols. (Paris, 1926–30), I: 106–11.

74. Usseglio calls Simon "più papista del Papa." *I marchesi di Monferrato*, II: 210.

75. Villehardouin, *Conquête de Constantinople*, sec. 81, I: 82.

76. Ibid., sec. 82, I: 82.

77. Ibid., sec. 83, I: 82–84.

78. Peter of Vaux-de-Cernay, *Hystoria Albigensis*, pp. 108–9; *Gesta Innocentii*, cols. 138–39. Robert of Clari says that Zara had secured a letter from Innocent saying that anyone who should attack them would be excommunicated, and they sent this letter to the doge and the pilgrims. *Conquête*, sec. 14, p. 14. This may have been the source of Abbot Guy's denunciation, or it may be a distortion by Robert of the facts as I have seen them, or there may have been two letters, one to the Zarans and one sent via the abbot of Locedio to the host.

79. Villehardouin, *Conquête de Constantinople*, sec. 83, I: 82–84.

80. Peter of Vaux-de-Cernay, *Hystoria Albigensis*, I: 109.

81. Robert of Clari, *La Conquête*, sec. 14, p. 14.

82. Villey, *La Croisade*, p. 142.

83. Villehardouin, *Conquête de Constantinople*, sec. 84, I: 84; Robert of Clari, *Conquête*, sec. 14, p. 14.

84. Robert of Clari, *Conquête*, sec. 14, p. 14; Peter of Vaux-de-Cernay, *Hystoria Albigensis*, I: 108.

85. Brunelli, *Storia di Zara*, p. 368.

86. Innocent III, *Epistolae*, v: 161, Migne, *PL*, ccxiv: 1178.

87. Villehardouin, *Conquête de Constantinople*, sec. 85, i: 84–86; Brunelli, *Storia di Zara*, p. 368.

88. Gunther of Pairis, *Historia*, p. 74.

89. Villehardouin says that the siege occupied five days. *Conquête de Constantinople*, sec. 85, i: 84–86. Gunther of Pairis says three. *Historia Constantinopolitana*, p. 74.

90. Villehardouin, *Conquête de Constantinople*, secs. 85–87, i: 84–88; Thomas of Spalato, *Historia*, p. 576; Robert of Clari, *Conquête*, sec. 117. xiv: 14–15; *Gesta episcoporum Halberstadensium*, p. 117.

91. Gunther of Pairis, *Historia*, p. 74.

92. Innocent III, *Epistolae*, v: 161, Migne, *PL*, ccxiv: 1178.

93. Thomas of Spalato, *Historia*, p. 576.

94. Hurter, *Papa Innocenzo III*, ii: 160–61; Brunelli, *Storia di Zara*, p. 369.

95. Innocent III, *Epistolae*, vii: 203, Migne, *PL*, ccxv: 511–12.

96. Runciman, *Crusades*, iii: 114; Vasiliev, *Byzantine Empire*, p. 454.

97. On Venice's allies, above, p. 54.

Chapter 6

1. Beazley, *Modern Geography*, ii: 410; Vriens, "De kwestie van den vierden kruistocht," p. 71.

2. Villehardouin, *Conquête de Constantinople*, sec. 86, i: 86–88. According to Robert of Clari, Dandolo told the crusaders that they would winter in Zara when he first proposed his plan to the host before leaving Venice. *Conquête*, sec. 13, p. 12.

3. Brunelli, *Storia di Zara*, pp. 36–37.

4. *Devastatio Constantinopolitana, M.G.H., SS*, xvi: 10 (Hopf ed., p. 87).

5. Villehardouin, *Conquête de Constantinople*, sec. 87, i: 88.

6. Blumenshine, "Zara," n. 29; Wiel, *Navy of Venice*, p. 136. I have found no source that says this explicitly, but it seems a probable cause of the fight between Venetians and Crusaders.

7. Villehardouin, *Conquête de Constantinople*, sec. 88–90, i: 88–90; Robert of Clari, *Conquête*, sec. 15, p. 15; *Devastatio Constantinopolitana, M.G.H., SS.*, xvi: 10 (Hopf ed., p. 87).

8. Ernoul-Bernard, *Chronique*, p. 350.

9. Innocent III, *Epistolae*, v: 161 in Migne, *PL*, ccxiv: 1178–79. As for the date of the letter, since it occasioned Bishop Nivelon of Soissons' supplicatory embassy, which probably arrived in Rome no later than mid-February, 1203, it must have been written around the New Year. Tessier, *Quatrième Croisade*, pp. 276–281; Alfred J. Andrea, "Innocent III and the Ban of Excommunication Incurred by the Fourth Crusade Army at Zara" (MS), pp. 9–10, n. 14. Contra: Roscher, *Papst Innocenz III*, p. 107.

10. Andrea, "Innocent III and the Ban of Excommunication," pp. 1–2.

11. Helene Tillmann, *Innocenz III*, p. 225.

12. Villehardouin, *Conquête de Constantinople*, sec. 91, I: 90.

13. Above, p. 10 and n. 12.

14. Robert of Clari, *Conquête*, sec. 17, p. 16. Riant, "Innocent III," *Revue des questions historiques* 364–65. Usseglio believed that this occurred before the army left Venice. *I marchesi di Monferrato*, II: 198, n. 1.

15. *Gesta episcoporum Halberstadensium*, p. 118; Villehardouin, *Conquête de Constantinople*, sec. 91, I: 90–92. Tessier, *Quatrième Croisade*, p. 155, makes a persuasive argument that this was the Hohenstaufen's first attempt to influence the course of the crusade. The German treason theorists, such as Riant, concede that it was the first *open* effort. "Innocent III," XVIII: 5–6.

16. Villehardouin, *Conquête de Constantinople*, sec. 91–94, I: 90–94; The *Devastatio Constantinopolitana* gives the date of the embassy's arrival as 1 January *M.G.H., SS.*, XVI: 10 (Hopf ed., p. 88).

17. Nicetas, *Historia*, pp. 539, 550–51.

18. *Chronicle of Novgorod*, p. 44.

19. Villehardouin, *Conquête de Constantinople*, sec. 72, I: 72–74.

20. Gunther of Pairis, *Historia Constantinopolitana*, pp. 76–77.

21. Riant, "Innocent III" *Revue des questions historiques* XVIII: 17.

22. Only the *Devastatio Constantinopolitana* links Simon with this disaccord *M.G.H., SS.*, XVI: 11 (Hopf ed., p. 87). Villehardouin does not mention his presence in the discussions over Alexius' proposals. Peter of Vaux-de-Cernay, *Historia Albigensis*, I: 110, and Robert of Clari, *Conquête*, sec. 14, p. 14, report that Simon departed in defiance of the army's decision to attack Zara, that is, before the discussions about Constantinople. Since Peter of Vaux-de-Cernay and the *Devastatio* link Simon and Guy of Vaux-de-Cernay together and we know from Villehardouin that the abbot took part in the Constantinopolitan argument, it is quite likely that Peter and Robert have confused the crusader quarrel over Alexius with the earlier one about Zara. Villehardouin, *Conquête de Constantinople*, sec. 95, I: 96, and sec. 97, I: 98.

23. The group was led by Renaud De Montmirail, Villehardouin, *Conquête de Constantinople*, sec. 101, I: 102; Riant, "Innocent III," *Revue des questions historiques* XVIII: 16.

24. Villehardouin, *Conquête de Constantinople*, sec. 97, I: 96–98.

25. Riant, "Innocent III," *Revue des questions historique* XVIII: 14–15. Faral, in support of Villehardouin's denunciation of those who went their own way, pointed out that the abbot of Vaux-de-Cernay, as well as Simon de Montfort, later took part in the Albigensian Crusade against Christians. In Villehardouin, *Conquête de Constantinople*, p. xxii. B. Ebels-Hoving, however, distinguishes the two cases. *Byzantium in Westerse Ogen, 1096–1204* (Assen, 1971), p. 223, n. 540.

26. Brown, "The Cistercians in the Latin Empire," p. 75. We do not know what role, if any, was played by the abbot of Perseigne.

27. Riant, "Innocent III," *Revue des questions historiques* XVIII: 13–14.

28. Villehardouin, *Conquête de Constantinople*, sec. 95, I: 94–96.

29. The church had made definite pronouncements on the subject on inter-

Christian warfare. The 1054 Council of Narbonne announced "Primo ergo ominum institutionum nostrarum, quae in hoc tomo scribenda sunt, monemus Dei, et nostrum, ut nullus Christianorum alium quemlibet Christianum occidit: quia qui Christianum occidit, sine dubio Christi sanquinem fundit." *Sacrorum conciliorum nova et amplissima collectio,* edited by Giovanni Mansi, 53 vols. (Paris, 1901–27), xix: 827. Peter Damian expresses a similar sentiment: "Quomodo ergo pro rerum vilium detrimento fidelis fidelem gladiis impetrat, quem secum utique redemptum Christi sanquine non ignorat?" *Epistolae,* iv: 9, Migne, *PL,* cxliv: 316. Cited by Villey, *La Croisade,* pp. 36–37.

30. Innocent had already pledged his support to Alexius III and had assured the emperor that the papacy considered the young Alexius' claims to the throne to be without foundation. *Epistolae,* v: 122, Migne, *PL,* ccxiv: 1123.

31. Charles Brand, "The Byzantines and Saladin, 1185–1192: Opponents of the Third Crusade," *Speculum* xxxvii (1962), 169–79. *Regesten der Kaiserurkunden des Oströmischen Reichs von 565–1453,* ed. Franz Dölger, 5 vols. (Munich and Berlin, 1924–65), ii, doc. 1591, p. 95.

32. For example, see Gunther of Pairis, *Historia Constantinopolitana,* p. 78. Gunther's estimation of the desires of the pope, of course, is at odds with the arguments of the anti-Hohenstaufen faction.

33. Villehardouin, *Conquête de Constantinople,* sec. 97, i: 96–98.

34. Above, p. 55.

35. Villehardouin, *Conquête de Constantinople,* sec. 96, i: 96. This argument from necessity is the only one put into the mouths of the proponents of the Hohenstaufen proposal by Hugh of St. Pol and Robert of Clari. *Epistola,* in *Annales Coloniensis maximi, M.G.H., SS.,* xvii: 812–14; *Conquête,* sec. 33, p.32. It is probably legitimate to conclude that this was the primary consideration, but that the proponents of the argument grasped at whatever straws they could to buttress their position seems probable, so I have recapitulated the obvious arguments.

36. Longnon, *L'empire Latin de Constantinople,* p. 31; Lodovico Sauli, *Della colonia genovese in Galata* (Turin, 1831), pp. 31–32.

37. Innocent III, *Epistolae,* vi: 211, in Migne, *PL,* ccxv: 238. The letter is from the crusaders to the pope.

38. Riant, "Innocent III," *Revue des questions historiques* xviii: 19–20; Alphandéry, *La Chrétienté,* pp. 81–82; Nicol, "Fourth Crusade," pp. 279–80. Robert of Clari, *Conquête,* sec. 39, p. 40.

39. Bede, *De locis sanctis,* chap. 20, in *Itineraria Hierosolymitana et descriptiones terrae sanctae bellis sacris anteriora,* edited by Titus Tobler and Augustus Molinier (Geneva, 1879), pp. 232–233.

40. Paul Riant, "Les dépouilles religieuses enlevées à Constantinople au XIIIe siècle," *Mémoires de la Société Nationale des Antiquaires de France,* Series 4 VI (1875): 11–12; Nicol, "Fourth Crusade," pp. 279–80. The difficulty with the emphasis put upon relics by Alphandéry and especially Frolow, and by Riant before them, is that it is impossible to prove that the desire for relics was a motive for the taking of Constantinople. There is ample evidence after the fact for the importance of the relics, but the desire to liberate relics is never used as an argument in the debates over the Constantinopolitan venture.

41. Gunther of Pairis, *Historia Constantinopolitana*, p. 78; Hurter, *Papa Innocenzo III*, II: 216, n. 365; Alphandéry, *La Chrétienté et l'idée de croisade*, pp. 88–89; Gerd Hagedorn, "Papst Innocenz III. und Byzanz am Vorabend des Vierten Kreuzzugs (1198–1203)," *Ostkirchliche Studien* XXIII (1974): 134; Schmandt, "Fourth Crusade and Just war," p. 212.

42. Gratian and Yves of Chartres, drawing upon Augustine's anti-Donatist writings and accounts of Jewish wars in the old Testament, developed a doctrine of the justice of warfare against infidels, heretics, schismatics, and excommunicates, who were all considered the enemies of God's chosen people, the orthodox believers. By making no distinction among the defense of the Holy Land, the defense of the structure and personnel of the organizational church, and the defense of the Catholic faith itself, the decretalists considerably expanded the variety of possible crusader missions. Russell, *Just War*, pp. 74–76, 112–19; Villey, *La Croisade*, p. 39. On the scholarly confusion of heretics and schismatics, see also Schmandt, "Fourth Crusade and Just War," p. 219.

43. Villey, *La Croisade*, p. 39.

44. Villehardouin, *Conquête de Constantinople*, sec. 98, I: 98.

45. Hugh of St. Pol, *Epistola*, in *M.G.H., SS.*, XVII: 812; Innocent III, *Epistolae*, VIII: 133, Migne, *PL*, CCXV: 710–11.

46. Innocent III, *Epistolae*, VIII: 133, Migne, *PL*, CCXV: 710–11. Since Capuano was not at Zara, if this occurred, it must have been at Venice when envoys of Alexius first contacted the leaders of the crusade.

47. Nicol, "Fourth Crusade and the Greek and Latin Empires," p. 280.

48. Villehardouin, *Conquête de Constantinople*, sec. 99, I: 99–101; Hendrickx, "Les chartes de Bandouin de Flandre," p. 70.

49. For example, when introducing the abbot of Vaux-de-Cernay and his party's argument against going to Constantinople, Villehardouin says of the faction, "Et parla l'abes de Vals, de l'ordre de Cystiaus, et cele partie qui voloit l'ost deprecier," *Conquête de Constantinople*, sec. 95, I: 94–96.

50. Ibid., sec. 99, I: 98–100. I know of no evidence supporting Brand's statement that the crusaders sent a deputation to gain the pope's approval of the project. *Byzantium Confronts the West*, p. 228. He appears to be relying upon Innocent's letter of 16 Nov. 1202, which refers to the earlier contact between envoys of Alexius and the crusaders at Venice. Innocent III, *Epistolae*, V: 122, Migne, *PL*, CCXIV: 1124.

51. Nicetas Choniates, *Historia*, p. 538. The translation is Brand's, *Byzantium Confronts the West*, pp. 203–4.

52. Giorgio Cracco, *Società e stato nel medioevo veneziano (secoli XII–XIV)* (Florence, 1967), pp. 46–47; Freddy Thiriet, *La Romanie vénitienne au moyen âge* (Paris, 1959), p. 42.

53. For example, Nicol's estimation of Dandolo is typical: "At worst the Doge of Venice stands out as the villain of the piece; at best as the only realist in a tale of confused aims and misdirected ideals." "The Fourth Crusade and the Greek and Latin Empire," p. 278.

54. Roger of Hoveden, *Chronica*, ed. William Stubbs 4 vols., *Rer. Brit. M. A. script.*, vol. LI, iv: 111.

55. *Devastatio Constantinopolitana, M.G.H., SS.*, xvi: 10 (Hopf ed., p. 88).

56. Ibid. The *Devastatio* places this before the arrival of the embassy from King Philip. I have assumed that it belongs with the defections placed by Ville-hardouin after the debate over the Constantinopolitan proposal (n.57), although it might refer to the same events as the Anonymous of Halberstadt. *Gesta episcoporum Halberstadensium*, p. 117. I do not believe however, that so many who had participated in the attack on Zara would be moved to defect without additional provocation.

57. The *Devastatio Constantinopolitana, M.G.H., SS.*, p. 10 (Hopf ed., p. 88) reports that two of the ships were lost. The drowning of the five hundred aboard one ship comes from Villehardouin, *Conquête de Constantinople*, sec. 101, I: 100.

58. Villehardouin, *Conquête de Constantinople*, sec. 101, I: 100–2. Clearly these defectors are not to be equated with those of the Anonymous of Halberstadt, because they did not reach their goal.

59. Ibid., sec. 102, I: 102, and sec. 315, II: 122–24; Tessier, *Quatrième Croisade*, p. 69.

60. Villehardouin, *Conquête de Constantinople*, sec. 109, I: 110–11; Robert of Clari, *Conquête*, sec. 14, p. 14. Robert, not to be much trusted on chronology, places Simon's defection before the debate on Alexius.

61. Peter of Vaux-de-Cernay, *Hystoria Albigensis*, I: 104–5.

62. The question of when Simon abandoned the army and where he went is a very vexed one. See Faral's discussion in Villehardouin, *Conquête de Constantinople*, I: 112, n. 1, and McNeal in Robert of Clari, *The Conquest of Constantinople*, trans. Edgar H. McNeal (1st ed., 1936; reprinted New York, 1966), p. 44, n. 27. Peter of Vaux-de-Cernay, *Hystoria Albigensis*, I: 110, and the *Devastatio Constantinopolitana, M.G.H., SS.*, xvi: 10 (Hopf ed., p. 88), are the best sources on this.

63. Villehardouin, *Conquête de Constantinople*, sec. 109, I: 112; Ernoul-Bernard, *Chronique*, p. 351. The Anonymous of Halberstadt tells us of "Quedam autem abbatum qui aderant, recedendum esse a Venetis propter hoc factum (the conquest of Zara) publice proclamabant, et quamplures peregrinorum versus Hungariam discesserunt." *Gesta episcoporum Halberstadensium*, p. 117. He must be dealing with the departure of Simon, because of his reference to the abbots. No abbots could be assigned to an earlier defection.

64. Peter of Vaux-de-Cernay, *Hystoria Albigensis*, I: 110.

65. Villehardouin, *Conquête de Constantinople*, secs. 48–49, I: 50–52, and sec. 103, I: 102–4. Some authors confuse the issue of the failure of the Flemish fleet to rendezvous with the main body by assuming that Countess Marie of Flanders was aboard. For example, Hurter, *Papa Innocenzo III*, II: 238, n. 491, and Riant, "Innocent III" *Revue des questions historiques* XVIII: 40. This is based upon a misinterpretation of Villehardouin, *Conquête de Constantinople*, sec. 317, II: 126. Villehardouin actually says that Marie took ship some time after the birth of Margaret from Marseilles, but he does not say that she joined the fleet under John of Nesle. That fleet, in fact, arrived in Palestine in the late spring or, at the latest, the early summer of 1203. Marie, Villehardouin tells us, arrived a year later, for she had just landed when messengers brought news of Baldwin's election as emperor. See also B. Hendrickx, "Het Regentschaap van Vlaanderen en Henegouwen na het

vertrek van Boudewijn IX (VI) op kruisvaart (1202–1211)," *Revue belge de philologie et d'histoire* XLVIII (1970): 386, n. 1. Incidentally, if Baldwin had been involved in a conspiracy to conquer Constantinople *instead of* Jerusalem, he would scarcely have allowed his wife to sail for Acre.

66. Villehardouin, *Conquête de Constantinople*, sec. 229, II: 28–30.

67. Above, p. 20. See Queller, Compton, and Campbell, "The Neglected Majority," pp. 441–42.

68. Ernoul-Bernard, *Chronique*, pp. 352–53. See Mas Latrie, *Histoire de Chypre*, I: 156–59.

69. Ernoul-Bernard, *Chronique*, p. 353.

70. Peter of Vaux-de-Cernay, *Hystoria Albigensis*, I: 110; Ernoul-Bernard, *Chronique*, p. 360. On the defectors in general, see Queller, Compton, and Campbell, "The Neglected Majority," pp. 441–65.

71. Innocent III, *Epistolae*, VI: 211, Migne, *PL*, CCXV: 238.

72. Ibid., V: 162, Migne, *PL*, CCXIV: 1180.

73. Villehardouin refers to him as "Chancellor," probably because he later became chancellor of the Latin Empire, for he was not chancellor of Flanders. B. Hendrickx, "Baudouin IX de Flandre et les empereurs byzantins Isaac II l'Ange et Alexis IV," *Revue belge de philologie et d'histoire* XLIX (1971): 484–85.

74. Villehardouin, *Conquête de Constantinople*, sec. 105, I: 104–6.

75. Ibid., sec. 106, I: 106; Robert of Clari, *Conquête* sec. 15, p. 15. Ernoul-Bernard has Robert as the single envoy. *Chronique*, p. 351. This is understandable, since he was the only one of the envoys to go directly to Palestine.

76. Gunther of Pairis, *Historia Constantinopolitana*, p. 74.

77. Ibid., p. 80; Riant, *Exuviae*, I: lxxxii, n. 2; Brown, "The Cistercians in the Latin Empire," pp. 75–76; Usseglio *I marchesi di Monferrato*, II: 213, n. 1; Alfred J. Andrea and Ilona Motsiff, "Pope Innocent III and the Diversion of the Fourth Crusade Army to Zara," *Byzantinoslavica* XXXIII (1972): 19, n. 66.

78. Above, p. 54–55.

79. Innocent III, *Epistolae*, VI: 102, Migne *PL*, CCXV: 107–8. Robert of Clari, *Conquête*, sec. 15, p. 15, is not credible in making the Venetians participate in the mission and in the absolution.

80. Gunther of Pairis, *Historia Constantinopolitana*, p. 76.

81. Villehardouin, *Conquête de Constantinople*, sec. 106, I: 106. My translation.

82. Innocent III, *Epistolae*, VI: 99, Migne, *PL* CCXV: 104.

83. Villehardouin, *Conquête de Constantinople*, sec. 106, I: 106.

84. Innocent III, *Epistolae*, VI: 232, Migne, *PL*, CCXV: 262.

85. See Andrea and Motsiff, "Pope Innocent III and the Diversion of the Fourth Crusade Army to Zara," p. 20. My attitude toward Innocent is somewhat harsher than theirs, due to the fact that the conditions of absolution were never met, and had never been likely to be performed, and yet Innocent did not revoke it. See the pope's letter of 15 Sept. 1204, in response to the Hungarian king, where he protests that he made them swear to adhere to his commands. Innocent III, *Epistolae*, VII: 127, Migne, *PL* CCXV: 417.

86. Innocent III, *Epistolae*, V: 162, Migne, *PL*, CCXIV: 1179–82. See

Innocent's later account of his action, ibid., VI: 232, Migne, *PL*, CCXV: 262. For contrary views on the relationship of letters V: 162, and V: 161, see Joseph Gill, "Franks, Venetians, and Pope Innocent III, 1201–1203," *Studi Veneziani* XII (1970): 93, n. 39, and Tessier, *Quatrième Croisade*, p. 284. On the question of who was to absolve the crusaders, see Faral in Villehardouin, *Conquête de Constantinople*, I: 109, n. 1.

87. Innocent III, *Epistolae*, VI: 99, Migne, *PL*, CCXV: 104.

88. Ibid., VI: 100, Migne, *PL* CCXV: 105.

89. This experience caused Innocent to issue a decretal on 20 June 1203, dealing with the problem of communication with excommunicates in special cases without incurring the automatic ban. This was incorporated into *Compilatio III* and later into the *Decretals* of Gregory IX. Brundage, *Medieval Canon Law and the Crusader* p. 155.

90 Innocent III, *Epistolae*, VI: 102, Migne, *PL*, CCXV: 109. The pope cited Gideon's punishment of the cities which would not give his army food (Judges 8:4–17) and Jesus' reference to the Pharisees of David's example in feeding his men with sacred bread (Luke 6:1–5). See also Gunther of Pairis, *Historia Constantinopolitana*, p. 79.

91. Gunther of Pairis, *Historia Constantinopolitana*, pp. 76–79.

92. *Gesta Innocentii*, chap. 88, col. 160.

93. Innocent III, *Epistolae*, VI: 48, Migne, *PL*, CCXV: 50.

94. Ibid., VII: 202, Migne, *PL* CCXV: 511. *Gesta Innocentii*, chap. 87, cols. 139–40.

95. Innocent III *Epistolae*, VI: 100, Migne, *PL*, CCXV 105. Riant reads *abbati Laudensi* as the abbot of Loos. "Innocent III," p. 15. Usseglio argues that it was the abbot of Locedio on the grounds of his close connection with Boniface. *I marchesi di Monferrato*, II: 213. I find it difficult to see the derivation of Locedio from a name with the dative form "Laudensi." In this same letter Boniface tells the pope that Dandolo and some Venetians had said that they were sending their own envoys to Rome.

96. *Gesta Innocentii*, chap. 88, col. 160.

97. Ibid., chap. 95, col 162.

98. Above, pp. 54–55.

99. Gunther of Pairis, *Historia Constantinopolitana*, p. 79.

100. Ibid., pp. 79–80.

101. Ibid., pp. 83, 104–5. See Faral's criticism of Gunther's account of Abbot Martin's role and movements. "Geoffroy de Villehardouin: la question de sa sincérité," *Revue historique* CLXXVII (1936): 542, n. 2.

102. Andrea Dandolo implies that the walls were destroyed before winter. *Chronica*, p. 277.

103. Villehardouin, *Conquête de Constantinople*, sec. 108, I: 110; *Gesta episcoporum Halberstadensium*, p. 118; *Historia ducum Veneticorum, supplementum*, p. 92; Thomas of Spalato, *Historia*, p. 576.

104. *Historia ducum Veneticorum, supplementum*, p. 93.

105. Villehardouin, *Conquête de Constantinople*, sec. 99, I: 100.

106. Ibid., sec. 111, I: 112–14; *Devastatio Constantinopolitana, M.G.H., SS.*,

xvi: 10 (Hopf ed., p. 88); Robert of Clari, *Conquête*, sec. xxxi: p. 31.

107. *Gesta episcoporum Halberstadensium*, p. 118.

108. Villehardouin, *Conquête de Constantinople*, sec. 112, i: 114; Alberic of Trois-Fontaines, *Chronica*, p. 880.

109. Villehardouin, *Conquête de Constantinople*, sec. 111, i: 112–14; *Gesta episcoporum Halberstadensium*, p. 118.

110. Villehardouin, *Conquête de Constantinople*, sec. 111, i: 114.

111. Villehardouin, *Conquête de Constantinople*, sec. 112, i: 115; *Gesta episcoporum Halberstadensium*, p. 118. Robert of Clari can be interpreted as saying that Alexius was led to Boniface's tent, which would emphasize the domination of the marquis over the young prince. *Conquête*, sec. 31, p. 31. Villehardouin is absolutely clear, however, that the marquis had his own tent pitched close by that of Alexius.

112. *Gesta episcoporum Halberstadensium*, p. 118.

113. Ibid., 118.

114. Riant argues that in this crisis Alexius was compelled to bribe the leaders to keep them to their agreement. "Innocent III," *Revue des questions historiques* xviii: 36–37.

115. Hugh of St. Pol, *Epistola*, p. 812.

116. *Conquête*, sec. 33, p. 32 (translation by Edgar H. McNeal); Hugh of St. Pol, *Epistola*, p. 812; Villehardouin, *Conquête de Constantinople*, sec. 113–14, i: 116–18.

117. Villehardouin, *Conquête de Constantinople*, sec. 113, i: 116.

118. Ibid., sec. 114, i: 118.

119. Hugh of St. Pol, *Epistola*, p. 812.

120. Robert of Clari, *Conquête*, sec. 39, p. 40; Usseglio, *I marchesi di Monferrato*, II: 216.

121. Hugh of St. Pol says that there were only a few more than twenty who advocated the Constantinopolitan expedition. *Epistola*, p. 812. One manuscript of this letter, the one published by Martène, lists the following names: Boniface of Montferrat, Louis of Blois, Matthew of Montmorency, Geoffrey of Villehardouin, Conon of Béthune, Miles the Brabantine, John Foisnon, John of Friaise, Peter of Bracheux, Anseau of Cayeux, Renier of Trith, Macaire of Ste. Menehould, Miles of Lille, the bishops of Troyes and Halberstadt, and John Faicete. There are two surprising omissions, undoubtedly erroneous, Baldwin of Flanders and Hugh himself. See B. Hendrickx, "Les Chartes," p. 70. Riant, "Innocent III," *Revue des questions historiques* xviii: 22, mistakenly places this at Zara. See Queller, Compton, and Campbell, "The Neglected Majority," p. 460, n. 102.

122. Villehardouin, *Conquête de Constantinople*, sec. 115–17, i: 118–20; Hugh of St. Pol, *Epistola*, p. 812.

123. Robert of Clari, *Conquête*, sec. 39, p. 40.

Chapter 7

1. Villehardouin, *Conquête de Constantinople*, sec. 119, i: 122. The *Devastatio Constantinopolitana* places the crusaders' departure one day later, on Whitsunday

itself. *M.G.H., SS.*, XVI: 10 (Hopf ed., p. 88).

2. Raimbaut de Vaqueiras, *Poems*, p. 218.

3. Villehardouin, *Conquête de Constantinople*, sec. 119–20, I: 122.

4. Innocent III, *Epistolae*, VI: 101, Migne, *PL*: CCXV, 106–7. Potthast dates it 20 June. The *terminus a quo* cannot be earlier than the beginning of May, according to Innocent's itinerary. *Regestum Pontificum Romanorum*, ed. August Potthast, 2 vols. (Berlin, 1874–75), vol. I, ep. 1948. p. 170. Schmandt speculates on the grounds of the silence of Villehardouin and Robert of Clari that the letter miscarried or was suppressed, but does not take into consideration the tardiness of its dispatch. "Fourth Crusade and Just War," p. 213.

5. E.g., Nicol, "The Fourth Crusade," p. 280.

6. *Historia Constantinopolitana*, p. 78. See also Alberic of Trois-Fontaines, *Chronica*, p. 880.

7. Gunther of Pairis, *Historia Constantinopolitana*, p. 78.

8. "Et quand le traité de Corfou est signé, il n'essaye pas, cette fois, d'empêcher leur départ par une nouvelle menace d'excommunication. Il laisse faire. C'est qu'il a conscience que toute opposition serait impuissante; qu'il est moins que jamais le maître de la croisade; et aussi que les propositions du jeune Alexis s'accordèrent après tout avec les visées séculaires de Rome sur l'empire grec et l'Eglise d'Orient. Tel est, autant que sa correspondance permet de l'entrevoir, l'état d'âme d'Innocent III." Luchaire, *Innocent III*, IV: 116. See also Nicol, "The Fourth Crusade," p. 280.

9. Nicetas, *Historia*, p. 541.

10. If these were some of those who had sailed under John of Nesle, they had had a very rapid voyage and return, allowing time for a *pro forma* appearance in the Holy Land at most. The Flemish fleet probably left Marseilles late in March 1203. Villehardouin, *Conquête de Constantinople*, sec. 103, I, 102–4. The journey to the Holy Land probably required close to two months. Roscher, *Papst Innocent III*, p. 57, n. 33. Thus the Flemings probably arrived in Syria in May, and the encounter between its remnants and the main crusading force took place in the first week of June. I doubt that these returning pilgrims were from the force under John of Nesle.

11. Villehardouin, *Conquête de Constantinople*, sec. 121–22, I: 124. The quotation is from the translation by M. R. B. Shaw, Villehardouin, *The Conquest of Constantinople* (1st publ. 1963; reprinted Baltimore, 1967), p. 57.

12. Villehardouin, *Conquête de Constantinople*, sec. 123–24, I: 124–26; Runciman, *Crusades*, III: 117.

13. Villehardouin, *Conquête de Constantinople*, sec. 125–26, I: 126–28. Recall that the pope had taken the position that if the emperor did not supply them, they might help themselves. Innocent III, *Epistolae*, VI: 102, Migne, *PL*, CCXV: 109–10.

14. Anonymous of Halberstadt gives a somewhat confused version of the journey omitting Negroponte. *Gesta episcoporum Halberstadensium*, p. 118. Alberic of Trois-Fontaines is utterly confused on the geography. *Chronica*, pp. 880–81.

15. M. F. Hendy has recently argued against the prevailing tendency to believe that twelfth-century Byzantium was in the throes of economic decay. "By-

zantium, 1081–1204: An Economic Reappraisal," *Transactions of the Royal Historical Society* xx (1970): 31–52. Hard evidence, however, is lacking on both sides of the question, as Hendy points out.

16. Freddy Thiriet, *Histoire de Venise*, 4th ed. (Paris, 1969), p. 40; Robert Lee Wolff, "Greeks and Latins," pp. 324–25; Antony Bryer, "The First Encounter with the West—AD, 1050–1204," in *Byzantium: An Introduction*, ed. Philip Whitting (New York, 1971); Donald M. Nicol, *The Last Centuries of Byzantium, 1261–1453* (London, 1972), pp. 8–9.

17. Nicetas, *Historia*, pp. 547–48.

18. Cf. Vasiliev, *Byzantine Empire*, p. 439; Ostrogorsky, *History of the Byzantine State*, pp. 408–9; Brand, *Byzantium Confronts the West*, pp. 105, 117.

19. Brand, *Byzantium Confronts the West*, p. 118; Nicetas, *Historia*, pp. 458–59.

20. Nicetas, *Historia*, p. 484.

21. Brand, *Byzantium Confronts the West*, p. 117; e.g., Nicetas, *Historia*, pp. 477–78.

22. Brand, *Byzantium Confronts the West*, p. 117.

23. Nicetas, *Historia*, pp. 530, 548.

24. Ibid., pp. 496–97; Brand, *Byzantium Confronts the West*, p. 117.

25. Nicetas, *Historia*, p. 460; Louis Halphen, "Le Rôle des 'Latins' dans l'histoire intérieure de Constantinople à la fin du XIIe siécle," *Mélanges Charles Diehl* (Paris, 1930), I: 145. Halphen believed that Euphrosyne was a member of a nationalistic faction and that she actually ruled in place of her weak husband.

26. Nicetas, *Historia*, p. 541.

27. The number seems fantastic, but is accepted by reputable authorities. Hélène Ahrweiler, *Byzance et la mer: la marine de guerre, la politique et les institutions maritimes de Byzance aux VIIe–XVe siècles* (Paris, 1966), p. 244; M. Şesan, "La flotte byzantine à l'époque des Comnènes et des Anges (1081–1204)," *Byzantinoslavica* xxi (1960): 52–53.

28. Şesan, "La flotte byzantine," 52–53.

29. Ibid., Ahrweiler, *Byzance et la mer*, p. 288. Sometimes the Byzantines unwillingly received such pirates into their services. Wolff reports an incident in which the Calabrian pirate Stirione forced the Greeks to pay him an indemnity and to make him an admiral in the Byzantine navy. "Greeks and Latins," p. 325.

30. Brand, *Byzantium Confronts the West*, pp. 147, 213–14; Nicetas, *Historia*, p. 482.

31. Usseglio, *I marchesi di Monferrato*, II: 218.

32. Nicetas, *Historia*, pp. 540–41.

33. Ibid.; p. 541; Brand, *Byzantium Confronts the West*, p. 147.

34. Runciman, *Crusades*, III: 117–18.

35. Cognasso, "Un imperatore bizantino della decadenza: Isaaco II Angelo," p. 52.

36. David Jacoby recently cast doubts on Ostrogorsky's identification of the *pronoia* and the fief. "The Encounter of Two Societies: Western Conquerors and Byzantines in the Peloponnesus after the Fourth Crusade," *American Historical Review* LXXVIII (1973): 876–77. For Ostrogorsky's description of the twelfth-

century *pronoia*, see his *History of the Byzantine State*, pp. 329–31, and his *Pour l'histoire de la féodalité byzantine* (Brussels, 1954), pp. 9–61.

37. Runciman, *Crusades*, III: 117–18; Brand, *Byzantium Confronts the West*, p. 4; Bréhier, *Vie et mort de Byzance* (Paris, 1947), p. 356.

38. Brand, *Byzantium Confronts the West*, p. 4.

39. Ibid., pp. 236–37; Innocent III, *Epistolae*, VI: 211, Migne, *PL*, CCXV: 238.

40. Usseglio, *I marchesi di Monferrato*, II: 218. Ernoul-Bernard reports that Alexius replied to those who questioned him about the defense of the city after the crusaders' landing on the north shore of the Golden Horn that he would allow them to land and camp under the walls. Then he would set all the prostitutes of Constantinople on a hill above their encampment, who would piss so much that all the invaders would be drowned in the torrent. *Chronique*, p. 363.

41. Benjamin of Tudela, *Itinerary*, p. 51; Cognasso, drawing upon John Cinnamus. "Un imperatore bizantino della decadenza: Isaaco II Angelo," pp. 31–32.

42. Usseglio, *I marchesi di Monferrato*, II: 218; Cognasso, "Un imperatore bizantino della decadenza: Isaaco II Angelo," p. 37.

43. Runciman, *Crusades*, III: 118.

44. Nicetas, *Historia*, p. 541.

45. Villehardouin, *Conquête de Constantinople*, sec. 127, I: 128. Robert of Clari, *Conquête*, sec. 40, p. 40; Hugh of St. Pol, *Epistola*, p. 812.

46. Villehardouin, *Conquête de Constantinople*, sec. 128, I: 130. Many scholars have estimated the population of Constantinople as high as a million, but J. C. Russell has recently argued that 200,000 is a more reasonable figure. "Population in Europe, 500–1500," *The Fontana Economic History of Europe* (London and Glascow, 1969), I: 9–10.

47. Villehardouin, *Conquête de Constantinople*, sec. 129–31. I: 130–32. For the tactical considerations influencing the doge's proposal, see Manfroni, *Storia della marina italiana*, I: 321.

48. Villehardouin, *Conquête de Constantinople*, sec. 132, I: 132–34.

49. *Fall of Constantinople*, p. 304.

50. Villehardouin, *Conquête de Constantinople*, sec. 133, I: 134; Robert of Clari, *Conquête*, sec. 40, p. 40; Nicetas, *Historia*, p. 542.

51. R. Janin, *Constantinople Byzantine* (1st ed. 1950), 2d rev. ed. (Paris, 1964), p. 1.

52. Villehardouin, *Conquête de Constantinople*, sec. 134–35, I: 134–36.

53. Ibid., sec. 136, I: 136–38; Hodgson, *Early History of Venice* (London, 1901), p. 371.

54. Villehardouin, *Conquête de Constantinople*, sec. 137, I: 138.

55. Hugh of St. Pol, *Epistola*, p. 812.

56. Villehardouin, *Conquête de Constantinople*, sec. 146, I: 148; Innocent III, *Epistolae*, VI, 211, Migne, *PL*, CCXV: 238.

57. Villehardouin, *Conquête de Constantinople*, sec. 137, I: 138.

58. This is according to Villehardouin. Nicetas places the scene at Damatrys on the Sea of Marmara southwest of Scutari. See Brand, *Byzantium Confronts the West*, p. 235.

59. Nicetas, *Historia*, p. 542, *in apparatu* (Bekker ed., *in textu*). On the iden-

tity of the Greek commander, see Faral, in Villehardouin, *Conquête de Constantinople*, I: 141, n. 2.

60. Villehardouin, *Conquête de Constantinople*, sec. 138–40, I: 138–42.

61. Axel Wallensköld, in Conon of Béthune, *Les Chansons de Conon de Béthune* (Paris, 1921), pp. iii–v; Rousset, *Histoire des croisades*, p. 205.

62. Queller, "L'évolution du rôle de l'ambassadeur," pp. 482–83, n. 11.

63. Villehardouin, *The Conquest of Constantinople*, trans. M. R. B. Shaw, p. 63.

64. Villehardouin, *Conquête de Constantinople*, sec. 141–44, I: 142–46. Robert of Clari, *Conquête*, sec. 41, pp. 40–41; Hugh of St. Pol, *Epistola*, pp. 812–13.

65. Villehardouin, *Conquête de Constantinople*, sec. 145–46, I: 146–48; Robert of Clari, *Conquête*, sec. 41, p. 41; Innocent III, *Epistolae*, VI: 211, Migne, *PL*, CCXV: 238. On the possibility of approaching within ten feet of the walls, see Pears, *Fall of Constantinople*, pp. 305–6.

66. Villehardouin, *Conquête de Constantinople*, sec. 147, I: 148.

67. Usseglio, *I marchesi di Monferrato*, II: 221.

68. Brand, *Byzantium Confronts the West*, p. 234.

69. Villehardouin, *Conquête de Constantinople*, sec. 147, I: 148.

70. For the armor worn by foot soldiers, see Smail, *Crusading Warfare*, pp. 115–16.

71. Faral, in Villehardouin, *Conquête de Constantinople*, p. ix.

72. Villehardouin, *Conquête de Constantinople*, sec. 379, II: 188. My translation.

73. Faral, in Villehardouin, *Conquête de Constantinople*, pp. xxxii–xxxv.

74. Villehardouin, *Conquête de Constantinople*, sec. 148–53, I: 148–52.

75. Innocent III, *Epistolae*, VI: 211, Migne, *PL*, CCXV: 239.

76. Villehardouin, *Conquête de Constantinople*, sec. 154, I: 152; Robert of Clari, *Conquête*, sec. 41, pp. 41–42.

77. Robert of Clari, *Conquête*, sec. 41, p. 42; Villehardouin, *Conquête de Constantinople*, secs. 155–56, I: 154–56.

78. Robert of Clari, *Conquête*, sec. 42, p. 42.

79. Ibid., sec. 42–43, p. 42; Villehardouin, *Conquête de Constantinople*, sec. 156, I: 156; Hugh of St. Pol, *Epistola*, p. 813. Clari makes it clear that the knights issued mounted from the transports. Probably lesser men led the horses down the bridge into the water.

80. Robert of Clari, *Conquête*, sec. 43, pp. 42–43; Villehardouin, *Conquête de Constantinople*, sec. 157–58 I: 156–58; Hugh of St. Pol, *Epistola*, p. 813. This Tower of Galata, located on the seashore, must not be confused with the fourteenth century tower, which still stands on the hillside at a considerable distance from the shore.

81. Villehardouin, *Conquête de Constantinople*, sec. 158, I, 158; Ernoul-Bernard, *Chronique*, p. 363.

82. Pears, *Fall of Constantinople*, p. 308.

83. Robert of Clari, *Conquête*, sec. XLIII, p. 43; Villehardouin, *Conquête de Constantinople*, sec. 159, I: 158.

84. Robert of Clari, *Conquête*, sec. 43, p. 43: Villehardouin, *Conquête de Con-*

stantinople, sec. 159, I: 158; Hugh of St. Pol, *Epistola*, p. 813; Manfroni, *Storia della marina italiana*, I: 323, n. 2. Hugh names as defenders of the tower "Anglici, Pysani, Leveniani, Dachi."

85. Robert of Clari, *Conquête*, sec. 44, p. 43; Villehardouin, *Conquête de Constantinople*, sec. 160–61, I 158–60; Hugh of St. Pol, *Epistola*, p. 813; Nicetas, *Historia*, pp. 542–43.

86. Robert of Clari, *Conquête*, sec. 75, p. 75, sec. 106, p. 102 (on the height of Peter). On the cloudy question of the right of a cleric to bear arms against the infidel, see Russell, *Just War*, pp. 105–12.

87. Villehardouin, *Conquête de Constantinople*, sec. 160, I: 160.

88. *Chronique*, p. 362.

89. Dandolo, *Chronica*, p. 322. The *Historia ducum Veneticorum*, p. 93, mentions a bridge over the chain by means of which men passed back and forth between Constantinople and Galata. It was supposedly struck and broken by the *Eagle*. This is wrong.

90. Robert of Clari, *Conquête*, sec. 44, p. 43; Nicetas, *Historia*, p. 543.

91. Alberic of Trois-Fontaines, *Chronica*, p. 881.

Chapter 8

1. Villehardouin, *Conquête de Constantinople*, sec. 162, I: 160–62; Robert of Clari, *Conquête*, sec. 44, pp. 43–44. Martino da Canale puts into the mouth of Dandolo in 1204 a remark concernig the French lack of experience in fighting from the flying bridges mounted on ships. *Les Estoires de Venise*, pt. 1, sec. 51, p. 57 (in the older ed., p. 332).

2. Villehardouin, *Conquête de Cosntantinople*, sec. 163, I: 162.

3. Above, p. 96.

4. Villehardouin, *Conquête de Constantinople*, sec. 163, I: 162–64; Robert of Clari, *Conquête*, sec. 44, p. 44; Hugh of Saint Pol, *Epistola*, p. 813. Brand ignores the demolition of the bridge by the Greeks. *Byzantium Confronts the West*, p. 238.

5. *Historia*, p. 543; Villehardouin, *Conquête de Constantinople*, sec. 164, I: 164–66; Ernoul-Bernard, *Chronique*, p. 364. Villehardouin says they could besiege one gate, which Faral identifies as the Blachernae Gate.

6. Hugh of Saint Pol, *Epistola*, p. 813; Robert of Clari, *Conquête*, sec. 44, p. 45; Nicetas, *Historia*, p. 544.

7. Janin, *Constantinople byzantine*, p. 284.

8. Ibid., p. 109: Pears, *Fall of Constantinople*, p. 310.

9. Pears, *Fall of Constantinople*, pp. 310–11.

10. Villehardouin, *Conquête de Constantinople*, sec. 166, I: 168; Hugh of Saint Pol, *Epistola*, p. 813; Nicetas, *Historia*, pp. 544–45.

11. Perhaps these bridges were operated by a pulley system similar to that used on a land-based siege tower in the Fifth Crusade at Damietta and described by Mayer. *Crusades*, p. 211.

12. At least one scholar has equated the terror inspired in medieval man by Greek fire to the modern psychological effects of atomic weaponry. While the comparison may be overdone, it does emphasize the very real "superstitious awe"

with which this device was regarded. H. R. Ellis Davidson, "The Secret Weapon of Byzantium," *Byzantinische Zeitschrift* LXVI (1973): 61.

13. Robert of Clari, *Conquête*, sec. 44, p. 44; Wiel, *Navy of Venice*, p. 142.

14. Robert of Clari, *Conquête*, sec. 92, p. 89; Gunther of Pairis, *Historia Constantinopolitana*, pp. 111-12.

15. Villehardouin, *Conquête de Constantinople*, sec. 165, I: 166.

16. Nicetas, *Historia*, p. 544.

17. Villehardouin, *Conquête de Constantinople*, secs. 165-66, 168, I, 166-70.

18. Ibid., sec. 169, I: 170.

19. Ibid.

20. Ibid., sec. 165, I: 166. Villehardouin, *Conquest of Constantinople*, trans. by Shaw, p. 69. The marshal estimates that they could maintain the siege for three weeks. In the letter of the crusading leaders to Innocent III, they estimate only fifteen days. Innocent III, *Epistolae*, VI: 211, Migne, *PL*, CCXV: 239.

21. Villehardouin, *Conquête de Constantinople*, sec. 170, I: 170-72; Hugh of Saint Pol, *Epistola*, p. 814.

22. Nicetas, *Historia*, p. 545. Although very strong, the walls in this area lacked a ditch or moat and a second wall. Janin, *Constantinople byzantine*, p. 283.

23. Villehardouin, *Conquête de Constantinople*, sec. 170, I: 170-72.

24. The conjecture is Alexander Van Millingen's. *Byzantine Constantinople: The Walls of the City and Adjoining Historical Sites* (London, 1899), p. 172.

25. Villehardouin, *Conquête de Constantinople*, sec. 171, I: 172-74.

26. Brand says "Three casts of a stone-thrower," but he is following Villehardouin incorrectly. *Byzantium Confronts the West*, p. 240. Villehardouin, *Conquête de Constantinople*, sec. 172, I: 174.

27. Quoted by Brand, *Byzantium Confronts the West*, p. 236.

28. Villehardouin, *Conquête de Constantinople*, sec. 172, I: 174.

29. Ibid., sec. 173-74, I: 174-76. For the status of Venetian rowers, see Lane, *Venetian Ships*, pp. 6-7.

30. Nicetas, *Historia*, pp. 544-45. Western chroniclers make no mention of the ram, and Raimbaut says specifically "the wall breached in many places without the battering ram. . ." Linskill, in Raimbaut de Vaqueiras, *Poems*, pp. 305, 310, and 332, n. to line 42.

31. Villehardouin, *Conquête de Constantinople*, sec. 175, I: 176, lists twenty-five towers, but Hugh of Saint Pol, *Epistola*, p. 814, says thirty.

32. Michael Maclagen, *The City of Constantinople* (New York and Washington, 1968), pp. 35-36.

33. Nicetas, *Historia*, pp. 544-45; Villehardouin, *Conquête de Constantinople*, sec. 175-76, I: 178.

34. Below, pp. 119-120.

35. Nicetas, *Historia*, p. 545; Villehardouin, *Conquête de Constantinople*, sec. 176, I: 278; Robert of Clari, *Conquête*, sec. 46, p. 47.

36. Villehardouin, *Conquête de Constantinople*, sec. 179, I: 180-82.

37. Ernoul-Bernard, *Chronique*, pp. 364-65.

38. Linskill, in Raimbaut de Vaqueiras, *Poems*, p. 332, n. to lines 43-45. Robert of Clari, *Conquête*, sec. 44, p. 45; Nicetas, *Historia*, p. 546; Hugh of Saint Pol,

Epistola, p. 814.

39. Villehardouin, *Conquête de Constantinople*, sec. 179, I: 180–82.

40. Ibid.

41. Ibid., sec. 177–79, I: 178–80.

42. Ibid., sec. 178, I: 180; Robert of Clari, *Conquête*, sec. 45–46, pp. 45–47. Brand, *Byzantium Confronts the West*, pp. 239–40, reverses the numbers of the attacking and guarding battalions.

43. Robert of Clari, *Conquête*, sec. 44, p. 45; Hugh of Saint Pol, *Epistola*, p. 814.

44. Robert of Clari, *Conquête*, sec. 45, p. 46.

45. Villehardouin, *Conquête de Constantinople*, sec. 180, I: 182.

46. Robert of Clari, *Conquête* sec. 47, pp. 47–49.

47. Ibid., sec. 48, pp. 50–51. The identification of Robert's canal was made by Brand, *Byzantium Confronts the West*, p. 240.

48. *The Alexiad*, trans. Elizabeth A. S. Dawes (London, 1928, reissued 1967), p. 342; Smail, *Crusading Warfare*, p. 115, n. 1.

49. Villehardouin has the emperor retreat to the Philopatrion, which was a palace outside the walls. *Conquête de Constantinople*, sec. 180, I: 182. Other sources, however, have him withdrawing into the city. Robert of Clari, *Conquête*, sec. 48, p. 51; Nicetas, *Historia*, p. 546; Innocent III, *Epistolae*, VI: 211, Migne, *PL*, CCXV: 239.

50. Raimbaut de Vaqueiras, *Poems*, pp. 305 and 310.

51. Robert of Clari, *Conquête*, sec. 48, p. 51.

52. Brand, on the other hand, arranges the chronology differently. He believes that it might have been the news of the Venetian success against the harbor wall that caused Alexius III to return to the city. *Byzantium Confronts the West*, p. 240. I do not think that this is quite as acceptable an interpretation, since the crusaders summoned the Venetians to rescue them, presumably when they learned that the emperor had come out of the city in force. The Venetian success had been achieved already at that time.

53. Villehardouin, *Conquête de Constantinople*, sec. 181, I: 182–84.

54. Robert of Clari, *Conquête*, sec. 50, p. 52.

55. Ibid., sec. 51, p. 52; Hugh of Saint Pol, *Epistola*, p. 814.

56. George Acropolita, *Annales*, in *Corp. Bonn* XXIX (Bonn, 1836): 7.

57. Nicetas, *Historia*, pp. 485–89.

58. *Qualiter caput beati Theodori martyris de Constantinopolitana urbe ad Caietam translatum est*, in *Exuviae*, I: 152.

59. Linskill, in Raimbaut de Vaqueiras, *Poems*, p. 335, n. to line 58.

60. Nicetas, *Historia*, pp. 546–47.

61. Ibid., pp. 549–50.

62. Such is Riant's estimation of Isaac. "Innocent III," *Revue des questions historiques* XVIII: 43–44.

63. Nicetas, *Historia*, p. 550; Villehardouin *Conquête de Constantinople*, sec. 182, I: 184.

64. Nicetas, *Historia*, pp. 550–51; Villehardouin, *Conquête de Constantinople*, sec. 182–83, I: 184–86.

65. Villehardouin, *Conquête de Constantinople*, sec. 184, I: 186–88; Robert of Clari, *Conquête*, sec. 52, p. 52.

66. Above, p. 72. A letter written by Isaac to Saladin and quoted by Raymond S. Schmandt gives some indication of the Byzantine emperor's duplicity: "[Barbarossa] has experienced every type of deception on the way; the sufferings he has endured and the shortage of his supplies have weakened and troubled him. He will not reach your country in any shape useful to himself or his army." "Orthodoxy and Catholicism: Public Opinion, the Schism, and the Fourth Crusade," *Diakonia* III (1968): 295.

67. Villehardouin, *Conquête de Constantinople*, sec. 184–85, I: 186–88. Van Millingen identifies their entry point as probably Gyrolimne. *Byzantine Constantinople*, p. 127.

68. Janin, *Constantinople byzantine*, pp. 126–27.

69. Nicetas, *Historia*, p. 452.

70. Villehardouin, *Conquête de Constantinople*, sec. 185, I: 188.

71. Ibid., sec. 186–89, I: 188–92.

72. Some western sources obfuscate the restoration of Isaac, probably deliberately. The letter of the crusaders to the pope had Alexius elected during the night and Isaac raised from prison by his son. Innocent III, *Epistolae*, VI: 211, Migne, *PL*, CCXV: 239. Robert of Clari also has Isaac rescued from prison by Alexius, although he does concede the imperial seat to his father. *Conquête*, sec. 52, pp. 52–53. Perhaps Robert tells the story as honestly as he knew it. See also *Devastatio Constantinopolitana*, in *M.G.H., SS.*, XVI: 11 (Hopf ed., p. 89), and Dandolo, *Chronica*, col. 322.

73. Villehardouin, *Conquête de Constantinople*, sec. 190, I; 192; Robert of Clari, *Conquête*, sec. 52, pp. 52–53; Nicetas, *Historia*, p. 551; Innocent III, *Epistolae*, VI: 211, Migne, *PL*, CCXV: 239.

Chapter 9

1. Villehardouin, *Conquête de Constantinople*, sec. 191, I: 194; Gunther of Pairis, *Historia Constantinopolitana*, p. 89; Innocent III, *Epistolae*, VII: 152, Migne, *PL*, CCXV: 447.

2. Robert of Clari, *Conquête*, sec. 55, pp. 55–56.

3. Faral in Villehardouin, *Conquête de Constantinople*, I: 228–29.

4. Brand, *Byzantium Confronts the West*, p. 241.

5. Such is also Riant's opinion. "Innocent III," *Revue des questions historiques* XVIII: 43–44; also in *Exuviae*, I: lxxxiii.

6. Villehardouin, *Conquête de Constantinople*, sec. 191, I: 194; Robert of Clari, *Conquête*, sec. 55, pp. 55–56; Gunther of Pairis, *Historia Constantinopolitana*, p. 89; Innocent III, *Epistolae* VII: 152, Migne, *PL*, CCXV: 447.

7. One wonders whether the date was chosen because of the association of Saint Peter with the Roman see.

8. Innocent III, *Epistolae*, VI: 211, Migne, *PL*, CCXV: 239; Villehardouin, *Conquête de Constantinople*, sec. 193, I: 196.

9. See Faral, in Villehardouin, *Conquête de Constantinople*, I: 229, and sources cited there.

10. Nicetas, *Historia*, p. 551.

11. Villehardouin says merely that the emperor began to pay some of the money due, and that each man was given the sum that it had cost him for transportation from Venice. *Conquête de Constantinople*, sec. 193, I: 196. Robert of Clari says that a hundred thousand marks of the two hundred thousand owed were promptly paid, of which fifty thousand went to the Venetians as their half and another thirty-six thousand out of the crusaders' half for payment of the long delinquent debt. The remainder, which (with typical Robertian arithmetic) he says was twenty thousand, was distributed among those who had loaned money to pay for the transportation of others. *Conquête*, sec. 56, p. 56. Robert cannot be correct, for we know from the treaty of March 1204 that the debt owed to the Venetians was not yet paid. Tafel and Thomas, *Urkunden*, I: 446. Faral, in my opinion, misinterprets a passage in a letter of the crusaders to the pope to say that at this point they also received provisions for a year and two hundred thousand marks. Villehardouin, *Conquête de Constantinople*, I: 197, n. 2. As I read the passage the emperor began to pay the sum of money promised under the treaty of Zara and made new promises in addition. "Hiis peractis, ad solutionem promissorum prosilit Imperator, et promissa rebus accumulat, victualia servitio Domini profutura nobis omnibus praebet in annum; ducenta marcarum millia nobis solvere pergit, et Venetis sumptibus suis stolium prolongat in annum, seque juramento astringit, quod erigere nobiscum debeat regale vexillum, et in passagio Martii nobiscum ad servitium Domini proficisci, cum quantis poterit millibus armatorum." Tafel and Thomas, *Urkunden*, I: 431 (Innocent III, *Epistolae*, VI: 211, Migne, *PL*, CCXV: 239). I translate the crucial passage as follows: "he offers supplies for us all for a year in the future for the service of God; he is proceeding to pay two hundred thousand marks to us." Both verbs are in the present tense. I admit, however, that Robert of Auxerre, also using the present, seems to say that Alexius had performed these things: "restituit precia navium, liberat nostros a debitis Venetorum, victualia omnibus copiose administratet sumptibus suis stolum prologat in annum, ducenta milia marchas argenti nostris et Venetis de imperiali munificentia dilargitur." *Chronicon*, pp. 265–66. Hendrickx, "Baudouin IX de Flandre et les empereurs byzantins," p. 486, n. 6, also reads the crusaders' letter as reporting that 200,000 marks had been paid. Dandolo refers to an earlier Venetian chronicle which states that the "Franks" were paid, but the Venetians were not. *Chronica*, pp. 278–79.

There is no contemporary evidence of the cession of Crete to Boniface at this time. If the sixteenth century chronicle of Galeotto del Carretto is correct, young Alexius promised it to him at Corfu. *Chronica di Monferrato*, ed. Gustavo Avrogado, in *Mon. Hist. patriae*, V: 1141. McNeal and Wolff accept this as probable. If so, it would seem to follow that he received it after the first conquest of the city. His transfer of it to the Venetians on 12 August 1204, after the second conquest, is well known. Tafel and Thomas, *Urkunden*, I: 512–15.

12. Villehardouin, *Conquête de Constantinople*, sec. 192, I: 194.

13. This is from the description given by the twelfth-century traveler, Benjamin of Tudela. *Itinerary*, trans. Asher, p. 54.

14. Cessi, "Venezia e la quarta crociata," pp. 2–3.

15. Hurter, *Papa Innocenzo III*, II: 219; quotation from W. B. Yeats, *Sailing to Byzantium*, as given in Maclagen, *The City of Constantinople*, p. 83.

16. Robert of Clari, *Conquête*, sec. 86, p. 86.

17. Van Millingen, *Byzantine Constantinople*, p. 269.

18. Janin, *Constantinople byzantine*, p. 115.

19. Hurter, *Papa Innocenzo III*, II: 225.

20. A Greek of this period, Nicholas Mesarites, tells how palpably the presence of Christ was felt in Constantinople, thanks to the innumerable relics, and especially the relics of the Nativity and the Passion. A. Frolow, *Recherches sur la déviation de la IVe Croisade vers Constantinople* (Paris, 1955), pp. 63–64. Constantinople did possess the greater part of the surviving remants of the Cross. Ibid., p. 50.

21. For a full interpretation of the importance of the True Cross to the crusaders' motivation, see ibid., pp. 59–71. The extremely knowledgeable and judicious historian of the crusades, Hans Eberhard Mayer, has accepted Frolow's argument. *The Crusades*, p. 188.

22. I am aware that Robert places his description of the marvels of the city after the account of the second conquest, but he does tell us that after the first conquest the crusaders went to the city whenever they wished. *Conquête*, sec. 82–92, pp. 81–90. The translated portions are from McNeal.

23. Anthony of Novgorod also saw it. See McNeal, ibid., p. 113, n. 120.

24. McNeal in Robert of Clari, *Conquest of Constantinople*, p. 17.

25. On Heraclius as a "crusader," see Frolow, *Recherches*, p. 75.

26. *Conquête de Constantinople*, sec. 192, I: 194.

27. Nicetas, *Historia*, p. 557. The Greek historian calls Alexius a "foolish, inexperienced child." Ibid., p. 551.

28. Ibid., p. 539. Runciman's observation that "Alexius IV soon found that an emperor cannot be as irresponsible as a pretender" is trenchant. *Crusades*, III: 119.

29. Nicetas, *Historia*, pp. 551–52.

30. Ibid., p. 552.

31. Brand, *Byzantium Confronts the West*, p. 140. Alexius III had, however, stripped the imperial tombs in the Church of the Holy Apostles of their precious ornaments to pay the so-called German tax to Henry VI. J. M. Hussey, "The Later Macedonians, the Comneni and the Angeli, 1025–1204," *CMH*, vol. IV, pt. 1 (Cambridge, 1966), pp. 247–48.

32. Innocent III, *Epistolae*, VI: 210, Migne, *PL*, CCXVI. Brand, *Byzantium Confronts the West*, p. 243, rightly observes that it would have been foolhardy to do so.

33. Innocent III, *Epistolae*, VI: 230, Migne, *PL*, CCXV: 260–61.

34. Gunther of Pairis, *Historia Constantinopolitana*, pp. 89–90.

35. Above, pp. 83–84.

36. Villehardouin, *The Conquest of Constantinople*, trans. Shaw, p. 77.

37. Villehardouin, *Conquête de Constantinople*, sec. 194–99, I: 196–202. As a further indication of the crusaders' good faith in fulfilling their vows in the Holy

Land, it must be pointed out that as late as 1205 Boniface still professed his intention to fight the infidel in Palestine. Innocent III, *Epistolae*, VIII: 133, Migne *PL*, CCXV: 710. Admittedly, Boniface might have been lying to the pope, but I do not think so.

38. Villehardouin, *Conquête de Constantinople*, sec. 201, I: 205.

39. Nicetas, *Historia*, p. 556.

40. Villehardouin, *Conquête de Constantinople*, sec. 201, I: 204–6. Robert of Clari, on the other hand, says that a good half of the host went with Alexius. *Conquête*, sec. 57, p. 57. Villehardouin, sec. 203, I: 206–8, and Robert of Clari in the passage just cited indicate that Alexius was out of the city with the expeditionary force before the time of the great fire, which broke out about 22 Aug. The letter from Alexius IV to Innocent III offering submission to Rome is somewhat troublesome, since it is dated in *Urbe Regia VIII Kal. Septembris*, which would seem to place Alexius in Constantinople at the time of the fire. Innocent III, *Epistolae*, VI: 210, Migne, *PL*, CCXV: 237. Could the document have been prepared before his departure, but issued with the date a few days later?

41. Villehardouin, *Conquête de Constantinople*, sec. 200, I: 204.

42. Nicetas, *Historia*, p. 556.

43. *Ibid.*; Villehardouin, *Conquête de Constantinople*, sec. 203, I: 206; Robert of Clari, *Conquête*, sec. 57, p. 57.

44. Nicetas describes the expedition after his account of the riot and the fire (*Historia*, pp. 552–56), but it is not clear that this is the correct chronological sequence. Nicetas frequently groups events together in a fashion not exactly chronological. Also see *Devastatio Constantinopolitana*, *M.G.H., SS.*, XVI: 11 (Hopf ed., pp. 89–90).

45. Nicetas, *Historia*, p. 553; *Devastatio Constantinopolitana*, *M.G.H., SS.*, XVI: 11 (Hopf ed., p. 89); Villehardouin, *Conquête de Constantinople*, sec. 203, I: 206–8.

46. Horatio Brown, "The Venetians and the Venetian Quarter in Constantinople to the Close of the Twelfth Century," *Journal of Hellenic Studies* XL (1920): 75–76.

47. Nicetas, *Historia*, p. 553.

48. Brand, *Byzantium Confronts the West*, p. 247.

49. Saint Peter and Saint Nicholas in the *Campo Pisanorum*. Hubaldus of Pisa, *Das Imbreviaturbuch des Erzbischöflichen Gerichtsnotars Hubaldus aus Pisa*, ed. Gero Dolezalek (Cologne-Vienna, 1969), p. 32.

50. Nicetas, *Historia*, p. 553.

51. *Ibid.*, p. 553. Nicol blames the fire on "some of the resident Latins in Constantinople," but Nicetas makes it clear that it was a band of Flemings, Venetians, and Pisans from across the harbor. "The Fourth Crusade and the Greek and Latin Empires," p. 283.

52. *Devastatio Constantinopolitana*, *M.G.H., SS.*, XVI: 11 (Hopf ed., p. 89).

53. Page 45.

54. Nicetas, *Historia*, pp. 553–55.

55 *Ibid.*, p. 553 and apparatus. Villehardouin says it continued for a whole week. *Conquête de Constantinople*, sec. 204. I: 210. Ernoul-Bernard says nine days and nights. *Chronique*, p. 367.

56. Nicetas, *Historia*, pp. 553–54.
57. Ibid., p. 587.
58. Ibid., p. 555.
59. Villehardouin, *Conquête de Constantinople*, sec. 204, I: 210–12.
60. Nicetas, *Historia*, p. 555.
61. Ibid.
62. Ibid., pp. 555–56.
63. Villehardouin, *Conquête de Constantinople*, sec. 205, I: 210.
64. Ibid.; *Devastatio Constantinopolitana*, *M.G.H.*, *SS.*, XVI: 11 (Hopf ed., p. 89).

Chapter 10

1. Robert of Clari, *Conquête*, sec. 57, p. 57. They returned on Saint Martin's Day, 11 Nov. Villehardouin, *Conquête de Constantinople*, sec. 207, II: 6. They had left the capital about the time of the fire. See p. 205, n. 40.

2. *Devastatio Constantinopolitana*, *M.G.H.*, *SS.*, XVI: 11 (Hopf ed., p. 90). The author adds that Boniface remained with the army with "a few Christians."

3. Robert of Clari, *Conquête*, sec. 57, p. 57.

4. Ibid.

5. Ibid., sec. 57, pp. 57–58.

6. Ibid., sec. 57, p. 58; Villehardouin, *Conquête de Constantinople*, sec. 207, II: 6–8.

7. *Conquête de Constantinople*, sec. 208, II: 8.

8. Usseglio, *I marchesi di Monferrato*, II: 229.

9. Brand distinguishes the contending parties, but doesn't emphasize their differing policies toward the Latins. *Byzantium Confronts the West*, pp. 242–43, and "A Byzantine Plan for the Fourth Crusade," p. 463.

10. Robert of Clari points out that during the absence of Alexius and Boniface Isaac had ceased payment. *Conquête*, sec. 57, p. 57. After their return Villehardouin also complains of postponements, payment of trivial sums, and finally cessation of payments. *Conquête de Constantinople*, sec. 208, II: 8.

11. See his words of caution to the mob against electing a new emperor in January, 1204. *Historia*, p. 562.

12. Letter of Baldwin of Flanders, in Innocent III, *Epistolae*, VII: 152, Migne, *PL*, CCXV: 447–48.

13. McNeal and Wolff, "The Fourth Crusade," p. 181, n. 62; Brand, *Byzantium Confronts the West*, p. 122.

14. Baldwin says that he was influenced by his father, the patriarch, and the mass of the nobles. In Innocent III, *Epistolae*, VII: 152, Migne, *PL*, CCXV: 447–48.

15. Nicephorus Chrysoberges, *Ad Angelos orationes tres*, ed. Maximilian Treu (Breslau, 1892), p. 28; trans. Charles Brand, "A Byzantine Plan for the Fourth Crusade," p. 467.

16. Nicetas, *Historia*, pp. 556–57.

17. Page 45. The context does not inspire confidence in the accuracy of details, although the author does have the gist of what happened.

18. Brand, "A Byzantine Plan for the Fourth Crusade," p. 473.

19. Above, n. 14.

20. Nicetas, *Historia*, p. 565.

21. Ibid., pp. 556–57.

22. Ibid., pp. 557–58.

23. Francesco Cognasso, "Un imperatore bizantino della decadenza: Isaaco II Angelo," *Bessarione* XXXI (1915): 40.

24. Nicetas, *Historia*, pp. 557–58. Nicetas tells a story, which he may have invented or retouched for dramatic effect, about how a seer named Basilakios, consulted by Isaac in 1195, before his imprisonment and blinding, poked out the eyes of the emperor's picture and tried to knock off his cap. Ibid., pp. 449–50. During the second rebellion of Alexius Branas in 1186, Isaac already had displayed his political and military ineptitude by retiring to the safety of monkish prayer to save himself from the rebel. Cognasso, "Un imperatore bizantino," p. 48.

25. Robert of Clari, *Conquête*, sec. 58, p. 58.

26. Villehardouin, *Conquête de Constantinople*, sec. 209, I: 8. The same sentiment occurs in the letter written by Baldwin of Flanders to the pope in 1204 after he had become the Latin emperor: "...et ex insperato seu innata malitia, seu graecorum seductus perfidia animo recedit a nobis, qui tanta beneficia contulimus, imperator, et in omnibus cum patre, patriarcho, et mole nobilium, nobis promissis periuris et mendax tot incurrit periuria, quot nobis praestitit iuramenta." Innocent III, *Epistolae*, VII: 152, Migne, *PL*, CCXV: 447–48.

27. Villehardouin, *Conquête de Constantinople*, sec. 208, II: 8.

28. Runciman, *Crusades*, III: 119.

29. Robert of Clari, *Conquête*, sec. 58, p. 58.

30. Nicetas, *Historia*, p. 89.

31. Villehardouin, *Conquête de Constantinople*, sec. 210, II: 8–10.

32. Ibid.

33. Ibid., secs. 211–16, II: 10–14; Robert of Clari, *Conquête*, sec. 59, p. 59. Faral suggests that Robert's account of a meeting immediately following the French embassy between Alexius and the doge is a confusion on Robert's part with such a conference held between the Venetian leader and Alexius Mourtzouphlus after the latter had ascended the Byzantine throne. In Villehardouin, *Conquête de Constantinople*, II: 15, n. 1. Even though I think that this meeting probably did not occur, Robert's account is worth quoting for its revelation of the feelings of the men in the ranks. Dandolo said: "Alexius, what do you think you are doing? Just think how we rescued you from great wretchedness, and made you lord, and crowned you emperor. Will you not keep your agreements with us?" To which Alexius replied that he would do no more for them. "No?" said Dandolo. "Evil boy! We pulled you out of shit, and into shit we will throw you back! I defy you, and let you know for certain that I will do you all the harm in my power." The translation is mine, and, because I want to reveal the feelings of the Latin troops, as reflected by Robert, I have rejected the customary euphemisms.

34. Gunther of Pairis, *Historia Constantinopolitana*, p. 53; Villehardouin, *Conquête de Constantinople*, sec. 262, II: 68; Robert of Clari, *Conquête*, sec. 80, p. 80.

35. Villehardouin, *Conquête de Constantinople*, sec. 147, I: 148.

36. Above, pp. 94 and 104.

37. Above, pp. 105–107.

38. Villehardouin, *Conquête de Constantinople*, sec. 216, II: 14; Nicetas, *Historia*, p. 741.

39. Nicetas, *Historia*, p. 560.

40. *Devastatio Constantinopolitana, M.G.H., SS.*, XVI: 11 (Hopf ed., p. 90). Brand believes that the victims were Latins "touring the city." *Byzantium Confronts the West*, p. 248. I think that the time for touring had passed. The *Devastatio*, is not completely unambiguous, but it seems to me to imply that they were the remaining Latin inhabitants. Runciman says that Mourtzouphlus "organized" the riot, for which I find no evidence. *Crusades*, III: 120.

41. Robert of Clari, *Conquête*, sec. 60, pp. 59–60; Baldwin of Flanders, in Innocent III, *Epistolae*, VII: 152, Migne, *PL*, CCXV: 448.

42. *Devastatio Constantinopolitana, M.G.H., SS.*, XVI: 11 (Hopf ed., pp. 90–91).

43. Villehardouin, *Conquête de Constantinople*, secs. 217–20, II: 16–18; Robert of Clari, *Conquête*, sec. 60, p. 60; *Devastatio Constantinopolitana, M.G.H., SS.*, XVI: 11 (Hopf ed., p. 91). Baldwin of Flanders in his letter to Innocent III and others (Innocent III, *Epistolae*, VII: 152, Migne, *PL*, CCXV: 449) places this second attack after the ascension to the throne of Alexius Ducas, probably erroneously. See Faral, in Villehardouin, *Conquête de Constantinople*, II: 17, n. 1.

44. Brand says that the location of the place is unknown today. *Byzantium Confronts the West*, p. 249. The Perforated Stone, however, was a well-known landmark located near the Blachernae Palace. Heyd, *Commerce du Levant*, I: 210, n. 1, and "Nuova serie di documenti sulle relazioni di Genova coll' impero bizantino," ed. Angelo Sanguineti and Gerolamo Bertolotto, *Atti della Società Ligure di Storia Patria* (1896–98), XXVIII: p. 346. Gerald Day called this positive information on the Perforated Stone to my attention.

45. Nicetas, *Historia*, p. 561.

46. *M.G.H., SS.*, XVI: 11 (Hopf ed., p. 91). Faral, at least, conjectures Nicetas and the *Devastatio* are recounting the same incident. Villehardouin, *Conquête de Constantinople*, II: 15, n. 2.

47. Robert of Clari, *Conquête*, sec. 60, p. 60.

48. Alberic of Trois-Fontaines, *Chronica*, p. 882.

49. Robert of Clari, *Conquête*, sec. 60, p. 60.

50. Alberic of Trois-Fontaines, *Chronica*, pp. 882–83.

51. Nicetas, *Historia*, p. 561, trans. Richard L. Bates.

52. The *Chronicle of Novgorod*, valuable, but often confused, tells us that this assembly was held after the death of Isaac (p. 45), but Villehardouin tells us that Isaac died a short time after the deposition of Alexius IV. *Conquête de Constantinople*, sec. 223, II: 22.

53. Nicetas, *Historia*, pp. 561-62; *Chronicle of Novgorod*, p. 45.

54. Nicetas, *Historia*, pp. 558–59. It is true that the Latins had sailed up the straits from the south, but they came from the West and were presently encamped

north of the harbor. R. J. H. Jenkins raises a doubt as to whether the statue was in fact the famous work of Phidias. "The Bronze Athena at Byzantium," *Journal of Hellenic Studies* LXVII (1947): 31–33. Marilyn Caldwell called this article to my attention.

55. Nicetas, *Historia*, p. 562; *Chronicle of Novgorod*, p. 45. Alberic of Trois-Fontaines wrongly dates this after the skirmish in which Mourtzouphlus lost the icon. *Chronica, M.G.H., SS.*, XXIII: 883.

56. Nicetas, *Historia*, p. 563; *Chronicle of Novgorod*, p. 45; Baldwin of Flanders, in Innocent III, *Epistolae*, VII: 152, Migne, *PL*, CCV: 448. Brand casts Mourtzouphlus as the crafty adviser who treacherously gave Alexius IV the idea of reintroducing the Latins. Mourtzouphlus' purpose, according to this theory, was to create an anti-Latin revolution which would put him on the throne in place of the tainted young emperor. *Byzantium Confronts the West*, p. 250, I cannot find the evidence supporting this theory. One indication that it is not true is the failure of Nicetas to mention it, thus passing up a good opportunity to vilify further his enemy, Mourtzouphlus. The question, of course, is not whether Mourtzouphlus was treacherous, but whether he initiated the embassy to Boniface.

57. Baldwin of Flanders, in Innocent III, *Epistolae*, VII: 152, Migne, *PL*, CCXV: 448; Nicetas, *Historia*, p. 563; Villehardouin, *Conquête de Constantinople*, sec. 221, II: 20.

58. Nicetas, *Historia*, p. 566.

59. For a brief sketch of Mourtzouphlus, see Usseglio, *I marchesi di Monferrato*, II: 230.

60. Nicetas, *Historia*, p. 566.

61. Ibid., p. 566.

62. Ibid., p. 571.

63. For example, according to Robert of Clari it was Mourtzouphlus who advised Alexius IV to suspend payment of the promised money and supplies to the crusaders. *Conquête*, sec. 58, p. 58.

64. Baldwin of Flanders, in Innocent III, *Epistolae*, VII: 152, Migne, *PL*, CCXV: 448.

65. Ibid.

66. Nicetas, *Historia*, p. 563; Villehardouin, *Conquête de Constantinople*, sec. 222, II: 20–22.

67. Baldwin of Flanders, in Innocent III, *Epistolae*, VII: 152, Migne, *PL*, CCXV: 148; Nicetas, *Historia*, pp. 563–64.

68. Robert of Clari, *Conquête*, sec. 61, p. 61.

69. Alberic of Trois-Fontaines, *Chronica*, p. 883.

70. According to the *Chronicle of Novgorod*, p. 46, Mourtzouphlus was crowned on 5 Feb. 1204. Villehardouin also places Ducas' coronation a little while after the palace coup. *Conquête de Constantinople*, sec. 222, II: 20–22. Nada Patrone dates the ascent of Alexius V to the empire in 1202! *La quarta crociata*, p. 42.

71. Nicetas, *Historia*, p. 564.

72. Page 45.

73. Nicetas, *Historia*, p. 564; Baldwin of Flanders, in Innocent III, *Epistolae*,

VII: 152, Migne, *PL*, CCXV: 448; Alberic of Trois-Fontaines, *Chronica*, p. 883; *Devastatio Constantinopolitana, M.G.H., SS.*, XVI: 12 (Hopf ed., p. 91).

74. Gunther of Pairis, *Historia Constantinopolitana*, p. 91.

75. Villehardouin, *Conquête de Constantinople*, sec. 224, II: 22.

76. In Innocent III, *Epistolae*, VII: 152, Migne, *PL*, CCXV: 449–50. Brand, *Byzantium Confronts the West*, p. 252, interprets this as taking place through correspondence, rather than a personal meeting, but this is not what the text says.

77. *Historia*, pp. 567–68. Nicetas has the interview sought by Boniface, while Baldwin has it sought by Mourtzouphlus. Brand interprets the incident described by Nicetas as a personal meeting distinct from the episode described by Baldwin. *Byzantium Confronts the West*, p. 252.

78. Villehardouin, *Conquête de Constantinople*, sec. 226, II: 24.

79. In Innocent III, *Epistolae*, VII: 152, Migne, *PL*, CCXV: 449.

80. Ibid.; Nicetas, *Historia*, p. 567.

81. *De terra Iherosolimitana*, ed. Paul Riant, *Exuviae*, I 6.

82. Nicetas, *Historia*, p. 567.

83. Robert of Clari, *Conquête*, sec. 66, p. 65. Alberic of Trois-Fontaines says a thousand men. *Chronica, M.G.H., SS.*, XXIII: 883. So does Baldwin. In Innocent III, *Epistolae*, VII: 152, Migne, *PL*, CCXV: 449. Villehardouin says that he took a great part of the best men. *Conquête de Constantinople*, sec. 226, II: 24. For once Robert's figures seem reasonable to me. He fixes the ambushing force of Mourtzouphlus as a thousand men, while Alberic says ten thousand and the *Devastatio Constantinopolitana* says fifteen thousand. *M.G.H., SS.*, XVI: 12 (Hopf ed., p. 91). Alberic says that he took so many because of fear that those remaining might try to prevent his reentry.

84. Villehardouin, *Conquête de Constantinople*, secs. 226–28, II: 24–28; Robert of Clari, *Conquête*, sec. 66, pp. 65–67; Nicetas, *Historia*, pp. 750–51; *Devastatio Constantinopolitana, M.G.H., SS.*, XVI: 12 (Hopf ed., p. 91); Baldwin of Flanders, in Innocent III, *Epistolae*, VII: 152, Migne, *PL*, CCXV: 449; Alberic of Trois-Fontaines, *Chronica*, pp. 882–83.

85. Robert of Clari, *Conquête*, sec. 66, p. 67.

86. Alberic of Trois-Fontaines, *Chronica*, p. 883.

87. Ibid.; Robert of Clari, *Conquête*, sec. 66, p. 67; Baldwin of Flanders, in Innocent III, *Epistolae*, VII: 152, Migne, *PL*, CCXV: 449.

88. Robert of Clari, *Conquête*, sec. 66–67, pp. 67–68.

89. This motive for Mourtzouphlus' action is the one attributed to him by Alberic of Trois-Fontaines, *Chronica*, p. 883.

90. Villehardouin, *Conquête de Constantinople*, sec. 223, II: 22; Nicetas, *Historia*, p. 564.

91. Baldwin of Flanders, in Innocent III, *Epistolae*, VII: 152, Migne, *PL*, CCXV: 450. The date is given by Nicetas as the sixth month, the eighth day of the reign of Alexius, which began officially on 1 Aug. 1203. *Historia*, p. 564.

92. Robert of Clari, *Conquête*, sec. 62, p. 61; Baldwin of Flanders, in Innocent III, *Epistolae*, VII: 152, Migne, *PL*, CCXV: 450; Villehardouin, *Conquête de Constantinople*, sec. 223, II: 22; Alberic of Trois-Fontaines, *Chronica*, p. 883; *Devastatio Constantinopolitana, M.G.H., SS.*, XVI: 12 (Hopf ed., pp. 91–92). Robert

incorrectly has Isaac strangled as well. A story reached Syria that Alexius had had a dream of being strangled by a wild boar of brass which was in the great palace. When he awoke he had the statue destroyed, but could not avert his fate. Ernoul-Bernard, *Chronique*, pp. 369–70.

93. Villehardouin, *Conquête de Constantinople*, sec. 223, ii: 22.

94. Ibid.

95. Brand, *Byzantium Confronts the West*, pp. 76, 114, and 115.

96. Hussey, "The Later Macedonians, the Comneni, and the Angeli, 1025–1204," p. 247. Hussey's judgment is harsher and lacks the nuances of Brand's.

97. Brand, *Byzantium Confronts the West*, pp. 113–14.

98. Nicetas, *Historia*, p. 441.

99. *Conquête*, sec. 62, p. 62; translated by McNeal in Robert of Clari, *Conquest of Constantinople*, p. 86.

100. A point made by Jeanette M. A. Beer, *Villehardouin: Epic Historian*, Geneva, 1968, pp. 45–46.

101. Robert of Clari, *Conquête*, sec. 62, p. 62.

102. Gunther of Pairis, *Historia Constantinopolitana*, i: 91–93. Gunther exaggerates, however, the strength of the Byzantines, especially of their fleet. Francis R. Swietek, "Gunther of Pairis and the *Historia Constantinopolitana*," pp. 5–6.

103. Witness the expedition of Henry of Hainaut to Philia. *Above*, pp. 134–135.

104. Alberic of Trois-Fontaines, *Chronica*, p. 883.

Chapter 11

1. It is strongly expressed in Dandolo's speech before the final assault on Constantinople as recounted by the sixteenth century manuscript chronicle of Gian Giacopo Caroldo: "Et io vi dico che siamo in alieno paese, et à noi è necessario vincèr o haver poca speranza de ritornar nella patria nostra." *Historia de Venetia*, Biblioteca Marciana, cl. ital. vii, cod. 127 (= 8034), f. 70v.

2. Manfroni, *Storia della marina italiana*, i: 329; Wiel, *Navy of Venice*, p. 147.

3. Raymond S. Schmandt, "Orthodoxy and Catholicism: Public Opinion, the Schism, and the Fourth Crusade," p. 297.

4. Villehardouin, *Conquête de Constantinople*, secs. 224–25, ii: 22–24.

5. Monk of San Giorgio, *Translatio corporis beatissimi Pauli martyris de Constantinopoli Venetias*, in Riant, *Exuviae*, i: 141.

6. Villehardouin, *Conquête de Constantinople*, sec. 225, ii: 24.

7. There are two texts of the treaty, one in the name of Dandolo, the other in the names of the crusading leaders. There are insignificant differences and one major discrepancy. In text B, the one in the names of the crusaders, it says that three quarters of the booty should go "nobis et hominibus Venetie," which is obviously a misreading of "vobis." Text A also has "nobis," in this case correctly. Tafel and Thomas, *Urkunden*, i: 444–52. Christopher G. Ferrard has become confused by trying to follow text B. "The Amount of Constantinopolitan Booty in 1204," *Studi Veneziani* xiii (1971): 102–3, n. 17.

8. Boniface of Montferrat remained the obvious candidate. He was the com-

mander-in-chief. The treaty itself seems to single him out, for it provides for its own amendment by the doge and his six councilors and Montferrat and his six. Tafel and Thomas, *Urkunden*, I: 448 and 452. After the election had fallen to Baldwin of Flanders and relations between the new emperor and the marquis had been patched up, Villehardouin refers to the marquis in glowing terms as "one of the most highly esteemed knights in all the world, and one whom his fellow knights loved most, since no one was more openhanded and generous than he." The *Conquest of Constantinople*, trans. Shaw, p. 97. The Venetians are usually considered instrumental in swinging the election to the count of Flanders, since the marquis of Montferrat was an old ally of the Genoese. Robert Lee Wolff, "The Latin Empire," pp. 76–77. Runciman, *Crusades* III: 121. Cessi challenged his position. "L'eredità di Enrico Dandolo," p. 10, n. 2. Riant speculated that the six Venetians voted for Baldwin, as well as John of Noyon, Baldwin's own chancellor of Hainaut, Peter, bishop of Bethlehem, legate of the pope, and Garnier, bishop of Troyes, who shared the bias of the Champenois against Boniface, leaving the marquis only Conrad of Krosigk, bishop of Halberstadt, Peter, abbot of Locedio, and Nivelon of Chérisy, bishop of Soissons. "Innocent III," *Revue des questions historiques* XVIII: 56. See also Antonio Carile, "Partitio Terrarum Imperii Romanie," *Studi Veneziani* VII (1965): 136–40, and especially n. 71. He thinks that the papal legate may have supported Boniface, but leaves the bishop of Soissons to Baldwin. It should be noted again that the marquis had lost status with the failure of his policy of support of young Alexius. Some authorities mention the possibility of a union of the two empires by the election of Philip of Swabia. Runciman, *Crusades*, III: 121; Frolow, *Recherches*, p. 21. I think that this was not a serious possibility. That Dandolo rejected the imperial title is a patriotic Venetian myth. Cessi, "L'eredità di Enrico Dandolo," p. 9. It can still be found, however, in less scholarly works. Elio Zorzi, *Venezia* (Milan, 1942), pp. 72–73.

9. Wolff has pointed out that the division of territories undercut, from the beginning, the foundations of the new state. *The Latin Empire*, p. 70.

10. In addition to the treaty, see Villehardouin, *Conquête de Constantinople*, sec. 235, II: 36.

11. Robert of Clari, *Conquête*, sec. 68, pp. 68–69.

12. Villehardouin, *Conquête de Constantinople*, sec. 251, II: 55. Hendrickx formulates an equation to determine the number of non-Venetian crusaders, which he finds insoluble. We are told by Villehardouin that among them they divided 100,000 marks (sec. 254, II: 58). He also tells us that the 100,000 marks were divided as follows: "II. serjanz a pié contre un a cheval, et .II. serjanz a cheval contre un chevalier," or a ratio of 1:2:4. The *Devastatio Constantinopolitana* and Ernoul-Bernard support this. According to the latter, Dandolo proposed to give each knight 400 marks, each mounted sergeant 200, and each sergeant on foot 100, but the actual distribution was 20 marks per knight, 10 per mounted sergeant, and 5 per sergeant on foot. (*Chronique*, pp. 375–76.) Hendrickx thus sets up the formula: $100,000 = 400x + 200y + 100z$, but he finds no way to arrive at numbers for x, y, and z. "Les troupes de la quatrième croisade," pp. 34–35. I think it should be $100,000 = 20x + 10y + 5z$, and I believe I see a way to solve the equation. If we assume that the proportions were in accord with the treaty of 1201, we can say

that $y = 2x$ and $z = 4.44x$, or
 $100,000 = 20x + 20x + 22.2x$
 $100,000 = 62.2x$
  $1,608 = x$
  $3,216 = y$
  $\underline{7,140} = z$
 11,964 non-Venetian crusaders.

Or, we might obtain a slightly different result by using the ratio 1:2:4, which is considered common for an army at this time. (I think this may be the right key, since it would mean that the 100,000 marks was divided into three equal shares for knights, mounted sergeants, and foot sergeants.) We would then have the equation:
 $100,000 = 20x + 20x + 20x$
 $100,000 = 60x$
  $1,667 = x$
  $3,334 = y$
  $\underline{6,668} = z$
 $11,669 =$ non-Venetian crusaders.

Neither of these is an unreasonable figure, if we interpret Villehardouin's one third of the anticipated number of crusaders actually arriving at Venice as a rather rough figure. Benjamin Hendrickx, "A propos du nombre des troupes de la quatrième croisade et de l'empereur Baudouin I," *Byzantina (Thessalonica)* III (1971): 34–35.
 McNeal calculates 9,900. Robert of Clari, *Conquête*, p. 131. Hans Jahn, *Die Heereszahlen in der Kreuzzügen*, pp. 50–51.
 13. Above, p. 118.
 14. Villehardouin, *Conquête de Constantinople*, sec. 245, II: 48.
 15. Ibid., sec. 162, I: 162.
 16. For description of some of these machines, see Nada Patrone's trans. of Robert of Clari, *Conquista de Costantinopoli*, p. 202, nn. 74–76, and McNeal, in Robert of Clari, *Conquest of Constantinople*, p. 92, n. 91.
 17. Robert of Clari, *Conquête*, sec. 69, p. 69; Manfroni, *Storia della marina italiana*, I: 335.
 18. Nicetas, *Historia*, p. 567.
 19. *Ibid.*; Villehardouin, *Conquête de Constantinople*, sec. 233, II: 32–34; Baldwin of Flanders, in Innocent III, *Epistolae*, VII: 152, Migne, *PL*, CCXV: 448–49; Robert of Clari, *Conquête*, sec. 61, pp. 60–61, and sec. 69, p. 69.
 20. Gunther of Pairis, *Historia Constantinopolitana*, pp. 92–93.
 21. *Chronica*, p. 883.
 22. Villehardouin, *Conquête de Constantinople*, sec. 236, II: 36.
 23. Carile has confused the dating: "Il 9 aprile, *joesdi aprés mi quaresme*, i crociati lanciarono l'attacco alle mura della città e dopo parecchie ore di lotta dovettero riparare al campo." "Partitio," p. 131. They *boarded* their vessels on 8 Apr. Thursday, and attacked at break of day on Friday, 9 Apr. Villehardouin, *Conquête de Constantinople*, secs. 236–37, II: 36–38. Inexplicably Runciman fixes the

attack on 6 April. *Crusades,* III: 122.

24. Villehardouin, *Conquête de Constantinople,* sec. 236, II: 36–38; Robert of Clari, *Conquête,* sec. 70, pp. 69–70.

25. Anonymous of Soissons, *De terra Iherosolimitana,* p. 6.

26. Villehardouin, *Conquête de Constantinople,* secs. 236–37, II: 36–38. Pears conjectured that the galleys and horse transports formed a first line and the transports a second. *Fall of Constantinople,* p. 347. Some MSS. support this interpretation, but Faral rejects it. In Villehardouin, *Conquête de Constantinople,* II: 39, n. 1.

27. Villehardouin, *Conquête de Constantinople,* sec. 237, II: 38.

28. Robert of Clari, *Conquête,* sec. 70, p. 70; Nicetas, *Historia,* p. 568.

29. Robert of Clari, *Conquête,* sec. 70, p. 70.

30. Van Millingen, *Byzantine Constantinople,* p. 183.

31. Robert of Clari, *Conquête,* sec. 70, p. 70; Nicetas *Historia,* p. 568.

32. Nicetas, *Historia,* p. 568. From the Palace of Blachernae to the monastery of Euergetes.

33. Ibid., pp. 568–69.

34. Robert of Clari, *Conquête,* sec. 71, p. 70.

35. Villehardouin, *Conquête de Constantinople,* sec. 237, II: 38.

36. Ibid., sec. 240, II: 42.

37. *Devastatio Constantinopolitana, M.G.H., SS.,* XVI: 12 (Hopf ed., p. 92).

38. Robert of Clari, *Conquête,* sec. 71, p. 70.

39. Villehardouin, *Conquête de Constantinople,* sec. 237, II: 38.

40. Ibid., sec. 238, II: 38.

41. Robert of Clari, *Conquête,* sec. 71, p. 70.

42. Baldwin of Flanders, in Innocent III, *Epistolae,* VII: 152, Migne, *PL,* CCXV : 450.

43. Robert of Clari, *Conquête,* sec. 71, pp. 70–71.

44. *Chronicle of Novgorod,* p. 46. The *Devastatio Constantinopolitana, M.G.H., SS.,* XVI: 12 (Hopf ed., p. 92), says that the losses were heavy on both sides. Baldwin of Flanders seems to say that the defeat occurred without much loss of Latin blood. In Innocent III, *Epistolae,* VII: 152, Migne, *PL,* CCXV: 450. Tafel and Thomas tentatively supply "non". *Urkunden,* I: 506. So does the version addressed to the archbishop of Cologne, but none of the others has it. Prevenier, *Oorkonden,* II: 570, 581 (Cologne version), 588, and 598. Villehardouin confesses that the Latins lost more men than did the Greeks. *Conquête de Constantinople,* sec. 238, II: 38–40.

45. Robert of Clari, *Conquest of Constantinople,* p. 93.

46. Villehardouin, *Conquête de Constantinople,* sec. 239, II: 40; Robert of Clari, *Conquête,* sec. 72, p. 71. Villehardouin himself was among those who thought that the Lord's wrath had fallen upon them, for he says: "Mais por noz pechiez furent li pelerin resorti de l'assault." *Conquête de Constantinople,* sec. 238, II: 38.

47. Robert of Clari, *Conquête,* sec. 72, p. 71.

48. Above, p. 85.

49. Villehardouin, *Conquête de Constantinople,* sec. 239, II: 40. Janin, *Constantinople byzantine,* p. 2, reports that the current, due to the overflow of the Black Sea, runs at 3–5 km./hr. For an appreciation of Dandolo's role in the crusade, see

Manfroni, *Storia della marina italiana*, I: 334–35. I cannot agree with Dufournet that Villehardouin glosses over the magnitude of the setback. *Villehardouin et Clari*, I: 151.

50. Villehardouin, *Conquête de Constantinople*, sec. 240, II: 240–42.

51. Ibid.

52. Robert of Clari names Abbot Simon of Loos among the preachers. *Conquête*, sec. 73, p. 71. Villehardouin has him dead in late autumn, 1203. *Conquête de Constantinople*, sec. 206, II: 7. See Brown, "The Cistercians in the Latin Empire," p. 76, and Schmandt, "Fourth Crusade and Just War Theory," p. 216, n. 67. The latter points out that Simon generally agreed with Villehardouin, for that reason received special attention, and would therefore have been mentioned by the chronicler were he living. On the eloquence of John Faicete, see Villehardouin, *Conquête de Constantinople*, sec. 290, II: 98.

53. Unfortunately for Frolow's argument concerning the attractive force of the relics of Constantinople, there is no evidence that the preachers exhorted their hearers to liberate the holy remains from the Greeks. There is plenty of evidence assembled by Riant in the *Exuviae* of the great importance of the relics after the conquest, but, although I have been alert throughout my research for documentation of the Frolow thesis, I have found no specific indication that the existence of the relics in Constantinople was used as an argument for attacking the city. Frolow, *Recherches*, p. 71. If Frolow's thesis is sound, it is difficult to understand why such an obvious appeal would not have been made.

54. Brand, *Byzantium Confronts the West*, p. 255.

55. Robert of Clari, *Conquête*, secs. 73–74, pp. 71–72.

56. *Chronicle of Novgorod*, p. 46.

57. Robert of Clari, *Conquête*, sec. 74, p. 73. Greek fire, it seems, was not a secret weapon of the Greeks.

58. Villehardouin,*Conquête de Constantinople*, sec. 241, II: 42; Nicetas, *Historia*, p. 569.

59. Robert of Clari, *Conquête*, sec. 74, p. 73.

60. Venetian tradition named him Pietro Alberti. See Zorzi Dolfin, *Chronica*, Biblioteca Marciana, cl. ital. VII, cod. 794 (=8503). Dolfin and the Venetian tradition generally, however, are not very reliable on the Fourth Crusade. Dolfin also has him bearing the standard of St. Mark.

61. Robert of Clari, *Conquête*, sec. 74, pp. 73–74; Villehardouin, *Conquête de Constantinople*, sec. 242 II: 42–44; Baldwin of Flanders, in Innocent III, *Epistolae*, Migne, *PL*, VII: 152 ccxv: 450; Nicetas, *Historia*, pp. 568–69; Ernoul-Bernard, *Chronique*, p. 372; Anonymous of Soissons, *De terra Iherosolimitana*, pp. 6–7. On the identity of Andrew, see Riant, *Exuviae*, I, lv.

62. Robert of Clari, *Conquête*, 74, p. 74; Ernoul-Bernard, *Chronique*, p. 372.

63. Villehardouin, *Conquête de Constantinople*, sec. 243, II: 44. I am aware that he says four towers, but it is not clear whether these are in addition to the first one.

64. Robert of Clari, *Conquête*, sec. 74, pp. 74–75.

65. Nicetas, *Historia*, pp. 569–70.

66. Robert of Clari, *Conquête*, secs. 75–78, pp. 75–77. In another position be-

neath the walls the poet-companion of Boniface of Montferrat, Raimbaut de Vaqueiras, was wounded. Linskill, in Raimbaut de Vaqueiras *Poems*, pp. 305 and
310, and notes. This gives a slight indication of the place of Boniface and his followers in the battle.

67. Robert of Clari, *Conquête*, sec. 78, p. 77; Villehardouin, *Conquête de Constantinople*, sec. 243, ii: 44–46.

68. *Historia*, p. 570. There was a massacre, at any rate. Gunther of Pairis,
Historia Constantinopolitana, p. 102; Anonymous of Soissons, *De terra Iherosolimitana*, pp. 6–7; Villehardouin, *Conquête de Constantinople*, sec. 244, ii: 46.

69. Villehardouin, *Conquête de Constantinople*, sec. 244, ii: 46.

70. Gunther of Pairis, *Historia Constantinopolitana*, pp. 102–3.

71. Robert of Clari, *Conquête*, sec. 78, p. 78.

72. Villehardouin, *Conquête de Constantinople*, secs. 243–44, ii: 46.

73. Ibid.; Robert of Clari, *Conquête* sec. 78, pp. 78–79.

74. Villehardouin, *Conquête de Constantinople*, sec. 245, ii: 46–48. I assume
that this is the meaning of "l'espés de la ville." Hodgson makes it out as the town
meadows, which he attempts to identify. *The Early History of Venice*, pp. 397–98.
This seems most unlikely.

75. Robert of Clari, *Conquête*, sec. 78, p. 78.

76. Villehardouin says only that the incendiaries were certain unknown persons. *Conquête de Constantinople*, sec. 247, ii: 48. Gunther of Pairis identified the
leader as "quidam comes Theotonicus." *Historia Constantinopolitana*, p. 101. Riant
conjectures Berthold. *Exuviae*, i: xxxiv, and "Innocent III," *Revue des questions
historiques* xviii: 52–53. In the latter he speculates that the fire was set by command of Boniface. Usseglio, *I marchesi di Monferrato*, ii: 237–38, and Brand, *Byzantium Confronts the West*, p. 257, follow Riant.

77. Villehardouin gives the duration of the fire. *Conquête de Constantinople*
sec. 247, ii: 48–50. Nicetas gives its extent. *Historia*, p. 570.

78. *Conquête de Constantinople* sec. 247, ii: 50.

79. Peter Charanis, "A Note on the Population and Cities of the Byzantine
Empire in the Thirteenth Century," *The Joshua Starr Memorial Volume* (New
York, 1953), pp. 137–38; Brand, *Byzantium Confronts the West*, p. 257.

80. Nicetas, *Historia*, p. 570; Baldwin of Flanders, in Innocent III, *Epistolae*,
vii: 152, Migne, *PL*, ccxv: 451; *Chronicle of Novgorod*, p. 47.

81. Nicetas, *Historia*, p. 571.

82. Nicetas has him escape the city in a small boat. *Historia*, p. 571. Villehardouin has him depart via the Golden Gate. *Conquête de Constantinople*, sec. 246,
ii: 48. Possibly these are not irreconcilable. After taking Eudocia and her mother
with him in his flight from Constantinople, Mourtzouphlus married her. Nicetas
Historia, p. 608; Demetrios I. Polemis, *The Doukai: A Contribution to Byzantine
Prosopography* (London, 1968), p. 146. Other writers regard him as the son-in-law
of Alexius III before his ascent to the throne. E.g., D. M. Nicol, "The Fourth
Crusade and the Greek and Latin Empires," pp. 283–84. See Runciman, *Crusades*
iii: 122.

83. Villehardouin, *Conquête de Constantinople*, sec. 246, ii: 48.

84. Nicetas, *Historia*, pp. 571–72. A fourteenth century manuscript, however

says that the two candidates were both named Theodore. B. Sinogowitz, "Über das byzantinische Kaisertum nach dem vierten Kreuzzuge (1204–1205)," *Byzantinische Zeitschrift* CLV (1952): 345–51, follows the Bonn ed., and now Van Dieten, in arguing that they were named Constantine. Robert Lee Wolff, "The Latin Empire of Constantinople," p. 201, n. 11, argues for Theodore. In the light of subsequent events, logic lies on Wolff's side, but I feel compelled to follow the editors' reading of what Nicetas says.

85. Nicetas, *Historia*, p. 572.

86. Ibid., pp. 572–73; Robert of Clari, *Conquête*, sec. 79, p. 79.

87. Villehardouin, *Conquête de Constantinople*, sec. 248, II: 50.

88. E. Frances contrasts the fall of Constantinople is 1204 in a short time to a meager force to its strong resistance to the overwhelming power of the Turks in 1453, arguing that the reason for the difference must be sought in the internal condition of the empire, and especially the capital, in 1204. "Sur la conquête de Constantinople par les Latins," *Byzantino-slavica* XXIX (1968): 22.

Bibliography

Primary Sources

Any discussion of the sources of the Fourth Crusade of necessity begins with the famous chronicle of Geoffrey of Villehardouin, the marshal of Champagne. The author was not only a participant, but stood in the second rank of leaders, right beneath the marquis of Montferrat and the counts of Flanders, Blois, and Saint Pol. More mature than many of the barons, he was greatly trusted and often employed as envoy and spokesman for the crusaders. He participated in the councils of the barons where the crucial decisions were made. In some passages he appears to have written with a copy of a treaty or other document before his eyes. It has been speculated that he wrote with the aid of a journal or diary. Even his critics concede that the marshal possessed a knowledge of events matched by no other chronicler. His very position among the leaders, however, has brought charges of bias and deliberate distortion upon him. For the last hundred years scholars have debated his veracity. His foes call him an "official historian," one who concealed facts damaging to the reputations of the leaders who diverted the crusade to Constantinople for their own ends. Others consider him a dupe, not implicated in a plot to divert the crusade, but foolish enough to overlook it. I strongly disagree with these interpretations, although he did possess a natural bias. It seems very clear to me that the marshal was much too wise and experienced a statesman to be duped. His judgment was clearly trusted by all who knew him. Only Dandolo, I think, commanded more respect in council. On the other hand, I do not believe that there was a conspiracy to divert the crusade in which Villehardouin could have been a conscious and crafty participant. Naturally he reports events from the viewpoint of the leaders and the party determined to hold the crusading army together. That was his station. His account, while it reports events quite fully and accurately, is lacking in analysis, and can thus be charged with a certain superficiality, but this also should not surprise us. He was a high military officer and diplomat writing his memoirs, not a modern historian removed by centuries from the events. He does feel defensive concerning the expedients adopted by the leaders to avoid dissolution of the army, for as principal negotiator of the treaty of Venice for the crusaders he was responsible for the hardship which faced them as a result of the shortage of men and money. He can be criticized for judging harshly and unjustly the motives of those who wished to abandon the leaders. Taking his chronicle for what it is, however, the memoirs of a well-informed leader, his account is one of the great historical sources of the Middle Ages. The Faral edition with modern French translation is the most recent and the best. Handy English translations by Shaw (Penguin) and Marzial (Everyman) are available.

The historian of the Fourth Crusade is extremely fortunate to possess another full eyewitness account by a participant far removed from the marshal of Champagne in rank and point of view, the chronicle of the poor Picard knight, Robert of Clari. He was not, of course, as well informed as Villehardouin on the plans and thoughts of the leaders. He is also extremely unreliable until the date of his own arrival in Venice, probably in June or July of 1202. Moreover, he is scandalously bad on chronology and figures. He tells an honest story, however, from a point of view which we would otherwise miss, for all the other sources stem from men of higher estate. He reflects the views of those in the ranks, including their resentment of the powerful and the wealthy. It is significant, therefore, that he shares Geoffrey's view that the assault upon Constantinople was the result of a series of accidents, not of a plot by the Venetians or the German party. Even where we know Robert to be wrong, his account has value for showing us what the common crusaders believed, based, perhaps, upon the rumors that circulated among them. He possesses one other outstanding virtue, for he provides color and human interest lacking in other sources—trumpets and banners, the splendor of the imperial city, close-ups of deeds of valor. Without him we would have a much poorer story. There is an English translation by Edgar McNeal, which should be employed even by those who read Old French for its modern and scholarly footnotes. The apparatus of the recent Italian translation is also very valuable.

Another source is the *Historia Constantinopolitana* by Gunther, a Cistercian monk of Pairis in Alsace. Gunther was not a participant in the crusade, but his account is based upon the reminiscences of his abbot Martin. The abbot of Pairis held an important place among the religious attached to the crusade, but he was not present from the time of his departure from Zara until he arrived before Constantinople on 1 January 1204. As one of those who accompanied the army to Zara reluctantly and then went his own way to the Holy Land Martin offers us yet another point of view. Within the mind of the abbot of Pairis, indeed, the conflicting claims of loyalty to the host and conscience met. The *Historia* was written between August 1207 and June 1208. It is marred by an exaggerated emphasis upon the role of Martin and by subversion of historicity in the interest of rhetoric. In a recent seminar paper, which is soon to be published in *Speculum* Francis R. Swietek convinced me that Gunther should be used with considerable caution. Comte Paul Riant's edition is the best (in Riant's *Exuviae* and published separately), but is unfortunately not very available. An older edition in the *Patrologia Latina* is possessed by good research libraries. There is a German translation by E Assmann.

The history of the Albigensian crusade by Peter, a monk of the Cistercian abbey of Vaux-de-Cernay, contains a section on the Fourth Crusade. Peter accompanied his uncle, Abbot Guy of Vaux-de-Cernay, and we thus have another narrative by an eyewitness. The abbot and his nephew were of Simon de Montfort's party, bitterly opposed to the attack upon Zara and determined to proceed to the Holy Land without further delay. The view held by Guy and Peter of Vaux-de-Cernay of their crusading obligation differs even more radically from

hat of Villehardouin and the leaders than does the view of Martin of Pairis. Pe-
er's account is especially valuable for presenting the side of the strongest dissidents, like the count of Montfort. The best edition is by Pascal Guébin and Ernest Lyon for the Société de l'histoire de France.

The *Devastatio Constantinopolitana* provides a brief, anonymous, and
informative account. Authorities differ concerning its author. The best edition is
in the *Chroniques Greco-Romanes*, edited by Charles Hopf, but the one contained
in volume XVI of the *Monumenta Germaniae Historica* is more available.

The letters of Pope Innocent III are extremely valuable for the crusade and
the relationship of the papacy to it. As official documents they offer compelling
evidence on the public postures of the pope. He was not, of course, an eyewitness
of the crusade itself, and in some respects he was not well-informed. On other
matters, however, the pope possessed unique first-hand knowledge.

The *Gesta Innocentii*, an adulatory biography of the pope written by a Ro-
nan cleric about 1208, is also useful, although it must be used with caution. It at-
tributes to the pope only the purest of motives and credits him with the acumen
to foresee the future. A modern edition is needed to supplant that published by
Migne in the *Patrologia Latina*.

The *Urkunden zur älteren Handels-und Staatsgeschichte der Republik Venedig*,
edited by Tafel and Thomas, contains many documents useful for the Fourth
Crusade, such as treaties, letters from the barons, and various minor sources.

Nicetas Choniates' *Historia* offers the viewpoint of a highly placed and responsible Byzantine statesman. He thought Alexius IV a young fool and he hated
Alexius V, who had removed him from office. Nicetas is our only substantial
source for the Greek point of view. The style is extremely complex and florid.
There is a new edition by Van Dieten. In the older, Bonn edition the Greek text
is accompanied by a Latin translation. There is also a German translation by
Franz Grabler.

The *Chronicle of Novgorod* gives a confused, but colorful account of the fall
and sack of Constantinople. Most authorities have believed the author to be a visiting Russian who witnessed the events he described. D. Freydank has recently argued that it is based upon a verbal account from a low-German cleric, probably
Bishop Conrad of Halberstadt. I am not yet convinced. The English translation of
the Russian work is in volume XXV of the Camden Third Series.

The *Chronique* of Ernoul-Bernard, a continuation of the great crusading history of William of Tyre, is based upon information received in the Holy Land. It
is to be expected that the Christians of the Holy Land would seek a villain to receive the blame for the failure of the crusade and that these feudal warriors
should select the mercantile Venetians for this role. Ernoul-Bernard should not be
taken seriously concerning the plans and motives of the crusading leaders, but he
provides unique material on the defectors who proceeded to Palestine, as well as
the opinions and prejudices of the Christians of the Levant.

Finally, attention should be called to a minor source that is little known and
used, the poems of Raimbaut de Vaqueiras. Raimbaut was the friend and companion of Boniface of Montferrat. He offers us some fine human interest material
on the feelings of those who took the cross. We also learn much about the charac-

ter of Boniface. Raimbaut's *Epic Letter* provides a few solid details concerning the conquest of Constantinople. The poems are edited, translated, and discussed by Joseph Linskill.

Literature

For an extended discussion of the literature on the Fourth Crusade see Donald E. Queller and Susan J. Stratton, "A Century of Controversy on the Fourth Crusade," *Studies in Medieval and Renaissance History* VI (1969): 235–77. The reader can sample the literature and the sources in *The Latin Conquest of Constantinople*, ed. Donald E. Queller. Here I shall discuss only the high points of the historiography.

For centuries historians of the Fourth Crusade simply followed Villehardouin, but in the second half of the nineteenth century, under the influence of nationalism, economic determinism, and the rise of a more critical historical method, they began to debate the straightforward narrative of the marshal. The first of the so-called treason theorists was Count Louis de Mas Latrie in his *Histoire de l'île de Chypre sous le règne des princes de la maison de Lusignan*. The editor of Ernoul, Mas Latrie chose to follow the Palestinian source, discovering a supposed Venetian plot in collusion with the sultan to divert the crusade from Egypt. Villehardouin is dismissed as a dupe of Venetian duplicity.

In his *Geschichte Griechenlands* the distinguished Byzantinist Carl Hopf appeared to have discovered the treacherous treaty which the Venetians signed with the sultan. There was no documentation, but Hopf's great scholarly reputation carried the day for a time. Gabriel Hanotaux shortly proved, however, that Hopf's evidence consisted only of certain conventions of a later date already published in the *Urkunden*, and that the supposed negotiations between the sultan and the Venetians could not have taken place. This should have laid the false treaty to rest, but it still pops up here and there.

A rival Swabian or German conspiracy theory took the field with Eduard Winkelmann's *Philipp von Schwaben und Otto IV. von Braunschweig*. According to Winkelmann the hard-pressed Philip diverted the crusade with the help of Boniface of Montferrat in order to embarrass Innocent III, who supported his rival for the German throne. He had not much power, but achieved his aim through skillful diplomacy—and the opportune appearance in the West of his refugee brother-in-law, Prince Alexius.

The Swabian treason was developed by Count Paul Riant in two articles in the *Revue des questions historiques* of 1875 and 1878. With great erudition and a massive command of minor sources, Riant wove a plot among Philip, Boniface, and young Alexius, who met at the German court at Christmas 1201. The Venetians, whose supposed treaty with Egypt was accepted by Riant upon the basis of Hopf's reputation, were easily gained for the conspiracy. Despite his great learning, Riant's work is flawed by excessive speculation and his too facile acceptance of the false treaty.

Ludwig Streit returned to the Venetians as the culprits in his *Venedig und die Wendung des vierten Kreuzzugs*, but he introduced a new element into Fourth Crusade historiography, an insistence upon setting the crusade in historical perspective by tracing the deterioration of relations between Venice and Byzantium in the twelfth century.

Edwin Pears' *The Fall of Constantinople* is not very good history. Unaware of Hanotaux's criticism of Hopf, Pears perpetuates the false treaty between the Venetians and the sultan. He regards Villehardouin as a suppressor of unpleasant facts, choosing to follow instead Robert of Clari, Ernoul-Bernard, and Nicetas. As the only book-length account of the Fourth Crusade in English, *The Fall of Constantinople* has been unfortunately influential in the English-speaking world. Pears does have the advantage of an intimate knowledge of Constantinople. A recent popularization, *The Sundered Cross*, by Ernle Bradford, follows Pears with lavish praise for a work that was inadequate when it was written over eighty years ago. Bradford has a lively style and a knowledge of ships and sailing lacking to armchair historians, but his history is atrocious.

Despite the treason theorists Villehardouin's theory of accidents retained supporters, among them the learned French scholar Jules Tessier. In his *La quatrième croisade: la diversion sur Zara et Constantinople* late nineteenth-century French patriotism took a peculiar turn. He resented the idea that the German king or the Venetian doge had been able to manipulate the barons of France like stupid dupes. Tessier follows Villehardouin, whom he affectionately calls "our old chronicler from Champagne." Tessier was too good a scholar, however, merely to retell the narrative of Villehardouin. He did take account of the critical work of the previous generation of scholarship, even though he rejected much of it.

A milestone in Fourth Crusade historiography was reached at the end of the nineteenth century with Walter Norden's *Der vierte Kreuzzug in Rahmen der Beziehungen des Abendlandes zu Byzanz*. The genuine political and economic insights of those who saw a conspiracy to divert the crusade and the sophisticated defense of Villehardouin by Tessier find fruition in what I call the modified theory of accidents. Like Streit, but more broadly, Norden places the Fourth Crusade in the framework of Western-Byzantine relations, not just those of Venice, but of Normans, Germans, Venetians, and crusaders of all Latin lands. No one could have possessed sufficient foreknowledge to conspire to divert the crusade, but there were underlying reasons and deep-seated causes which predisposed the crusaders and Venetians to grasp at the opportunity offered by young Alexius. Villehardouin was essentially truthful, in the eyes of Norden, but superficial. Norden's thesis has become extremely influential.

Achille Luchaire's *Innocent III: la question d'Orient* interprets the Fourth Crusade as the triumph of increasing secularism over the moral concerns of the church. Innocent did not wish the diversion, but was himself enough of a secularist to draw advantage from events he was powerless to prevent. Among writers on the Fourth Crusade Luchaire is best known for his dictum that "historical science has something better to do than to discuss indefinitely an insoluble problem," the question of the diversion. It is, of course, impossible even for Luchaire to write of the Fourth Crusade without discussing it. The debate over the diversion, moreover, is not a mere jumble of conflicting views, but an orderly process in which later scholars, although still unable to agree, profited from the debates of their predecessors to write more and more sophisticated history.

Leopoldo Usseglio's common-sense approach to the Fourth Crusade in *marchesi di Monferrato in Italia ed in Oriente durante i secoli XII e XIII* is much too little known. Solidly in the tradition of Norden, this is an admirable scholarly work.

The most ardent defender of Villehardouin since Tessier is Edmond Faral, the marshal's most recent editor. His article on Villehardouin's sincerity in the *Revue historique* of 1936 scores off all Geoffrey's rival chroniclers and detractors. Faral follows Villehardouin's theory of accidents with the barest nod in the direction of Norden and his disciples.

Henri Grégoire, on the other hand, like other Byzantinists, continued to see a conspiracy behind the attack on Constantinople. He sought to lay the groundwork for a new attempt to prove a Swabian plot by showing that young Alexius arrived in the West in 1201, not 1202 as Villehardouin seems to say, thus allowing time for the meeting at Hagenau and the development of a conspiracy. His article in *Byzantion* in 1941, which was not entirely convincing to some of us, has been decisively confirmed by J. Folda in *Byzantino-Slavica* in 1965. In my opinion the question of the date of the arrival of Alexius is now closed: it was 1201. Folda does not, however, incline very much toward the treason theory and he explains the discrepancy in Villehardouin as an error made in good faith.

Another famous Byzantinist, Charles Diehl, represented over his long career a gradual softening of the theory of Venetian responsibility. In his rather romantic *Une republique patricienne* (1915) he clearly pointed the finger at Dandolo, a man "capable of every self-sacrifice, careless also of every scruple when the greatness of the Republic was at stake." In more recent works, however, Diehl showed appreciation for the various underlying factors which made the diversion attractive to northern crusaders, as well as Venetians, and he did not attempt to prove that the Venetians planned the diversion as early as April 1201, when the treaty of Venice was signed. He did still hold a moderate belief in Venetian responsibility.

As far as the Fourth Crusade is concerned the popularity and influence of Sir Steven Runciman's *A History of the Crusades* are somewhat unfortunate, for the author failed to integrate into his account the several generations of scholarship on the diversion question. There are a number of errors on details. He is also inexplicably reluctant to give up the false Venetian-Egyptian treaty. More unfortunate is D. M. Nicol's chapter in the new *Cambridge Medieval History*, which not only follows other Byzantinists in blaming the Venetians, but contains far too many errors.

At the opposite pole of opinion stood the eminent Venetian historian Roberto Cessi, whose various articles on the subject (notably in *Archivio Veneto* of 1951 and 1960) attempt to justify his beloved Venice. There was, for example, no plan to go to Egypt, and, for another, no request that the northern crusaders join in the Venetian undertaking at Zara. Cessi's great knowledge of Venetian history commands attention, and respect, but his startling interpretations are not convincing.

The most satisfactory synthesis of Fourth Crusade scholarship is found in the chapter by Edgar McNeal and Robert Lee Wolff in the multi-authored *A History* of the Crusades edited by Kenneth M. Setton. McNeal and Wolff possess a notable command of the sources and literature and they weigh motives and causes judiciously.

Quite recently Sibyll Kindlimann's *Die Eroberung von Konstantinopel als politische Forderung des Westens im Hochmittelalter* has contributed to the placing of the Fourth Crusade within a framework of long-range causes and motivations. She traces the rise of the feeling in the West that Byzantium was an obstacle to the crusading movement unworthy to survive. Although notably weak on the Venetian relations with the Greeks, she successfully confirms and extends the tradition of Walter Norden.

Setting the stage from the Byzantine point of view is Charles M. Brand's excellent book, *Byzantium Confronts the West, 1180–1204.* I have used it especially for the events of late 1203 and early 1204, but it has provided much other information useful to counterbalance to a degree my own Western orientation.

William M. Daly offered in *Medieval Studies* in 1960 a discussion of the breakdown of the sense of Christian community joining the East and the West and the failure of the medieval peace movement. The gradual divergence of ideals and interests culminated in the conquest of Constantinople.

The most recent trend in the historiography of the Fourth Crusade has been the effort to get inside the minds of the mass to crusaders to attempt to capture the interior history of the expedition. A. Frolow has examined the influence of the cult of relics upon the minds of the crusaders in his *Recherches sur la deviation de la IVe croisade vers Constantinople.* Riant had suggested this long ago, but historians preoccupied with modern nationalism and economic causation failed to grasp this key to medieval mentality.

Paul Alphandéry went much further in *La Chrétienté et l' idée de croisade.* He attempted to plumb other religious and psychological factors which moved the crusaders. These factors, such as the twelfth century emphasis upon the humanity of Christ and expectations of the Last Judgment, were peculiarly medieval, and Alphandéry scorned the imposition of modern stereotypes upon medieval men. He is especially concerned with the thoughts and feelings of the anonymous mass of crusaders inspired by Fulk of Neuilly.

Primary Sources

I accept as standard the abbreviations for the collections of sources given in the new Potthast. *Repertorium fontium historiae medii aevi.* Vol. I (Rome, 1962.)

Acropolita, Georgius. *Annales.* Ed. Immanuel Bekker. Bonn, 1836. In *Corp. Bonn.* Vol. XIX.

Alberic of Trois-Fontaines. *Chronica.* Ed. P. Scheffer-Boichorst. *M.G.H., SS.,* XXIII: 631–950.

Anonymous of Gaeta. *Qualiter caput beati Theodori martyris de Constantinopolitana urbe ad Caietam translatum est.* Ed. Paul Riant. *Exuviae,* I: 150–55.

Anonymous of Halberstadt. *De peregrinatione in Greciam et adventu reliquiarum de Grecia libellus.* Ed. Paul Riant. *Exuviae,* I: 10–21. (Riant urges that the *De* peregrinatione in Greciam should be detached, as it is here, from the Chronicle of Halberstadt.) Also in the *Gesta episcoporum Halberstadensium*. Ed. Ludewicus Weiland, in *M.G.H., SS.*, XXIII: 73–123. (I have used both versions, but have cited the one in the *M.G.H., SS.* for the convenience of the reader, since the *Exuviae* is hard to find.)

Anonymous of Langres. *Historia translationum reliquiarum s. Mamantis*. Ed. Paul Riant. *Exuviae*, I: 22–34.

Anonymous of Soissons. *De terra Iherosolimitana et quomodo ab urbe Constantinopolitana ad hanc ecclesiam allate sunt reliquie*. Ed. Paul Riant. *Exuviae*, I: 1–9.

Arnold of Lübeck. *Chronica Slavorum libri VII*. Ed. J. M. Lappenberg. *M.G.H., SS.*, XXI: 115–250.

Baldwin of Flanders. *Epistola* (addressed to Innocent III). In Prevenier, *Oorkonden*, II: 564–77, no. 271; in Migne, *PL*, CCXV: 447–54; in Tafel and Thomas, *Urkunden*, I: 502–11: (the same, addressed to Adolph, Archbishop of Cologne). In Prevenier, *Oorkonden*, II: 577–83, no. 272; in *Annales Coloniensis, M.G.H., SS.*, XVII: 815–18: (the same, addressed to the abbot of Cîteaux and other abbots of the order). In Prevenier, *Oorkonden*, II: 583–91, no. 273: (the same, adressed to all Christians). In Prevenier, *Oorkonden*, II: 591–603, no. 274; in Arnold of Lübeck, *Chronica Slavorum, M.G.H., SS.*, XXI: 226–30. I have customarily cited the version addressed the pope, assuming it to be the original, and have cited the version in Migne, *PL*, because it is widely accessible, although Prevenier is to be much preferred.

Baldwin of Flanders, Louis of Blois, Hugh of Saint Pol, and other barons and knights. *Epistola*. In Prevenier, *Oorkonden*, II: 542–45, no. 260; in *Rec. Hist. Gaules*, XVIII: 515–16; (with a different address) in Arnold of Lübeck, *Chronica Slavorum, M.G.H., SS.*, XXI: 224–26.

Bede, *De locis sanctis*; chap. 20 in *Itineraria Hierosolymitana et descriptiones terrae sanctae bellis sacris anteriora*. Ed. Titus Tobler and Augustus Molinier. 3 vols., Geneva, 1879.

Benjamin of Tudela. *The Itinerary*. Trans. and ed. A. Asher. London and Berlin, 1840.

Caroldo, Gian Giacopo. *Historia de Venetia*. Biblioteca Marciana, cl. ital. VII, cod. 127 (= 8034).

Chronica regia Coloniensis (Annales maximi Colonienses). Ed. Georgius Waitz. *M.G.H., Script. rer. Germ.*, XXX (1880).

Chronicle of Novgorod (1016–1471), The. Trans. Robert Michell and Nevill Forbes in Camden Third Series. Vol. XXV. London, 1914.

Chronicon Hanoniense quod dicitur Balduini Avennensis. Ed. Joh. Heller. *M.G.H., SS.*, XXV: 419–67.

Chronique de la conquête de Constantinople. Trans. J. A. Buchon. Paris, 1825.

Chronique de Morée. Ed. Jean Longnon. Paris, 1911.

Codice diplomatico della Repubblica di Genova. Ed. Cesare di Imperiale. *Font. stor. Italia*. Vol. LXXIX. Rome, 1936–42.

Comnena, Anna. *The Alexiad*. Trans. Elizabeth A. S. Dawes. London, 1967.

Conon of Béthune. *Les chansons de Conon de Béthune*. Ed. Axel Wallensköld, *Paris. 1921.*

Cronaca Bemba. Biblioteca Marciana, cl. ital. vii, cod. 125 (= 7460).

Crusaders as Conquerors: the Chronicle of Morea. Trans. Harold E. Lurier. New York, 1964. (See Livre de la conqueste . . . .)

Da Canal, Martin. *Les estoires de Venise: Cronaca veneziana in lingua francese dalle origini al 1275.* Ed. Alberto Limentani. Florence, 1972. An older edition (1845) is found in *Archivio Storico Italiano,* ser. 1, viii (1845): 229–776.

Dandolo, Andrea. *Chronica.* Ed. E. Pastorello. *R.I.S.*², Vol. xii, i: 1–327.

———, *Chronica brevis.* Ed. E. Pastorello. *R.I.S.*², Vol. xii, i: 329–73.

Del Carretto, Galeotto. *Cronica di Monferratto.* Ed. Gustave Avrogado. In *Mon. hist. patriae.* Vol. v: 1081–1300.

Devastatio Constantinopolitana. Ed. Charles Hopf. *Chroniques Greco-Romanes.* Berlin, 1873. pp. 86–92. (Also in the *Annales Herbipolensis, M.G.H., SS.,* xvi: 9–12; and, with introduction, translation and notes, Ed. M. A. C. de Muschietti and B. S. Díaz Pereyra. In *Anales de historia antigua y medieval* xv (1970): 171–200.)

Documenti del commercio veneziano nei secoli XI–XIII. Ed. Raimondo Morozzo della Rocca and Antonino Lombardo. 2 vols. Turin, 1940.

Documents relatifs au comté de Champagne et de Brie (1172–1361). Ed. Auguste Longnon. 2 vols. Paris, 1901–14.

Dolfin, Zorzi. *Chronica.* Biblioteca Marciana, cl. ital. VII, cod. 794 (= 8503).

Ernoul et Bernard le Trésorier. *Chronique.* Ed. Louis de Mas Latrie. Paris, 1871. (Consult M. R. Morgan, *The Chronicle of Ernoul and the Continuations of William of Tyre,* Oxford, 1973. We do not have the original chronicle of Ernoul, which, in any case, ends in 1197. For the Fourth Crusade all the texts are almost the same, and all should be used with some caution.)

Exuviae sacrae Constantinopolitanae. Ed. Paul Riant. 3 vols. Paris, 1877–1904.

Gesta Innocentii PP. III. Ed. in Migne, *PL.* ccxiv: 18–228.

Guillaume le Bréton. *Gesta Philippi Augusti.* In *Rec. hist. Gaules,* xvii: 62–116.

Gunther of Pairis. *Historia Constantinopolitana.* Ed. Paul Riant. *Exuviae,* i: 57–126. Trans. into German by Erwin Assman, Köln-Graz, 1956.

Historia ducum Veneticorum. Ed. H. Simonsfeld. *M.G.H., SS.,* xiv: 72–97.

Hubaldus of Pisa. *Das Imbreviaturbuch des Erzbischoflichen Gerichtsnotars Hubaldus aus Pisa.* Ed. Gero Dolezalek. Cologne-Vienna, 1969.

Hugh of St. Pol. *Epistola.* Ed. in *Annales Coloniensis maximi, M.G.H., SS.,* xvii: 812–14. (Also in Tafel and Thomas *Urkunden,* i: 304–11, and in *Rec. hist. Gaules,* xviii: 517–19.)

Innocent III. *Epistolae.* In Migne, *PL,* cciv–ccxvii.

———. *The Letters of Pope Innocent III (1198–1216) concerning England and Wales.* Ed. C. R. Cheney and Mary G. Cheney. Oxford, 1967.

———. "Lettres inédites d'Innocent III." Ed. Léopold Delisle. *Bibliothèque de l'Ecole des Chartes,* xxxiv (1873): 397–419.

———. *Regestum Innocentii III papae super negotio Romani imperii.* Ed. Friedrich Kempf. Rome, 1947.

———. *Die Register Innocenz' III.* Ed. Othmar Hageneder and Anton Haidacher. vol. 1. Graz-Cologne, 1964.

———. *Registrum de negotio Romani Imperii.* In Migne, *PL,* CCXVI.

————. "Rubriche Registri litterarum secretarum fel. rec. Domini Innocentii pape tertii de anno pontificatus sui III. IV. (XVIII. et XIX.)." In *Vetera monumenta Slavorum meridionalium historiam illustrantia*. Ed. Augustin Theiner, Rome, 1863, pp. 47–70.

Jacques of Vitry. *The Historia Occidentalis of Jacques de Vitry: A Critical Edition.* Ed. John F. Hinnebusch. Fribourg, 1972.

Kreuzzugsdichtung. Ed. Ulrich Müller. Tübingen, 1969.

"Lai de la dame de Fayel." In *Recueil de chants historiques français*. Ed. Antoine le Roux de Lincy, lre série, Paris, 1841, pp. 105–08.

Lectiones Longipratenses. Ed. Paul Riant. *Exuviae*, ii: 10–22.

Livre de la conqueste de la princée de l'Amorée: Chronique de Morée (1204–1305). Ed. Jean Longnon. Paris, 1911. (There are Greek and other versions.) Trans. Harold E. Lurier as *Crusaders as Conquerors: the Chronicle of Morea*. New York, 1964.

Lorenzo de Monacis. *Chronicon de rebus venetis ab u. c. ad annum MCCCLXV.* Ed. Fl. Cornelius. Venice, 1758.

Matteo d' Amalfi. *Translatio sancti Andreae.* Ed. Paul Riant. *Exuviae*, i: 165–78.

Monk of San Giorgio. *Translatio corporis beatissimi Pauli martyris de Constantinopoli Venetias.* Ed. Paul Riant. *Exuviae*, i: 141–49.

Nicephorus Chrysoberges. *Ad Angelos orationes tres.* Ed. Maximilian Treu. Programm des Konigl. Friedrichs Gymnasiums zu Breslau. Vol. CXXVII. Breslau, 1892.

Nicetas Choniates. *Historia.* Ed. Aloysius van Dieten. 2 vols. Berlin and New York, 1975. The old edition by Immanuel Bekker, *Corp. Bonn.*, vol. XXXIII, Bonn, 1835, contains a Latin translation. There is also a German translation by Franz Grabler, Graz-Vienna-Cologne, 1958.

"Nuova serie di documenti sulle relazioni di Genova coll' impero bizantino," Ed. Angelo Sanguineti and Gerolamo Bertolotto, *Atti della Società Ligure di Storia Patria*, xxviii (1896–98).

Nuovi documenti del commercio veneto dei secoli XI–XIII. Ed. Raimondo Morozzo della Rocca and Antonino Lombardo, in Monumenti Storici della Deputazione di Storia Patria per le Venezie, n.s., vol. vii, Venice, 1953.

Ogerius Panis. *Annales Ianuensis.* Ed. Luigi Tommaso Belgrano and Cesare Imperiale. *Fonti per la storia d'Italia.* xii: 67–154. Rome, 1901.

Oorkonden der graven van Vlaanderen (1191–aanvang 1206), De. Ed. W. Prevenier. 3 vols. Brussels, 1964.

Otto of Sanit Blaise. Continuation of Otto of Freising. *Chronicon.* Ed. Roger Wilmans. *M.G.H., SS.*, xx: 302–37.

Peter of Vaux-de-Cernay. *Petri Vallium Sarnaii monachi hystoria Albigensis.* Ed. Pascal Guébin and Ernest Lyon. 3 vols. Paris, 1926–30.

Raimbaut de Vaqueiras. *The Poems of the Troubadour Raimbaut de Vaqueiras.* Ed. Joseph Linskill. the Hague, 1964.

Ralph of Coggeshall. *Chronicon Anglicanum.* In *Rer. Brit. M. A. script.*, lxvi: 1–208.

Recueil de chants historiques français. Ed. Antoine le Roux de Lincy. lre série. Paris, 1841.

Regesta Pontificum Romanorum. Ed. August Potthast. 2 vols. Berlin, 1874–75.
Regesten der Kaiserurkunden des Oströmischen Reichs von 565–1454. Ed. Franz Dölger. 5 vols. Munich and Berlin, 1924–1965.
Rigord. *Gesta Philippi Augusti Francorum Regis.* In *Rec. Hist. Gaules,* XVII: 1–62.
Robert of Auxerre. *Chronicon.* Ed. O. Holder-Egger. *M.G.H., SS.,* XXVI: 219–76.
Robert of Clari. *La Conquête de Constantinople.* Ed. Philippe Lauer. Paris, 1924. (Eng. trans. by Edgar H. McNeal, New York, 1936; new Italian trans. with valuable introduction and apparatus by Anna Maria Nada Patrone, Genoa, 1972.)
Roger of Hoveden. *Chronica.* Ed. William Stubbs. 4 vols. *Rer. Brit. M. A. script.,* LI. London, 1868–71.
Rostaing de Cluni. *Exceptio capitis S. Clementis.* Ed. Paul Riant. *Exuviae,* I: 127–40.
Sabellico, Marcantonio. *Rerum venetarum ab urbe condita libri XXIII.* Venice, 1718.
Sacrorum conciliorum nova et amplissima collectio. Ed. Giovanni Mansi. 53 vols. Paris, 1901–27.
Sanudo, Marino. *Le vite dei dogi.* Ed. G. Monticolo. *R.I.S.²,* Vol. XXII, iv
Sanudo, Marino (Torsello). *Istoria del regno di Romania.* Ed. Charles Hopf. *Chroniques Gréco-Romanes.* Berlin, 1873. pp. 99–170.
————. *Liber secretorum fidelium crucis super Terrae Sanctae recuperatione et conservatione.* Hanover ed. of 1611. Toronto and Buffalo, 1972.
Thomas of Spalato. *Historia Spalatina.* Ed. L. de Heinemann. *M.G.H., SS.,* XXIX: 570–98.
Urkunden zur älteren Handels- und Staatsgeschichte der Republik Venedig. Ed. G. L. Fr. Tafel and G. M. Thomas. 3 vols. 1st ed., 1856–57, reprinted, Amsterdam, 1967.
Venetiarum historia vulgo Petro Iustiniano Iustiniani filio adiudicata. Ed. Roberto Cessi and Fanny Bennato. Deputazione di Storia Patria per le Venezie. Venice, 1964.
Vetera monumenta Slavorum meridionalium historiam illustrantia. Ed. Augustin Theiner. Vol. 1. Rome, 1863.
Villehardouin, Geoffrey of. *La Conquête de Constantinople.* Ed. Edmond Faral. 2 vols. Paris, 1938–39. (Also several editions beginning in 1870 by Natalis de Wailly and the 1891 ed. by Emile Bouchet. Trans. M. R. B. Shaw, 1963, reprinted, Baltimore, 1967. Also by Sir Frank Marzials, London and New York, 1908, and later reprints.)

Literature*

Ahrweiler, Hélène. *Byzance et la mer: la marine de guerre, la politique et les institutions maritimes de Byzance aux VIIe–XVe siècles.* Paris, 1966.
Alphandéry, Paul. *La Chrétienté et l'idée de Croisade.* Completed from the author's notes by Alphonse Dupront. 2 vols. Paris, 1954 and 1959.

*Dr. Janet Rabinowitch read the Russian works, marked with asterisks, and made copious notes for me.

Andrea, Alfred J. "Innocent III and the Ban of Excommunication Incurred by the Fourth Crusade Army at Zara." Unpublished MS.

———. and Ilona Motsiff. "Pope Innocent III and the Diversion of the Fourth Crusade Army to Zara." *Byzantinoslavica* XXXIII (1972): 6–25.

———."Pope Innocent III as a Crusader and Canonist: His Relations with the Greeks of Constantinople, 1198–1216." Ph.D. diss., Cornell Univ., 1969.

Arbois de Jubainville, Henri d'. "Catalogues d'actes des comtes de Brienne (950–1356)." *Bibliothèque de l'Ecole des Chartes* XXXIII (1872): 141–86.

———. *Histoire des ducs et des comtes de Champagne*. Vol. IV. Paris, 1865.

Ashtor, Eliahu. *A Social and Economic History of the Near East in the Middle Ages*. Berkeley-Los Angeles-London, 1976.

Atiya, Aziz S. *Crusade, Commerce and Culture*. Bloomington, Ind., 1962.

———. *The Crusade: Historiography and Bibliography*. Bloomington, Ind., 1962.

———. "The Crusades: Old Ideas and New Conceptions." *Cahiers d'histoire mondiale* II (1954): 469–75.

Bagley, C. P. "Robert of Clari's *La Conquête de Constantinople*." *Medium Aevum* XL (1971): 109–15.

Baldwin, Marshall W. "The Decline and Fall of Jerusalem, 1174–1189." In *History of the Crusades*. Vol. I. Ed. Kenneth M. Setton.

———. "The Latin States under Baldwin III and Amalric I, 1143–1147." In *History of the Crusades*. Vol. I.

Beasley, C. R. *The Dawn of Modern Geography*. Vol. II. London, 1901.

Beck, Hans Georg. "Byzanz und der Westen im 12. Jahrhundert." *Probleme des 12. Jahrhunderts*. Vortrage und Forschungen vom Konstanzer Arbeitskreis für mittelalterliche Geschichte, XII. Constance-Stuttgart, 1968.

Beer, Jeanette M. A. *Villehardouin: Epic Historian*. Geneva, 1968.

Berry, Virginia G. "The Second Crusade." In *History of the Crusades*. Vol. I.

Besta, Enrico. "La cattura dei Veneziani in Oriente per ordine dell'imperatore Emanuele Comneno, e le sue consequenze nella politica interna ed esterna del commune di Venezia." *Antologia Veneta* I (1900): 35 ff.

Bithell, Jethro. *The Minnesingers*. London, 1909.

Blake, E. O. "The Formation of the 'Crusade Idea,'" *Journal of Ecclesiastical History* XXI (1970): 11–31.

Bloch, Marc. *The Historian's Craft*. Trans. Peter Putnam. Vintage ed. New York, 1964.

Blumenshine, Gary. "Cardinal Peter Capuano, the Letters of Pope Innocent III, and the Diversion of the Fourth Crusade to Zara." Seminar paper, Univ. of Illinois, 1968–69.

———."The Election and Confirmation of Boniface of Montferrat as Leader of the Fourth Crusade." Seminar paper, Univ. of Illinois, 1968–69.

Boase, Thomas Sherrer Ross. *Kingdoms and Strongholds of the Crusaders*. London, 1971.

Bormans, S., and Halkin, J., eds. Vol. XI pt. 1, of *Table chronologique des chartes et diplomes imprimés concernant l'histoire de la Belgique*. Brussels, 1907.

Borsari, Silvano. "Per la storia del commercia veneziano col mondo bizantino nel XII secolo." *Rivista storica italiana* LXXXVIII (1976): 104–26.

Brader, David. *Bonifaz von Montferrat bis zum Antritt der Kreuzfahrt (1202),* in *Historische Studien.* Berlin, 1907.

Bradford, Ernle. *The Sundered Cross: The Story of the Fourth Crusade.* Englewood Cliffs, N. J., 1967.

Brand, Charles M. *Byzantium Confronts the West, 1180–1204.* Cambridge, Mass., 1968.

———. "A Byzantine Plan for the Fourth Crusade." *Speculum* XLIII (1968): 462–75.

Bréhier, Louis. *L'église et l'orient au Moyen Age: les croisades.* 1st ed., 1906; 6th ed. Paris, 1928.

———. *Vie et mort de Byzance.* Paris, 1947.

Brown, Elizabeth A. R. "The Cistercians in the Latin Empire of Constantinople and Greece, 1204–1276." *Traditio* XIV (1958): 63–120.

Brown, Horatio. "The Venetians and the Venetian Quarter in Constantinople to the Close of the Twelfth Century." *Journal of Hellenic Studies* XL (1920): 68–88.

Brundage, James A. *Medieval Canon Law and the Crusader.* Madison, Milwaukee and London, 1969.

———. "Recent Crusade Historiography: Some Observations and Suggestions." *Catholic Historical Review* XLIX (1964): 493–507.

———. *Richard Lion Heart.* New York, 1974.

———. "A Transformed Angel (X. 3.31.18): the Problem of the Crusading Monk." *Studies in Medieval Cistercian History Presented to Jeremiah F. O'Sullivan.* Spencer, Mass., 1971.

———. "The Votive Obligations of Crusaders: The Development of a Canonistic Doctrine." *Traditio* XXIV (1968): 77–118.

———. ed. *The Crusades: Motives and Achievements.* Boston, 1964.

Brunelli, Vitaliana. *Storia della città di Zara.* Venice, 1913.

Bryer, Anthony. "The First Encounter with the West — A.D. 1050–1204." In *Byzantium: An Introduction.* Ed. Philip Whitting, New York, 1971.

Burdach, Konrad. "Walter von der Vogelweide und der vierte Kreuzzug." *Historische Zeitschrift* CXLV (1931): 19–45.

Byrne, Eugene. *Genoese Shipping.* Cambridge, Mass., 1930.

Cardini, Franco. "Gli studi sulle crociate dal 1945 ad oggi." *Rivista storica italiana* LXXX (1968): 79–106.

Carile, Antonio. "Alle origini dell'impero latino d'Oriente. Analisi quantitativa dell'esercito crociato e ripartizione dei feudi." *Nuova rivista storica,* LVI (1972): 285–314.

———. *La cronachistica veneziana (secoli XII–XVI) di fronte alla spartizione della Romania nel 1204.* Florence, 1969.

———. "Partitio Terrarum Imperii Romanie." *Studi Veneziani* VII (1965): 125–305.

———. Review article of Charles M. Brand, *Byzantium Confronts the West, 1180–1204.* In *Studi Veneziani* XI (1969): 237–264.

Cerone, Francesco. "Il papa e i Veneziani nella quarta crociata." *Archivio veneto* XXXVI (1888): 57–70 and 287–98.

Cessi, Roberto. *Le colonie medioevali italiane in Oriente.* Bologna, 1942.

————. "L'eredità di Enrico Dandolo." *Archivio veneto*, ser. 5, LXVII (1960): 1–25.

————. "Politica, economia, religione." In *Storia di Venezia, vol. II, dalle origini del ducato alla IV crociata*, Venice, n.d.

————. *La Repubblica di Venezia e il problema adriatico*. Naples, 1953.

————. *Storia della Repubblica di Venezia*. 2 vols. Milan and Messina, 1944–46.

————. "Venezia e la quarta crociata." *Archivio veneto*, ser. 5, XLVIII–XLIX (1951): 1–52.

————. "Venice on the Eve of the Fourth Crusade." *Cambridge Medieval History*. Vol. IV, pt.i. Cambridge, Eng., 1966.

Charanis, Peter. "Aims of the Medieval Crusades and How They Were Viewed by Byzantium." *Church History* XXI (1952): 123–34. Reprinted in *Social, Economic and Political Life in the Byzantine Empire*. Ed. Peter Charanis. London, 1973.

————. "A Note on the Population and Cities of the Byzantine Empire in the Thirteenth Century," *The Joshua Starr Memorial Volume*. New York, 1953.

Cheney, C. R. "Master Philip the Notary and the Fortieth of 1199." *English Historical Review* LXIII (1948): 342–50.

Cognasso, Francesco. *Storia delle crociate*. Milan, 1967.

————. "Un imperatore bizantino della decadenza: Isaaco II Angelo." *Bessarione* XXXI (1915): 29–60.

Costa, Eugene A., Jr. "Alexius IV, the Latins, and the Greeks, July, 1203– January, 1204." Seminar paper, Univ. of Illinois, 1968–69.

Cracco, Giorgio. "Il pensiero storico di fronte ai problemi del comune veneziano." In *La storiografia veneziana fino al secolo XVI: Aspetti e problemi*. Ed. Agostino Pertusi, Florence, 1970.

————. *Società e stato nel medioevo veneziano (secoli XII–XIV)*. Florence, 1967.

Daly, William M. "Christian Fraternity, the Crusaders, and the Security of Constantinople, 1097–1204: the Precarious Survival of an Ideal."*Mediaeval Studies* XXII (1960): 43–91.

Da Mosto, Andrea. *I dogi di Venezia nella vita pubblica e privata*. Milan, 1960.

Daniel-Rops, Henri. *Cathedral and Crusade: Studies of the Medieval Church, 1050–1350*. Trans. John Warrington. London, 1957.

Davidson, H. R. Ellis. "The Secret Weapon of Byzantium." *Byzantinische Zeitschrift* LXVI (1973): 61–74.

Dawkins, R. M. "The Later History of the Varangian Guards: Some Notes." *Journal of Roman Studies* XXXVII (1947): 39–46.

Diehl, Charles. *Byzance: grandeur et décadence*. Paris, 1919.

————. "The Fourth Crusade and the Latin Empire." In *Cambridge Medieval History*. Vol. IV. Cambridge, Eng., 1923.

————. "The Government and Administration of the Byzantine Empire." In *Cambridge Medieval History*.IV (old).

————. *Histoire de l'Empire Byzantin*. Paris, 1919.

————. *Histoire du Moyen Age*. vol. IX. Paris, 1945. In *Histoire générale*, Ed. Gustave Glotz. Paris, 1928–47.

————. *Une République patricienne: Venise*. Paris, 1915.

Duby, Georges. *The Early Growth of the European Economy: Warriors and Peasants from the Seventh to the Twelfth Century.* Trans. from the French 1st ed. of 1973 by Howard B. Clarke. Ithaca, N.Y., 1974.

Dufournet, Jean. *Les écrivains de la Quatrième Croisade: Villehardouin et Clari.* 2 vols. Paris, 1973.

———. "Villehardouin et Clari, juges de Boniface de Montferrat." *Revue des langues romanes* LXXVIII (1969): 29–58.

———. "Villehardouin et les Vénitiens." *L'information littéraires* XXI (1969): 7–19.

Dupront, Alphonse. "Croisade et eschatologie." In *Umanesimo e esoterismo.* Padua, 1960.

Ebels-Hoving, B. *Byzantium in Westerse Ogen, 1096–1204.* Assen, 1971.

Englebert, Omer. *St. Francis of Assisi.* Trans. from the 2nd French ed. by Eve-Marie Cooper. 2nd Eng. ed. revised and augmented by Ignatius Brady and Raphael Brown. Chicago, 1965.

Ensslin, W. "The Government and Administration of the Byzantine Empire." *Cambridge Medieval History* IV (new), pt. 2.

Erdmann, Carl. *Die Entstehung des Kreuzzugsgedanken.* Stuttgart, 1935.

Esprit de croisade, L'. Ed. Jean Richard. Paris, 1969.

Faral, Edmond. "Geoffroy de Villehardouin: la question de sa sincérité." *Revue historique* CLXXVI (1936). 530–82.

Fasoli, Gina. "Nascita di un mito." In *Studi storici in onore di Gioacchino Volpe.* Florence, 1958, vol. I.

Ferrard, Christopher G. "The Amount of Constantinopolitan Booty in 1204." *Studi veneziani* XIII (1971): 95–104.

Fliche, Augustin, Thouzelliers, Christine, and Azais, Yvonne, *La Chrétienté romaine (1198–1274).* In Fliche and Martin, *Histoire de l'église.* Vol. x Paris, 1950.

Folda, J. "The Fourth Crusade, 1201–1204: Some reconsiderations." *Byzantinoslavica* XXVI (1965): 277–90.

Fotheringham, J. K. "Genoa and the Fourth Crusade." *English Historical Review* XXV (1910): 26–57.

Frances, E.. "Alexis Comnène et les privilèges octroyés à Venise." *Byzantinoslavica* XXIX (1968): 17–23.

———. "Sur la conquête de Constantinople par les Latins." *Byzantinoslavica* XV (1954): 21–26.

Freydank, D. "Die altrussische Erzählung über die Eroberung Konstantinopels, 1204." *Byzantinoslavica* XXIX (1968): 334–59.

Frolow, Augustin. *Recherches sur la déviation de la IVe croisade vers Constantinople.* Paris, 1955.

Gardner, A. *The Lascarids of Nicaea.* London, 1912.

Gerland, Ernst. "Der vierte Kreuzzug und seine Probleme." *Neue Jahrbücher für das klassische Altertum und für Pädagogik* XIII (1904): 505–14.

Gill, Joseph. "Franks, Venetians, and Pope Innocent III: 1201–1203." *Studi veneziani* XII (1970): 85–106.

———. "Innocent III and the Greeks: Aggressor or Apostle?" In *Relations between East and West in the Middle Ages.* Ed. Derek Baker. Edinburgh, 1973.

Giry, A. *Manuel de diplomatique.* Paris, 1894.

Gottlob, Adolf. *Die Päpstlichen Kreuzzugssteuern des 13. Jahrhunderts.* Heiligenstadt, 1892.

Goimard, Jacques, ed. *Venise au temps des galères.* Paris, 1969.

Grégoire, Henri. "The Question of the Diversion of the Fourth Crusade." *Byzantion* xv (1941): 158–66.

Grossman, Ronald P. "The Financing of the Crusades." Ph.D. diss., Univ. of Chicago, 1965.

Grousset, René. *L'empire du Levant.* Paris, 1949.

———. *Histoire des croisades et du Royaume Franc de Jérusalem.* 3 vols. Paris, 1934–36.

Gutsch, M. R. "A Twelfth Century Preacher — Fulk of Neuilly." In *The Crusades and Other Historical Studies Presented to Dana C. Munro.* Ed. Louis J. Paetow. New York, 1928.

Hagedorn, Gerd. "Papst Innocenz III. und Byzanz am Vorabend des Vierten Kreuzzugs (1198–1203)." *Ostkirchliche Studien* xxiii (1974): 3–20 and 105–36.

Haidacher, Anton. "Beiträge zur Kenntnis der verlorenen Registerbände Innocenz' III." *Römische Historische Mitteilungen* iv (1961): 37–62.

Halphen, Louis. "Le rôle des 'Latins' dans l'histoire intérieure de Constantinople à la fin du XIIe siècle." In *Mélanges Charles Diehl.* Vol. i. Paris, 1930.

Hanotaux, Gabriel. "Les Vénitiens ont-ils trahi la Chrétienté en 1202." *Revue historique* iv (1877): 74–102.

Hart, Henry H. *Marco Polo: Venetian Adventurer.* Norman, Okla., 1967.

Hazlitt, W. C. *The History of the Origin and Rise of the Venetian Republic.* 4th ed., 1915. Reprinted, 2 vols., New York, 1966.

Hellweg, M. "Die ritterliche Welt in der französichen Geschichtschreibung des vierten Kreuzzuges." *Romanische Forschungen* lii (1938): 1–40.

Hendrickx, Benjamin. "À propos du nombre des troupes de la quatrième croisade et de l'empereur Baudouin I." *Byzantina (Thessalonica)* iii (1971): 29–40.

———. "Baudouin IX de Flandre et les empereurs byzantins Isaac II l'Ange et Alexis IV." *Revue belge de philologie et d'histoire* xlix (1971): 482–89.

———. "Boudewijn, de vrome keizer von Konstantinopel." *Ons Geestelijk Erf* xliv (1970): 227–32.

———. "Les chartes de Baudouin de Flandre comme source pour l'histoire de Byzance." *Byzantina (Thessalonica)* i (1969): 59–80.

———. "Recherches sur les documents diplomatiques non conservés concernant la Quatrième Croisade et l'Empire Latin de Constantinople pendant les premières années de son existence (1200–1206)." *Byzantina (Thessalonica)* ii (1970): 107–84.

———. "Het Regentschap van Vlaanderen en Henegouwen na het vertrek van Boudewijn IX (VI) op kruisvaart (1202–1211)." *Revue belge de philologie et d'histoire* xlviii (1970): 337–93.

———. "Wat vonden de kruisvaarders in 1203/4 in Constantinopel en wat dachten zij over de Griekse schatten en het Griekse verleden?" *Hermeneus* xli (1970): 72–79.

Hendy, M. F. "Byzantium, 1081–1204: An Economic Reappraisal." *Transactions* of the Royal Historical Society xx (1970): 31–52.

Heyd, Wilhelm von. *Histoire du commerce du Levant au moyen âge.* 1st ed. in Germ., 1879. Trans. by Furcy Raynaud and revised and augmented by the author, 1885. Reprinted, 2 vols., Leipzig, 1936.

History of the Crusades, A. Ed. Kenneth M. Setton. Vols. I and II. Philadelphia, 1958 and 1962. Reprinted by the University of Wisconsin Press.

Hodgson, F. C. *The Early History of Venice.* London, 1901.

Hoeck, Johannes M., O.S.B., and Loenertz, Raymond J., O.P. *Nikolaos-Nektarios von Otranto, Abt von Casole: Beitraege der Ostwestlichen Beziehungen unter Innocenz III and Friedrich II.* Passau, 1965.

Hopf, Carl. *Bonifaz von Montferrat und der Troubadour Rambaut von Vaqueiras.* Ed. Ludwig Streit. Berlin, 1877.

————. *Geschichte Griechenlands.* In J. S. Ersch and J. G. Gruber. *Encyclopädie.* Vols. LXXXV–LXXXVI. Leipzig, 1867; reprinted, New York, n.d.

Hurter, Friedrich. *Storia di Papa Innocenzo III.* Trans. from the 3rd Germ. Ed. T. Giuseppe Gliemone. 4 vols. Milan, 1857–58.

Hussey, J. M. "The Later Macedonians, the Comneni and the Angeli, 1025–1204," *Cambridge Medieval History.* Vol. IV pt. i. Cambridge, 1966.

*Ivanov, A. "Zakhvat Konstantinopolia Latinianami v 1204 godu."*Zhurnal Moskovskoi Patriarchii* (1954), pp. 64–73.

Jacoby, David. "The Encounter of Two Societies: Western Conquerors and Byzantines in the Peloponnesus after the Fourth Crusade." *American Historical Review* LXXVIII (1973): 873–906.

Jahn, Hans. *Die Heereszahlen in den Kreuzzügen.* Berlin, 1907.

Janin, R. *Constantinople byzantine.* 2nd rev. ed., Paris, 1964.

Jenkins, R. J. H. "The Bronze Athena at Byzantium." *Journal of Hellenic Studies* LXVII (1947): 31–33.

John, E. "A Note on the Preliminaries of the Fourth Crusade." *Byzantion,* XXVIII (1958): 95–103.

Johnson, Edgar A. "The Crusades of Frederick Barbarossa and Henry VI." In *History of the Crusades,* Ed. Setton. Vol. II.

Kandel, M. "Quelques observations sur la Devastatio Constantinopolitana." *Byzantion* IV (1927–28): 79–88.

Kantorowicz, Ernst. *Frederick II.* Trans. E. O. Lorimer. London, 1931.

Kennan, Elizabeth. "Innocent III and the First Political Crusade: A Comment on the Limitations of Papal Power." *Traditio* XXVII (1971): 231–49.

Kindlimann, Sibyll. *Die Eroberung von Konstantinopel als politische Forderung des Westens im Hochmittelalter.* Zurich, 1969.

King, Archdale A. *Cîteaux and her Elder Daughters.* London, 1954.

Kirfel, Hans Joachim. *Weltherrschaftsidee und Bündnispolitik: Untersuchungen zur auswärtigen Politik der Staufer.* Bonn, 1959.

Klimke, C. *Die Quellen zur Geschichte des vierten Kreuzzuges.* Breslau, 1875.

Krehbiel, Edward B. *The Interdict: Its History and Operation.* Washington, D.C., 1909.

Kretschmayr, Heinrich. *Geschichte von Venedig.* Vol. I 1st ed., 1905; reprinted, Gotha, 1964.

Lamma, Paolo. *Comneni e Staufer: ricerche sui rapporti fra Bisanzio e l'Occidente nel secolo XII.* 2 vols. Rome, 1955–57.

——. Venezia nel giudizio delle fonti bizantine dal X al XII secolo." *Rivista storica italiana* LXXIV (1962): 457–79.

Lane, Frederic Chapin. "From Biremes to Triremes." In *Venice and History: The Collected Papers of Frederic C. Lane.* Baltimore, 1966.

——. *Venetian Ships and Shipbuilders of the Renaissance.* Baltimore, 1934.

——. *Venice: A Maritime Republic.* Baltimore, 1973.

——. *Venice and History: Collected Papers of F. C. Lane.* Baltimore, 1966.

Langlois, Charles-V. *La vie en France au Moyen Age d' après quelques moralistes du temps.* 2nd ed. Paris, 1911.

Larmat, Jean. "Sur quelques aspects de la religion chrétienne dans les Chroniques de Villehardouin et de Clari." *Moyen Age* LXXX (1974): 403–27.

Lemerle, Paul. "Byzance et la croisade." In *Relazioni del X Congresso Internazionale di Scienze Storiche.* Vol. III Florence, 1955.

Lewis, Archibald R. "The Danube Route and Byzantium, 802–1195." In *Actes du XIVe Congrès International des Études Byzantines.* Bucharest, 1975.

——. "The Economic and Social Development of the Balkan Peninsula during Comneni Times, A.D. 1081–1185." In *Actes du IIe Congrès International des Études du Sud-Est Européen.* Athens, 1972.

——. "Merchants in the Indian Ocean, 1000–1500 A.D." Forthcoming in *Journal d'histoire sociale et économique.*

Lippincott's Gazetteer. Philadelphia, 1873.

Longnon, Jean. "Domination franque et civilisation grecque." In *Mélanges d'archéologie et d'histoire offerts à Charles Picard.* Vol. II. Paris, 1949.

——. *L'Empire Latin de Constantinople et la Principauté de Morée.* Paris, 1949.

——. *Les Français d'Outremer au Moyen Age.* Paris, 1929.

——. *Recherches sur la vie de Geoffroy de Villehardouin, suivies du catalogue des actes des Villehardouin.* Paris, 1939.

Lopez, Robert S. "Foreigners in Byzantium," *Miscellanea Charles Verlinden.* In *Bulletin de l'institut historique belge de Rome* XLIV (1974): 341–52.

Lot, Ferdinand. *L'art militaire et les armées au Moyen Age.* Paris, 1949.

Luchaire, Achille. *Innocent III: la question d'Orient.* Paris, 1907.

Lunt, William E. *Financial Relations of the Papacy with England to 1327.* Cambridge, Mass., 1939.

——. *Papal Revenues in the Middle Ages.* 2 vols. New York, 1934.

Luykx, Theo. *De graven van Vlaanderen en de kruisvaarten.* Louvain, 1947.

Luzzato, Gino. *Storia economica di Venezia dall' XI al XVI secolo.* Venice, 1961.

Maccarone, Michele. *Studi su Innocenzo III.* Italia sacra XVII. Padua, 1972.

Maclagen, Michael. *The City of Constantinople.* New York and Washington, 1968.

Manfroni, C. *Storia della marina italiana dalle invasioni barbariche alla caduta di Costantinopoli.* Vol. I. Leghorn, 1899.

Maranini, Giuseppe. *La costituzione di Venezia dalle origini alla Serrata del Maggior Consiglio.* Venice, 1927.

Martini, Giuseppe. "Innocenzo III ed il finanziamento delle crociate." *Archivio della Deputazione romana di Storia patria.* n.s. X (1944): 309–35.

Mas Latrie, Louis de. *Histoire de l'île de Chypre sous le règne des princes de la maison de Lusignan.* 3 vols. Paris, 1852–61.

Mayer, Hans Eberhard. *Bibliographie zur Geschichte der Kreuzzüge.* Munich, 1960.

———. *Geschichte der Kreuzzüge.* Stuttgart, 1965. Engl. trans., John Gillingham, rev. and up-dated by the author. New York and Oxford, 1972.

———. "Literaturbericht über die Geschichte der Kreuzzüge." *Historische Zeitschrift,* Sonderheft 3 (1969): 641–731.

McNeal, Edgar H., and Wolff, Robert Lee. "The Fourth Crusade." In *A History of the Crusades.* Ed. Setton. II, 153–185.

McNeal, Edgar H. "Fulk of Neuilly and the Tournament of Ecry." *Speculum,* XXVIII (1953): 371–75.

Mollat, Michel. "Problèmes navals de l'histoire des croisades." *Cahiers de civilisation médiévale* X (1967): 345–59.

Moore, J. C. "Count Baldwin of Flanders, Philip Augustus and the Papal Power." *Speculum* XXXVII (1962): 79–89.

Morgan, M. R. *The Chronicle of Ernoul and the Continuations of William of Tyre.* Oxford, 1973.

Morris, Colin. "Geoffroy de Villehardouin and the Conquest of Constantinople." *History* LIII (1968): 24–34.

Mundo Lo, Sara de. *Cruzados en Bizancio: la cuarta cruzada a la luz de las fuentes latinas y orientales.* Buenos Aires, 1957.

Munk, Connie. "Papal Financing of the Fourth Crusade." Seminar paper, Univ. of Illinois, 1968–69.

Munro, Dana C.. "The Popes and the Crusades." *Proceedings of the American Philosophical Society* LV, no. 5, (1916): 348–56.

Nada Patrone, Anna Maria. *La quarta crociata e l'impero latino di Romania (1198–1261).* Turin, 1972.

Naslund, Sebastian. "The Crusading Policy of Innocent III in France, 1198–1202: An Evaluation from Secular and Ecclesiastical Sources." Seminar paper, Univ. of Illinois, 1968–1969.

Nesbit, John W. "The Rate of March of Crusading Armies in Europe: A Study and Computation." *Traditio* XIX (1963): 167–81.

Nicol, Donald M. "The Fourth Crusade and the Greek and Latin Empires, 1204–1261." *Cambridge Medieval History* Vol. IV, pt. i. Cambridge, 1966.

———. *The Last Centuries of Byzantium, 1261–1453.* London, 1972.

Norden, Walter. *Das Papstum und Byzanz.* Berlin, 1903; reprinted, New York, n.d.

———. *Der vierte Kreuzzug im Rahmen der Beziehungen des Abendlandes zu Byzanz.* Berlin, 1898.

O'Brien, John M. "Fulk of Neuilly." Diss., Univ. of Southern California, Los Angeles, 1964.

———. "Fulk of Neuilly." *Proceedings of the Leeds Philosophical and Literary Society* XIII (1969): 109–48.

Ohnsorge, Werner. *Abendland und Byzanz.* Weimar, 1958.

Oman, Charles. *The Art of War in the Middle Ages.* 1885; rev. and ed. John H. Beeler. Ithaca, 1953.

Ostrogorsky, George. *History of the Byzantine State.* Trans. from the 2nd Germ.

ed. of 1952 by Joan Hussey with revisions by the author. New Brunswick, 1956.

——. "The Paleologi." In *Cambridge Medieval History*. Vol. IV, pt. i. Cambridge, 1966.

——. *Pour l'histoire de la féodalité byzantine*. Brussels, 1954.

Packard, Sidney R. *Europe and the Church under Innocent III*. New York, 1927.

Painter, Sidney. "The Third Crusade: Richard the Lionhearted and Philip Augustus." In *History of the Crusades*. Ed. Setton. II, 45–85.

Passant, E. J. "The Effects of the Crusades upon Western Europe." *Cambridge Medieval History*. Vol. V. Cambridge, 1948.

Pauphilet, Albert. "Robert de Clari et Villehardouin." In *Mélanges de linguistique et de littérateur offerts à M. Alfred Jeanroy*, Paris, 1928.

——. "Sur Robert de Clari." *Romania* LVII (1931): 289–311.

Pears, Edwin. *The Fall of Constantinople*. London, 1885, and New York, 1886 (same, but with differing pagination).

Pertusi, Agostino. "Quedam regalia insignia: ricerche sulle insegne del potere ducale a Venezia durante il medioevo." *Studi Veneziani* VII (1965): 3–123.

Polemis, Demetrios J. *The Doukai: A Contribution to Byzantine Prosopography*. London, 1968.

Potthast, August. *Regestum pontificum romanorum*. 2 vols. Berlin, 1874–75.

Powicke, F. M. "The Reigns of Philip Augustus and Louis VIII of France." *Cambridge Medieval History*. Vol. VI. Cambridge, 1936.

Prawer, Joshua. *The Crusaders' Kingdom: European Colonialism in the Middle Ages*. New York, 1972.

Previté-Orton, C. W. "The Italian Cities till c. 1200." *Cambridge Medieval History*. Vol. V. Cambridge, 1948.

Primov, Borislav. "The Papacy, the Fourth Crusade and Bulgaria." *Byzantinobulgarica* I (1962): 183–211.

Purcell, Maureen. "Changing Views of Crusade in the Thirteenth Century." *Journal of Religious History* VII (1972): 3–19.

Queller, Donald E., and Stratton, Susan J. "A Century of Controversy on the Fourth Crusade." *Studies in Medieval and Renaissance History* VI (1969): 235–77.

Queller, Donald E. "Diplomatic 'Blanks' in the Thirteenth Century." *English Historical Review* LXXX (1965): 476–91.

——. "L'évolution du rôle de l'ambassadeur: les pleins pouvoirs et la traité de 1201 entre les Croisés et les Vénitiens." *Le Moyen Age* XIX (1961): 479–501.

——. Compton, Thomas K.; and Campbell, Donald A. "The Fourth Crusade: The Neglected Majority." *Speculum* XLIX (1974): 441–65.

——. "Innocent III and the Crusader-Venetian Treaty of 1201." *Medievalia et Humanistica* XV (1963): 31–34.

——. "A Note on the Reorganization of the Venetian Coinage by Doge Enrico Dandolo." *Rivista Italiana di Numismatica* LXXVII (1975): 167–72.

——. Ed. *The Latin Conquest of Constantinople*. New York, London, Sidney, Toronto, 1971.

——. and Day, Gerald W. "Some Arguments in Defense of the Venetians on the Fourth Crusade." *The American Historical Review* LXXXI (1976): 717–37.

Renouard, Yves. *Les hommes d'affaires italiens du moyen age.* Rev. according to the author's notes by Bernard Guillemain. Paris, 1968.

———. "Les voies de communication entre pays de la Méditerranée et pays de l'Atlantique au Moyen Age." In *Mélanges d'histoire du Moyen Age dédiés à la mémoire de L. Halphen.* Paris, 1951.

Riant, Paul. "Le changement de direction de la quatrième croisade." *Revue des questions historiques* XXIII (1878): 71–114.

———. "Les dépouilles religieuses enlevées à Constantinople au XIIIe siècle." *Mémoires de la Société Nationale des Antiquaires de France,* ser. 4, VI (1875): 1–214.

———. "Innocent III, Philippe de Souabe et Boniface de Montferrat." *Revue des questions historiques* XVII (1875): 321–75, and XVIII (1875): 5–75.

Richard, Jean. *Le Royaume Latin de Jérusalem.* Paris, 1953.

Robbert, Louise Buenger. "Reorganization of the Venetian Coinage by Doge Enrico Dandolo." *Speculum* XLIX (1974): 48–60.

———. "The Venetian Money Market, 1150–1229." *Studi Veneziani* XIII (1971): 3–94.

Roscher, Helmut. *Papst Innocenz III. und die Kreuzzüge.* Göttingen, 1969.

Rousset, Paul. *Histoire des croisades.* Paris, 1957.

Runciman, Steven. *Byzantine civilization.* London, 1933.

———. "The Byzantine Provincial Peoples and the Crusade." In *Relazioni del X Congresso Internazionale di Scienze Storiche.* Vol. III, Florence, 1955.

———. "The Decline of the Crusading Idea." *Ibid.*

———. *The Eastern Schism.* Oxford, 1955.

———. *A History of the Crusades.* 3 vols. Cambridge, 1954.

Russell, Frederick Hooker. *The Just War in the Middle Ages.* Cambridge, London, New York, Melbourne, 1975.

Russell, Josiah C. *Late Ancient and Medieval Population.* Transactions of the American Philosophical Society, vol. XLVIII, pt. 3. Philadelphia, 1958.

———. "Population in Europe, 500–1500." *The Fontana Economic History of Europe.* Vol. I. London and Glasgow, 1969.

Sauli, Lodovico. *Della colonia genovese in Galata.* Turin, 1831.

Saunders, J. J. *Aspects of the Crusades.* Christchurch, New Zealand, 1962.

Schaube, Adolf. *Handelsgeschichte der Romanischen Völker des Mittelmeergebiets bis zum Ende der Kreuzzüge.* Munich and Berlin, 1906.

Schmandt, Raymond H. "The Fourth Crusade and the Just War Theory." *The Catholic Historical Review* LXI (1975): 191–221.

———. "Orthodoxy and Catholicism: Public Opinion, the Schism, and the Fourth Crusade." *Diakonia* III (1968): 284–99.

Schneider, A. M. "Brände in Konstantinopel." *Byzantinische Zeitschrift* XLI (1941): 382–403.

Şesan, M. "La flotte byzantin à l'époque des Comnènes et des Anges (1081–1204)." *Byzantinoslavica* XXI (1960): 48–53.

Setton, Kenneth M. *The Papacy and the Levant (1204–1571).* Vol. I. Philadelphia, 1976. I have been able to read the first chapter on "Innocent III and the

Fourth Crusade" just before returning my revised manuscript to the press.

Shaked, Shaul. *A Tentative Bibliography of Geniza Documents.* Paris, 1964.

Sinogowitz, B. "Über das byzantinishce Kaisertum nach dem vierten Kreuzzuge (1204–1205)." *Byzantinische Zeitschrift* XLV (1952): 345–56.

Smail, R. C. *Crusading Warfare (1097–1193).* Cambridge, 1956.

Strayer, Joseph R. "The Political Crusades of the Thirteenth Century." in *History of the Crusades.* Ed. Setton, II, 377–428.

Streit, Ludwig. *Venedig und die Wendung des vierten Kreuzzugs gegen Konstantinopel.* Anklam, 1877.

Sweeney, James Ross. "Innocent III, Hungary and the Bulgarian Coronation: A Study in Medieval Papal Diplomacy." *Church History* XLII (1973): 320–44.

———. "Papal Hungarian Relations During the Pontificate of Innocent III, 1198–1216." Ph.D. diss., Cornell Univ., 1976.

Swietek, Francis R. "Gunther of Pairis and the Historia Constantinopolitana." Seminar paper, Univ. of Illinois, 1976. To appear shortly in *Speculum.*

Swift, E. H. "The Latins at Hagia Sophia." *American Journal of Archeology*, ser. 2, XXXIX (1935): 458–74.

Tessier, Jules. *La quatrième croisade: la diversion sur Zara et Constantinople.* Paris, 1884.

Thayer, William R. *A Short History of Venice.* Boston and New York, 1908.

Thiriet, Freddy. "Les chroniques vénitiennes de la Marcienne et leur importance pour l'histoire de la Romanie gréco-vénitienne." *Mélanges d'archéologie et d'histoire: Ecole Française de Rome* LXVI (1954): 241–92.

———. *Histoire de Venise.* 4th ed. Paris, 1969.

———. *La Romanie vénitienne au Moyen Age.* Paris, 1959.

Tillmann, Helene. *Papst Innocenz III.* Bonn, 1954.

*Uspenskii, F. I. *Istoriia Vizantiskoi Imperii.* Vol. III. Moscow and Leningrad, 1948.

Usseglio, Leopoldo. *I marchesi di Monferrato in Italia ed in Oriente durante i secoli XII e XIII.* Vol. II. Turin, 1926.

Van Cleve, Thomas C. *The Emperor Frederick II of Hohenstaufen: Immutator Mundi.* Oxford, 1972.

Van Millingen, Alexander. *Byzantine Constantinople.* London, 1899.

Vasiliev, A. A. *History of the Byzantine Empire, 324–1453.* 2nd Eng. ed. rev. Oxford and Madison, 1952.

*Vasilievskii, V. G. Review of Fedor Uspenskii, *Obrazovanie votorogo Bolgarskogo tsarstva.* In *Zhurnal Ministerstva Narodnogo Proshveshcheniia* CCIV (1879): 337–48.

Verbruggen, J. F. *Het leger en de vloot van de graven van Vlaanderen vanaf het ontstaan tot in 1305.* Brussels, 1960.

Verlinden, Charles. *Les empereurs belges de Constantinople.* Brussels, 1945.

Villey, Michel. *La croisade: essai sur la formation d'une théorie juridique.* Paris, 1942.

———. L'idée de la croisade chez les juristes du moyen âge." *Relazioni del X Congresso Internazionale di Scienze Storiche.* Vol. III. Rome, 1955.

Vriens, H. "De kwestie van den vierden kruistocht." *Tijdschrift voor Geschiedenis* XXXVII (1922): 50–82.

Waas, Adolf. *Geschichte der Kreuzzüge.* 2 vols. Freiburg, 1956.

Wailes, Bryan. "The Fighting Galley." *History Today* XVIII (1968): 337–43.

Wiel, Alethea. *The Navy of Venice.* London, 1910.

Williams, Patrick A. "The Assassination of Conrad of Montferrat: Another Suspect." *Traditio* XXVI (1970): 381–88.

Winkelmann, Eduard. *Philipp von Schwaben und Otto IV von Braunschweig.* 2 vols. Leipzig, 1873–78.

Wolff, Robert Lee. "Baldwin of Flanders and Hainaut, First Latin Emperor of Constantinople: His Life, Death and Resurrection, 1172–1225." *Speculum* XXVII (1952): 281–322.

———. "Greeks and Latins before and after 1204." *Ricerche di storia religiosa* I (1957): 320–34.

———. "The Latin Empire of Constantinople (1204–1261)." Ph.D. diss., Harvard Univ., 1947.

———. "The Latin Empire of Constantinople." In *A History of the Crusades.* Ed. Setton. II, 187–233.

———. "The Organization of the Latin Patriarchate of Constantinople, 1204–1261: Social and Administrative Consequences of the Latin Conquest." *Traditio* VI (1948): 33–60.

Wright, John Kirtland. *Geographical Lore of the Time of the Crusades.* New York, 1925.

*Zaborov, M. A. "Krestovye pokhody v russkoi burzhuaznoi istoriografii." *Vizantiiskii Vremennik,* n.s. IV (1951): 177–80.

*———. "K voprosu o predistorii chetvertogo krestovogo pokhoda." *Vizantiiskii Vremennik,* n.s. VI (1953): 223–35.

Index

The Middle Ages
Edward Peters, *General Editor*

Christian Society and the Crusades, 1198–1229. Sources in Translation, including The Capture of Damietta by Oliver of Paderborn. Edited by Edward Peters

The First Crusade: The Chronicle of Fulcher of Chartres and Other Source Materials. Edited by Edward Peters

The Burgundian Code: The Book of Constitutions or Law of Gundobad and Additional Enactments. Translated by Katherine Fischer Drew

The Lombard Laws. Translated, with an Introduction, by Katherine Fischer Drew

Ulrich Zwingli (1484–1531). Selected Works. Edited by Samuel Macauley Jackson. Introduction by Edward Peters

From St. Francis to Dante: Translations from the Chronicle of the Franciscan Salimbene (1221–1228). G. G. Coulton. Introduction by Edward Peters

The Duel and the Oath. Part I and II of Superstition and Force, Henry Charles Lea. Introduction by Edward Peters

The Ordeal. Part III of Superstition and Force, Henry Charles Lea. Introduction by Edward Peters

Torture. Part IV of Superstition and Force, Henry Charles Lea. Introduction by Edward Peters

Witchcraft in Europe, 1110–1700: A Documentary History. Edited by Alan C. Kors and Edward Peters

The Scientific Achievement of the Middle Ages. Richard C. Dales. Introduction by Edward Peters

History of the Lombards. Paul the Deacon. Translated by William Dudley Foulke. Introduction by Edward Peters

Monks, Bishops and Pagans: Christian Culture in Gaul and Italy, 500–700. Edited, with an Introduction, by Edward Peters

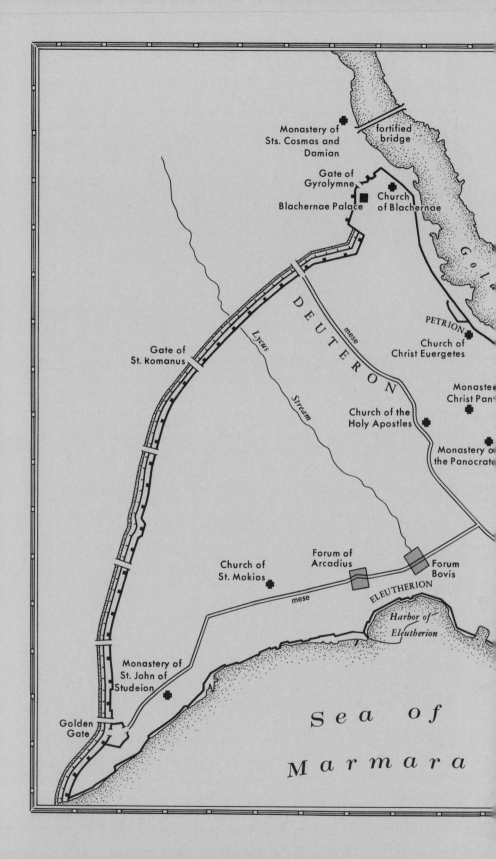

Monastery of
Sts. Cosmas and
Damian

fortified
bridge

Gate of
Gyrolymne

Church
of Blachernae

Blachernae Palace

D E U T E R O N

mese

PETRION

Church of
Christ Euergetes

Lycus

Monaste
Christ Pan

Stream

Gate of
St. Romanus

Church of the
Holy Apostles

Monastery o
the Panocrat

Church of
St. Mokios

Forum of
Arcadius

Forum
Bovis

mese

ELEUTHERION

Harbor of
Eleutherion

Monastery of
St. John of
Studeion

S e a   o f

Golden
Gate

M a r m a r a

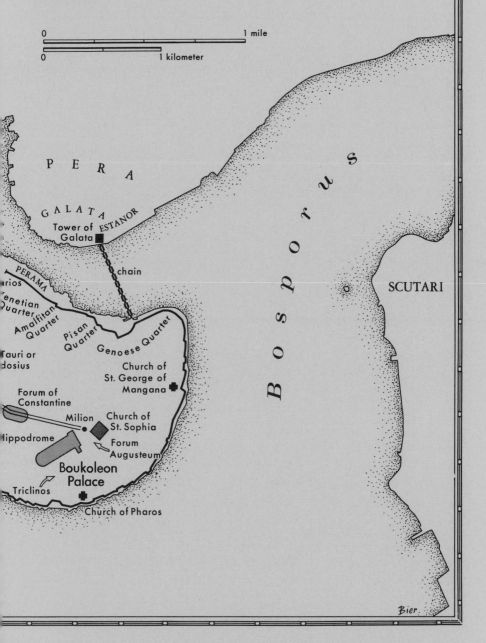

CONSTANTINOPLE

In the Time of the Fourth Crusade
1203-1204

0   1 mile

0   1 kilometer

P E R A

G A L A T A

ESTANOR

Tower of
Galata

PERAMA

chain

...rios

...enetian
Quarter

Amalfitan
Quarter

Pisan
Quarter

Genoese Quarter

...auri or
...dosius

Church of
St. George of
Mangana

Forum of
Constantine

Milion

Church of
St. Sophia

...lippodrome

Forum
Augusteum

Boukoleon
Palace

Triclinos

Church of Pharos

B o s p o r u s

SCUTARI

Bier.